Also by Blu Greenberg

ON WOMEN AND JUDAISM

BLU GREENBERG

How to Run a Traditional Jewish Household

SIMON AND SCHUSTER • NEW YORK

10 9 8 7 6 5 4 3 2 1

LIBRARY OF CONGRESS CATALOGING IN PUBLICATION DATA
GREENBERG, BLU, DATE.
    HOW TO RUN A TRADITIONAL JEWISH HOUSEHOLD.
    BIBLIOGRAPHY: P. 503
    INCLUDES INDEX.
    1. JUDAISM—CUSTOMS AND PRACTICES. I. TITLE.
BM700.G734   1983   296.7'4   82–19702
ISBN 0-671-41700-2

ACKNOWLEDGMENTS

There is a great deal of personal material in this book. Since I refer to members of my family quite often, let me describe them briefly: my husband, Irving Greenberg, is an Orthodox rabbi. In the book, I refer to him as Yitz, which is short for his Hebrew name, Yitzchak. His contribution to this book goes far beyond his sustained encouragement, his corrections and suggestions on each and every page, his taking up the slack in running this traditional Jewish household as I immersed myself in work. Among other things, he has been my mentor and dearest friend for over two decades. For all this—and much more—words seem inadequate.

Also, my children, to whom this work is dedicated: Moshe, David, Deborah, J.J., and Goody. Each helped in the completion of this manuscript in his or her own way, but more important, they have provided much of the anecdotal material in this book—as in my life.

In the work below, I also describe my beloved parents and parents-in-law, Rabbi Sam and Sylvia Genauer, Rabbi Eliahu Chaim Greenberg of blessed memory, and Sonia Greenberg. They are the primary links in our chain; without their teachings and their commitment to tradition, none of this would have been possible. Regarding this immediate work, I am especially grateful to my father, for his innumerable halachic contributions; and to my mother, for teaching me most of what I know about running a Jewish household.

There are many others to whom I owe a debt of gratitude. For an entire year, the Bellin family of Riverdale, New York, provided me with everything I needed: a quiet room away from home, where I could work in isolation for several hours each day; a tree-lined pond beneath my window, where I could find a moment's serenity and calm after a stretch of writing that produced nothing but anxiety; and eight-year-old Hudi Bellin, who worked with Charlotte Sheedy in pacing me. Upon her return from school each afternoon, starting with Day One, Hudi would ask, "Did you finish your book yet?" And special thanks to my friend from high-school days, Rosalind Bellin, who not only offered me space, quiet (and lunch)—but whose common sense and wisdom influenced this writing in many places.

I want to express my great gratitude to the *klei kodesh*, the religious leaders of our synagogue, the Riverdale Jewish Center, and to the teachers, principals, deans, and *roshei yeshiva* of our children's schools. The shul and the yeshiva schools are an integral part of our family's life. They are always there for us, and while we sometimes tend to take our community and its institutions for granted, we well know how important they are to us, how they help us to raise our children and enable us to live as Orthodox Jews. That the names of all the people involved are too numerous to mention here is a symbol of how much work goes into giving over the chain of tradition from one generation to the next.

There are many others who had a direct hand in this work and to whom I am most grateful: Dan Green, publisher at Simon and Schuster, whose creative imagination sparked this entire project; Charlotte Sheedy, my literary agent, who gently but persistently nudged me toward completion; Francine Klagsbrun, who generously recommended me for this work; Vivian Oleen, who forced me to clarify for her, and by extension, the unknown reader; Moshe Greenberg, Roslyn Siegel, and David Szonyi whose editorial skills were widely used and much appreciated; Deborah Greenberg, who carefully constructed the Glossary. Sophie Sorkin, director of copyediting at Simon and Schuster, who gave me wise counsel throughout; and Dan Johnson, my editor at Simon and Schuster. It was Dan with whom I worked most extensively throughout this project. I came increasingly to rely on his kindness, humor, patience, and good judgment.

And to many other teachers and friends whose paths I have been fortunate to cross throughout these years—my deep gratitude. No woman is an island; this work, except for its mistakes, is theirs, too.

ת.ו.ש.ל.ב.ע.

Sivan 5742
Spring 1982

TO MOSHE, DAVID, DEBORAH, J.J., AND GOODY

Who fill our lives with love and laughter, wisdom and goodness, humor and spirit. To me they are sufficient proof of a benevolent and loving God.

Hebrew has a guttural sound that does not appear in English. It is the consonant *ch* pronounced as in the German *ach*. Whenever *ch* appears in a Hebrew word, it is pronounced as a guttural and *not* like the English *ch* in chapter.

CONTENTS

ACKNOWLEDGMENTS   5
PREFACE   13

Part I   THE JEWISH WAY   23

1 Shabbat, 25
2 Kashrut, 95
3 Taharat Hamishpachah: The Laws of Family Purity, 120
4 Daily Prayer and Blessings, 137
5 Parenting and Education, 166
6 Dress, 185
7 Speech, 198
8 Mezuzah: Symbol of a Jewish Household, 208

Part II   SPECIAL STAGES OF LIFE   *213*

9 Marriage, 215
10 Birth, 233
11 Abortion and Birth Control, 255
12 Bar Mitzvah—Bat Mitzvah, 264
13 Divorce, 283
14 Death and Mourning, 287

Part III   CELEBRATION AND REMEMBERING   *299*

15 Jewish Rhythm, 301
16 Elul, the Month of Repentance, 309
17 Rosh Hashanah and Yom Kippur, 317
18 Sukkot, Shemini Atzeret, Simchat Torah, 342
19 Chanukah, 374

12 • Contents

20 Purim, 387
21 Pesach (Passover), 398
22 Yom HaShoah—Holocaust Remembrance Day, 443
23 Yom Ha'Atzmaut—Israel Independence Day, 449
24 Shavuot, 457
25 Tisha B'Av and Other Fasts, 468

AFTERWORD
RECIPES
GLOSSARY
SELECTED BIBLIOGRAPHY FOR A HOME LIBRARY
INDEX

PREFACE

Traditional Jews come in a wide variety of types in America today. Chasidic Jews number their ranks; so do some right-wing anti-Zionists; left-wing profeminists; middle-of-the-road conventional modern Orthodox; "born again" ba'alei teshuva; spiritual neo-Kabbalists; the sectarian yeshiva crowd; some havurah Jews; some Conservative rabbis; and so on. Twentieth-century American Jewry being what it is, the institutional frameworks in which most of the above would locate themselves are the institutions of Orthodox Jewry; and the self-label they would be likely to choose is—Orthodox Jew. Hence, my use of the terms "traditional" and "Orthodox" almost interchangeably throughout the text.

Despite the great diversity within traditional or Orthodox Judaism, however, the basics are essentially the same for all: an underlying belief that there is a personal God, Who revealed Himself in history, Who gave us the Torah, Who commanded— and commands—us to live in a certain way. That "special way" includes, among other things, observance of the Sabbath and the holidays, daily prayer, kosher food laws, a well-defined code of morality and sexual ethics, and a very high value placed on Torah learning and education of the young. It is these very things, these modes of behavior, that make the traditional Jewish household so overtly different from any other.

But that is only part of the picture. Other differences exist.

Perhaps they are less obvious or less open to tabulation and quantification, but they are persistent characteristics, nevertheless. In great measure, they are linked to the special ritual life of an Orthodox Jew.

One is the strong commitment to community. Orthodox Jews understand that without sturdy communal structures, most of the observances—such as kashrut, Torah education of children, Sabbath and holidays, daily prayer—would be infinitely more difficult to carry out.

Another feature of traditional Jewish households is the cohesiveness of the family unit. Much of "family time" is organized around the required observances. A typical Orthodox Jewish family is quite likely to celebrate together home rituals, synagogue life, and community events.

An unspoken but underlying assumption of all this is that individual needs will at times be subordinate to the claims of family and community. I would even suggest that one of the subtle side effects of required ritual is that children are taught in a natural way to respect their parents and respect authority. The matter-of-fact attitude that parents must assume in teaching ritual to children has, I believe, broader implications for the general task of parenting.

Moreover, the content as well as the practices of Orthodox Judaism provide some measure of insulation against the overwhelming force of contemporary values. Because traditional Jews have not been deracinated, they remain anchored to a moral system of another era in human history. In such matters as drugs, premarital sex, extramarital affairs, pornography, and alcoholism, the views and practices of a typical Orthodox Jew would be considered old-fashioned. And he/she would take this as a compliment.

One more characteristic of Orthodox Judaism—one which gives it all meaning—is an overarching sense of history and tradition of, say, the past thirty-five hundred years. . . .

Having briefly defined the essence of Orthodox Judaism, I hasten to add that, even within the basics, there is considerable room to maneuver. For example, some Orthodox Jews believe that every last ritual we observe was given in one form or another at Sinai, while others subscribe to a theory of human initiative in rabbinic interpretation of divine law. For the former group, this latter view borders on heresy. For the latter group, the fundamentalist view allows no room for coming to terms with new realities, such as Israel reborn as a nation-state without intervention of a supernatural messiah.

Nor are the differences restricted to theology alone. When my cousins from the Lakewood (New Jersey) Yeshiva come to visit, I buy special milk for them, for unlike me, they will not drink brand-name milk. Thus, they would reject the definition of kashrut in this book; yet another Orthodox Jew would think that what I have said below is much too strict.

To simplify the tasks at hand, however, and because this is the universe I know best, throughout this book I have generally limited myself to a discussion of the modern Orthodox. So let us take a moment to examine this group more closely.

By simple definition, modern Orthodoxy sounds like an anomaly. How can one be modern and Orthodox at the same time? Certainly, no one would deny that Orthodoxy was established in the nineteenth century as a defense against those modern secular values that gave rise to the more liberal Reform and Conservative movements.

The answer lies in a historic redefinition of the term "Orthodoxy." In the late nineteenth and early twentieth centuries, certain traditionalist rabbis began to reassess the fruits of Emancipation. And they found its social and ethical values not so wanting. Individualism, liberalism, and universalism—the hallmarks of modernity—turned out to have some redeeming social value, for traditional Jews as much as for anyone else. The goal of this new orthodoxy, then, was to somehow integrate these modern values, yet do so in a manner that would not diminish the authority and integrity of the tradition. Thus, in the mind of its standard-bearers, "Orthodox" came to be synonymous with "authentic bearers of rabbinic tradition," rather than with "defenders of a beleaguered faith." One can hardly underestimate the difference in psychological valence between these contrasting self-views.

Modern Orthodox Jews can—and do—live squarely in two worlds: one of traditional Judaism, the other of modern Western society. One can lead the religious life and still be a "modern" man or woman.

The key element in the whole process is the nature of halacha.

Halacha is the means whereby we understand the details of that "special way" I spoke of earlier. The word *halacha*, in fact, means "the way." It is the corpus of Jewish law and ethics, revealed at Sinai, elaborated by the Rabbis of the Talmud, further developed in the medieval codes and commentaries, and explicated continuously through the generations until this very day. It is halacha that defines one as a member of the covenantal community. Acceptance of the authority of halacha—that's a shorthand way of defining an Orthodox Jew.

Yet, for the modern Orthodox Jew, embracing halacha doesn't rule out membership in the broader society. Nor does it imply flat rejection of modern Western values or a modern style of life. Joseph Soloveitchik, the leading theologian-halachist of modern Orthodoxy, argues that confrontation between contemporary human norms and Torah values can be positive. It can lead to mutual enhancement. Rabbi Soloveitchik speaks with a passion of the modern "man of faith" who feels a dialectical tension between the pull of the covenantal community and the socioethical responsibilities of modern life. Interaction, and not withdrawal, is the creative response.

What distinguishes modern from "right-wing" Orthodoxy, then, is its attitude to modern culture and, by extension, to all groups beyond its own periphery. At times, the signals are almost imperceptible; at times they are as blatant as the clothing one wears. For example, unlike Chasidic Jews whose garb clearly says to the world, "I am not one of you," the modern Orthodox will fine-tune the Jewish codes of dress so as to be more or less in step with the fashions of the times.

How else does modern Orthodoxy manifest itself in the lives of its practitioners? Not necessarily in global affirmations of this sort or that, but rather in the various choices Orthodox Jews make as they synthesize Torah and contemporary culture. For example, an Orthodox Jew refrains from work on the Sabbath, doesn't drive his or her car to the synagogue, spends the day in prayer, study, feast, rest, leisure, community, and family time. But on Monday, he or she may work as a lawyer in a large Chicago law firm, or a teacher in a Philadelphia public school. Modern Orthodox Jews will educate their children in religious schools, but also will be more than happy to help their sons and daughters through Harvard Medical School, expecting that these very same offspring will continue to keep kosher, pray daily, "pick up a *sefer*" (study a religious text) on a regular basis, and date only Jewish women or men. A modern Orthodox Jew will cooperate in certain endeavors with Conservative and Reform Jews, the very denominations to which Orthodoxy once set itself in opposition. This is in contrast to right-wing Orthodox Jews who are not informed by this same spirit of coexistence or cooperation.

As I write these words, my sixteen-year-old son has just entered the dining room from the kitchen. He asks for thirty dollars to pay for his karate lessons this month. What distinguishes J.J. from his more traditional counterpart at this moment is not the yellow-sashed white gi he wears so handsomely on his tall, slender frame (although the other might consider karate a form of *avodah zarah*, idolatry). What distinguishes J.J. from another sixteen-year-old karate fan is not the finely crocheted maroon kepah that covers his head. No, at this moment, what is different about J.J. is that as he walked through the door separating kitchen and dining room, eyes aglow with thoughts of a coveted green belt he will test for next month, his hand automatically reached up to touch the mezuzah affixed to the doorpost. The mezuzah, in this case a brass cylinder, contains a parchment inscribed with several sacred passages from the Torah. There is one on every doorpost in our house. In a brief instant, J.J. has brought his fingertips to the mezuzah and then back to his lips to kiss. I know his mind is on other things right now, yet some part of his soul is informed by the ancient Biblical passage "and these words that I command you this day shall be in your heart . . . and you shall inscribe them on the doorposts of your house . . ." (DEUT. 6:4–7). Modern Orthodoxy includes many things. But in 1982, it also includes gi-clad mezuzah kissers.

To generalize, one can live a distinctive life, one can eat, dress, pray, marry, have sex, celebrate rites of passage, raise children, study, think, relate to others, and mark holy time all in a special way, yet still not find oneself terribly at odds with contemporary culture. Of course, there are conflicts in being a citizen of the world and a member of the convenantal community, conflicts in embracing universalist and particularist values almost simultaneously. But the tensions are quite bearable and the impasses are generally negotiable.

Still, I must say it one last time. As the reader will see below, even within modern Orthodoxy, there is great range—both in attitude toward society and in personal practice. Despite others' perception of Orthodoxy as lockstep, there is considerable room for individual style, personal nature, and each person's unique world view.

All this diversity in such a small group! The story is told of a Jew who was shipwrecked many years ago. He had swum ashore to an uninhabited island and had somehow managed to subsist all those years. Finally he is found. Overjoyed at the arrival of his rescuers, he takes them on a tour of the islands: the little hut he built for himself, a comfort station, and—two shuls! "Why two shuls?" they ask him. "After all, you're the only person on the island." He points to one and says, "This is the shul where I pray every day. And that shul? I wouldn't go into it if you paid me!"

All this diversity, however, is not a symbol of religious anarchy, but rather a sign of the vitality and dynamism of Orthodoxy. The fact that there are no neatly drawn lines is a sign of health and not of disorder. Within certain parameters, there is room for everyone. . . .

This book, then, attempts to describe the way a modern Orthodox Jewish household functions. I hope its content will satisfy the interests of four different groups of readers:

For those who are experienced faithful practitioners, the book offers some reminders of the meaning behind the rituals we perform.

For the growing number of ba'alei teshuva—"born again" Jews who are in the process of recovering tradition in their lives and are creating their own Jewish households—the text contains step-by-step descriptions of how things are done.

For those who are simply curious about the interior space of this exotic species, this work offers some glimpses into the inner workings of family and community.

Finally, for the large segment of American Jews who are reopening questions of their own Jewish identity, their Jewish feelings, or their ties to tradition, I hope this book will enlarge their sense of the unlimited Jewish possibilities that do exist.

So as to make the work of practical value, each chapter has been formulated as an independent entity, requiring only occasional reference to the Glossary for terms that were explained in an earlier chapter. So as to parallel the normal flow of life, I have begun with daily life experience and have moved gradually through the text to celebration of special events in history. The reader, however, may start anywhere.

One caveat: this book happens to be about traditional practices and rituals. It happens not to be focused on the larger subject of the ethics of being a Jew. I am aware of the great danger in this approach, for I know that some people mistakenly define an Orthodox Jew by ritual criteria alone. Sometimes, even Orthodox Jews make the same mistake—as if ritual behavior can be separated from ethical behavior.

But that is as far from the truth as is the notion that one can approach God through ethics alone. The essence of Judaism is that all of life is rooted in the divine; we are commanded by God to live in a special way. The commandment not to steal is as central to Judaism—indeed, more central—as the commandment not to eat pork. What comes out of one's mouth (that is, speech and words) is as stringently regulated in Jewish law as what goes into it (kosher food). The Rabbis point out that half of the Ten Commandments deal with ethical laws—behavior between one human being and another—and half deal with behavior between human beings and God.

The essential Orthodox Jew, then, must be honest, ethical, respectful of other human beings, responsible in relationships, reliable in their word. Are all Orthodox Jews this way? Of course not. They are only human, and no system—even a divine one—can guarantee absolutely correct, perfect, human behavior. By the same token, the misbehavior of any individual Jew, then, does not prove anything about the validity or viability of this system of Jewish law. It simply demonstrates the failure of an individual to internalize the entire set of obligations. An observant Jew who wears a kepah and who cheats his customers does not represent a breakdown of the apparatus; he represents a breakdown in human conscience. If an Orthodox Jew violates the ethical laws, he has violated a part of the Torah he was pledged to keep in its entirety.

Thus, although I have taken liberties in narrowing the focus, I hope the reader will understand its limits. Further, I hope the reader will fill in the large gaps and search within every description of halachic minutiae for their ethical interface. That, and not only what I have written below, is what the essential Orthodox Jew is all about.

I was very grateful to have had the opportunity to work on this topic, for I learned many things. Most of us, I daresay, have neither the time nor impetus to examine the meaning of our acts, to reflect in a moment's repose on our habits, to put the pieces of our lives into some coherent whole. While I cannot claim to have achieved such grandiose ends, this work has generously afforded me the first steps.

I have also learned to articulate something which I, as a Jewish woman highly involved in process and preparation, had always sensed but have never before expressed: that process and preparation are part of the spiritual payoff. It is not only the celebration of the Passover Seder itself; it is also the prior experience of vacuuming out pretzel crumbs from the keyholes, products of the silly game of a three- and a five-year-old the week before. It is not only going to shul on Shabbat morning with my family; it is my fifteen-year-old daughter borrowing my cashmere sweater for shul, which she knows she cannot borrow on an ordinary school day. In preparing for this book, I became much more sensitive to the thousand and one little actions—often mundane and barely noticeable—that create the ambiance of an Orthodox Jewish household. As is probably true of most things in life, the lines between preparation and celebration are often blurred. Or, more accurately, preparation is also celebration—of life, of spirit, of family, of community, even of the holy.

Third, I have come to realize, too, how much of a transition woman I am. I live not only in two worlds—Orthodoxy and modernity—I live also in the world of feminist values, which sometimes do not sit well with the former. It would have been much easier for me to write this book ten years ago, before feminism challenged me to come out of so many of my comfortable parochial hiding places. Nevertheless, I do want to tell about Orthodoxy as it is, so in most instances I describe how something has always been done in a traditional home, and in some I add how it might be done incorporating new values for women.

And finally, I have learned that one need not apologize for mixing the unmixable—devotion and humor, piety and irreverence, spirituality and a bit of spoof, faith and lapses, fidelity to practice and backsliding in intent. There are some who can invest every act with ultimate meaning; but there are others, like myself, who cannot help but engage a critical eye and a loving heart at one and the same time. Somehow, we can be deadly serious about our commitment, yet not take ourselves so seriously at every given moment. Human beings live with all kinds of contradictions and inconsistencies, and the perfect faith is no more free of these than the perfect world view or the ultimate in ideologies.

Still, I hope I will not offend the spiritual sensibilities of others with the occasional humor, irreverent anecdote, or personal impious reflection. Instead I hope what will come through, as I have felt it in this writing and as I have lived it all my life, are a great faith in this system, a love of its community, an awe and fear of its Creator, and a profound appreciation for the traditional Jewish way of life. Poking fun, at myself so to speak, is part of that love and appreciation. It is even part of the awe.

But how, the reader might ask, can one perform ritual without perfect and pure intent? Is it not a sham? The answer might be, "Once more, with feeling." Even so, should ritual or rite happen to be devoid of inner spirit at a given moment, it does not imply that it is devoid of meaning. Sometimes, in ritual, we simply feel part of the community, and that is enough. Sometimes, ritual serves but to generate a sense of self, and that is enough. Sometimes, it strengthens the family unit, and that is enough. And sometimes, it connects us to the Divine, and that is enough.

The Jewish Way

One of the most remarkable qualities of the Jewish religion is its ability to sanctify everyday life—the routine, the mundane, the necessary bits and pieces of daily existence. This is achieved through the guidelines of halacha, the body of Jewish law and ethics that defines the Jewish way through life. What Judaism says in effect is this: Yes, commemorating a unique event in history is a holy experience, but so is the experience of waking up alive each morning, or eating to nourish the body, or having sex with one's mate; so is the act of establishing clear demarcations between work and rest or investing everyday speech and dress with a measure of sanctity. Judaism takes the physical realities of life and imposes on them a set of rules or rituals. By doing so, it transforms this reality or that basic necessity of life into something beyond itself. That is the heart of the Jewish Way.

CHAPTER 1

SHABBAT*

THE SEVENTH DAY

Time. Jews have an amazing way with time. We create islands of time. Rope it off. Isolate it. Put it on another plane. In doing so, we create within that time a special aura around our everyday existence. Carving out special segments of holy time suits the human psyche perfectly, for ordinary human beings cannot live constantly at the peak of emotion. Thus, Shabbat, holy time, gives us an opportunity to experience that emotional peak, to feel something extraordinary in an otherwise ordinary span of time.

You would not think of time as having texture, yet in a traditional Jewish household it becomes almost palpable. On Shabbat, I can almost feel the difference in the air I breathe, in the way the incandescent lamps give off light in my living room, in the way the children's skins glow, or the way the trees sway. Immediately after I light my candles, it is as if I flicked a switch that turned Shabbat on in the world, even though I know very well the world is not turned on to Shabbat. Remarkable as this

---

* In writing of the Sabbath, I have used interchangeably its two Hebrew pronunciations: Shabbat or Shabbos. I chose one or the other depending on what I believe to be its most common pronunciation in that particular context.

experience is, even more remarkable is that it happens every seventh day of my life.

How does it happen? There will always be an element of mystery in transforming time from ordinary to extraordinary, but the human part of the process is not mysterious at all. It is not one great big leap or one awesome encounter with the Holy, but rather just so many small steps, like parts of a pattern pieced together.

Why do I or any other Orthodox Jew take these steps, week after week, month after month, year after year, with never a slipup? The first answer falls hard on untrained ears. I observe Shabbat the way I do because I am so commanded. Somewhere in that breathtaking desert, east of Egypt and south of Israel, Moses and the Jewish people received the Torah, including the commandment to observe Shabbat. Since I am a descendant of those people, my soul, too, was present at Sinai, encountered God, and accepted the commandments.

Now, I don't for a moment believe that God said at Sinai, "Do not carry money in your pockets on Shabbat," or, "Do not mow thy front lawn," or even, "Go to synagogue to pray," but the cumulative experience of Revelation, plus the way that experience was defined and redefined in History for a hundred generations of my ancestors, carries great weight with me.

The Biblical commandment to observe Shabbat has two reference points: God's creation of the world, and the Exodus/freedom from slavery. True, these are events in history, yet, linked as they both are to Shabbat, they also suggest something else about the human condition: that there is a tension between the poles of one's life, mastery at the one end and enslavement at the other; mastery in drive, energy, creativity—and enslavement to the pressures and seduction of the hurly-burly world.

To some extent, Shabbat achieves what the song title suggests: "Stop the World, I Want to Get Off." Let me paraphrase the Biblical injunction, as it speaks to me, a contemporary person:

Six days shall you be a workaholic; on the seventh day, shall you join the serene company of human beings.
Six days shall you take orders from your boss; on the seventh day, shall you be master/mistress of your own life.

Six days shall you toil in the market; on the seventh day, shall you detach from money matters.

Six days shall you create, drive, create, invent, push, drive; on the seventh day, shall you reflect.

Six days shall you be the perfect success; on the seventh day, shall you remember that not everything is in your power.

Six days shall you be a miserable failure; on the seventh day, shall you be on top of the world.

Six days shall you enjoy the blessings of work; on the seventh day, shall you understand that being is as important as doing.

A friend has this bumper sticker affixed to the front of her refrigerator: HANG IN THERE, SHABBOS IS COMING. There definitely are weeks in my life when I feel that I will barely make it, but the prize of Shabbat carries me through.

It doesn't always work this way. There are times on Friday night that my best ideas come to me. I feel the urge to take pen in hand and write my magnum opus, but I am not allowed to write. There are those weeks when I am just not in the mood for a big Friday-night family dinner. There have been some Shabbat mornings when it might have been more fun on the tennis court than in shul, and there were some Saturday afternoons when I had to miss what I was sure was the world's best auction.

Happily, the negative moods are the exception and the positive ones the rule. (Were it otherwise, commanded or not, I might have walked away as most modern Jews have done—without, I am well aware, being struck down.) But more important is the fact that I never have to think about picking and choosing. I am committed to traditional Judaism. It has chosen me and I have chosen it back. And just as I am commanded to observe the laws on a Shabbat that rewards, pleases, heals, or nurtures me, so I am commanded on a Shabbat when it doesn't strike my fancy. So when that auction rolls around each year, I don't really suffer serious pangs of temptation. I go to shul, which might even happen to be tedious that particular Shabbat, but which offers me that which I could not buy for a bid of a hundred million dollars anywhere—community, family, faith, history, and a strong sense of myself.

There is something, too, about the power of habit and routine, regimentation and fixed parameters—stodgy old words—that I increasingly have come to appreciate. There are some things that spontaneity simply cannot offer—a steadiness and stability which, at its very least, has the emotional reward of familiarity and, at best, creates the possibility of investing time with special meaning, experience with special value, and life with a moment of transcendence.

And that goes for feelings, too. Those occasional Shabbat dinners when I am just not in the mood? When I don't feel like blessing anyone? Simply, I must be there. Involuntarily, almost against my will, a better mood overtakes me.

I find it fascinating that the Rabbis * of the Talmud speak of *kavannah* as the emotion that should accompany performance of ritual. Kavannah means intent, or directed purposefulness, rather than spirituality. Even in those more God-oriented times, the Rabbis knew you couldn't always drum up feeling. Try, they said, but it's all right, too, if it doesn't come. Often, meaning and feeling will come after the fact, and not as a motivating force.

While it may sound sacrilegious, one can experience a beautiful Shabbat without thinking a great deal about God. Peak for a Jew does not always mean holy or having holy thoughts. Rather ordinary experiences often become sublime because of the special aura created by Shabbat.

On a recent Shabbat, in shul, my peak experience had nothing to do with prayers, God, Shabbat, or the Torah. As we all stood to sing a prayer toward the end of the service, my eye caught sight of Henri V. holding his two-year-old granddaughter Jordana in his arms. In that same line of vision, twenty rows ahead, I saw Lou B., whose wife was just recovering from surgery, holding his two-year-old grandson Jeremy in his arms. For a few seconds I felt a surge of spirit, a misting of the eyes, a moment of joy in the heart. For me that was Shabbat.

My peak experience the week before (and I don't have them every week) was even more "unholy." Three of our children had friends for Shabbat lunch. After zemirot and before the closing Grace, Moshe and two of his yeshiva high-school friends reviewed their terrible pranks of yesteryear. For an hour at the

---

* At times the word rabbi is spelled with a capital R. This signifies a special group of rabbis, those of the Talmudic period whose decisions served as the basis for rabbinic activity throughout history, including modern times.

Shabbat table we all laughed over their antics. It wasn't very "Shabbosdik," but neither could it have happened at any other time—the warmth, the closeness, the leisure . . .

No system that engages a variety of human beings can be absolutely perfect. But, to the average Orthodox Jew, Shabbat comes very close to perfection. It is a day of release and of reenergizing; a day of family and of community; of spirit and of physical well-being. It is a day of prayer and of study; of synagogue and of home; a day of rest and self-indulgence; of compassion and of self-esteem. It is ancient, yet contemporary; a day for all seasons. A gift and a responsibility. Without it I could not live.

Activities Proscribed on Shabbat

The Shabbat laws we observe today are a fine example of how Jews have remained tied to the Torah even as we have enlarged its literal mandates. The Torah enjoins us to set aside a day of rest, to remember both divine creation of the world and the Exodus. But it gives us very few cues as to what shape the day takes. In fact, the Torah explicitly forbids activities in three broad categories: leaving one's place (EXOD. 16:29); kindling fire (EXOD. 35:2–3); and engaging in work (EXOD. 20:10; DEUT. 5:14). But what does leaving one's place mean? And what is work?

The ancient Rabbis, in setting down the oral tradition of generations before them, have defined the day for us. Work is understood to be all those activities that were associated with building the sanctuary in the desert, and include the following categories:

I. Growing and preparing food
  1. Plowing
  2. Sowing
  3. Reaping
  4. Stacking sheaves
  5. Threshing
  6. Winnowing
  7. Selecting out (as, for example, the chaff)
  8. Sifting
  9. Grinding
  10. Kneading
  11. Baking (cooking)

II. Making clothing
  12. Sheep shearing
  13. Bleaching (washing)
  14. Combining raw materials
  15. Dyeing
  16. Spinning
  17. Threading a loom
  18. Weaving
  19. Removing a finished article
  20. Separating threads
  21. Tying knots
  22. Untying knots
  23. Sewing
  24. Tearing

III. Leatherwork and writing
 25. Trapping an animal
 26. Slaughtering
 27. Flaying skins
 28. Tanning
 29. Scraping
 30. Marking out
 31. Cutting
 32. Writing
 33. Erasing
IV. Providing shelter
 34. Building
 35. Demolishing

V. Creating fire
 36. Kindling a fire
 37. Extinguishing a fire
VI. Work completion
 38. Giving the "final hammer stroke," that is, completing some object or making it usable
VII. Transporting goods
 39. Carrying in a public place

In order to preserve the spirit of the Sabbath and to prevent its violation, the Rabbis specified three other prohibited categories.

1. Muktzeh—things that are not usable on Shabbat (such as work tools) should not be handled.
2. Sh'vut—an act or occupation that is prohibited as being out of harmony with celebration of the day. For example, if an act is prohibited to Jews on Shabbat, then a Jew may not ask a non-Jew to do it for him. (However, on occasion there are ways of getting around this latter restriction—see p. 37.)
3. Uvdin d'chol—(weekday things). Some activities are "weekday" in spirit even though they do not involve direct labor or prohibited work. Discussing business or reading papers from the office are prohibited on these grounds. Similarly, most sports are considered uvdin d'chol even though they are technically permissible, as, for example, when tennis is played inside an area enclosed by an eruv. (An eruv halachically transforms public areas into private domain. Thus, technically, one is permitted to carry racquet and ball on a tennis court located within the eruv area. But all that exertion and sweat—it's uvdin d'chol.)

Beyond the thirty-nine prohibitions and the three rabbinic categories, there was also the very large principle of "the honor of Shabbat," creating a special spirit of the day as the Torah intended. Rabbis of the Talmudic times and of later generations took this principle most seriously, and they proceeded to do everything in their interpretive powers to set aside the Sabbath from the weekday.

Thus, even after the oral law was finally committed to writing (the Talmud, sixth century), the process of defining the Sabbath day continued, including the addition of relevant prohibitions. These were all part of the attempt to remain faithful to tradition and create a special day. Today, we observe a variety of restrictions on Shabbat: no turning on electricity (which is considered a form of kindling fire), no use of television, radio, telephone, vacuum cleaner, food processor, public transportation, or automobile; no cutting paper or fabric, sewing, mending, laundry, writing, playing a musical instrument; no home repair jobs, arts and crafts, sports activities of a certain type, or business activity of any sort; no cooking, baking, squeezing a sponge, opening sealed mail, pushing electric buttons such as doorbell or elevator; no shopping.

There is some variation in practice. For example, some Orthodox Jews will not play tennis, but will play catch in an area that has an eruv. Some will set their dishwashers on a Shabbos clock; others would not wash dishes even by hand, unless they are needed for the next Sabbath meal.

There are certain apartment buildings and even Orthodox synagogues where the elevator is pretimed, that is, it stops at each floor automatically, so that no one has to operate it; and there are some people who will not use these Shabbos elevators, as they are called. Some Orthodox Jews will tear foil, toilet paper, and so forth. Some will open paper wrappings of food. Some will do neither, and will therefore pretear any sort of paper and open all boxes and cans of food on Friday afternoon before sundown.

The Rabbis interpreted not leaving one's place as not going out of the city limits beyond a distance of two thousand cubits. A cubit is approximately twenty-two inches, so two thousand of them equal roughly a quarter of a mile. City limits do not signify a municipal boundary. They refer to the last house in a built-up locality. If one has to go beyond, it is possible to do so by preparing beforehand. If some sort of food is placed at the outermost limit of the two thousand cubits, this is considered a "dwelling place," and the person is allowed to walk another two thousand cubits. This is called an eruv techumim, an eruv of limits. In the European towns where Jews were farmers, this kind of eruv was set up between the edge of the farm and the synagogue, so that a Jew could walk there even though it was beyond the formal distance limit.

PREPARATION

Islands of time do not appear on their own, nor merely as a result of imagination. There is a great deal of planning and preparation that goes into creating an island of time. For the well organized, this means starting on Wednesday; for most of us, it also includes a last-minute madness, the tension-producing countdown before candlelighting each week.

One should definitely not approach Shabbat the way I do, and each year I try to change my ways. But human nature being what it is, I suspect half the Orthodox Jews enter it leisurely and the other half pump adrenaline on Friday afternoons. The amazing thing is that when the moment of Shabbat descends upon us —as it inexorably does, for the sun will not stay another moment despite our pleas—an utter serenity falls over the frantic and the reposed alike. After I light my candles, always at the very last moment, I feel a sense of relaxation sweep through me, more total than I could ever dream of achieving in a yoga exercise class.

What must one do in advance to prepare for Shabbat? Everything!

On Shabbat itself, there is no cooking, no cleaning, no laundry, no shopping, no business, so literally everything needed for Saturday must be done before Friday evening candlelighting. Some of these tasks can be done only at the last moment, although far fewer fall into this category than a brinkmanship mentality would allow. In fact, mental preparation for the coming Shabbat really begins early in the week. For example, if on Monday morning you are ordering something from a department store, unless it were essential, you would request not to have it delivered on Saturday. Receiving a chance delivery that doesn't involve an exchange of money is not forbidden; it's simply that the United Parcel Service man—his uniform, his truck, his department-store packages—intrudes the workaday world into a Sabbath household that has temporarily set that world aside.

The physical tasks fall into three broad categories: (1) getting the house in order, (2) preparing the meals, and (3) getting oneself ready. One would be hard put to call these tasks spiritual (who can find godliness in polishing a silver challah tray?). Yet, without this kind of preparation, one could not as easily be transported into holy time.

THE HOUSE (APARTMENT)—CLEANING UP

The house should be cleaned or tidied well so that family, guests, the Sabbath angels and the Sabbath Queen will notice the difference. No, Jews don't really believe in angels looking for dust on the coffee table. I speak here of the aura of Shabbat. If your house is spotless all the time, then bring in fresh flowers or something else to distinguish and honor the day.

You can't swab the kitchen floor or shovel the snow after dinner Friday night, or run the washing machine, or pick the tomatoes on Saturday morning, so plan ahead. Polish whatever silver you'll be using for Shabbat, such as wine cups, challah tray and knife, candlesticks, wine bottle, cake knife, and serving pieces; silver polishing is prohibited on Shabbat, and cannot be done after sunset. Many families try to change their bed linens on Friday in honor of Shabbat, although it gets a little tough to do everything on those short winter Fridays.

SETTING A SHABBAT TABLE

The table should be set with a clean, fresh cloth, the best china, crystal, silver, and flowers. (If you happen to be a paper-plate user, then get special paper plates for Shabbat, just as you would for a party.)

The Shabbat table is set with these special items:

Wine	Challah knife
Wine cups (bechers)	Challah cover
Two challot	Candlesticks
Challah tray	

Nearby, there should be booklets for each person containing zemirot (Sabbath table songs) and Birkat Hamazon, the Grace recited after meals.

The illustration shows what a traditional Shabbat table will generally look like.

For Shabbat lunch, the table will be set up exactly the same way as in the illustration, except that the candles will have burned down and will not be replaced. When another male-head-of-household guest is expected, a wine becher and two covered challah loaves or two challah rolls might also be placed at his setting. Orthodox tradition is strongly male-oriented, and this reflects itself in things large and small. However, there is more room for sharing the head-of-household role yet still remain within the boundaries of tradition than one would think.

For example, in an egalitarian home, there might be a wine cup at each plate, or wine at the father's plate and challah at the mother's, or reversed—wine at the mother's plate and challah at the father's.

Most Orthodox families, however, even feminist ones, stick to the ancient model where husband-father leads the rituals. It's hard to change time-hallowed custom that carries weight equal to Mosaic law.

CANDLESTICKS AND CANDLES

In many homes, mine included, the candlesticks are set up on a side table nearby, rather than directly on the dining table. The reason for this is that candlesticks cannot be removed all during Shabbat even though the candles have long since burned out. Candlesticks fall into the category of muktzeh—items that cannot be handled on Shabbat. Any item whose use is forbidden on Shabbat may not be handled, despite the fact that one has not the slightest intention of using it. (For this same reason, one would not lean up against a car on Shabbat nor sit inside of it, even though the motor is off.)

But wait! What about the candles and candlesticks we light especially for Shabbat? Why can't we touch them during Shabbat? The answer is one of those fine points of Jewish law: it is permitted to light the candles *for* Shabbat but not *on* Shabbat, for that would constitute kindling of fire, which is proscribed. The candles may burn during Shabbat, for it is a mitzvah, a requirement, to enjoy light and heat on that day; however, they must be lit before Shabbat actually starts.

Since there is no guarantee against spills, and since I haven't been able to come up with a magic trick to exchange Friday night's soiled tablecloth with a fresh one for Shabbat lunch without touching the candlesticks—I'll have to continue lighting my candles on a sideboard. (In the old days, the Shabbat candlesticks, or "Shabbos lights" as they were called, were suspended over the table from the ceiling, but nowadays we all have electrical fixtures up there.)

Although most any candles may be used, generally we use special Sabbath candles that are sold as such. They can be purchased in most supermarkets in a Jewish neighborhood or in a religious articles store. Their size is such that they burn approximately two hours, or three if refrigerated beforehand. This is sufficiently long to get through Shabbat dinner, but not that long so as to burn unattended while the family sleeps.

APPLIANCES

All radios, phonographs, TVs, hair dryers, washing machines, and dryers are turned off before candlelighting. No need, however, to disconnect electric clocks.

SETTING THE LIGHTS AND THE SHABBOS CLOCK

One of the distinguishing characteristics of Orthodox Judaism is the approach to electricity on Shabbat. It isn't that we don't use electricity, it's that we don't operate it. So in preparation, we set the lights we'll be needing for the next twenty-five hours, and turn off all other unnecessary lights. That includes the automatic refrigerator and closet lights whose bulbs we unscrew slightly, for otherwise they would go on each time the door is opened.

Every Orthodox Jew has some kind of Shabbos clock in his/her home. A Shabbos clock is a timer, to which any number of lights in the house are attached, to go off and on at preset times. Shabbat symbolizes light and warmth, and yet one does not want the lights burning all night. In our house, for example, we installed a master Shabbos clock (connected to the central fuse box) that controls living room, dining room, kitchen, and some bedroom fixtures. Every Friday afternoon, we set the off-on times and turn the clock on. The lights are usually timed to go off at midnight on Friday (sometimes a gentle hint for guests who might stay too late on this night) and on again at noon on Saturday when we come home from shul. Some people have their houses wired differently; every light switch in every room has its own timer, and can be set independently. Nevertheless, certain lights are generally left on all twenty-five hours—bathroom lights, hallway lights, outside light for guests.

THE SHABBOS GOY

Before Shabbos clocks were invented, another solution was used —the Shabbos goy, whom the rabbis "invented" to resolve problems of restrictions on Shabbat. According to Jewish law, a non-Jew—which is what the word goy means and which should not be used derogatorily—was not bound by any of the prohibitions of Shabbat. As long as a Jew didn't explicitly instruct a non-Jew during the Shabbat itself to perform this or that forbidden activity, a goy was permitted to do it. Thus, the name Shabbos goy. I remember our Shabbos goy in Seattle, a nice teenaged Catholic boy who would stop by every Friday afternoon to receive his instructions—and some coins—from my mother. Later that night, after dinner, he would return to our house and go independently about his switch-flicking business.

REFLECTIONS

I must admit to a bit of ambivalence about the electric-light situation. While I wouldn't want the law reinterpreted—as Conservative and Reform Judaism have done—I do feel conscious of the problems of energy waste under a system that doesn't permit the flexibility of flicking a switch. For example, we don't use the upstairs hall lights or bathroom lights except for occasional moments throughout the Shabbat, yet you can't program when someone is going to walk through the hall or use the toilet, so the light must burn continuously.

We have done two things. One is to cut down. Unless it's an emergency, or a special situation, such as the need to do a lot of quiet reading, we don't leave on the lights in the bedrooms. In our hallway, we turn on a wall lamp that uses half of what the regular ceiling fixtures use. In our bathrooms, we unscrew all but one bulb of the three- to four-bulb fixtures. Unspiritual as it is, that, too—going into a dimly lit bathroom—is part of the ambiance. If we've invited guests who are not Sabbath observant and who would automatically turn off the bathroom lights, we tape the switch in its on position before Shabbat begins.

The second thing I do is rationalize. I say to myself that, by and large, our family, as a unit, doesn't use any more light than we would on an ordinary weekday if everyone went up to his/her own bedrooms after dinner and switched on the lights.

Whatever the arrangement, at times it can be rather inconvenient, such as when you want to read in bed in the middle of the night and forgot to set up your bed lamp on a Shabbos clock, or worse, when someone thoughtlessly leaves the light on in the bedroom and you have to sleep with a pair of bleepers over your eyes all night. (One thing we've learned: never put a white, cotton bedspread over a lamp to block out the light. Fall into a deep sleep and the whole place will go up in smoke.)

Moreover, of all the restrictions of Shabbat that are linked to the Biblical categories of labor, creativeness, and the kindling of fire, this one seems most remote of all.

Nevertheless! Electric lights are part of the total package, one piece of the whole gift of Shabbat. It is a commitment of our own choosing, one that we have lovingly made; it is the manner in which we identify ourselves. Having done so, then if our lights should happen to be on or off inappropriately, we simply take that in our stride.

On the positive side, inconvenience or not, somehow walking into a room and not being able to flick a light switch does contribute to the total mood and feeling of the day. And in a covert sort of way, it serves another function: it generates a sense of family time that goes beyond special mealtimes. There is something nice about family and associated friends gathering in the living spaces of the house, instead of each going his or her own way. Sometimes two or three of us sit in the living room on Friday night after dinner, reading or talking quietly, while we hear the sounds of laughter from the breakfast room where some of the children sit and snack with their friends, or two or three of them lie sprawled out on the carpet under the lamp in the hallway, playing a board game.

And finally, lest you think Orthodox Jews can't find a way in every instance to observe the law in comfort, some enterprising souls have invented a Shabbos lamp (as opposed to Shabbos clock), a fluorescent lamp with a shade that slides over it to block out the light. Some say this is a legal fiction which circumvents the law. I prefer to see it as a technique by which one finds oneself relatively undiscomfited, yet reminded that the day and all of its human actions are special.

To one who is completely unfamiliar with the law, it almost seems petty and silly to go to such lengths over such a little thing as throwing a light switch. But this is one of the many basic steps in creating that special aura of Shabbat.

PRETEARING

Prepare facial tissues or Shabbat toilet tissue for the bathroom, precut paper towels, sheets of aluminum foil. Tearing, changing something from an unusable form to a usable one, was forbidden on Shabbat. Later, the halachic discussion arose as to whether this injunction extended to household paper goods, items such as paper towels and toilet paper which are perforated, or aluminum foil and plastic wrap which are used in connection with food serving and storage. Today, some Orthodox Jews do tear perforated paper on Shabbat; others do not, depending on whose interpretation of the law one follows. In dense Jewish neighborhoods, special paper supplies for Shabbat are sold.

When I was a child, and tissues were a luxury to be used only for colds, it was my job each Friday to prepare the Shabbat paper. Until I was ten or eleven, I used to tear it into threes by hand and it would take me ten minutes. Suddenly I invented the wheel. Using a razor blade, I could slice through an entire roll of toilet paper in thirty seconds. How clever!, I said to myself each week. Growing up in a traditional Jewish household in the forties had its own unusual gratifications.

Preparing paper in advance seems so remote from holy time. The objective outsider might say: "This is pure legalism and highly ridiculous besides; there's no work involved in tearing a piece of perforated toilet paper on the Sabbath." To which an insider might respond, "Look how clever the Rabbis were: even in as mundane a place as a bathroom, one is reminded of the uniqueness of the day."

THE TELEPHONE

People will generally know not to call an Orthodox Jew's home on Shabbat. Our phone rings every ten minutes on a normal evening, but rarely ever does it ring on Shabbat. However, even an occasional jangling can interrupt the mood. Rather than take it off the hook altogether, before Shabbat we put the ringer on low and stick the phone into a drawer so it is barely audible.

Some people think the lack of use of phone is constricting and inconvenient. It surely sometimes is, as when you're expecting company and you don't know whether or not they'll come in this driving rain, or how your mother is fighting the flu bug that attacked her yesterday.

But as one who does a lot of business—social, managerial, and professional—on the telephone, to be released from it on Shabbat is worth the entire effort. On Shabbat, I am freed from the ringing of the telephone. I am simply not available to whoever might want the immediate access a telephone brings. I have the freedom to savor the peace and privacy of my family and my home.

Emergencies notwithstanding, my mother doesn't expect or want me or anyone else to call her on this day; and our friends will know that we will wait half an hour for them and then conclude that they've decided not to weather the storm.

However, in case of medical emergency, the Sabbath not only may be violated, it must be violated. Lifesaving comes above everything else, and there's a good deal of leeway in interpreting what lifesaving means. Once, when J.J. was fifteen he began fighting with his sister over who would cut the cake. He grabbed the knife and sliced a deep cut through his finger. It bled heavily for about twenty minutes. We called the doctor (a friend who is Orthodox), he came immediately, and said the finger must be stitched. We asked if it could wait five hours until Shabbat was over. "No," was the answer, there was a measure of risk. He called the surgeon, who said come right over. J.J. and his father walked; if it hadn't been close by, J.J. would have taken a cab. Despite what the New Testament says about Jewish legalism, this is just how our ancestors, the Pharisees, would have done it.

Having said all that, modern Jews have gone a step further. The same ingenious scientists and scholars who invented the Shabbos lamp have invented a Shabbos telephone. These are members of the Institute for Science and Halacha in Jerusalem, whose basic principle is that there is nothing that needs to be done that cannot be done according to halacha. Inventing something called a "grama switch," they are able to activate electricity in a manner that is consonant with halacha. The grama switch turns on an electrical device without violating the Sabbath. How? It works like this: an electric capacitor stores voltage from a constant power source. From somewhere nearby, an electric eye beams light rays at the capacitor, dissipating the voltage. To activate the switch, a Sabbath observer slides a piece of plastic between the two devices, blocking the light rays from reaching the capacitor. The voltage then builds up unhindered, until it reaches the necessary level to start whatever is hooked up to it.

What makes this a Shabbos telephone? It does not directly generate electricity; instead, it acts by preventing it—the pieces of plastic inhibit rather than activate. This, the modern rabbis have determined, is permissible. They base their contemporary interpretation on a Talmudic precedent: one may close a window on the Sabbath in order to stop a breeze that might blow out a candle, even though closing the window makes the candle burn more brightly.

However, even a Shabbos telephone must conform to another principle of Jewish law—the spirit of Shabbat. So while it may be used for medical and other urgencies, its use is checked in order to preserve the sanctity of the holy day.

Some of what we have learned from Shabbat carries over to the weekday, and the telephone is a good example. Why not preserve an island of family time each day? we asked ourselves. With five teenagers the phones are always ringing. First we told our children to ask their friends not to call at dinnertime, and then we lower the ringer and just ignore the thing until we're all through with our meal. Four of them accept it nicely. The fifth gives us a song and dance every night about the possible emergencies we are missing by not answering—but I've noticed his litany is becoming less dramatic.

FOOD PREPARATION—SHOPPING

All the shopping must be done before sundown. If you've forgotten a jar of mayonnaise, you cannot run out on Saturday morning to buy one, nor call the deli downstairs and have it sent up. And if you don't have an eruv (see p. 47) in your community, you can't even borrow it from a kosher neighbor.

If there is some special food newly available, buy it for Shabbat. Your first avocado of the season should be saved for Shabbat. The first watermelon of the season is cause for Shabbat afternoon rejoicing in our backyard. Halibut and salmon are expensive, but we prepare these for our vegetarians for Shabbat.

COOKING

All cooking for Shabbat must be completed before sundown. This means more work on Thursday and Friday, but the bonus is "paid" on Shabbat.

BUY OR BAKE CHALLOT, THE SPECIAL SABBATH LOAVES

You'll need two challot for Friday night, two for Shabbat lunch; add two more if you'll be serving shaleshudos, the third meal, at home; however, if one of the Friday-night challot is unsliced, it can do double duty for Shabbat lunch or shaleshudos. Where there is no one to eat all that challah, either rolls or whole squares of matzah can be used as substitute for one or both of the challot.

CHILL THE WINE

It is proper to use red wine, sweet or dry, on Friday night. For Shabbat lunch, there's a little more flexibility, and many Jews use white wine or schnapps.

SETTING UP THE BLECH (THE STOVE-TOP COVERING)

If all the food is cooked beforehand, and one cannot ignite the fire, does that mean one must serve cold food? Not at all. In fact, the Pharisees and the Sadducees fought over the issue of maintaining light and heat during Shabbat. The Pharisees were the prolight and proheat faction, and, happily, their interpretation of the law prevailed. The same debate came up eight centuries later, between the Karaites and the Rabbinites. The Karaites, like the Sadducees, held the strict and literal view of Exodus 35:3, "You shall not burn any fire in all your dwellings on the Sabbath day"; they interpreted this to mean there could be no fires, and, therefore, no hot food. The Pharisees, on the other hand, and their descendants the Rabbinites, interpreted Scripture to mean that, "you shall not *burn* (that is, ignite or regulate) a fire" and not that "no fire shall burn." Thus, any heat source lit before Shabbat may be maintained as long as one does not have to reignite it on Shabbat. An oven or top-of-the-stove flame that is turned on before candlelighting and kept burning throughout fits this category. So does a boiler that is controlled by thermostat, or electric lights that are set with a timer. The difference, then, between a rabbinic Shabbat and a Sadducean one is a warm, well-lit family experience versus a cold, dark, forbidding taboo day.

In addition to the proscription against lighting fire, there is another ban of Shabbat: food may not be cooked on Shabbat, but it may be heated. In order to avoid the possibility of actual cooking, the flame is kept low and a blech (the *ech* pronounced gutturally as in *Mad* magazine's yecch) is placed over it. A *blech* is simply a solid tin or copper sheet that covers a burner, or several burners. Most people have it cut to fit right across the entire top of the stove so that it diffuses heat to several pots, and one can rotate these to its hottest spot as the need arises. A tinsmith will cut a *blech*, or it can be ordered from a hardware store in a Jewish neighborhood.

FOODS

There are many traditional foods associated with Shabbat. Among them are:

Chicken soup	Tsholent
Roast chicken	Potato kugel
Chopped liver	Noodle kugel
Gefilte fish	

(See Recipes, p. 481.)

It is traditional to serve poultry or other meat for the two main Shabbat meals: Friday-night dinner and Saturday lunch. However, this is not a hard-and-fast rule: there are plenty of Jewish vegetarians who still qualify for a place in the world to come.

Some foods like tsholent have a special association with the light-heat issue mentioned above. Tsholent is a bean/meat/potato stew that is cooked before Shabbat and sits warming on the blech or in a low oven all night long, until Shabbat lunch. One source has it that when you eat tsholent you score a political point for the Pharisees, who made hot food on Shabbat day a litmus test of Pharisaic loyalty. The authoritative medieval code of Jewish law informs us that "One who disbelieves the words of the Sages, and forbids hot food to be eaten on Shabbat, is suspected of being an apikores [renegade Jew]" (SHULCHAN ARUCH, ORACH HAYYIM 257.8). The word "tsholent" perhaps derives from the Hebrew *sheh-lon*—that which rested on the heat source all night long.*

Another tradition about tsholent is that it symbolizes the unquenchable optimism of the Jewish people. You eat all that heavy tsholent for lunch, and then you lie down for your Shabbat afternoon nap, and you think you're going to get up again. . . .†

One of my fondest memories as a child is coming home from school on a wintry Friday afternoon into a house full of delicious smells of Shabbat food—and sitting right down to a piece of potato kugel. My mother would always prepare an extra large one so that we could all enjoy a pre-Shabbat snack. We weren't permitted to nosh the other foods prepared for Shabbat; the custom is to eat lightly on Friday, to savor the special Shabbat meals all the more. But kugel—that was our erev Shabbat (Friday-afternoon) treat.

There is no partaking of food from the time candles are lit until Kiddush is recited at dinner, so if you are having weekend guests who come from a distance, prepare a light snack for them before Shabbat begins.

BOILED WATER

A kettle of water that will be used for tea or coffee throughout Shabbat must be boiled in advance of candlelighting. Some people use electric coffee urns which they keep on all of Shabbat. You cannot boil water during Shabbat itself, nor add to the kettle, so put up as much as you'll need for the entire Shabbat. In Israel, wonderful large Shabbat kettles are made that hold three or four gallons of water, yet sit compactly on the blech.

* Courtesy Rabbi Ralph Pelcovitz of Far Rockaway, New York.
† Courtesy Rabbi Yitz Greenberg.

They have a neat spigot from which to fill a teapot or teacup, and they come with flat covers so that you can place another pot on top to also keep warm. These are sold in hardware stores in Jewish neighborhoods.

TEA ESSENCE

There is a difference of opinion as to whether making tea is cooking. Most people prepare tea essence beforehand, others use instant tea or steep teabags on Shabbat. Whichever form one chooses, during Shabbat the boiled water is poured first into the cup, and then the tea is added; not the reverse. Pouring the hot water into a secondary utensil (a tea cup) sufficiently reduces the heat so as not to constitute "cooking tea." In the case of teabags, however, some authorities require the boiled water to be poured into a tertiary utensil. Which is why, if you like your tea hot, it is best to prepare strong essence before Shabbat.

FRESH SALADS AND FRUITS

Preparation of fruits and vegetables which don't require cooking can be done during Shabbat. So as not to have to clean up afterward, however, many people prepare salads or fruit dishes in advance.

PREPARING ONESELF

There are two ways to prepare oneself—spiritually and physically—and the two are intertwined. Nevertheless, I shall attempt to distinguish between them.

PHYSICAL PREPARATION

Shower, shampoo, blow dry, shave, haircut: these are all common Friday-afternoon preparations in an observant Jew's life. Each of us carries special associations with the day, associations that have nothing to do with creation and freedom, and yet have everything to do with Shabbat. For me, a mother of five teenagers, one of my strongest associations with Friday afternoon is of shining, sweet-smelling hair.

Prepare your nice clothes for Shabbat. If you bought something new that's appropriate for this special day, wear it first on Shabbat. Do whatever laundry is necessary, pick up the suit from the dry cleaner, sew on the button, put up the hem, cut off the tags from new clothes, polish the shoes. My father used to get us to polish his shoes on Friday afternoon by calling out to my sisters and me, "Girls, which one of you wants a mitzvah?" (of honoring parents).

Mail off the letter you've written, call up that friend you've been meaning to call all week; otherwise, it'll have to wait until Saturday night.

Put your wallet in a drawer, take your favorite lipstick out of your handbag, for a handbag is muktzeh on Shabbat. Empty your pockets of money and other items, and remember to check your coat pockets too. Orthodox Jews do not handle money on Shabbat, nor do they carry things out of doors on Shabbat, unless there is an eruv.

THE ERUV

A few words about the eruv are in order here. Jewish law forbids the carrying of objects into the public domain on Shabbat; it doesn't matter if the object is as light as a handkerchief or house key or as heavy as a book of Talmud. Nor can one push a baby carriage or stroller, or even carry a baby who cannot walk by himself or herself.

This law can definitely clip one's wings! Particularly with babies, one can feel "locked in" on a Shabbat. But Jews have found a way to resolve it; or, rather, several ways. One way is by having objects that one needs outside of the home available at the other end of the line. For example: having prayer books and Bibles at a synagogue for everyone who comes is a solution to a Jew's not being permitted to carry his/her own siddur (prayer book) through the streets.

When I was a teenager, I would periodically apply my talents toward finding a good safe hiding spot for my comb and lipstick in the small ladies' room of my shul. I couldn't carry these items with me, and yet there was no way on earth I would walk into shul without recombing after the ten-minute walk there. So I had to provide for these things properly. Best friends were those girls to whom you would tell where your "Shabbos comb and lipstick" were hidden. When I married, and moved away, I left my comb and lipstick in place. It was like leaving a small part of me behind in the shul of my youth. I wonder if it's still in place. I know no one is looking anymore, because an eruv has since been put up in that neighborhood.

A second solution is to have craftsmen create things like Shabbos keys. A key, nicely gilded, is affixed to a belt buckle or tie clip or pin back; thus, it becomes part of a person's clothing or jewelry on which there is no restriction of carrying. One would also tie a handkerchief around the wrist rather than carry it in a pocket. Some of this seems ludicrous to an outsider, but it is all part of the total commitment of an Orthodox Jew.

Still, neither of those solutions addresses the larger problem of taking babies out of doors on Shabbat. But an eruv does. An *eruv* is a symbolic act by means of which the legal fiction of community or continuity is established. An eruv symbolically transforms a public domain into a large private one; this allows a Jew to carry outside the house items that would normally be permissible to carry from place to place inside the house. In other words, where there's an eruv enclosure, one may carry on Shabbat, within reason, any item which is not muktzeh. An eruv encircles a town, and makes it all private property, even though we all know it isn't private property. An eruv is sometimes nothing more than a wire connected at appropriate points to existing telephone wires, in order to completely close the perimeter. There are eruv checkers and eruv hot lines—to see if the eruv is in order.

In recent years, many communities have constructed eruvin (plural), putting Shabbos keymakers and Shabbos baby-sitters out of business, but, in general, making life much less complicated and more pleasant for traditional Jews.

For most of my early married and childraising years, I lived in a community that had no eruv; and therefore, if I didn't plan ahead for a baby-sitter to mind the babies at home or take them out in the carriage, there was no way that I could go to shul or take an afternoon walk with Yitz and the bigger children. For the most part, I took it with great equanimity. When I look back on those times, I can only wonder in amazement why it didn't bother me more and why I didn't organize a huge rally of all Orthodox mothers of young children. Although no eruv has come out of a women's protest group, I think the increase in eruvin has something to do with the new perception women have of themselves, their needs, and their place in community life.

In Riverdale, New York, where we live, it took five years to get that eruv up. There were people who resisted the idea, fearing it would lead to transgression of Shabbat—that is, the domino theory of sinning. Also, the law is very complicated, and there are very few eruv experts around. And, like all things, it costs money. But, finally, it was accomplished. I was very pleased to see it go up, even though it came too late for me to benefit personally. However, in a way I, too, reap its benefits every week. It's very satisfying on Shabbat morning to see all those baby carriages and strollers parked outside of shul, and to see all the beautiful new young life inside.

SPIRITUAL PREPARATION

Some Jewish men, Chasidim in particular, go to the mikvah (ritual bath) on Friday afternoon. It is a lovely custom, for mikvah not only symbolizes a spiritual cleansing, it also offers a few moments of private time to reflect, to relax, to disengage from the past week, to think about the coming experience of Shabbat. However, if their wives are home frenziedly preparing for Shabbat, caring for eight kids, it's not altogether fair, nor is it in the spirit of the day. Similarly, in those families where a woman has the leisure to sit in a beauty parlor for three hours on a Friday afternoon, while her husband is frantically winding up a hard week, there might be a better distribution of responsibility so that a man will have the time to come a bit more restfully into Shabbat.

Before Shabbat begins, it is a custom to put some money into a pushke, a charity box. Nowadays, tzedakah (charity) being a bigger business, what with appeals, dinners, guests of honor, checks and IRS deductions, this custom of slipping a few coins into a slotted tin box is of less impact. Yet, it is a sweet thing for children to observe, to do, and to learn from. And it's one more act associated with the special preparations for Shabbat.

Some people also are able to set aside time to meditate, or study quietly before Shabbat. These are wonderful ways to prepare spiritually for the day. My husband often studies his daily quota of Talmud right before Shabbat. Somehow, I never have the time or discipline to distance myself this way until the very last minute. Perhaps this is my conditioning as a woman who, like most women, has been largely responsible for the physical preparations in the home, and who gleans the sense of sacredness and holiness from those endeavors; but for those who can get themselves spiritually as well as physically ready, there is a different foretaste altogether of Shabbat.

Inasmuch as one should review the Biblical portion of the week at least once before it is read in shul on Shabbat morning, this is an excellent subject for quiet study on a Friday afternoon.

HACHNASAT ORCHIM—HOSPITALITY

Although tradition requires that Jews fulfill the mitzvah of hachnasat orchim whenever the opportunity or need presents itself, for most of us modern urbanites Shabbat and holidays seem to be the preferred times for inviting guests. There is more time to spend leisurely with old friends, and more time to get to know acquaintances better. In addition, Shabbat and holidays are experiences of sacred time and of family tone. Those are added gifts to share with people who are lonely or unconnected to family and/or tradition.

And finally, hachnasat orchim is a wonderful mitzvah for children: a) it is a concrete model from which to learn the art of sharing; b) children have an opportunity to become acquainted with all different kinds of people, including non-Jews; c) it reminds them, periodically, that they are not the center of the universe. . . .

Like all good things, we must learn to balance openness and sharing with our own needs for privacy and rest. Like all good things, we must plan ahead to fulfill this mitzvah. Erev Shabbat is too late to invite guests for that evening, but it is a good time to think ahead and act. It is easy to invite people we like; but, occasionally, we have to extend ourselves and invite those who otherwise might not have, yet would greatly appreciate, the experience of a family Shabbat. Most often, they, too, become our friends. In other words, Shabbat is a great occasion for enlarging one's circle of friends.

ONE FAMILY'S PREPARATIONS

Preparation for Shabbat fits Parkinson's Law, and then some. On several occasions, in the year 1981, I kept a diary of our own preparations. In comparing them, I find it almost hard to believe it's the same household. I have selected two here: one, during the time we had a live-in housekeeper who had been with us almost a year; the other, with the family fending pretty much for itself.

SHABBAT I

On Thursday and Friday I called the butcher, the baker, the fish store, the vegetable man, and gave them my orders, most of which were delivered. I made up a menu and talked it over with my housekeeper. When I returned home on Friday afternoon, everything had been done, except for the following: setting the lights and the Shabbos clock, picking up the bakery order, fish order, and some last-minute supermarket items, checking the tissues and towels in the bathroom, baking a homemade cake, chilling the wine, putting up the kettle of water, burning in the candles' bottoms, prodding the kids, getting the blech set up, and everyone showering, polishing shoes, and dressing. All of these tasks were divided, and the last-minute tensions were kept to a bare minimum. (Without a little hysteria, it just wouldn't be a real erev Shabbat.)

I can't say that I missed the cooking, cleaning, and setting up, no matter how much it heightened the difference between week work and Shabbat. If someone else fills my house with Shabbat cooking odors and spanking cleanliness, that's just fine. Several years ago, I was assigned to supervise a lab that officially closed at 4:00 P.M. on Fridays. I ordered most of my food ready-made, and would stay as late as possible toward closing time. This meant that on certain Fridays of the year I didn't get home until twenty minutes before Shabbat. I remember once coming home to find my candles lit for me. It was a half hour before Shabbat, and I couldn't figure out who had done it. Yitz had picked me up at school so I knew it wasn't he. The children were all under seven, so it couldn't have been any of them. It turned out that the housekeeper, who had been with me only three weeks and had seen me light candles during the previous weeks, wanted everything to be just perfect for Shabbat when I arrived home.

I recall my father was very unhappy about my Friday-afternoon routine that entire year, with so little personal preparation on my part. He felt that it just wasn't the same, and that I wasn't creating for the children the proper memories and associations and smells of Friday in a traditional Jewish home, memories my mother certainly gave me. I wasn't quite liberated at that time, and it would never have occurred to me to say, even respectfully, to my father, "If you think it's so wonderful, how come men don't take over the preparations for Shabbat?" All I could tell him was that my appreciation of Shabbat after a hard day at work was as great as it was staying home all day and preparing. I still feel that way, even though I know that our children don't get the same flavor of the day unless all of us are involved.

SHABBAT II

The second Shabbat was somewhat more harried. It went something like this: *On Wednesday, at 10:00 P.M.*, I call the wife of my vegetable man. (A little thing like having a vegetable man take telephone orders—at night, no less—can save at least a hundred hours a year.) He will leave my order on the porch, and I'll leave him an approximate check in the mailbox. The temperature is just right and the produce will hold until I get home. Thank God that Juno, the dog down the block, doesn't scavenge fruit and vegetables.

Thursday morning: I prepare my menu. I should have done it on Wednesday because I forgot to order mushrooms and Mr. I. is already out with his vegetable truck. Here's my menu:

Friday dinner	*Saturday lunch*
Vegetable soup	Grapefruit
. . . . .	. . . . .
Tossed salad	Tsholent with brisket
. . . . .	
Chicken	Parve tsholent (meatless for the vegetarians)
Baked salmon (main course for the vegetarians)	Tofu with mushrooms and onions (for the vegetarians)
Potato kugel	Cole slaw
Sweet carrots	Tomato/cucumber salad
. . . . .	. . . . .
Tea	Tea
Seven-layer cake	Brownies, rhubarb pie

For fifteen years I prepared five- or six-course meals for Friday night, starting with fish or fruit in season, soup, salad, main course, dessert, tea and pastry. That's how my mother did it, so that's how I did it. Most Orthodox families still eat that way on Shabbat. About eight years ago, Jane Brody, health columnist of *The New York Times*, wrote an article that made me ask myself whether it is actually a commandment from Sinai to push six courses on the table. So we cut that first course, and the dessert, and surprise! It's still a "Shabbos meal." I've even found that those summer Shabbat lunches at which I serve dairy have, more or less, taken on the feeling of a traditional meal.

Next, I call my kosher butcher. He'll deliver my chicken and meat at 6:00 P.M. on his way home (I can't take a chance with that mutt, Juno). "Very clean," I tell him. "No feathers, please, and cut into eighths."

Three of our children are vegetarians. If I wait until Friday, I'll forget them and they'll be stuck with hard-boiled eggs for Shabbat, so I call the fish and the health food stores (for tofu) to put my orders aside for tomorrow afternoon, when Moshe will pick everything up.

Thursday night: I had planned to do a bit of Shabbat preparation after dinner. But I am too tired, having put in a full day's work. So, after we clean up the dairy dishes (there's no law about this, but it's customary to serve dairy on Thursday evening; it heightens the taste for chicken and meat on Shabbat), I announce that everyone must come home immediately after school tomorrow and we will all do the job together. Working woman and all, I am still pretty much in charge of the whole plant and its day-to-day functioning. David says he has to go to the library for an hour after school, so he does his job—vacuuming and dusting—on Thursday night. He knows he's getting off easy.

Friday morning: I call the bakery to get my order ready. There are some compensations in shopping for a large family. The clerk in the bakery wouldn't take a phone order for two challot, but for six loaves plus, everything will be ready for whichever Greenberg comes by, usually at an hour when the challot are all gone.

Friday morning: the cleaning woman comes. She will stay for half a day, washing the bathrooms, changing the linens, and cleaning the kitchen, only to have us come home after she leaves and mess the whole thing up.

Friday afternoon is countdown, with mostly cooking to be done. Goody and I are the first ones home. After a snack, she brings the TV into the kitchen, plunks it down on the counter, turns on her favorite "soap," and begins to polish the silver wine cups, challah plate, challah knife, and serving pieces. What with Luke and Laura (of the soap opera *General Hospital*) inching romantically toward each other, Goody's work gets done only during commercials. Then Goody starts peeling potatoes—five pounds for kugel and tsholent. Her friend Seth has just come over to visit, and he sweetly offers to help, so we give him another peeler. If only his mother could see him . . . Moshe takes the car and goes out to do the errands: the bakery, the fish store, the health food store, the cleaners, and so forth. Deborah is baking brownies and a pie, and preparing popcorn for her friends, who will visit during Shabbat. Meanwhile, with Deborah's help I have made the vegetarian soup, cleaned and put the chickens into the oven—ignoring the few feathers the butcher missed—and prepared the two tsholents—one with meat and bones, the other, vegetarian. I have also called my guests, to inquire whether any of their children are vegetarian (and really to remind them of our date tomorrow, since I haven't spoken to them in a month). Goody and I feed the rest of the potatoes into the food processor for the kugel. I don't feel like hassling an onion, so I cut off the ends and throw it into the processor with its skin on. But it doesn't work, and I have to scoop that one out, take another onion, and do it the right way, tears and all. I mutter aloud my old motto, "Haste works only seventy-five percent of the time," and Goody cleverly tells me those are still better odds than "Haste makes waste." J.J. takes out the garbage, sets the Shabbos clock, and begins to set the dining-room table. He gets as far as cleaning my papers off the table into a carton, spreading out a new cloth and placing on it the stack of dishes. Then he vanishes. As I come to set up my candlesticks a few moments later, I see that he has not finished the job. I set out the plates and goblets, also the challah plate, knife, challah cover, and wine cups so at least the table will look Shabbosdik. I save the rest for later. If I remember, J.J. will hear from me.

The phone rings; it's my mother-in-law calling to wish me a good Shabbos. I should have called her first, but I was waiting for her son to come home to speak to her as well. She gets upset when he has to be out of town for Shabbat. He's scheduled to arrive from Detroit one hour before Shabbat. If all goes well, he'll be home forty minutes before candlelighting. It's pretty hairy; there are often long lines for taxis on a Friday afternoon, so we've arranged for the local car service to be waiting there for him. His plane is actually five minutes early; he calls from the airport to find out where to meet the driver. So far, so good, I think to myself. Everything, except J.J., seems to be working.

Ninety minutes to candlelighting. I call my parents to wish them a good Shabbos. Moshe comes back with the last-minute groceries, which he proceeds to put away. He's hungry, and heats up some spaghetti for himself, and then starts to tip the string beans, J.J.'s job. I prepare the fish and the tofu/mushroom/onion dish. All four burners are going. My sister calls to say hello. Some of the kids have gone up to shower and shampoo and dress. What's still left? I check my menu and my Shabbat countdown list taped to the inside of my pantry closet: cook the string beans, and the carrots, prepare the salad, boil a kettle of water, prepare the tea essence, set up the blech, and turn on necessary lights. Deborah and I split the tasks. We scratch coleslaw from the menu. No time. We'll open a jar of pickles instead.

David walks in, famished, and despite the pressure of time, he sits down to a bowl of dry cereal and a leisurely reading of the cartoons on the box. I prod him along, give him a speech about how he shouldn't save library work for Friday, and I tell him to go quickly upstairs. He grins and says, "You know I'll be ready before you." "Right, Flash," I answer, and up he goes. J.J. saunters in. Our neighbor was leaving for a ski weekend and good-natured J.J. spotted him through the window and went out to help him load the car. I want to say, "You should help your mother first," but instead I give him a long look and we call it a draw: Knowing how slowly he moves, I tell him to forget his other jobs and go up and get ready.

There is no time to clean up the cooking and baking utensils, so Deborah removes the racks and loads the dishwasher cavity with dirty pots and pans, which we will tackle tomorrow night. Dreadful, I say to myself, but I will put it out of my mind for the next twenty-five hours.

I go up to shower and dress while Deborah stays down to clean off the counters. I wanted to be down when Yitz walked in the door, but the timing didn't work. While I'm upstairs he arrives, calls out hello to everyone, makes two phone calls, slits open two days of mail, and sets aside the personal mail to read later in a moment of leisure. He unpacks his suitcase, polishes his shoes, showers, and shaves. We'll talk later. The best water-saver in the world is the erev Shabbat shower. Seven people, and the water isn't cold yet. It may not be the most relaxing shower in the world, but it works. As I dress quickly, I think about my cousin by marriage, a professor of social work, who goes to the mikvah in Forest Hills every Friday afternoon; then he comes home and helps his wife prepare for Shabbat. Now that's the way to do it.

I call everyone on the intercom. Ten minutes left to candle-lighting. J.J. can't polish his Shabbat shoes because he can't find them. His father tells him to reconstruct. Sure enough, last week our guests used J.J.'s room, and J.J. left his shoes in the attic bedroom beneath Moshe's bed. No matter what, J.J. will be late. We've tried punishing, bribing, ignoring. They all have about the same effect. We try to stay cool.

I put on my long skirt, wrap a scarf around my head, which is still wet, and go down for the last-minute details. There's a smell of gas in the kitchen: the kettle of water boiled over and extinguished the flame. I check the lights again and put on the front-porch light for after-dark visitors. Yitz takes care of the upstairs lights and checks to see if there are tissue and fresh towels in each bathroom. He hurries everyone along.

The intercom sings out, "Five minutes to licht-bentschen" (Yiddish for blessing the candles). The tension mounts. Am I the only one who feels it?

David is the first one down, all ready except for blazer in one hand and blazer button in the other. "You forgot to sew my button on during the week." "I can't remember everything," I tell him; "you have to remind me during the week. Besides, next week I'm going to teach you how to sew by hand." (He knows how to machine-sew.) He reminds me that he already knows, and has sewed on his own buttons in camp. "So why don't you do it yourself?" "Please," he says. Who can resist that? I take the needle and thread and tell David to fix the blech. There's no place to set down the hot pots for a moment, so he takes today's *Times*, places it on the counter and puts the pots on top, spoiling pages 1 and 2 for me, which I haven't yet read.

"Thirty seconds to candlelighting. Who's ready to light candles with me?" "I'm coming," Goody calls back on the intercom, but she doesn't get there in time. David is the only one with me as I light the candles. Afterward, I heave a sigh of relief, give David a kiss, and feel the stress and strain of the week begin to drain out of my body.

There is hardly a thing we could not have done earlier to ease the pressure. We have fallen into bad ways. I hope our children will do it differently, like their grandparents, ready by midmorning. Nevertheless within ten minutes, everyone else is down, on their way to shul with Yitz or ready to daaven (pray) at home with me. Once again, we've made it. . . .

Celebrating Shabbat

SHABBAT

Not only do we read from right to left, but we start our day at night. More confusing, erev Shabbat, which literally means the evening of Shabbat, in actual fact refers to daytime Friday.

The reason for this is that the Jewish calendar is a lunar one, with the new month beginning at the first sighting of the sliver of new moon. If the first day begins at night (as did the first day of Creation), so do all the days that follow. And if the "day" begins at night, the "eve" of any given day is what immediately precedes it—daytime.

Shabbat, therefore, begins and ends at a particular moment of evening. On the general principle of "adding on to the good" (in this case, from weekday to holy), Shabbat begins eighteen minutes before sunset on Friday and ends forty-two minutes after sunset on Saturday. All in all, Shabbat is approximately twenty-five hours long. Tied as it is to the setting sun, Shabbat starts at a different hour each week. The earliest it begins is the week of the winter solstice, the shortest Friday of the year.

In the summertime, the sun sets as late as nine o'clock. During spring and summer months, many communities begin Shabbat at seven in the evening so as not to have to wait until ten to sit down to Kiddush and a five course meal. Moreover, during these weeks of advanced onset time, the Sabbath evening prayers are recited during daylight hours (only the Shema is repeated later) rather than after dark as is normally required for evening prayers. These are examples of sensible rabbinic modification that enable traditional Jews to live according to the law, comfortably.

Since we may only add weekday time onto Shabbat and never subtract, no matter what time Shabbat is advanced on Friday, it will not end earlier than forty-two minutes after sunset on Saturday.

The onset of Shabbat is marked by a ceremony of candlelighting. This probably started as a very practical response to "Thou shalt not kindle fire . . ." In order to have the supply of oil burn longer into Shabbat, the lamps were lit at the very last moment. So, too, with candles.

Candlelighting can advance the Shabbat but it cannot delay it. Shabbat comes automatically, with the setting of the sun. In fact, if candles have not been lit on time, they may not be kindled later, for it is already Shabbat. Thus, the Rabbis established that candles be lit close to but earlier than sunset.

Traditional Judaism, with its heavy emphasis on role definition, assigned nerot, candlelighting, to women—although not all candles, it must be added. The Havdalah candle, which concludes the Sabbath, and Chanukah candles, the more "public" candles, go to men.

A minimum of two candles are lit, symbolic of the two forms of the commandment—"remember" and "observe" the Sabbath day. Many women light one candle for each member of the family. My mother's candelabrum has five branches. As a child, I used to wonder whether she bought it before or after she had three children.

A woman covers her hair for candlelighting. (Some Orthodox women cover their heads all the time, some only on Shabbat, some only for candlelighting and synagogue attendance.) She then lights the candles but does not blow out the match, laying it down in a safe spot to burn itself out, because the act of candlelighting has ushered Shabbat into her household, and extinguishing the match is no longer permitted.

The ceremony is very simple. A woman encircles the light three times with her hands and repeats with each encircling:

בָּרוּךְ הוּא וּבָרוּךְ שְׁמוֹ.

Baruch hu u'varuch shemo.

Blessed be He and blessed be His name.

She then covers her eyes with both hands and recites the blessing:

בָּרוּךְ אַתָּה יְיָ, אֱלֹהֵינוּ מֶלֶךְ הָעוֹלָם, אֲשֶׁר קִדְּשָׁנוּ בְּמִצְוֹתָיו, וְצִוָּנוּ לְהַדְלִיק נֵר שֶׁל שַׁבָּת.

Baruch ata Adonai Elohainu melech ha'olam asher kidshanu b'mitzvotav v'tzivanu l'hadlik ner shel Shabbat.

Blessed are You, Lord our God, Ruler of the universe, Who has sanctified us with His commandments and commanded us to kindle the light of the Sabbath.

For the last few hundred years, Jewish women have added another brief prayer to the candlelighting blessing. It is the Yehi

Ratzon, the prayer for return to the Temple, which is really a prayer for messianic times:

יְהִי רָצוֹן מִלְּפָנֶיךָ יְיָ אֱלֹהֵינוּ וֵאלֹהֵי אֲבוֹתֵינוּ שֶׁיִּבָּנֶה בֵּית הַמִּקְדָּשׁ בִּמְהֵרָה בְיָמֵינוּ. וְתֵן חֶלְקֵנוּ בְּתוֹרָתֶךָ. וְשָׁם נַעֲבָדְךָ בְּיִרְאָה. כִּימֵי עוֹלָם וּכְשָׁנִים קַדְמוֹנִיּוֹת. וְעָרְבָה לַיְיָ מִנְחַת יְהוּדָה וִירוּשָׁלָיִם כִּימֵי עוֹלָם וּכְשָׁנִים קַדְמוֹנִיּוֹת.

Yehi ratzon milfanecha Adonai Elohainu ve'Elohai avotainu, sheh'yibaneh bet ha'mikdash bimheyra veyamenu, vetain chel'kaynu betorah'techa, ve'sham na'avad'cha beyira kimey olam uchshanim kadmoniot, ve'arva la'Adonai minchat yehuda vee'yerushalayim kimey olam uch'shanim kadmo'niyot.

May it be Your will, Lord, our God and God of our fathers, that the Temple be speedily rebuilt in our days, and grant our portion in Your Torah. And there we will serve You with awe as in days of old and as in ancient years. And may the offerings of Judah and Jerusalem be as pleasing to You as ever and as in ancient times.

The reason for covering the eyes is this: blessings are usually recited prior to the act; the blessing over the candles, however, like the lighting of the candles, ushers in the beginning of Shabbat. This being so, after having recited the blessing, we would no longer be permitted to light candles. So we light the candles, cover our eyes so we don't see the light or have "benefit" from it, as if the candles are not lit. Then we recite the blessing, uncover our eyes, and presto, the candles are lit.

I treasure my moment of candlelighting. When we speak today of men and women sharing rituals that have been traditionally male, such as Kiddush and aliyot (calling men up for the Torah blessings in the synagogue), a little fear creeps up inside of me. I don't want Shabbat candles to be taken from me. . . . If I were starting out now, I might do it a bit differently. I would expect all the family to be in attendance as I light, much as they are for Kiddush and Havdalah. But having done it this way for so many years, my pleasure comes from the private rather than the public experience, enhanced if some of the family are there at the moment, but not diminished if I light alone.

For many years my husband would stand by while I lit, but that ended when he became a pulpit rabbi and had to leave early for shul. When the children all were younger, I used to let each of them light a candle or ignite the match (which, to a five-year-old, is an even bigger prize). Now that they are grown, and I have less control over their time, their presence at candlelighting is a sometimes thing. A friend, a young widow with three teen daughters, sets up a pair of candlesticks for each to light, and they all do it together every Friday night. It's a lovely sight to behold.

Some Jews, particularly the Lubavitch Chasidim, have embarked on a campaign to have all young Jewish girls light one Shabbat candle. Though Jewish law does not explicitly require it, many consider it important for educational training purposes. This practice is still not universally observed. In most Orthodox homes, the mother will light for the entire household. However, when an unmarried woman sets up her own household, she is responsible for Shabbat candles. So is a man, when there is no woman in the household. There are many Jewish college students living in dormitories who light Shabbat candles every week. A pair of candlesticks make a fine gift for a student, male or female, going away to college.

If one has women guests, at least two candles should be prepared for each of them. If there are young girls present, it is thoughtful to inquire whether they, too, wish to light their own candles. One doesn't need a whole lot of extra candlesticks. Almost anything flat and lined with aluminum foil will do. Shabbat candles are short and stubby, and if the bottoms are burned in, they will stand safely on just about anything. But do not use thin glass as a base. When the candles burn down, their heat will shatter that beautiful Limoges bonbon tray. . . .

I've added another brief ritual to my candlelighting, a very private one. Several years ago I was chatting one evening in

Jerusalem with a middle-aged couple who had settled in Israel four years earlier. They had come without their three children, and had left America as their youngest daughter was entering Barnard College. Planning ahead for the day when our children go their own ways, I asked Mrs. F., "Do you miss them? Do you think about them a lot? Do you imagine what they are doing at any given moment?" "No," she said. "I love seeing them" (usually twice a year as things worked out), "receiving their letters, and writing to them, but I don't miss them. . . . In fact, I began to realize that if I didn't remind myself of them, a week or two could go by without my thinking about them at all. So I decided that at candlelighting each Friday night, I would let my thoughts dwell for a moment on each child, picture their faces, and think about their lives. I once mentioned it to them, and now they all light candles on Friday night and think for a few moments about us."

So as I light my candles each week, I reflect for a few seconds about my husband and about each child, and then I remove my hands from my eyes and say, "Good Shabbos," and kiss whoever happens to be standing by.

After candlelighting, the men go off to shul for Minchah, Kabbalat Shabbat, and Maariv prayers. Minchah, the afternoon prayer, really belongs to the weekday, but it is scheduled back to back with the evening prayer for convenience. Minchah is recited at the last possible moment of the afternoon, and Maariv, the evening prayer, at earliest evening, with the Kabbalat Shabbat service (welcoming the Sabbath) as the highlight wedged between the two. In an urbanized society, it is difficult to run back and forth to shul three times a day, especially on a short Friday, and the Rabbis took these practical problems into consideration as they formulated ritual.

Some women go to shul for Friday-evening services, but far fewer than go on a Shabbat morning. Most of the Friday-night women's crowd consists of little girls, teenagers, and older women. At times our daughters go, but often they stay home, and the three of us pray together. We should go more often, because the Friday-night shul daavening (prayer) is the most beautiful of all, with more communal singing than at any other time. But on Friday night I like to luxuriate in the sudden peacefulness of the house between candlelighting and dinner and in the prayer with my daughters, parts of which we sing together.

One of the special prayers of Kabbalat Shabbat is the Lecha Dodi, welcoming the beloved Sabbath. There are several beautiful melodies for these words. On Friday nights, as I sing the Lecha Dodi, an image of the sixteenth-century mystics of Safed springs into my mind.* I picture them as lean men, dressed in white caftans, their fine faces tanned from sun and wind, and glowing from their ritual immersion. I see them standing atop the mountain crest, facing toward Jerusalem and the setting sun, and singing Lecha Dodi. Could they ever have imagined that four hundred years later a New York Jew, in a modern house, would be singing "their" song? I wonder if the Beatles will have such longevity.

Even better than shul is my mother-in-law's Friday-night daavening. Occasionally, she spends a Shabbat with us. As I lurk around a corner, and listen intently, I feel as if I am privy to a private audience with God. She finishes up the regular Friday-night prayers, and then, in a barely audible whisper, and looking into her siddur all the while, she proceeds to carry on a one-way conversation with Him.

With eighty-five years behind her, my mother-in-law brings God up-to-date on the whereabouts and doings of each child, grandchild, and great-grandchild, occasionally summing up past favors and events of yesteryear. Once, more than fifteen years after I had been married, she reminded God that her son had married a nice yiddishe maidele (Jewish girl). After describing what each of us was doing, she turned His attention to the grandchildren—which school each attended, who was graduating, who was in a cast with a torn cartilage, and who was going to camp for a month. Rarely does she make an outright plea, but once she mentioned in passing that my brother-in-law's blood pressure was too high. Yet another time, she informed her beloved God that her grandson, then twenty-eight, chief resident at Peter Bent Brigham Hospital in Boston, was working very hard

---

* In the sixteenth century, Jewish mystics, known as the Kabbalists, went up to settle in the Holy Land in the city of Safed. It was they who created the Kabbalat Shabbat service, including in it the Lecha Dodi prayer which was written by one of their own.

and had no time yet to look for a wife (hint, hint). Systematically, every Friday night she parades the entire family before God. Without ever using those words, it is a prayer of thanksgiving. May I be forgiven for eavesdropping, hers are truly among the most moving prayers I have ever heard.

As soon as the shul contingent returns, the family sings Shalom Aleichem together, greeting the Shabbos angels who have accompanied them home:

Shalom aleichem
mal'achei hashareit
Mal'achei elyon
Mimelech malechai hamelachim
Hakadosh baruch Hu.

Bo'achem leshalom
mal'achei hashalom
Mal'achei elyon
Mimelech malechai hamelachim
Hakadosh baruch Hu.

Barchuni leshalom
mal'achei hashalom
Mal'achei elyon
Mimelech malechai hamelachim
Hakadosh baruch Hu.

Tzeitchem leshalom
mal'achei hashalom
Mal'achei elyon
Mimelech malechai hamelachim
Hakadosh baruch Hu.

Peace unto you
Angels of peace
Angels of the most High
Angels of the King Who is King of Kings
The Holy One, blessed be He.

Come in peace
Angels of peace . . .

Bless us in peace . . .
Angels of peace . . .

Go in peace,
Angels of peace . . .

People have different customs regarding Shalom Aleichem. Some families sing each stanza three times, others, only once. Some families sing while seated about the living room; others, while standing around the dining room table immediately before Kiddush. When our children were very young, we developed a simple custom, which has persisted, even though sometimes I feel we've outgrown it. We join hands and move about in a circle as we sing. Since there are four stanzas, we've upped the choreography to reversing direction after the first two stanzas. Years ago, we would put a baby in the center or sometimes two; and of course the birthday boy or girl always stood in the middle as we circled about. This is how family rituals begin. Our future grandchildren will probably assume it's a two-thousand-year-old ritual.

Another fine Shabbat custom is for parents to bless their children with the Biblical blessings of Ephraim and Manasseh. The parent (traditionally the father but in many homes now both father and mother) places the two hands on the child's head and says:

To a son:

יְשִׂמְךָ אֱלֹהִים כְּאֶפְרַיִם וְכִמְנַשֶּׁה.

Yesimcha Elohim k'Ephraim ve'chiMenashe.

May God make you [a symbol of blessing] as He did Ephraim and Manasseh.

To a daughter:

יְשִׂמֵךְ אֱלֹהִים כְּשָׂרָה, רִבְקָה, רָחֵל וְלֵאָה.

Yesimech Elohim k'Sarah, Rivka, Rachel, v'Leah.

May God make you [a symbol of blessing] as He did Sarah, Rebekah, Rachel, and Leah.

Some add the priestly blessing:

יְבָרֶכְךָ יְיָ וְיִשְׁמְרֶךָ. יָאֵר יְיָ פָּנָיו אֵלֶיךָ וִיחֻנֶּךָ. יִשָּׂא יְיָ פָּנָיו
אֵלֶיךָ, וְיָשֵׂם לְךָ שָׁלוֹם.

> *Yevareche'cha Adonai ve'yishmerecha*
> *Ya'er Adonai panav eleycha viyechuneka*
> *Yissah Adonai panav eleycha veyasem lecha shalom.*

May God bless you and keep you
May God cause His face to shine upon you and be gracious unto
   you
May God lift up His face upon you and give you peace.

—NUMBERS 6:24–27

My husband adds another blessing, the one with which his father would bless him as he departed for summer camp, college, or a journey away from home:

כִּי מַלְאָכָיו יְצַוֶּה לָּךְ. לִשְׁמָרְךָ בְּכָל דְּרָכֶיךָ.

> *Ki malachav yetzave lach lishmorcha bechol derachecha.*

He shall command His messengers to guard over you wherever you go.

And then, as he hugs the children afterward, he adds a word or two about something special in their lives this week.

When Moshe was eight, he decided he wanted to bless us back. His younger siblings copied him—and that's how another ritual started in our house.

Before Kiddush is recited, a husband sings to his wife the

words of Ayshet Chayil (A Woman of Valor) from Proverbs, chapter 31. The translation is as follows:

A good wife who can find?
She is worth far more than rubies.
Her husband trusts in her,
And he never lacks gain.
She brings him good and not harm,
All the days of her life.

She seeks out wool and flax,
And works with her willing hands.
She is like the merchant ships—
She brings her food from afar.
She rises while it is yet night,
And gives food to her household,
And rations to her maids.

She considers a field and buys it;
With her earnings she plants a vineyard.
She girds herself with strength,
And braces her arms for work.
She finds that her trade is profitable;
Her lamp goes not out at night.
She sets her hands to the distaff;
Her fingers hold the spindle.

She stretches out her hand to the poor;
She reaches out her arms to the needy.
She is not afraid of the snow for her household,
For all her household is clad in scarlet wool.
She makes her own tapestries;
Her clothing is fine linen and purple.

Her husband is known at the gates,
As he sits among the elders of the land.
She makes linen cloth and sells it;
She supplies the merchants with wraps.
Dignity and honor are her garb;
She smiles looking at the future.

She opens her mouth in wisdom
And she speaks a language of loving-kindness
She watches her family's comings and goings
And partakes not from the bread of idleness.

Her children arise and bless her
Her husband sings her praises
Many women are marked by greatness
But you have surpassed them all
Charm is false, beauty emptiness
A woman who fears the Lord shall be praised
Give her the fruits of her labors
And let her accomplishments be a source of praise.

Several years ago, our family spent Shabbat at a retreat with a group of young Jews who were in the process of fusing Jewish tradition with the counterculture. We were the only married couple, and when Yitz sang the Ayshet Chayil to me, several people clucked their tongues in protest: how could we, feminists both, at that (a man, too, can be a feminist), persist in carrying on with this sexist song? Later, the group discussed it at some length. I cannot recall the arguments now, but they could not convince me that it was sexist, nor could they convince me that I didn't enjoy having it sung to me every Friday night.

I think it's beautiful and romantic and my only complaint is that while he's singing he's also getting the wine ready. Instead, he should be looking into my eyes. Without undue modesty, I can say there is always some wonderful part that applies especially to me that week (although sometimes it's none other than the phrase "her husband is known at the gates").

Kiddush, the formal sanctification of the day, is recited over a brimming cup of wine. Kiddush retells how God completed creation on the sixth day and then set aside—and sanctified—the seventh day as a day of rest. We bless God for giving us the Shabbat by which to remember Creation and the Exodus from Egypt. We also express gratitude that God chose us from among all other people to be His special people.

וַיְהִי עֶרֶב, וַיְהִי־בֹקֶר,

יוֹם הַשִּׁשִּׁי. וַיְכֻלּוּ הַשָּׁמַיִם וְהָאָרֶץ וְכָל־צְבָאָם. וַיְכַל אֱלֹהִים בַּיּוֹם הַשְּׁבִיעִי, מְלַאכְתּוֹ אֲשֶׁר עָשָׂה, וַיִּשְׁבֹּת בַּיּוֹם הַשְּׁבִיעִי, מִכָּל מְלַאכְתּוֹ אֲשֶׁר עָשָׂה. וַיְבָרֶךְ אֱלֹהִים אֶת יוֹם הַשְּׁבִיעִי, וַיְקַדֵּשׁ אֹתוֹ, כִּי בוֹ שָׁבַת מִכָּל מְלַאכְתּוֹ, אֲשֶׁר בָּרָא אֱלֹהִים לַעֲשׂוֹת.

סָבְרִי מָרָנָן וְרַבּוֹתַי.

בָּרוּךְ אַתָּה יְיָ, אֱלֹהֵינוּ מֶלֶךְ הָעוֹלָם, בּוֹרֵא פְּרִי הַגָּפֶן.

בָּרוּךְ אַתָּה יְיָ, אֱלֹהֵינוּ מֶלֶךְ הָעוֹלָם, אֲשֶׁר קִדְּשָׁנוּ בְּמִצְוֹתָיו וְרָצָה בָנוּ, וְשַׁבַּת קָדְשׁוֹ בְּאַהֲבָה וּבְרָצוֹן הִנְחִילָנוּ, זִכָּרוֹן לְמַעֲשֵׂה בְרֵאשִׁית. כִּי הוּא יוֹם תְּחִלָּה לְמִקְרָאֵי־קֹדֶשׁ, זֵכֶר לִיצִיאַת מִצְרָיִם. כִּי בָנוּ בָחַרְתָּ וְאוֹתָנוּ קִדַּשְׁתָּ מִכָּל הָעַמִּים. וְשַׁבַּת קָדְשְׁךָ בְּאַהֲבָה וּבְרָצוֹן הִנְחַלְתָּנוּ. בָּרוּךְ אַתָּה יְיָ, מְקַדֵּשׁ הַשַּׁבָּת.

Vayehi erev vayehi voker yom hashishi. Vayechulu hashamayim veha'aretz vechol tzeva'am vayechal Elohim bayom hashevi'i melachto asher asa, vayishbot bayom hashevi'i mikol melachto asher asa. Vayevarech Elohim et yom hashevi'i vayekadesh oto, ki vo shavat mikol melachto asher bara Elohim la'asot.

Savree maranan verabotie:
Baruch ata Adonai. Elohainu melech ha'olam, borai pri hagafen.
Baruch ata Adonai. Elohainu melech ha'olam, asher kidshanu bemitzvotav veratza vanu, veShabbat kodsho be'ahava uveratzon

hinchilanu, zikaron lema'asei vereishit; ki hu yom techila lemi-kra'ei kodesh, zeicher litziyat mitzrayim: ki vanu vacharta ve'otanu kidashta mikol ha'amim veShabbat kodshecha be'ahava uveratzon hinchaltanu. Baruch ata Adonai, mekadesh haShabbat.

There was evening, and there was morning, the sixth day.

The heavens, the earth, and all their array were finished. And on the seventh day God finished the work He had been doing and rested on the seventh day from all the work which He had done. Then God blessed the seventh day and set it aside, for on it He rested from all the work of creation which was to be done by God.

Blessed are You, Lord our God, Ruler of the universe, Who creates the fruit of the vine.

Blessed are You, Lord our God, Ruler of the universe, Who made us special with Your commandments, wanted us, and lovingly and willingly gave us Your holy Sabbath, a commemoration of the work of creation. For it is the culmination of special events, a remembrance of the going out from Egypt. For You chose us among all the nations, made us special, and lovingly and willingly gave us Your holy Sabbath. Blessed are You, God, Who makes the Shabbat holy.

By and large, in an Orthodox household, the husband-father will recite the Kiddush. He will then pour a bit of wine from his cup into other cups, one for each person at the table. In some households, the entire family will sing Kiddush together, each over his/her own cup of wine. This, one must admit, is still quite rare, though halachically a woman is permitted to recite Kiddush.

Before we proceed with our meal, we ritually wash our hands and recite the hamotzi, the blessing over bread. The ritual washing of the hands is symbolic of the ritual washing in the Temple. It suggests that the table is like an altar. As such, it commands respectful behavior.

The ritual is as follows:

Over the sink or a large basin (most people do this standing at the kitchen sink), fill a glass or cup with water. There are special "washing cups" for this ritual, but any cup or glass will do. With the left hand, pour the water over the right hand and then reverse. This is done two or three times over each hand.

As this is being done, many people quietly recite this brief meditation:

שְׂאוּ יְדֵיכֶם קֹדֶשׁ וּבָרְכוּ אֶת־יְיָ. וְאֶשָּׂא כַפַּי אֶל־מִצְוֹתֶיךָ אֲשֶׁר אָהַבְתִּי וְאָשִׂיחָה בְחֻקֶּיךָ.

*Se'uh yedaychem kodesh
u'varchu et Adonai, ve'esah kappai el mitzvotecha
asher ahavti ve'asicha be'chukecha.*

Lift up your hands to the Holy and bless the Lord; and I shall lift up my hands to Your commandments which I love and I shall reflect on Your laws.

—PSALMS 134:2

The blessing is then recited:

בָּרוּךְ אַתָּה יְיָ, אֱלֹהֵינוּ מֶלֶךְ הָעוֹלָם אֲשֶׁר קִדְּשָׁנוּ בְּמִצְוֹתָיו, וְצִוָּנוּ עַל נְטִילַת יָדָיִם.

Baruch ata Adonai Elohainu melech ha'olam asher kidshanu b'mitzvotav v'tzivanu al netilat yadayim.

Blessed are You, Lord, our God, Ruler of the universe, Who has sanctified us with His commandments and commanded us on the washing of hands.

It is customary to remain silent from the moment of ritual washing until after the challah blessing is recited and the challah is eaten.

When everyone is reseated at the table, the challah cover is removed from the two loaves. Two challot are used to evoke the memory of the double portion of manna which the Jews received every Friday in the desert in order that they not have to go food gathering on the Sabbath.

Every gesture one makes during performance of ritual has meaning. Before slicing the challot, the head of the household will hold the two loaves together with one hand, and with the other hand will draw the knife across the loaves in a symbolic cutting gesture. The head of household will then recite the blessing and slice the bread through. In these simple gestures lie the resolution of a rabbinic conflict: on the one hand, one is supposed to cut the challah first, then say the blessing and eat the bread. The blessing is on the eating of the bread, not the slicing, said the Rabbis. On the other hand, on Friday night the blessing is said over two whole challot, not only on the one that is sliced. Solution: symbolically slice the two challot, recite the blessing over two, cut one, and eat.

בָּרוּךְ אַתָּה יְיָ, אֱלֹהֵינוּ מֶלֶךְ הָעוֹלָם, הַמּוֹצִיא לֶחֶם מִן הָאָרֶץ.

Baruch ata Adonai Elohainu melech ha'olam hamotzi lechem min ha'aretz.

Blessed are You, Lord our God, Ruler of the universe, Who brings forth bread from the earth.

Usually the head of household recites the blessing, while all others answer Amen. Each person receives a slice of challah, and eats it on the strength of the blessing of the head of household. That is based on the rabbinic principle that listening to a blessing with full intention to participate, and answering Amen, is equivalent to saying the blessing yourself. In most other instances, one recites an individual blessing over an individual act, such as eating a piece of bread. In this particular case—the Shabbat and holiday meals—the mitzvah is to recite the blessing over the two loaves. Thus, whoever has two loaves at his/her plate holds both loaves together and recites the hamotzi blessing. All others respond with Amen.

Over the past decade, I have tried to resolve the issue of how to serve a four-course meal to family and guests yet not be absent from the table for long periods of time myself. In the course of this writing, I've tried to learn what other modern Orthodox women do. Some do all the serving and have no problem with it, but most struggle with the issue exactly as I do.

In my parents' home, my father always sat through the entire meal while my mother, my two sisters, and I alternately got up from the table to serve and clear. It was the natural order of things. It never occurred to me that it could be otherwise. But from the post-factum perspective of a raised consciousness, that scene now appears sexist. My gentle father is the last person in the world one would describe as macho, yet Jewish tradition cast him unwittingly in that role. As head of household he was to be served.

I've still not resolved the problem of serving in my own home. For a while, my husband at his own initiative would get up to help serve. But I didn't like the idea of two of us leaving the table in between courses. It made our guests uncomfortable to see him get up; and even without guests, it broke the thread of continuity, an anchored quality the Shabbat meal takes on when there is one constant head of household seated throughout. Nor was I into programming whose week or whose course it was to serve, or for my feminist ax to grind away at every pleasurable moment for the family. Buffet wasn't nice to serve for Shabbat, and the children were too young to dish the food onto serving platters. Besides that, there's a part of me that derives deep satisfaction in serving my husband dinner, much as he serves me in other ways.

So for many years of Shabbat dinners, I have served, willingly and lovingly for the most part, and only occasionally with resentment, yet all the while becoming increasingly conscious that my husband and I, in our distinct roles, are probably perpetrating a questionable model for our children and their future spouses. Now that the children are older, they help a great deal more, with no distinction between son and daughter in the various tasks. And I am able to sit through most of the meal. Yet, the general issue remains unresolved.

Mealtime on Shabbat is leisurely, easily double the time of weekday dinners. Families talk about everything families talk about, except financial matters. At the table, they also speak words of Torah, and sing zemirot. Zemirot are an unusual invention. These are special songs for Shabbat, sung a cappella, as the family sits around the table. Somehow, if anyone were to suggest to me that my family sing songs at the dinner table during the week, I would think him/her strange. On Shabbat, however, zemirot are perfectly beautiful, natural, in order, and a lovely family experience. Some families sing them in between all courses, others at the end of the meal before Grace; some families harmonize; in others there are solos—the possibilities are endless.*

For the most part, the themes are connected to Shabbat. There are special zemirot for Friday-night dinners and others for Shabbat lunch, but no hard-and-fast rules. Some of the modern Israeli songs have been incorporated into zemirot, and so have some of the old Yiddish songs. Often a guest will bring a new tune which will become a family heirloom in time.

One of my favorites is the Ya Ribon Olam, probably the most popular of zemirot. It, too, was composed in Safed in the sixteenth century. The words are Aramaic; it is a song of praise to the King of the world, Who rules the world in His endless power and glory. Mention is made of the Chosen People, and the song closes with a plea to God to bring back the Chosen from exile to Jerusalem, to the Holy Temple. While the words are beautiful, since they are in Aramaic I hardly ever think about them. What I like most about Ya Ribon is the knowledge that it was sung in

---

* Zemirot are best learned at another's table. Barring that, zemirot records, which can only be played before and not during Shabbat, are available in book and record shops. In addition to records, there are several books of zemirot, including ones with transliteration and musical scores. See Bibliography, p. 506.

my grandparents' home, and in their grandparents' home, and is now sung in the homes of all my cousins and their children on this night. Not a law, but merely a custom, it is a simple song that has filled the homes of Jews on Friday nights for four hundred years in every remote corner of the world.

There are records from which to learn zemirot (records are not played on the Shabbat itself in an Orthodox home), and there are several books available for zemirot, including ones with transliteration (see Bibliography, p. 506).

The meal concludes with Birkat Hamazon, the Grace, which is usually sung aloud and in unison on Shabbat. Typically, the ba'al habayit, the head of household, will ask a guest to lead the Grace. In traditional Judaism, women do not count as part of the mezuman, the quorum of three to introduce the Grace, even though women are required to recite it. However, again, in response to contemporary values and new images of women, a few "avant garde" Orthodox Jews do count women as part of the quorum and allow them to lead the Grace.

After dinner on Friday night, Orthodox Jews relax, talk, study the Torah portion of the week with Rashi,* read, play board games, go for a walk, learn with their children, visit with friends, or go to sleep early. Some synagogues have occasional guest lecturers on Friday night; others hold classes or gatherings called Oneg Shabbat (literally, the joy of Sabbath). Activities are scheduled depending on whether Shabbat starts early or late. Often, the community's high-school and college students will schedule an Oneg Shabbat program on Friday night—a discussion group, Hebrew songs, and that which guarantees a good teenage turnout the next time—snacks.

Over the centuries, Friday night earned the reputation as "mitzvah" night; it was customary for husband and wife to make love on Friday night. The Rabbis understood that this was an ideal night to have sex because people were more relaxed, there was more time, the pressures of the morrow were simply not there. Some Orthodox Jewish couples . . . ; others . . .

---

* Rashi, an acronym for Rabbi Isaac ben Shlomo, was a scholar and exegete of eleventh-century France. His commentary on the Bible, known simply as Rashi, was culled largely from rabbinic texts. Rashi is the most important and widely used commentary on the Torah.

SATURDAY

Shabbat morning is spent mostly in shul; services usually begin between eight and nine and end between eleven and twelve, depending on local custom. Jewish law does not permit one to eat before reciting the morning prayers. This is fine on a weekday, when morning prayers start early and are over in forty-five minutes; but on Shabbat, one would come into lunchtime Kiddush on a near-empty stomach and fade right out with that first cup of wine were it not for the widely accepted practice of drinking juice or coffee, eating a bit of cake or fruit before leaving for shul. No real breakfasts, however, and no bread.

People are expected to dress nicely for shul. Men wear suits with ties; women wear their best clothes, although not what we would call formal or evening wear, which would be out of place. Females never wear pants to the synagogue. Children wear their nicest clothes, which are often called Shabbos dresses or Shabbos pants or Shabbos shoes. Married women all wear hats to the synagogue.

As soon as a man comes to shul, he wraps his tallit (prayer shawl) around him, reciting the appropriate blessing and kissing the tallit as he does. In most Orthodox shuls, in contrast to Conservative or Reform, only married men wear the tallit.

The service starts with some warm-up prayers known as the Pesukai Dezimra. These prayers, selected mostly from Psalms, also provide an extra twenty-five minutes for the stragglers to arrive before Shacharit, the morning service, begins. The Pesukay Dezimra do not need a quorum of ten men, but the Shacharit service does. The synagogue is in trouble if it doesn't have a minyan by then (that's the origin of "waiting for the tenth man"). On the other hand, people keep coming in to join all through the morning; the ratio of worshipers present when Shacharit begins is probably one to ten of the number at service's end.

The Shacharit of weekday emphasizes the Exodus and Revelation. Shacharit of Shabbat—the same only more so. It is a fitting prelude to the center point of the whole morning—the Torah reading. The Torah, the five books of Moses, is read in entirety, in consecutive fashion, once each year. The Torah is divided into fifty-four portions, each called a parshah. One parshah a week—or sometimes a double reading—gets us through the annual cycle smoothly. In the Jewish calendar, the weeks of the year are named according to the appropriate parshah of the Torah. For example, a Jew writing a letter on a particular Wednesday in October would head his letter: the fourth day of Parshat Noah (that is, the week preceding the Sabbath on which we shall read the story of Noah and his ark). Shabbat is the seventh day, so Sunday is the first day and Wednesday is the fourth day.

By the time we get to the Torah reading, the shul is quite full. Most of the men have arrived by now, as have many of the women and children. Women, who are not counted as part of the required minyan, and who sit behind a mechitza—a divider separating men and women—tend to arrive after their husbands. Traditional Jewish law requires separate seating for men and women. Since men have a primary role in the synagogue, they always sit center and front. The mechitza is one characteristic that distinguishes Orthodox from Conservative, Reform, and Reconstructionist synagogues. Separate seating, plus the absence of formal roles for women in synagogue ritual, have conditioned women to assume fewer liturgical responsibilities than are halachically required of them. Thus, an Orthodox woman can arrive midway through the service and hardly an eyebrow will be raised, whereas a man must hastily catch up from the beginning of the prayers (if he arrives late) and must take care not to arrive too late, lest he be judged by his fellows.

Children come to synagogue with their fathers or with their mothers, or on their own. The fact that Orthodox Jews don't drive on Shabbat, and therefore must live within reasonable walking distance, adds to the flexibility of each person's arriving on his/her own. One of my fond memories as a teenager is of walking to shul, keeping a distance but within earshot of a certain woman in our congregation. She was exceedingly thin, and not too attractive; her skin had wrinkled prematurely. But she had a magnificent voice, and she and her daughter would sing all the Hit Parade songs on their way to shul together. Somehow, the incongruous combination of "A Slow Boat to China" coming from this middle-aged pious woman on her way to shul caught my fancy.

In the synagogue, young children can sit with either parent, even of the opposite sex. By the time they reach nine or ten, however, little boys will sit with their fathers or their friends in the men's section and little girls with their mothers or friends in the women's section. Most children understand this on their own, but some have to be told, "It's time . . ."

Many synagogues have junior congregation services geared to the appropriate age level. Not only do these help maintain decorum in the main synagogue sanctuary, but they also give children an opportunity to take on certain roles such as opening the ark, leading a prayer, and so forth. Junior congregation services always end before the main service does, so that children have some time to be in the main sanctuary with the full congregation.

Though families arrive at shul in spurts, and husbands and wives sit apart, and children pray with friends, it still doesn't seem to diminish the family feeling of a traditional shul. Perhaps it's the presence of little children circulating between parents; perhaps it's simply the presence of young ones altogether; or quite possibly it's the associated spirit of the entire day—an Orthodox shul always feels like a family shul.

In general, even though the service is very formal and structured, there is an air of informality and camaraderie about the Orthodox synagogue. It is not at all uncommon to see people wandering in and out during various parts of the service. But for those in the know, even these "wanderings" take place at appropriately sanctioned times. One would never walk out, for example, during the opening of the ark, or the recital of Kedusha, a prayer extolling God's holiness.

There is a special ceremony for opening the ark, taking the Torah out, and carrying it through the congregation for people to adore and kiss before setting it down on the reading table to unroll and read. Surely the most beautiful scene on a Shabbat morning is that of fathers—and in some shuls, mothers—carrying their young children to the aisle or to the mechitza where they can kiss the Torah as it is carried past them. Adults kiss the Torah, too. They touch their siddur to the Torah, and then kiss the siddur; or wrap the fringe of the tallit around their finger, touch it to the Torah and kiss that; or kiss the Torah directly. A stranger observing this five-minute ceremony would quickly understand that the Torah is the most beloved treasure a Jew has.

The reading of the Torah parshah is divided into seven parts, each called an aliyah. A man is honored by being called up to the Torah to recite a blessing before and after an aliyah (see p. 266).

This honor itself is also called an aliyah. The first aliyah is reserved for those of priestly descent (Kohen); the second aliyah for Levites (of the tribe that assisted the priests in the Temple); and all the rest are reserved for Israelites—that is, anyone who is neither Kohen nor Levi. These aliyot are often distributed for special occasions. The Bar Mitzvah boy and his family will be honored with several aliyot. But other events in life also warrant this honor: on becoming a groom, the engagement of a daughter, the yahrzeit (anniversary of death) of a parent or an in-law, the birth of a new baby, thanksgiving for saving from a near mishap, a wife recovering from an operation, someone in the family returning from a long trip, and so forth. One often pledges a contribution to the synagogue upon receiving an aliyah. (This steady source of donations is an important supplementary source of income for synagogues whose membership dues and fund-raising activities do not generally cover the budget.) Since no moneys are handled on the Sabbath, payment is made later.

In addition to the seven aliyot, the last few verses of the parshah are repeated. They constitute an eighth aliyah called the Maftir. This eighth aliyah is typically reserved for the Bar Mitzvah boy; however, the Maftir can be used for any other purpose, or by any other male over thirteen.

After a person has an aliyah, he waits at the reading table until the next aliyah is completed, then shakes hands all around, and returns to his seat. Along the way, those in his reach will extend a hand, wish him a yasher koach—may your strength increase. He responds with the expression baruch ti'he'yeh—may you be blessed.

Who reads the Torah? That, too, varies. It is read with special cantillations, special intonations for different words. But that's not all. The reader must memorize beforehand the cantillation associated with each word, because the Torah scroll for ritual use is written without vowels and without cantillation marks. So the reader must be skilled. Many communities have a regular Torah reader; however, he defers to a Bar Mitzvah boy when the latter has prepared the entire parshah himself.

Although the reading is completed, the Torah is not put back just yet. First comes hagbah (lifting the Torah) and gelila (wrapping it), followed by the Haftorah, a reading from one of the books of the Prophets. Hagbah is an honor a reasonably strong man is called upon to perform. A full-sized Torah scroll is a hefty object. It must be held aloft, on its two rollers (called "trees of life"), and held open to the section just read. The person honored with hagbah must hold the Torah high and must swivel around so that all the congregation can look upon it and sing out together, "This is the Torah that Moses placed before the people of Israel according to the Word of God, through the hand of Moses." Since the scroll is rolled from one end to the other over the course of the year, its weight can be distributed very unevenly, depending on what part of the year it is. I never checked it out, but I suspect that butchers must have strong left arms because the kosher butcher in our congregation, may he rest in peace, was always given Hagbah during the first periods of the new reading cycle, when all the weight of the Torah scroll was on the left. (We read the Torah from right to left, and unroll it bit by bit as we move along each week.) After swiveling around, Mr. Hagbah then sits in a seat nearby, holding the Torah upright on his lap while Mr. Gelila (the roller-upper) rolls the two trees of life closed, ties a cord around the waist of the scroll, covers the Torah with a Torah wrap (usually made of embroidered velvet), and tops it off with the rest of its finery—silver crowns for the trees of life, and a silver breastplate hung across the Torah wrap. Mr. Gelila then goes back to his place, shaking all extended hands en route, while Mr. Hagbah remains seated, holding the Torah comfortably in his arms while the Haftorah is recited.

The Haftorah portions were chosen two thousand years ago to correspond to a theme in the Torah reading. The Rabbis didn't want the people to neglect the Prophets altogether, what with such great emphasis placed on the Torah, but it was unrealistic to attempt a reading of the entire Prophets; so a chapter from this book and a chapter from that were selected. It is fascinating to see the counterpoint of the two readings. A Torah portion dealing with the sacrifices is matched by a prophetic portion stressing the idea that God prefers heart and feeling to animal sacrifices. Another week, a Torah reading that heavily warns of punishment is tempered by a prophecy of consolation and redemption. (Compare, for example, Deuteronomy, chapters 26–28, with its Haftorah, Isaiah, chapter 60.) Some weeks, the connection is not obvious and the amateur Haftorah sleuths speculate thoughtfully on the connections.

The Haftorah is read from a printed book, not from a scroll. In ancient times it, too, was read from special scrolls, but that art is mostly gone. Many Bar Mitzvah boys read both the Torah and Haftorah readings; some read only the Maftir portion of the Torah plus the Haftorah. Or the Haftorah may be read by any male over thirteen for any special occasion. The psychiatrist in our congregation always reads the Haftorah on his wedding anniversary. (No need to analyze; it's simply a Jewish way to honor a special day in his life.)

After the Haftorah reading is completed, the circuit with the Torah scroll is made again; with equal pomp it is returned to the ark.

What comes next in the service is that invention of modern Jewry, the rabbi's sermon. Introduced first by Reform Jews, the sermon is an adaptation of premodern Orthodox services where the rabbi or the most learned worshiper would review for the congregation some highlight from the Torah, adding the traditional commentaries. Today's sermon is connected to the parshah but not restricted to it. Modern rabbis have a knack for finding something in the parshah to link with current political situations, a contemporary social issue, or an overall religious or ethical problem.

Sometimes the search for relevance goes too far. In recent years, as criticism has grown that the sermon too often sounded like an editorial from *The New York Times* or *The New Republic*, rabbis have tried to recover the eternal message of the tradition. Instead of being second-rate news commentators, the rabbis strive to be first-rate teachers of Torah and rabbinic wisdom. Some rabbis have shifted to teaching a text from the Torah or some other classic source. Others have opened it up to questions and answers from the congregation. In any event, the key to a good sermon seems to be the balance between wisdom and text and the ability to apply it to personal, communal and societal concerns.

The sermon is less central in the Orthodox synagogue, for people come primarily to fulfill the obligation to pray or to be with the community. Some Orthodox synagogues will manage without a rabbi altogether. However, a rabbi with a consistently good sermon can be a major draw in the Orthodox synagogue as well. A barometer of the rabbi's speaking ability is the direction of traffic immediately before and after sermon time. A good speaker will often bring in a whole group who pack the shul at that moment. With a poor speaker, a perceptible exodus will frequently occur at that point, with people filing back in right after the talk. Outsiders are sometimes embarrassed, but the informality and individualist mood of Orthodox synagogues seem to allow for it.

The sermon is followed by Mussaf, the special additional service for Shabbat. It begins with a silent prayer called the Amidah or the Shmoneh Esreh and concludes with several prayers sung in unison or responsively.

Unlike its more liberal counterparts, in an Orthodox shul the members say all the prayers individually. Whatever the rabbi is required to recite, so is the least of his congregants. However, individuals do pray at different speeds. Thus, in order to avoid total chaos, the Rabbis of ancient times instituted the requirement for a special shaliach tzibbur, messenger of the congregation. His expressed function is to carry the sentiments of the entire congregation to God in a special way, but his real function is to keep prayers on track. At the end of each prayer, he will repeat the last few words out loud, and when he finishes everyone moves on to the next prayer. The device of shaliach tzibbur was really an act of genius on the part of the ancient Rabbis. It allows for individual prayer within a cohesive congregational setting, quite a remarkable dialectic. In most Orthodox congregations a professional chazzan (cantor) is the shaliach tzibbur, but there are many shuls that get by very nicely with a ba'al tefila (a prayer leader), often a lay member of the congregation who has a pleasant voice and knows how to lead.

After the service, a Kiddush is occasionally held in the shul, to celebrate a particular simcha (happy event). A Kiddush can range from wine and cake to elaborate catered spreads. One of my favorite stories is about Jed A., a former student of my husband's at Yeshiva University in New York City. After graduation, Jed became a Peace Corps worker, serving in Ethiopia for two years. He spent his first weekend back in the States with us. It so happened, just that Shabbat, a family in our congregation was making a Kiddush reception in honor of their son's Bar Mitzvah. It was a very lavish reception, and the entire congregation was invited. Jed got down to the social hall early, heaped his plate with four different kinds of fish, two or three salads, a piece of potato kugel, a piece of noodle kugel—more food than he had seen in two years of Shabbatot (plural) in Ethiopia. As he stepped away from the table, he realized he had forgotten horseradish for his gefilte fish. By now, the lines at the serving tables were four deep, but Jed was not to forgo horseradish, his first in a long time. So, plate in hand, he got back in line. The woman in front of him happened to turn around. She looked at his plate, then looked him straight in the eye and in a tone of utter disgust said, "For God's sake, finish that one first!"

After shul, everyone returns home for the second Shabbat meal. Even if one has recited or heard Kiddush in shul, it is still customary to recite it again at one's own table. The Kiddush on Shabbat morning is quite different from that of Friday night. It is a much shorter Kiddush, the essence of which is the single blessing over the wine; in some homes, Kiddush is recited over schnapps, for which there is a separate blessing. The Rabbis, with their exquisite sensitivity, dubbed it Kiddush Rabbah—the Great Kiddush, or the Large Kiddush, so that its feelings (that's right, the Kiddush's feelings) should not be "hurt" by being so much more abbreviated than the Friday-night Kiddush. Nowadays, the trend in many homes is to add several preliminary passages, in accordance with the interpretation of this or that scholar. Thirty years ago, most Orthodox Jews would recite only one short traditional verse ("And therefore God blessed the Sabbath day and sanctified it"), followed by the one-line blessing over wine or schnapps. Today, some men recite a Kiddush as long as Friday night's. Like much else in tradition, Shabbat morning Kiddush grew in stages.

וְשָׁמְרוּ בְנֵי יִשְׂרָאֵל אֶת הַשַּׁבָּת, לַעֲשׂוֹת אֶת הַשַּׁבָּת

לְדֹרֹתָם בְּרִית עוֹלָם. בֵּינִי וּבֵין בְּנֵי יִשְׂרָאֵל אוֹת הִיא

לְעֹלָם, כִּי שֵׁשֶׁת יָמִים עָשָׂה יְיָ אֶת הַשָּׁמַיִם וְאֶת הָאָרֶץ,

וּבַיּוֹם הַשְּׁבִיעִי שָׁבַת וַיִּנָּפַשׁ.

(Some people start here:)

עַל כֵּן בֵּרַךְ יְיָ אֶת יוֹם הַשַּׁבָּת וַיְקַדְּשֵׁהוּ.

בָּרוּךְ אַתָּה יְיָ, אֱלֹהֵינוּ מֶלֶךְ הָעוֹלָם, בּוֹרֵא פְּרִי הַגָּפֶן.

Veshamru venai Yisrael et haShabbat la'asot et haShabbat ledo-rotam berit olam. Baynee uvayn b'nai Yisrael ot hi le'olam, ki shayshet yamim asa Adonai et hashamayim ve'et ha'aretz uvayom hashevi'i shavat vayinafash.
Al kayn bayrach Adonai et yom haShabbat vayekadeshaihu.

Baruch ata Adonai, Elohainu melech ha'olam, borai pri hagafen.

The children of Israel shall keep the Sabbath, to observe the Sabbath throughout their generations as an everlasting covenant. It is a sign between Me and the children of Israel forever that in six days the Lord made heaven and earth, and on the seventh day He rested and ceased from His work (EXOD. 31:16–17).

. . . Therefore the Lord blessed the Sabbath day and made it holy (EXOD. 20:11).

Blessed are You, Lord our God, Ruler of the universe, Who creates the fruit of the vine.

If an alcoholic beverage other than wine is used, the following blessing is substituted for the one over wine:

בָּרוּךְ אַתָּה יְיָ, אֱלֹהֵינוּ מֶלֶךְ הָעוֹלָם, שֶׁהַכֹּל נִהְיֶה בִּדְבָרוֹ.

Baruch ata Adonai Elohainu melech ha'olam she-hakol nee-yeh bidvaro.

Blessed are You, Lord our God, Ruler of the universe, by Whose will all things exist.

The hamotzi is recited over two challot, the same as Friday night. Meat is generally served for Shabbat lunch. Zemirot and Birkat Hamazon are similar to those of Friday night.

"Sleep on Shabbat is pure pleasure," tradition tells us. So it is that after lunch or after a walk, the custom is to take a nap. A Shabbat afternoon nap is the most delicious sleep of all. Perhaps it's because a Sabbath-observant Jew doesn't care if the world runs on while he/she sleeps.

Not everybody naps. But let me tell you about a whole city that naps, and the sheer power of custom in the Jewish world. Some years ago, we spent Shabbat with a cousin in B'nai Brak. B'nai Brak is the heart of Israel's Orthodox community as Jerusalem is its soul. My cousin and his wife have seven children. So do many of their neighbors. Six, eight, or ten—four children in B'nai Brak is considered zero population growth. And these families all live in apartment houses, with four bedrooms at the most. So the streets and apartment terraces are filled with children, all day long, hundreds of children on every street. You can hear the sounds of laughter and the crying of small voices at every turn. Suddenly, at about two o'clock on Shabbat afternoon, the sounds recede. At two-thirty you might hear an occasional baby cry, but that's about all. It is as if there was not a single child in all of B'nai Brak. Now I know firsthand that you cannot force a six-year-old to nap if he/she is bursting with energy, and I know that the parents in B'nai Brak love their children dearly, consider children their greatest blessing, and their greatest wealth. They would never force a child to sleep. But somehow the magic, the appeal, the necessity, and above all the inviolability of a Shabbat afternoon nap is communicated to thousands upon thousands of young B'nai Brak children, who themselves have learned to nap or to rest or read or play very, very quietly. And if you ever want to see a city come suddenly to life again, a city streaming back to life, teeming with young life, just be in B'nai Brak any Shabbat afternoon at four.

What happens after naptime depends on how late Shabbat ends, and in which community one finds oneself. Every Orthodox community varies. My shul offers youth groups on Shabbat afternoon, led by the community's own youth. When I was a teenager, for years I led an Oneg Shabbat group, with girls barely two years younger than I. My two sisters did the same thing, and among the three of us we knew every kid in the community. We used to tell stories about Jewish heroes, sing songs, talk about Zionism or Israel, or the parshah. And we would play games. There's a whole slew of Shabbos games, mostly mental ones, since one cannot write on Shabbat. I think my sister Judy invented most of them. Now, some of my own children lead youth groups, and they do pretty much the same thing. In my daughter's group is the daughter of a woman whose youth leader I once was.

On Shabbat afternoon, for adults, there are classes in Torah, also in Mishnah and Gemara (the two layers of the Talmud); there are classes for men, simultaneous classes for women, or mixed classes with different subject matter. In some communities no formal classes at all are scheduled, but individuals will find a few friends to study with on a regular basis. Several years ago, in our town, an artist-photographer-mother-of-five on her own initiative started teaching a women's Mishnah class, scheduled at the same time as the rabbi's Gemara class. It still meets regularly in shul every Shabbat afternoon, October through June, and has grown from year to year.

Shabbat Minchah service, once again attended mostly by males, has the special feature of introducing the Torah portion of the coming week. Three men are called up for aliyot. These aliyot, however, are different from those of Shabbat morning. Each is but a few sentences long, altogether adding up to one seventh of the entire parshah to be read next Shabbat. Still, the symbolism there is too good to miss. Jews never stop learning Torah. No sooner do they finish this week's portion than they begin next week's, which should be studied a bit every day, so that by the following Shabbat, one will have reviewed the entire parshah.

During spring and summer months, the afternoon is longer. It is traditional between Minchah and Maariv to study a work called Pirke Avot or the Ethics of the Fathers. Pirke Avot, which is part of the Mishnah, contains aphorisms and choice ethical statements of the Sages of the Talmud. Hundreds of commentaries have been written on the six chapters of this book. In many communities, lay people will take turns with the rabbi in teaching "Perek," as this work is affectionately called.

All this learning makes Shabbat a mind-stretching day—and the linchpin of a remarkable, popular adult education system.

The mood of Minchah is supposed to be messianic in tone. Shabbat will soon be over, it's back to the real world, and one hopes for the Messiah to come along and help straighten out the real world.

This mood continues at shaleshudos—more properly called shalosh seudot or seudah shelishit, the third of three Shabbat meals. Shaleshudos is served between Minchah and Maariv. The meal is light; one has eaten enough and the emphasis is spiritual rather than physical. But still, a little physical never hurts: challah and herring, egg salad, club soda and ginger ale, sponge cake or a few kichel. There will be zemirot; perhaps a few words from an out-of-town Jewish dignitary or scholar who happens to be spending Shabbat with relatives, or a Dvar Torah from the rabbi; or a talk by a meshulach trying to raise money for a struggling yeshiva in Israel, then Birkat Hamazon and seudah shelishit is all over in forty minutes.

There is a certain male camaraderie about the shaleshudos served in the subterranean mahogany or walnut channels of the shul—but it is gentle, subdued—and messianic. Nor is there any rejection of the few women who come.

It's hard to capture this same spirit over shaleshudos in one's home, but for those who don't return to shul late Shabbat afternoon, a light meal is served at home: challah, fruit, salads, a cold-fish platter, soda—or coffee if there's hot water still left in the kettle. . . . In the summer months, when Shabbat ends late, shaleshudos is often a nice time for inviting guests.

After shaleshudos, the congregants return to the sanctuary for Maariv. Maariv is very brief (the Rabbis understood it's enough of shul already); its theme is one of separation of night and day, holy and mundane time.

Shabbat closes with the ceremony of Havdalah (literally, separation). Immediately after Maariv, Havdalah is recited by the rabbi (or cantor, or sexton) for those assembled. Essentially a home ceremony, it is recited again when all the family members have returned home from shul. Although Havdalah is one of the most ancient blessings—over twenty-five centuries old—some of its attendant customs grew throughout history. The custom of reciting Havdalah in shul has a history that itself could fill a book. One piece of the story is this: Havdalah, like Kiddush, is optimally recited over wine. But some Jews could not afford a third cup of wine. So the custom arose to recite Havdalah, over wine, in shul, where all could hear it. Then they could return home and substitute juice or some other liquid, as many do today.

A brimming cup of wine (or other liquid), a multiwick candle, and aromatic spices are essential to the ceremony. The Havdalah candle is unique. It is made of at least two separate wicks, intertwined into one candle. (One can also use two candles, with the wicks held together in one flame.) A child is usually given the candle to hold; girls were supposed to hold it as high as they wanted their future husbands to be tall. (I used to hold it very high; and it worked!)

Kindling the fire, that which was forbidden on Shabbat, is a most logical way to distinguish between Shabbat and weekday. Fire is also a symbol of all the things we do all week long.

The spices are usually cloves, cinnamon, bay leaves, or others that have a sweetness to them. In the Havdalah ceremony, we thank God for creating such a great variety of spices; immediately we take a sniff of whatever spices we are using. Tradition tells us that the spices are to remind us of the fragrance of Shabbat that is now departing; also that the spices are compensation for the special soul of Shabbat that is leaving us. To me, the whiff of besamim suggests the full use of all our senses we now put to work for the coming week.

The spices—besamim—have given rise to an art form called the besamim box. Of silver, and other materials, all kinds of unusual and decorative spice holders have been fashioned by craftsmen throughout the ages, and many museums have exquisite besamim box collections. In our house, we use a variety of besamim boxes, including some small Israeli and Italian pillboxes.

Our favorite besamim is a pomander etrog (citron) whose scent is divine. We have several of these, mostly homemade. To make an etrog besamim: Save the etrog after Sukkot has ended. With a nail or compass point puncture the etrog with holes, filling each hole as you go with a clove. (Pinch off the head and four leaves of each clove before inserting.) Make the holes close to each other so the etrog skin will be completely covered with cloves and will not shrink. This etrog besamim will last a long time. We have one that is three years old and is still magnificent. (It is also a great weekday dietary aid. Just fill your plate with cloves and work quietly at the dinner table with compass and etrog while everyone else is consuming calories. It takes about eight weekday family dinners to complete one.)

So much for the Havdalah props; now the service. In an Orthodox home the service is recited by the husband-father, with all the members of the household present. In our home, we turn off the lights so that only the candle glows as everyone stands close by. How beautiful are the faces by the light of the Havdalah candle!

The Havdalah service begins with eight brief verses culled from Isaiah, Psalms, and the Book of Esther:

הִנֵּה, אֵל יְשׁוּעָתִי, אֶבְטַח, וְלֹא אֶפְחָד, כִּי עָזִּי וְזִמְרָת יָהּ,
יְיָ, וַיְהִי לִי לִישׁוּעָה.

Hinei eil yeshuati evtach velo efchad.
Ki azi vezimrat Ya Adonai, vayehi li lishuah.

Behold, God is my deliverer: I trust in Him and am not afraid
For God is my strength and my stronghold, the source of my
deliverance.

וּשְׁאַבְתֶּם מַיִם בְּשָׂשׂוֹן, מִמַּעַיְנֵי הַיְשׁוּעָה. לַייָ הַיְשׁוּעָה;
עַל עַמְּךָ בִרְכָתֶךָ, סֶּלָה.

Ushavtem mayim besason mima'ainei hayeshuah.
La-Adonai hayeshuah al amcha birchatecha selah.

With joy shall you draw water from the wells of salvation.
In God there is salvation; Your blessing is on Your people.

יְיָ צְבָאוֹת עִמָּנוּ, מִשְׂגָּב לָנוּ, אֱלֹהֵי יַעֲקֹב, סֶלָה.
יְיָ צְבָאוֹת, אַשְׁרֵי אָדָם בֹּטֵחַ בָּךְ.

Adonai tzeva'ot imanu misgav lanu elohei ya'akov selah.
Adonai tzeva'ot ashrei adam botei'ach bach.

The Lord of hosts is with us; the God of Jacob is our stronghold.
Lord of all the universe, happy is the one who trusts in You.

יְיָ, הוֹשִׁיעָה; הַמֶּלֶךְ יַעֲנֵנוּ בְיוֹם קָרְאֵנוּ.

לַיְּהוּדִים הָיְתָה אוֹרָה וְשִׂמְחָה, וְשָׂשׂוֹן, וִיקָר. כֵּן תִּהְיֶה
לָנוּ. כּוֹס יְשׁוּעוֹת אֶשָּׂא, וּבְשֵׁם יְיָ אֶקְרָא.

Adonai hoshiah hamelech ya'aneinu veyom kareinu.
Layehudim hie'ta ora vesimcha vesason vee'y'kar; kein tiyeh lanu.
Kos yeshu'ot esa, uvesheim Adonai ekra.

Save us, O Lord; Let the King answer us in the day we call upon Him.
The Jews [in the deliverance of Purim] had lightness and joy, happiness and honor; let it be so for us.
I shall lift the cup of salvation and I shall call in the name of the Lord.

The heart of the Havdalah service is its four blessings:
Over wine:

בָּרוּךְ אַתָּה יְיָ, אֱלֹהֵינוּ מֶלֶךְ הָעוֹלָם, בּוֹרֵא פְּרִי הַגָּפֶן.

(over other liquid) (שֶׁהַכֹּל נִהְיֶה בִּדְבָרוֹ).

*Baruch ata Adonai Elohainu melech ha'olam borai pri hagafen
(she-hakol nee-yeh bidvaro).*

Blessed are You, Lord our God, Ruler of the Universe, Who creates the fruit of the vine (by whose Will all things exist).

Over spices which are held in hand while reciting the blessing:

בָּרוּךְ אַתָּה יְיָ, אֱלֹהֵינוּ מֶלֶךְ הָעוֹלָם, בּוֹרֵא מִינֵי בְשָׂמִים.

Baruch ata Adonai Elohainu melech ha'olam borai minai b'samim.

Blessed are You, Lord our God, Ruler of the universe, Who creates diverse spices.

After this blessing is recited, the besamim are passed around for each person to smell.
Over the candle:

בָּרוּךְ אַתָּה יְיָ, אֱלֹהֵינוּ מֶלֶךְ הָעוֹלָם, בּוֹרֵא מְאוֹרֵי הָאֵשׁ.

Baruch ata Adonai Elohainu melech ha-olam borai m'orai ha-esh.

Blessed are You, Lord our God, Ruler of the universe, Who creates the light of the fire.

As this blessing is recited, all extend their fingers toward the flame, straight out or cupping them with the palms facing up, so that the light of the candle is reflected in the fingernails and in the shadows cast by the bent fingers over the palms.

Finally, the fourth blessing, over divine acts of separation, of distinguishing one thing from another. The Havdalah leader holds the cup as he recites this blessing:

בָּרוּךְ אַתָּה יְיָ, אֱלֹהֵינוּ מֶלֶךְ הָעוֹלָם, הַמַּבְדִּיל בֵּין קֹדֶשׁ לְחֹל, בֵּין אוֹר לְחֹשֶׁךְ, בֵּין יִשְׂרָאֵל לָעַמִּים, בֵּין יוֹם הַשְּׁבִיעִי לְשֵׁשֶׁת יְמֵי הַמַּעֲשֶׂה. בָּרוּךְ אַתָּה יְיָ, הַמַּבְדִּיל בֵּין קֹדֶשׁ לְחוֹל.

*Baruch ata Adonai Elohainu melech ha'olam, hamavdil bayn ko-
desh l'chol, bayn or l'choshech, bayn Yisrael l'amim, bayn yom
hashvi-i leshaishet y'may hamaaseh. Baruch ata Adonai, hamavdil bayn kodesh l'chol.*

Blessed are You, Lord our God, Ruler of the universe, who
distinguishes holy time from weekday, light from dark, Israel
from the nations, the seventh day from six days of labor.

After all the blessings are completed, the leader drinks the
wine. The candle is blown out directly, or some people pour a
few drops of wine into a saucer and extinguish the candle in the
wine. I remember my grandfather would dip his two pinkie fingers into the wine in which the candle had just been extinguished. Then he would dab his eyes, ears, and nostrils. Come
to think of it, perhaps that is why sniffing the spices suggests to
me the full-blooded use of all the senses.

Many families linger a moment longer before extinguishing
the candle to sing several Havdalah songs. The three classics are:

"Eliyahu Hanavi" ("Elijah the Prophet")

Eliyahu hanavi
Eliyahu hatishbi
Eliyahu hagiladi
Bimhera yavo eileinu
Im mashiach ben daveed.

This is a song about Elijah who will herald the Messiah. What's
the connection between Elijah, the Messiah, and Havdalah? The
answer is percentages. We learn from tradition that the Messiah
won't come on Shabbat—the world is perfect on Shabbat; besides, the Messiah wouldn't ride on the Sabbath. Being thus
detained on one day, the odds of his arriving on the next day
increase from one in seven to two in seven. In recognition of
that fact, and to help the odds along, we sing a song reminding
ourselves that Elijah will come and bring the Messiah with him,
"speedily and in our day."

"*Shavua tov*" ("A Good Week")

Shavua tov is repeated eight times.

It is a simple song in which we wish everyone a good week. Some families sing this song in several languages, such as the Yiddish "A Guteh Voch," or "A Good Week."

"Hamavdil" ("He Who Makes Distinctions")

Hamavdil beyn kodesh lechol
Chatoteinu hu yimchol
Zareinu vechaspeinu yarbeh kachol
Vecha'kochavim balielah.

"Hamavdil" is an earthy rhymed verse whose very first stanza gets right to the heart of the matter:

May He Who separates holy from mundane
Forgive us our sins
And multiply our children
And our wealth
Like the sands of the sea
And the stars of the sky.

Who could ask for anything more!

The holiness of Shabbat has ended. Some Jews, however, particularly Chasidim, extend its spirit a bit longer through the Melaveh Malkah (accompanying the Queen). They make a small feast, like a farewell banquet, honoring the departure of the Shabbat Queen. In some Chasidic communities, this Melaveh Malkah lasts until midnight.

Shabbat is now over. Much as I love the Shabbat and could not live without it, I am happy to see it go. I feel rested, relaxed, and raring to go. Perhaps I shall keep a bit of the Shabbat serenity with me during the week. But I doubt it. If not, I shall rely on the coming Shabbat to restore an added measure of dignity and peace to my life.

Shabbat is over, and that is good. I have gone on much too long. I chose to do so for two reasons: Shabbat in a traditional Jewish household is distinctive from Shabbat in any other setting. And second, it comes fifty-two times more often than any other special day in a Jew's life. As such, it occupies, preoccupies, and marks our lives in ways more pervasive and more encompassing than one would ever imagine. Although we are often not conscious of it ourselves, our very lives revolve around Shabbat, even as we throw ourselves with full energy into the weekday world.

CHAPTER 2

KASHRUT

You are what you eat.

You are also
> What you cook
> How you shop
> Where you dine
> How you crack an egg
> What you burn up
> How long you wait between meals
> And the way you slaughter a calf.

Kashrut is not simply a set of rules about permitted and forbidden foods; kashrut is a way of life. As with any life-style we adopt, we know we are successful at it when it becomes second nature to us.

The basic laws of kashrut are given in the Bible, and are further expanded in the Talmud. The laws fall into two categories:

1. Food prohibited under any circumstances
2. Foods that are not categorically prohibited but which may be eaten only if prepared in a certain way

The laws of kashrut fall into the category of statutes, *chukkim*, Biblical laws for which no reason is given. In other words, we don't know why this food is forbidden and that one not.

It is obvious, however, that what is involved is the holiness quotient. Most of the laws of kashrut are given in the context of the holiness code. For example, immediately following the laws of forbidden kinds, we read: "For I am the Lord your God, sanctify yourselves and be holy, for I am holy" (LEV. 11:44).

What does it mean for a human being to be holy? Several things come to mind: special, set aside, more pure, on a special plane of existence. These are not mere words; they have resonance in the daily life of a Jew. Holiness has something to do with the way we consume food, the profound implications of killing for food, and the nature of the community with whom we share this same value system.

By extension, one who keeps kosher should not eat with crude table manners, gobble food down, or talk while chewing. There should be an aura of dignity, a component of holiness in the act of appeasing appetite and satisfying hunger. The theme of table-as-altar is expressed in other practices as well: ritually washing the hands before eating bread; reciting a blessing over bread, which symbolizes a meal; salting the bread, symbolic of the salting of Temple offerings; and reciting Grace after the meal.

Second, when we buy food, prepare it, and eat it, we are reminded that we live not by laws of human beings but by the law of the One Who creates life and gives food. Moreover, it is only by divine sanction that we are given the right to take the life of an animal for food.

Third, the Rabbis tell us, the laws of kashrut come to teach us compassion. This is true of laws regarding ritual slaughter, draining of blood, and separation of meat and milk. Even as we eat that which comes of another life, we must do it with a sensitivity to what life means. We may not callously take the life of an animal nor become inured to the pain of a beast. We may not take the bird from its nest with its mother hovering nearby, nor seethe a kid in its mother's milk. These would be acts of cruelty and uncaring. The laws of kashrut are often pointed to as examples of pure ritual. Truly, however, they should be considered as prime examples of the ethical sensitivity of Jewish law. It does not surprise me in the least to come across a tradition that suggests we will all be vegetarians when the Messiah comes, just as Adam and Eve once were in the Garden of Eden.

But all of those things are more elusive and harder to keep continuously in mind than a fourth meaning of kashrut—community. Somehow, an awareness of others who operate within identical and very specific parameters creates a strong bond of kinship. Just as Shabbat and holiday celebration foster a sense of "community," so does personal observance of kashrut become a tie that binds us to each other. Nowhere do I feel more connected to my community than on those rare occasions when I find myself in a non-kosher restaurant, eating half a cantaloupe while my companions dab at their shrimp cocktails or paté de foie gras.

FORBIDDEN FOODS

All four-footed animals that do not chew their cud and/or do not have a split hoof. Thus, for example, pigs (which have split hooves but don't chew cud), horses (chew cud but no split hooves), and dogs (neither), are forbidden.

All animals which are not ritually slaughtered. This includes animals that died a natural death and animals that died an unnatural death, such as from attack by other animals.

All wild beasts that attack.

All animals that are found to be diseased after they have been ritually slaughtered.

All fish that do not have fins and scales (including all shellfish).

All birds of prey.

All creeping animals.

All products derived from these forbidden animals such as bone meal, animal gelatin, and so forth.

All blood of an animal.

Certain kinds of fat and sinews from animals which are otherwise permitted.

What is permitted, then, is meat of the most common domesticated herbivores, such as beef or lamb; the most common fowl, such as chicken, duck, and turkey; also, the most common type of fish, except for shellfish. All fruits and vegetables are permitted, as are all nuts and grains. Basic dairy products that are derived from kosher animals are also permitted.

PREPARATION AND EATING

Kosher (permitted) animals must be slaughtered in a prescribed manner and prepared in a way that removes the blood. Obviously, one cannot drain all the blood from the meat without completely dehydrating it, and that is not required. But all of the arterial blood and at least some of the capillary blood is removed.

Meat and milk products may not be prepared or eaten together.

Permissible foods may be prepared only in utensils that are themselves kosher; in other words, utensils that are used exclusively to cook or serve kosher foods.

RITUAL SLAUGHTER

Judaism is an earthy religion and not an ascetic one. But great care is taken to prevent this earthiness from spilling over into torpor, butchery, brutality. Ritual slaughter is a superb example of this process of restraint.

First and foremost, meat must be slaughtered by a shochet, one who is an expert at shechitta (ritual slaughter), who understands the laws of kashrut in fine detail, one who is personally a pious Jew.

A shochet knows his knife must be razor-sharp and absolutely free of nicks or dents. It must be twice as long as the throat of the animal, so that it can be drawn through only once. He must examine the knife both before and after each shechitta, and if it fails inspection, the shechitta is not kosher. Before each act of shechitta, he must recite a benediction which reminds him that his act is both sanctioned and sanctified in a special way.

The shochet knows how to sever the carotid artery and jugular vein in the neck with one deft stroke so that the chicken or calf loses consciousness instantaneously and dies a swift and painless death. I wonder whether the requirement that the animal be conscious before shechitta is to prevent the shochet—and by extension the community he serves—from losing sight of the fact that animal life is also life.

My father-in-law, of blessed memory, was a shochet. He came from Europe, an ilui, a genius at Talmudic studies; but immediately he had to start saving money to bring over his wife and three young children. The only secure job he could find was as a shochet. He qualified because, although he had no prior experience in Europe, he was a man of piety, of morality, and he knew the intricate and multifaceted laws of shechitta as he knew the Shema Yisrael—backward, forward, blindfolded. Every morning he would leave for the slaughterhouse at 5:30 A.M. By early afternoon he had completed his shechitta. He would return home to wash, eat, and then go off in a fresh white shirt to the synagogue's beis medrash (study hall) where he would pray with a minyan. Then, seated at a long oak table, exquisitely buffed and scarred by the heavy black tomes, he would teach a daily Talmud class to a dozen or so men who were transported into another world for an hour each day by this brilliant scholar-shochet. This is what he did every day for forty years, and in all those years his sense of the inviolability of life and of reverence for life were never blunted.

Following shechitta, the animal is hung upside down so that the arterial blood can drain out. The shochet then searches the body for "signs." Any sign of possible disease or discoloration of the lungs will render the animal trefeh, unfit for kosher use. Obviously, if the animal is truly diseased, then U.S. Food and Drug Administration regulations and business practice would prohibit its use by everyone. But there are borderline situations where possible faults or ritual disqualification rule out use for kosher but not for non-kosher consumption. This is why many people who don't keep kosher have come to associate kashrut with purity and quality control.

The arteries and sinews of beef are removed, as are the intestines of fowl. The sinews in the hindquarters, which are hard to get at, are also prohibited; since these are too labor-intensive to remove economically, most kosher meat processors simply do not bother. Thus, the hindquarters of an animal, from which filet mignon is made, are usually separated and sent to a non-kosher meat market. There are some kosher meat processors who do make the effort, for there is a small market for filet mignon: some posh kosher restaurants and caterers want to serve these special meats and are willing to pay the extra costs.

Still, the animal is not quite ready. It must be properly kashered, that is, made kosher for cooking by further eliminating the capillary blood. This applies to fowl and red meat alike. It is a process of soaking and salting:

Rinse the meat well under cold water.

Soak a half hour in cold water, with the meat completely immersed. The pail used for soaking should not be used for anything else.

Salt the meat lightly but thoroughly with coarse salt; place the salted meat on a perforated or slanted drainboard and let the blood drain off. The meat should drain for an hour.

Rinse off the meat thoroughly.

The meat, or fowl, is now ready for cooking.

There is another way to kasher meat, and that is by broiling it on a rack so that the blood drains onto the pan below. This is always done with liver, because liver is so rich in blood it cannot be kashered by soaking and salting. Broiling can also be used to kasher other meats, such as steaks and chicken quarters. This is fine for people who are restricted to salt-free diets. A separate broiling rack is used for any of these meats or poultry that have not been soak/salt kashered. You would not use the same broiling rack for hamburgers made of kashered ground meat as you would for unkashered ground meat. The concern is that the kashered meat may reabsorb some flavor of blood from the rack that has been used to broil unkashered meat (meat not previously drained of capillary blood).

It is ironic that, over the course of history, anti-Semites invented the "blood libel," claiming that religious Jews have used blood of Christian children to bake their matzot. It is a classic case of lying—or should I say, projection. Kashrut stringently prohibits blood in any form. Even a blood spot on a raw egg is forbidden, so we buy eggs that are candled, and we crack them one by one into a clear glass to make sure they have no blood spot in them. Blood is a symbol of life and it seems inhuman to partake of it in any form or fashion. For the same reason, traditional Jews tend to cook or broil meat to the point where people think of kosher meat as automatically well done or overcooked. (In actual fact, kosher meat can be prepared rarer than most people realize, but the tradition of removing blood is so well established that even many observant people don't know this.) It only proves that the humane aspects of kashrut are not well known.

Few Jews do their own kashering anymore. Most kosher butchers will kasher the meat and poultry as a routine service. But it wasn't that way twenty-odd years ago.

Shortly after Yitz and I were married we moved to Waltham, Massachusetts. I ordered from a kosher butcher in Roxbury, twenty miles away. He agreed to deliver, but only if it were a large order. When my order arrived on a Friday afternoon, all thirty pounds of it, I thought I would just cook one chicken and efficiently pop the rest into the freezer. But the chicken looked a little pinker than the ones my mother used to prepare. A nervous phone call to Roxbury ensued. "But you didn't ask me to kasher your order," he said. I tried to pull the new bride routine on him, but to no avail. I didn't even have kosher (coarse) salt in the house. I can't recall now how I handled it; all I remember is that it was a minor disaster. (The law suggests that I could have washed off the meat, held it until after Shabbat, and then kashered it within the next day or two, but, in retrospect, that seems too simple.)

The saying goes, once you establish a relationship with a kosher butcher it's like being married to him. So it pays to shop around a bit before settling down to one lasting relationship; that is, if there is a choice. The local rabbi can supply information on kosher butchers. One relies heavily on a kosher butcher. He must be a man of reliability and integrity and, like the shochet, he, too, must be knowledgeable in the laws of kashrut and must be personally observant of halacha.

SEPARATION OF MEAT AND MILK

Laws of Kashrut require total separation of meat and milk products. This means not only separating foods in cooking and eating, but separating everything that is used in the process: a completely separate set of dishes, flatware, knives, pots, pans— one for meat and another for dairy. It's like outfitting two separate kitchens.

Jews who keep kosher often have six sets of dishes, none of

which are there just for show: an everyday set of meat, an everyday set of dairy, a good set of meat, a good set of dairy, a set of dairy Passover, a set of meat Passover. That's a lot of cupboard space.

Where it is possible, a kosher kitchen will contain two sinks: one for meat and one for dairy. Where there is only one sink, the dishes are never put directly into the sink. Instead, separate racks are used for meat or dairy, likewise, separate sponges, scouring pads, dish towels, counter drain racks, and so forth. For convenience, everything is color-coded—for example, red for meat, blue for dairy. Counters made of Formica can be used for meat or dairy as long as the food is cold and the counter is perfectly clean. However, many Jewish housewives set aside special counter sections for meat or dairy.

Stove burners can be used for either meat or dairy, as can an oven. However, meat and dairy foods should not be cooked simultaneously in an oven. Refrigerators, where everything is cold, can be used to store both meat and dairy as long as the foods are sealed and are kept separate; one would not stack, say, a salami on top of a container of butter.

Dishwashers are an interesting story, part of the "politics" of kashrut. Depending on which rabbi one asks, dishwashers may or may not be used consecutively for meat and dairy. If the interior basin is metal, some rabbis will say the dishwasher can be used for meat and dairy (consecutively), as long as it is cleaned by running a full cycle before each use. Most require that different racks be used. For a decade now, individual Israeli rabbis have ruled that not only metal-interior dishwashers but porcelain enamel ones as well may be used for meat and for dairy if there has been an interim cleaning cycle and a change of racks. However, one is required to ask a rabbi. And having asked, one must abide by his decision.

Should a mishap occur, under certain conditions Jewish law provides a remedy. Restoring something to its kosher state is not magical. The general principle is that the flavor of meat or dairy is absorbed in utensils or surfaces only when the contact is through heat but not through cold. For example, if cold dairy food is placed inadvertently on a meat plate, all that is required is to wash the plate very clean in cold water and to rinse it well;

it can then be used immediately. If, on the other hand, hot dairy foods were involved, and the utensil is porous, such as china or pottery or earthenware, it is assumed that because of the heat, some of the dairy flavor has been absorbed into a dish that has previously been saturated with meat flavor. Since meat and milk are now mixed in this porous dish, it cannot be kashered, and therefore can no longer be used. If the dish is not porous, such as glassware, it is assumed that no flavors have been absorbed; therefore, it needn't be kashered. In fact, glassware, as long as it is perfectly clean, can be used for meat or dairy since it is non-porous. However, if it were to be used continuously for both types of food, the Rabbis were concerned that people might get sloppy. So they prohibited routine use of glass utensils for both meat and milk. Water glasses, however, may be used for both.

If a pot was inadvertently made trefeh—such as using a meat pot for dairy—in certain instances it can be kashered. Pots not made of one piece, and which therefore are impossible to clean perfectly at all points of joining, cannot be kashered. Most pots with soldered handles cannot be kashered.

If a pot qualifies for kashering, it must first be completely cleaned so there is no macroscopic mixing of meat and milk. Next, the absorbed flavor of the forbidden ingredient must be removed by heat. There are two heat kashering processes for utensils: hagalah and libun.

In hagalah, an oversize pot or vessel is filled with water and heated to boiling. The trefeh pot is completely submerged in the water. Since the addition of the pot will often cool the water to below the boiling point, two things can be done: (1) Keep the pot in the larger vessel until the water has boiled up again. (2) Heat a rock or stone to a very high heat on another burner and toss it into the large vessel. This superheats the water and immediately causes it to boil in the presence of the pot. Through this process, any absorbed flavors are assumed to be removed and the trefeh pot becomes kosher. There is no minimum time limit for the boiling. All it takes is a second for the trefeh pot to be completely submerged in boiling water.

A further requirement is that the volume of water used to boil the trefeh utensil be at least sixty times the volume of the actual metal to be kashered. (This can be measured carefully through

displacement, but most people make a reasonably generous estimate.) This ensures that any flavor of meat or dairy present will
be so diluted (a one-to-sixty solution maximum) that it becomes
too insignificant to make the large kashering pot trefeh.

Libun is a firing process, using a blowtorch, the kind that can
be purchased in a hardware store for ten or fifteen dollars. The
flame is passed over the entire pot or utensil. At times, libun and
hagalah are used in combination to kasher an item, for example,
a pot with a certain kind of handle that can be cleaned only by
libun while its insides are best kashered by hagalah.

Although technically one could switch something on a permanent basis from meat to dairy using these processes, this is
not permitted. Repairing mistakes, okay, but not switching.

In general, a rabbi is always reading and willing to answer
questions of kashrut. Rabbis don't have as much opportunity to
use their expert knowledge of kashrut these days, since things
are more clearly labeled, more easily available. It used to be quite
different. A rabbi would get ten, fifteen, twenty questions about
kashrut in an average week. As a matter of fact, a great proportion of his rabbinic training dealt with the laws of kashrut—
practical preparation for meeting the needs of his constituency.
Today if he gets one question a week it's a lot.

TEVILAH

In addition to kashering, there is a process called tevilah, ritual
immersion for utensils. Technically, it has nothing to do with
kashrut, but rather with sanctification of vessels as ownership
passes to a Jew. It is based on the Biblical passage (NUM. 31:23)
describing how the vessels the Jews captured from Midianites
had to be purified in the ritual waters. Dishes or pots or flatware
that are made of metal or of glass require this tevilah in the
mikvah (ritual bath), or in a body of moving water such as ocean
or river. Immediately before the tevilah, this blessing is recited:

בָּרוּךְ אַתָּה יְיָ, אֱלֹהֵינוּ מֶלֶךְ הָעוֹלָם אֲשֶׁר קִדְּשָׁנוּ
בְּמִצְוֹתָיו, וְצִוָּנוּ עַל טְבִילַת כֵּלִים.

*Baruch ata Adonai Elohainu melech ha'olam asher kidshanu
b'mitzvotav v'tzivanu al tevilat kelim.*

Blessed are You, Lord our God, Ruler of the universe, Who has
sanctified us with His commandments and commanded us on
the immersion of vessels.

Chinaware or ceramic doesn't require tevilah, but some Orthodox Jews "tovel" these items anyhow. However, they do not say
the blessing. Interestingly, utensils that had not previously been
immersed are not considered non-kosher, which explains why
it's never too late to immerse a vessel that wasn't ritually immersed before. Tevilah is done during the day at the mikvah;
one must call ahead for an appointment.

WAITING BETWEEN MEALS

Not only are foods separated in preparation and eating, but also
in "digesting." After a dairy meal, you wait thirty minutes before
eating meat. Some people wait several hours after eating hard
cheeses, since these take longer to digest, but most authorities
say all dairy is the same and rule half an hour wait after hard
cheeses too.

After a meat meal, it's a different story altogether. Most traditional Jews wait six hours before eating a dairy product. Nevertheless, there is some variation in custom. Some Jews of German
origin wait three hours after eating meat. Many Dutch Jews wait
one hour, as was the custom in that community.

The origin of these variations has its source in the Talmud.
One Rabbi states that after eating meat, one waits "from one
meal to another" before eating dairy foods. Other Rabbis interpreted this to mean a six-hour wait, since in those days people
typically ate two meals a day, about six hours apart. The communities that followed these interpretations wait six hours.
Later, other rabbis ruled that "one meal to another" denotes a
three-hour wait, approximately the time we wait from breakfast
to lunch. Still others ruled that "one meal to another" means
finish one meal, wait a decent interval (that is, one hour) so your
mouth will not be full of meat or its flavor, and then you may eat

another (dairy) meal. However, other rabbis emphasized that the flavor of meat remains longer in one's mouth and thus one should wait a full six hours. This latter custom has always been the most widespread one among Orthodox Jews. Interestingly, recent nutrition studies have shown that it takes the digestive tract approximately five and one-half hours to digest animal protein.

When J.J. was thirteen, he decided to become a vegetarian. Not only did he want to emulate an older brother and sister, but he also couldn't stand having to wait six hours after lunch on Shabbat for ice cream or a glass of milk. Now, the rest of the family carnivores envy him as he finishes Shabbat lunch and goes off to help himself to a big bowl of ice cream.

HOUSEHOLD HELP AND KASHRUT

The laws, though they seem complex to the uninitiated, are really quite simple. Some years ago I discovered the factor that makes the difference between complex and simple. That factor is the seriousness with which one takes the whole thing. That is truly all there is to it. Since the time I discovered this secret I have applied it several times and invariably it works. Here's what happened. Years ago, I had a woman working for me in my home. She had received no education beyond the eighth grade, but she was a very decent woman with an average level of common sense. Her tasks involved preparation of food. I explained to her the laws of kashrut, and worked with her for several days, explaining and repeating and watching to make sure that there would be no mistakes. Everything was labeled and in its proper cabinets. She seemed to be catching on, but there were one or two slipups that I caught just in time. One evening as I came in to supervise how things were proceeding, I saw that she had taken a meat pot to cook string beans for a dairy meal and had put some butter in the pot. Again, I explained to her that we couldn't cook in a meat pot anything that was to be used for a dairy meal. Moreover, putting butter in the pot had now made the pot trefeh. This particular pot could not be kashered either. Therefore, if she didn't mind, she should take the pot home with her on her day off, for I could no longer use it in my home. She felt awful. "I'm sorry," I said, "please don't feel bad about the pot. I can replace it, but these are my laws." That's all it took for her to understand. Suddenly, she knew I meant business; she grasped the seriousness with which we approach halacha. The notion of separation became absolutely clear to her, and she never made another mistake. I don't panic anymore when I think of having to train household help in the laws of kashrut. All it takes is one dish or pot, irreversibly trefehed and banished from my kitchen forever, to uncomplicate these laws. But it won't work unless everything is labeled clearly.

PARVE

In addition to classifications of meat and dairy which must be completely separate, there is a large category called parve— foods that are neither meat nor dairy and can therefore be used in conjunction with either of them. All fruits, vegetables, nuts, and grains are parve (pronounced pahr'vuh, but also spelled pareve), as are eggs and fish, and staples such as flour, sugar, tea, coffee, and spices; most condiments and relishes such as ketchup, mustard, jams and jellies; most oils and juices. Many of these parve items, however, need rabbinic supervision to determine whether they are really parve or even kosher, which brings us to the subject of how we shop.

BUYING KOSHER

What we bring into our homes in addition to kosher meat is as important as how we prepare it. Oddly enough, the more sophisticated and extensive the prepared-food industry becomes, the more cautious an Orthodox Jew must be about reading labels. Not only must we ascertain if a food is meat or dairy, but nowadays there are preservatives and additives used in almost every type of prepared food that is on the market. Some of these additives are made of dairy or meat or non-kosher by-products such as gelatin from a non-kosher animal. A seemingly harmless little olive thrown casually into a salad could disqualify that salad for a meat meal: olives are often prepared with lactic acid, which makes them dairy, and therefore unusable with a meat meal; or shortening marked pure vegetable shortening can contain stearic acid, which is derived from non-kosher animals; or peanut butter, which might include a glyceride of non-kosher origin.

So there is an art to buying kosher. The easiest way is to "let Chaim Yankel do it." To save any hassle, some Jews will shop only in a store that sells kosher products exclusively. One doesn't have to read fine-print labels; even the words meat, dairy, or parve are stamped in legible letters on all prepared foods.

The alternative is to buy in regular supermarkets but to check all prepared foods for the seal of rabbinic supervision. What it means is that there is a reliable independent supervisor (mashgiach), a person who is knowledgeable in laws of kashrut, who spends time at the plant overseeing the entire process from receipt of the new foodstuffs to shipment of the finished products. There are a number of registered kashrut symbols to look for. Among them are:

Ⓤ —the Union of Orthodox Jewish Congregations, New York, New York. (Inasmuch as the Ⓤ is under the aegis of a large communal organization, this is the best known and most widely used symbol of kashrut.)

Ⓚ —O.K. (Organized Kashrut) Laboratories, Brooklyn, New York.

Ⓜ —(K.V.H.) Kashrut Commission of the Vaad Horabanim (Rabbinical Council) of New England, Boston, Mass.

⒦ —Rabbi J. H. Ralbag, New York, New York.

⒦ —Kosher Supervision Service, Hackensack, New Jersey.

◄ —Kosher Overseers Association of America, Beverly Hills, California.

Ⓥ —Vaad Hoeir of St. Louis, St. Louis, Missouri.

▟ —Board of Rabbis, Jersey City, New Jersey.

☆ —Vaad Hakashrus of Baltimore, Baltimore, Maryland.

None of these symbols should be confused with ® , which does *not* mean Orthodox rabbis; it means registered trademark. For reliability of the above certifications, one should check with one's own rabbi.

In addition to the symbols above, there is the ubiquitous K . The U.S. Food and Drug Administration law permits the K to be used where there is rabbinic supervision. However, the K is no more reliable than the individual rabbi who grants it. K on some foods is fine according to Orthodox standards, but not on others. The local rabbi—or the individual—will write to the company to get the name of the supervising rabbi, and then take it from there. Within the Orthodox community there are differences of opinion among rabbis as to whether on certain breakfast cereals is adequate. Some say yes, some say no.

There is also a range of response as to what kinds of items need rabbinic supervision in the first place. Some will say anything that is packaged, for even the food containers for vegetables and fruits could contain derivatives of non-kosher monoglycerides. At the other end are those who say any uncooked product whose listed ingredients are not unkosher is okay. For most Orthodox Jews the answer lies somewhere in between. Generally speaking, we look for rabbinic certification on all baked goods, cheeses, cake mixes, candies, desserts, puddings, breakfast cereals, dressings, frostings, ice creams, relishes, condiments, preserves, sauces, ground spices, pastas, canned fish, margarine and all prepared foods (for example, French fries and soups).

The tricky things to look for in seemingly harmless foods are monoglycerides and diglycerides, shortening, gelatin, and stearic acid, which could be derived from non-kosher animals or from dairy sources. That is why rabbinic supervision is needed on so many processed foods. Happily, today there is little of any given type of food that is not available in strictly kosher form. Even kosher "bacon," (made of soybean derivatives), parve cheesecake, and kosher paté de fois gras. Thank God no one has come out with kosher pork. However, it must be noted that the Rabbis of the Talmud said that for every forbidden food, including pork, there is something exactly equivalent in taste that is kosher. (How did they know??)

Another restriction of kashrut, which is followed very strictly by some Jews, less so by others, is the law concerning wine produced or handled by a non-Jew.

The Torah prohibited use of any wine which a non-Jew produced for idol worship libations. The Rabbis extended this ban not only to wine produced by a non-Jew, but also to any Jewish-made wine that was touched or handled by a non-Jew. This was done to discourage social contact.

In the medieval period, when the Jews of France were deeply involved with their non-Jewish neighbors in the wine industry, many of these laws were reexamined. Moreover, by that time the use of wine for idol worship was very rare. Thus, certain rabbinic authorities permitted Jews to deal in *stam yainam*, as non-Jewish wine was called.

Nevertheless, the restriction on drinking still obtained, for the social reason. The *Shulchan Aruch* (sixteenth-century code of law) stressed that the prohibition is enforced to prevent drinking and social contact between Jews and non-Jews. This, it was felt, would lead to intermarriage.

Today, some authorities permit use of Jewish wine handled by non-Jews as long as it has been pasteurized (boiled during its production process). The reason for this is that the original prohibition exempted boiled wine, which was not used for libations or social drinking. On the other hand, some authorities forbid wines that are touched even by a non-Sabbath-observant Jew. Most Orthodox Jews drink only kosher wines, which are simply wines produced by Jews under rabbinic supervision. These wines are generally packaged under double seals to prevent any prohibited form of handling.

The prohibition extended to any by-product of grapes—such as grape juice or grape jelly. However, it did not extend to whiskey, for whiskey is a grain product; it wasn't used for idol worship purposes, so there was nothing on which to peg a prohibition. Thus it is that there are times when Orthodox Jews drink kosher wines and regular whiskey in "mixed" company, but you won't catch them eating pure grape candies that have no kosher label.

There is also debate as to extent of rabbinic supervision over dairy products. Most modern Orthodox Jews drink milk and use butter and creams from Gentile-owned farms that are not rabbinically supervised, because the danger that the milk comes from a non-kosher animal no longer exists. It is against U.S. law to sell as "milk" anything other than what comes from a cow.

However, some Jews will drink only milk that is produced by a Jewish-owned, rabbinically supervised dairy.

On hard cheeses, however, there is little debate; the enzyme, rennet, that is used to harden cheese comes from the lining of a calf's stomach. The enyzme is considered a meat product and may not be used together with cheese. Moreover, since it is a powerful chemical, it is considered not to be diluted, so that even a minute amount (less than one part in sixty) is still prohibited. However, some rabbis ruled that the rennet is so treated chemically (isolated and purified) that it is no longer considered a meat product. Others disagree with this ruling, arguing that the rennet is not denatured in the course of preparation. Almost all Orthodox Jews will eat only hard cheeses (such as Swiss and Gouda) that are rabbinically certified. Many of the soft cheeses (cream cheese, cottage cheese) are prepared by physical separation, not rennet. In such cases, certification would not be needed. The marginal case is American cheese—some Orthodox Jews eat American cheese without kosher labels based on the rennet ruling mentioned above or because much American cheese is prepared by nonchemical process. Most, however, insist on certification for American cheese as well—if for no other reason than to avoid a situation in which the kashrut of their home would be questionable or inadequate in the eyes of others.

Regarding bread: one of the three special mitzvot assigned to women is the law of *challah*, removing a token amount of dough (the size of an olive) from a yeast batter, and throwing it into the oven fires while reciting the proper blessing (see p. 482). This is a residual practice, symbolic of ancient Temple rites of gift offerings to God from nature's bounty. The law of challah is binding only upon Jews; thus, the bread of a bakery owned by non-Jews, whose products are kosher and have rabbinic supervision, does not require challah to be taken. A Jewish-owned and rabbinically supervised bakery will take challah as will a woman or man baking bread at home.

One of the bonuses of living in an intensive Jewish neighborhood is the presence not only of a kosher bakery but of a Sabbath observant (Shomer Shabbat) one as well. This means the owners are personally observant of halacha. Accordingly, they close the bakery before sundown Friday and don't reopen until early Sunday morning. There is never any worry whether or not challah was taken or whether Sunday morning's bread or Monday morning's cookies were baked by another Jew on Shabbat (which would not be permitted).

FISH

In all but very intensive Jewish neighborhoods, the fish store will sell both kosher and non-kosher fish. However, if there is a Jewish clientele, the fishman will keep two sets of knives for cutting and cleaning.

The most common kosher fish in the United States are:

Anchovies	Sardines
Bluefish	Sea bass
Carp	Shad
Chubs	Smelts
Cod	Striped bass
Flounder (and Sole)	Trout
Herring	Tuna
Mackerel	Whitefish
Red snapper	Whiting
Salmon	Yellow perch

Non-kosher fish include:

Clams	Oysters
Crabs	Scallops
Crayfish	Shrimp
Lobster	Sturgeon
	Swordfish

There has been some debate among the denominations over swordfish. Swordfish is deemed non-kosher by Orthodox authorities while many Conservative rabbis rule that it is kosher. Swordfish are born with fins and scales, but as they mature, they lose the scales. The Orthodox maintain that the kind of scales swordfish are born with could not be removed without damaging the underlying skin and therefore do not qualify for the Biblical criterion of scales.

TRAVEL

Now that Orthodox Jews travel more than ever before, kashrut has moved into the jet-setting scene. There is a kosher hotel in Majorca and one in Aruba, a kosher restaurant in downtown Amsterdam, and even a small kosher sandwich shop in Creve Coeur, Missouri. There are many books on Jewish travel, and most Orthodox organizations can supply the get-up-and-go types with a list of places to dine.

Still, what to do if you are strictly kosher and your travels take you to a place where there is no kosher restaurant?

One can manage even under the most dire circumstances. In 1976, Yitz and I traveled to the Soviet Union to visit refuseniks, Jews who are held in a state of limbo once they have applied to leave. Allowed neither to emigrate nor to live as free citizens, they are very much dependent on each other and on visitors from abroad for emotional support.

Our plans were to stay for two weeks, traveling to different cities in the U.S.S.R. As far as food went, it didn't matter, one city or another: there would be no kosher food anywhere. So we packed some staples and figured we'd fill in with fruits and vegetables. Russian bread, which is not considered kosher by our Free World standards (a Sabbath-observant bakery or kosher-certified packaged bread), was, under the circumstances, deemed permissible by Israeli and American rabbinic boards. (We didn't know how delicious Russian bread would be—I felt the urge to hop on the counter of the Moscow bakery every morning and shout, "Have some more, friends, it's on us!" knowing that we Americans were heavily subsidizing the only thing that "works" in Russia—bread!)

At any rate, into our suitcases went an immersion heater, two mugs, two sets of cutlery, a can opener, several dozen instant soups in foil packages, and a Kiddush cup. In a separate, compact overnight bag, all prepared so that all I'd have to do was take it out of the refrigerator at the last minute, I packed two salamis, two bottles of wine for Kiddush, six large cans of tuna, a large jar of peanut butter (protein), and a dozen bars of halvah (I married a halvah freak; and besides, it, too, has protein).

As one might expect, halfway to the airport I realized who

would be eating the salami in a day or two—and it wasn't us. We managed to pick up two bottles of kosher wine at a package store en route, but when we got to the airport, I didn't even have time to attack the candy counter. The airline officials, of a national carrier that shall remain forever nameless, made us hurry onto the plane so that we could sit on the runway for the next six hours locked in a noisy, nonair-conditioned cabin, and marvel at the periodic lies that came over the PA system as to how soon this or that "minor" problem would be repaired. Three A.M.: we hadn't even taken off and I was starved. I contemplated drinking the two bottles of wine on an empty stomach and spending the next two days in a blessedly drunken stupor, but my dear husband wouldn't allow! "Pull yourself together," he said gently, for the fortieth time, as I threatened to bite the flight attendant.

So! Forty packages of instant broth and two hungry kosher Jews in Moscow with two weeks to go. But we didn't starve. And we didn't drink only tea and instant soups. Food was not the main item on our agenda, nor did we want to spend time or money in restaurants where we couldn't eat much anyhow. We quickly found out what we could eat inexpensively and easily. Every morning for breakfast we ate in the workers' cafeteria. For a few pennies we filled up on a delicious sweet buttermilk drink, a staple in the Russian workers' diet. At the bakery near our hotel, we bought fresh Russian pumpernickel, better than Ratner's. Next door we purchased butter, and sour cream and yoghurt and fresh milk—and no long lines. A few times we boiled eggs in our mugs, using our immersion heater. Fresh fruits and vegetables, a staple in our diet at home, required waiting on long queues with not much to buy when your turn came. On day two, I waited twenty minutes, only to get to first place in line when 2:00 P.M. struck and the farmer closed his street stall in the middle of my sentence. We never waited again; juices and fruits and fresh salads we ate in our hotel dining room, not much of a selection, but more than the average Russian gets from a street stall. To my great happiness, I lost five pounds during those two weeks, but it was because we ran all day long and not because there was nothing for us to eat. A kosher Jew can manage anywhere in the world.

The principle in dining out is the same principle that operates at home: the food must be kosher, it must be prepared in a kosher way, and it must be served on kosher utensils. That would not allow one to eat any meat in a non-kosher restaurant, nor any forbidden fish, nor any permitted food cooked in non-kosher pots and served on non-kosher dishes. Does that mean it is possible to eat nothing in a restaurant that serves non-kosher food? Some say one should not enter a non-kosher eating place because of the principle of marit ayin—the prohibition of giving the wrong impression to someone else. I must admit that I get a little rattled when I see—as I've seen—a man wearing a kepah (skullcap) sitting near the windows of a McDonald's. I say to myself:

1. The fellow wears a kepah as a sign of belonging but not of commitment to the tradition.
2. He's just drinking a coke and nothing more.

Marit ayin is an important principle, but it is also a relative judgment. When parve margarine was first introduced, it was always served in its wrapper at a meat meal so that no one mistakenly would think it to be butter and draw the wrong conclusion or follow the wrong example. Similarly, when parve cream first came on the market, we all served it in its original container because of marit ayin. Now, one can go to a meeting at an Orthodox home or a dinner at a kosher restaurant and everyone knows that the cream-looking liquid served in the small crystal pitcher after a meat meal—is parve. As more and more Orthodox Jews dine out—on business and vacations—and as more of them wear kipot (with women you can't tell), eating in a non-kosher restaurant does not mean one is not keeping strictly kosher.

Marit ayin aside, then, there is another principle that makes it possible to eat certain things in an eating place that is not otherwise kosher. The principle is that food absorption is transferred through heat and not through cold: a fresh vegetable salad or fresh fruit, a mound of cottage cheese, a glass of milk, a bowl of dried cereal, an individual can of tuna or salmon, kosher-brand ice cream (many of the large ice-cream companies have rabbinic certification), fresh juices, liquor: these are some of the things that an Orthodox Jew will feel comfortable eating or drinking from a cold clean plate or glass or disposable ware. The larger the establishment is, the safer it is, because it is more likely that the knife used to slice the tomato is not the same knife used to cut the bacon—something which would make the tomato inedible for a kosher Jew. However, in a small establishment it is easier to ask and to oversee what the staff is doing. Even in a large restaurant, one can ask, for example, if the salad preparation counter is separate. . . .

Many restaurants are quite willing to accommodate the special dietary needs of any person, including a kosher one. Once, on a business lunch with a young woman, I ordered an avocado vinaigrette. I asked the waitress to find out what the dressing was made of, since wine vinegar, undoubtedly made of non-kosher wines, was not in my kosher repertoire. Wine vinegar it was, so she brought me lemon and Italian olive oil. The woman I was with, a non-Jew, was curious about the whole thing, but we didn't have time to talk about it. A week later I received a bottle of champagne from her, celebrating our mutual success. It was kosher champagne, with this note: "If you can't eat their vinegar, you sure as hell can't drink their champagne!" It's a lot easier to take a non-kosher friend to a kosher restaurant, but if that's not possible, with a little care, one can do more than nurse a glass of ginger ale the entire time.

There are some Orthodox Jews who take matters a step further —eating fish in non-kosher restaurants or hotels. This process is not as complicated as it seems:

1. Order a kosher fish, that is, one of the permitted kinds, let us say red snapper.
2. Ask the maître d' or the chief cook to rinse the fish well and to wrap it tightly in two separate layers of aluminum foil, completely closed, and then bake it. It can be baked with seasoning such as butter, sour cream, lemon juice, salt and pepper, cloves (wonderful with baked fish).
3. It should be served exactly the way it is baked, closed, in its aluminum foil wrapping, just as the kosher flight food packs are served on airlines.
4. Since it is hot, it cannot be eaten from a non-kosher dish nor with non-kosher cutlery. Therefore, the waiter will bring plastic cutlery and a paper plate—or the fish can be eaten out of

its own foil container. Some hotels keep on hand brand-new flatware which they bring for first-time use in these circumstances.

I tried this once at a health spa, where the management was most accommodating and even asked me to come to the kitchen to see that everything was "kosher." I must admit I was a bit apprehensive, and every time the waiter passed I reminded him not to open the aluminum foil but that I would do it myself. However, there are Orthodox Jews who travel a lot and find it works without a hitch. A friend suggests that a telephone call to the chef in the quiet hours of the afternoon to explain the whys and wherefores makes it much simpler.

The same procedures can be followed when people who observe kashrut are invited to the homes of people who do not. True, some hosts will feel awkward about serving a guest a fresh salad when others get roast duck, but by extending themselves and by agreeing not to be embarrassed on either side, justice can be done to both kashrut and the need to socialize.

The above suggestions will enable one to eat out with friends or in business situations while meeting the technical requirements of kashrut. Some Jews would object on the principle of marit ayin. Others might point out that the dishes used had not been immersed. Still others would argue that the very purpose of kashrut was to discourage excessive socializing with people who don't observe the laws. However, none of these objections are flaws in the basic condition of being kosher.

I believe that the purpose of kashrut is to make eating a special experience and to serve as a reminder of a Jew's ethical conscience as well as of the other unique teachings of Judaism. To me, distinctiveness and not separation is the Jew's calling. This feeling is possible in the presence of nonobservant Jews and of non-Jews. The values of friendship, human solidarity, and socializing are highly esteemed Jewish values; making a living and exchanging professional service (sometimes performed over a meal) also are respected in Jewish culture. One of the great qualities of the Jewish tradition is its ability to balance contradictions—idealism and realism, Jewish particularism and unusual concern for humanity. Similarly, in the act of eating, one can strike that balance between fidelity to one's own principles and shared friendship and respectful contact with others.

How does it feel to be strictly kosher?

I have given a good many words to eating kosher in non-kosher eating places. It would seem to suggest that there are some Orthodox Jews who keep strictly kosher yet who underneath it all are dying to eat non-kosher. The truth? For 99.9 percent of my life, the thought simply never crosses my mind. I was born into a kosher home, have lived that way all of my life, and have never really felt deprived. I have shopped, cooked, and eaten according to the laws of my faith—and I do so out of love and not a sense of oppression. I have never tasted shrimp nor eaten at Regine's and it is all the same to me. To be sure, there have been a dozen times in my life when I've had a passion to eat something I wasn't permitted to have—marshmallows, as a child growing up in Seattle; dark chocolate mousse being served at a non-kosher neighbor's birthday party while I smile sweetly over my poor bowl of strawberries; feeling a huge craving for a gourmet meal prepared by Jean Banchet of Le Français that I read about in TWA's *Ambassador* magazine (February 1981); or when I've eaten a bad meal at a kosher restaurant whose banquettes smell slightly of mildew—well, I can't always say kosher is the best thing in the world.

And yet, I like keeping/being kosher, for as I've said earlier, it is not only a way of eating, it is a way of life. Kashrut is like a portable faith, perhaps more so for a woman than for a man who has tangible religious paraphernalia to remind himself and others who he is. An Orthodox Jewish woman, having no such visible symbols as kepah and tzitzit, tallit and tefillin, feels a heightened sense of Jewish awareness as she goes about her worldly business, all the while carrying with her this elaborate and very special discipline. Strange, but walking past a hot-dog stand or reading labels in the supermarket aisles or breaking raw eggs into a glass one by one makes me feel—Jewish!

I like it, too, because it says something to me about the generations. Not just the past but the future. When Moshe scrutinizes the label of something I've bought and tells me he won't eat it, I don't consider it the one-upmanship of an adolescent. Instead, I am very proud of him, for he has done what we had hoped—he has taken the laws of kashrut as his own serious responsibility. Yitz and I now know that Moshe could travel anywhere around the world or find himself in any social circumstance—and he would remain a faithful Jew, inextricably tied to *his* people and to *his* tradition. What more could a parent want!

Though I might dwell a few moments on thoughts of dinner at Le Français, a dispensation for a day is not something I would ever consider. I've kept this body filled with kosher food all these years—and it has served me pretty well—body and soul. I intend to keep doing the same for as long as I live. Someday I'll find my kosher Monsieur Banchet and have my elegant orgy. Meanwhile, no one makes chicken soup and knaidlach like Sylvia G.

CHAPTER 3

TAHARAT HAMISHPACHAH: THE LAWS OF FAMILY PURITY

In traditional Jewish literature, one can find both positive and negative attitudes toward sex. There are statements made by great rabbis that are thoroughly positive and wholesome:

Where there is no union of male and female, men are not worthy of beholding the Shekhinah, the Divine Presence.

—*The Zohar*

. . . when you are ready for sexual union, see that your wife's intentions combine with yours. Do not hurry to arouse her until she is receptive. Be calm . . . as you enter the path of love and will.

—*The Holy Letter,*
attributed to Nahmanides

Yet, turn a page or two, a century or two, and you will find more circumspect attitudes. But as with all things in Judaism, no matter what the attitude or the interpretation of certain laws, there is a special way to behave. So it is with marital sex.

If I were asked to list the central rituals that characterize and regulate the life of an Orthodox Jew, I would swiftly recite my catechism: Shabbat, kashrut and taharat hamishpachah, the laws of family purity. Taharat hamishpachah is a fairly accurate euphemism for those laws that prohibit sexual intercourse each month during a woman's menses and during the seven days following menses; the entire period of abstinence is concluded with ritual immersion. Two other equally good code words that summon up this body of laws are mikvah (ritual bath) and niddah (woman in a state of sexual unavailability).

Of all the laws that govern an Orthodox Jew's life, these are the most private, the most secretive, and without contest, the most difficult. Which explains, in part, why Conservative, Reconstructionist, and Reform denominations, though retaining varying degrees of observance of Shabbat and kashrut, have all but discarded taharat hamishpachah from their ritual agendas.

Not so Orthodox Jews. That is not to say that some individuals have privately decided not to adhere, or, more likely, have simply defaulted. On the one hand, the secrecy and privacy allow that only a woman and her husband know for sure whether they observe the laws or not. On the other hand, locking horns with something as powerful as the sex drive makes it a surety that the law will not always prevail. Nevertheless, despite a measure of noncompliance among Jews who consider themselves Orthodox and are so identified, taharat hamishpachah remains a basic assumption of Orthodox Jewish family life.

Taharat hamishpachah is given great weight in the tradition: (1) Niddah is one of three mitzvot assigned primarily to women —the other two being challah and nerot (candlelighting). (2) The laws of niddah and mikvah are Biblical in origin. The Torah even gives us the exact punishment for a man and a woman who have sex during menstruation; it is the dreaded and mysterious *karet*, a divine punishment of cutting off their souls from the Jewish people. (3) Most surprising of all, constructing a mikvah, a ritualariam as it is sometimes called, takes precedence over many other mitzvot. For example, where there is no mikvah, community leaders are required to sell the Torah scroll in order to pay for building a mikvah. And if communal resources are such that a choice must be made between a synagogue or a mikvah, the latter comes first. (It doesn't usually happen that way, but that's how it is on record.)

What is it all about? Why such secrecy? Why such import? And what does it say to us today?

The Torah gives the law, not once but three times:

1. "And if a woman have a bodily flow and this flow from her flesh be blood, she shall be in her impurity for seven days. And whosoever touches her shall be unclean until the evening" (LEV. 15:19).
2. "And unto a woman while she is impure by her uncleanness you shall not approach to uncover her nakedness" (LEV. 18:19).
3. "And if a man shall lie with a woman having her flow and shall uncover her nakedness—her source he has uncovered and she has uncovered [to him] the fountain of her blood; both of them shall be cut off from among their people" (LEV. 20:18).

The Biblical laws appear in two different contexts: one (1) in a list of ritual impurities, the other (3) as part of a litany of forbidden sexual unions. The middle verse, Leviticus 18:19, seems to be the bridge phrase interweaving the two themes. But it is important to keep in mind that there is a distinction between impurity, taboos, and forbidden relationships, for it affects the way we use language regarding niddah as well as the way we understand the meaning of the laws today. More about that later.

The Bible requires a minimum of seven days of abstinence, beginning with the onset of flow and concluded by purification in the mikvah. The Rabbis expanded the minimum from seven to twelve days—five-day minimum for the flow and seven "white" days following the last day of flow. In the Talmud, we read that it was the women themselves who increased the severity of the law, that is, extended the off limits time.

Briefly, it works this way: as soon as menstruation begins each month, the woman and her husband separate from each other sexually. A woman should keep track of her menstrual rhythm so as to anticipate onset day. Toward the end of her menstrual flow, she will begin to examine herself to see exactly on what day the flow stops. At the end of the last day of staining, she begins to count the seven "white" days, days that are free of any staining. If her menses lasts longer than five days, or if she stains for a long while after the end of the regular flow, she and her husband have an extra burden. However, there are numerous rabbinic qualifications as to what constitutes staining, and the rabbis took extenuating circumstances into consideration as they legislated.

I have used the term "whites," a literal translation of the Talmudic *levanim*, rather than the more commonly used term "clean," as in "seven clean days," because clean implies unclean. I would like to get away from categories of unclean. Menstruation is natural and healthy. At worst, it is a nuisance, but it is not unclean and impure. In Temple times, those words were appropriate. They meant ritually impure and unclean, that is, unfit for Temple access. Today, however, they summon up negative associations of "not clean" or "dirty," which the term "whites" does not. I, for one, don't consider my body impure just because I am a niddah. I might feel *more* pure after immersion in the mikvah, but I didn't feel unclean or impure before it. It's a shade of difference, but it matters.

The law proscribes all physical contact during niddah. This harks back to Temple times when impurity could be transferred by touch. The prohibition of bodily contact can also be explained by the domino theory of sexual passion, a la Victorian novels— for example, he touches her earlobe and inevitably, four pages later, they're down on the grassy green riverbank.

Thus, not only intercourse, but everything short of it is also forbidden. That is why you will never see in an Orthodox home only one bed in the master bedroom: twin beds, or occasionally a queen and a twin, but never only one bed. For at least twelve days of every menstrual cycle, a niddah woman and her husband must sleep in separate beds. In some homes, twin beds are pushed apart for the duration. Not only is sleeping together prohibited, but also kissing, holding hands, touching, and so forth.

There is, however, a range of behavior among Orthodox with regard to all physical contact. Some men will never shake hands with a member of the opposite sex, because of the possibility of it being her time of niddah. But some Orthodox rabbis will shake every woman's hand every Shabbat. Some couples will not hand the car keys directly to one another during niddah, but rather one will put the keys down on a neutral surface and the other will retrieve them; other Orthodox Jews will hold hands and display other gestures of affection. There is, as one might expect, a good deal of personal packaging of this very private mitzvah.

In the evening, at the end of the seventh "white" day, a woman goes off to the mikvah. The mikvah is sometimes housed in the synagogue, but more often it is a discreet, nondescript building apart, a kind of brown-wrapper edifice, much as taharat hamishpachah is kind of a brown-wrapper mitzvah, replete with tones of modesty, taboo, innuendo, privacy, and great secrecy. (One is expected to speak of niddah and mikvah in hushed tones, which, to my mind, does not exactly help to gain adherents.)

At the mikvah, the woman prepares herself, immerses in the mikvah waters, and recites the blessing over this Mitzvah. A couple is expected to resume sex that night, although there is no law that directly says, "Thou shalt . . . ."

For a woman who has just given birth—and is considered to be a niddah—the procedures are quite similar, although the count of days for flow is different. If she has given birth to a boy, she counts a minimum of seven days for flow or staining, plus seven full white days, after which she goes to the mikvah. If she has given birth to a girl, she counts a minimum of fourteen days for the flow, followed by seven whites. There are numerous explanations for the gender differential in the length of impurity state. Some of these explanations are sexist, some apologetic, some irrelevant, some elegiac. Whatever, Orthodox men and women have been trained to wait as the law prescribes. A week earlier, a week later, the new baby is a sufficiently large distraction that no one has mounted a protest at what many outside the community consider to be theoretically discriminatory. Besides, most gynecologists require their patients to wait even longer.

PROCEDURES AT THE MIKVAH

What happens at the mikvah deserves a fuller description. Contrary to uninformed assertions (for example, "I can take a bath at home"), the mikvah is not for bathing or cleansing. One must be perfectly clean before entering the mikvah, which is why there is a regular bathtub in the very same chamber as the mikvah pool, or in a room adjacent to it. The first type of setup is called a "private"; the second type is called "semiprivate"—two or three individual bathing rooms open onto a small vestibule that leads to the mikvah basin room, which the semiprivate clients share in consecutive fashion. In order to ensure maximum privacy for each semiprivate client, all doors are closed immediately after entry or exit. It sometimes feels like we're playing musical doors in going to and from the mikvah room.

The mikvah is not just an ordinary pool of warm water: its waters must be live waters, that is, from a living source, such as rain, river, or ocean. The water must be in its natural state—not drawn in by pumps and plumbing. The ideal (and original) mikvah would be an actual lake or river. Since it would be virtually impossible to gather such large amounts of fresh water every day for indoor mikva'ot (plural), the Rabbis allowed that only a portion need be live waters and the rest may be tap drawn. When the tap-water portion is connected to the live-water source, it is considered, by means of a legal fiction, to be as one living water source. Constructing a kosher mikvah * is quite complex, and certain engineering skills are needed. But one doesn't have to reinvent the wheel. Jewish law being as ancient as it is, there are many ready-made architectural and plumbing designs—some dating as far back as the Talmud—that make it relatively easy to construct a mikvah today. Every American city with a sizable Jewish population has at least one mikvah.

A woman prepares herself for the mikvah in a special way: she removes anything that would constitute a barrier between the water and her body—all jewelry, bandages, dentures, makeup, nail polish, and so forth. She brushes her teeth; she clips her

---

* Kosher can refer not only to food but to what conforms to halachic (legal) requirements.

finger- and toenails and brushes them in order to dislodge any particles of dirt beneath them. (The fingernail injunction has caused some women to complain.) Unlike women of ancient times, when long nails were a sign of unkemptness, modern Orthodox women pride themselves on long, beautiful nails. Many an argument has been waged in the mikvah chamber over the length to which a woman must cut her fingernails. My father-in-law, a great Talmudic scholar, was once summoned to the mikvah in Boro Park, to give a p'sak, a rabbinic decision. The mikvah lady wanted the nails cut and the "client" balked. The only authority they could both agree upon was my father-in-law, who came armed with his legal codes. He calmed the "client" and eased the mikvah lady's mind by showing her in fine Hebrew print that as long as the nails were perfectly clean, their length made no difference. Vanity was a perfectly legitimate reason for post-Talmudic rabbinic authority to interpret ancient law.

After a woman has prepared herself, she steps into a bath that has been drawn for her. She bathes for a few minutes, washes herself, shampoos, and then rinses off thoroughly with a shower. She then combs out her hair free of knots, rinses her mouth with a cup of water, wraps a large white sheet around herself, and presses a buzzer. The buzzer will summon that unique and special functionary in the Jewish community, the mikvah lady.

In larger mikva'ot there are several mikvah ladies, ladies of the lake, I call them. Nice Jewish women all, there is something of a pecking order: the one who supervises the immersion is at the top—the professional. Next come the attendants (assistants) who draw the baths, supply the sheets, towels, soap, and so forth. At the bottom are those who scour the tubs and wash the floors to prepare the room for the next niddah. Even in the most busy mikva'ot, there are never more than five women in attendance, and in many smaller mikva'ot one woman does all three jobs, with just an occasional bit of assistance. We, the community, take these trusty soldiers for granted. (I wonder what it must be like to inspect thirty bodies a night for loose hairs and trimmed toenails, or to wash thirty bathtubs a night.) They serve the community quietly, modestly, seriously, and with dignity; understandably, mikvah jokes are distasteful to them.

If the mikvah is not crowded on a given evening, the mikvah lady will come to the room immediately after the buzzer sounds. If it is crowded, one might have to wait five or ten minutes, but generally no longer than that, except for that one evening every few years when the mikvah looks as though it's giving away something free.

I have observed that the most crowded time seems to be when Shabbat precedes or follows two days of Shavuot. This is particularly true in a mikvah that serves several adjacent communities and is thus not within walking distance of many of its clients. For example, all the women whose cycle would have ended on Wednesday, Thursday, and Friday night, as well as those whose "regular" night that month happened to be Saturday night, would all come together. Four nights of niddah enders crowded into one—and on a night, no less, when Shabbat ends late and the mikvah hours are foreshortened. The mikvah opens for business as soon as three stars are out. In winter, this means five o'clock; in June, the month of Shavuot, it means nine P.M.

One such night, after waiting fifteen minutes from buzzer time and still no lady of the lake had appeared on the scene, I went out in my damp white sarong to take back a *Vogue* from the waiting-room coffee table. But everyone else had the same idea. Even *Popular Mechanics* was gone. So I slipped back to my room and waited another ten minutes. I knew full well it was no one's fault, but I was very impatient nevertheless. I must have tucked this night away in my brain somewhere. When a similar situation occurred a few years later, I was prepared. The mikvah was very crowded, but my husband and I also wanted to catch the ten o'clock movie. As soon as the attendant who had led me into my room and had drawn my bath closed the door behind her, I buzzed. My room number went right up on the board, and just as I finished my shower came a knock on my door for immersion. My husband was more dazzled that night by my speed than by my purity.

The immersion: Standing near the mikvah basin, a woman will remove her white sheet and the mikvah lady will check to see if she has any loose hairs on her body and if she's clipped her nails, simultaneously asking, "Brushed your teeth? Rinsed your mouth?" This inspection takes fifteen seconds. The woman then walks down four or five steps into the mikvah pool, which is approximately five feet square and filled with water four feet high. Standing with legs spread slightly apart, her hands loose and not touching the sides, she immerses herself completely underwater. Only the soles of her feet touch the mikvah basin. Immediately she rises. If every bit of her body and every strand of hair was below the waterline, the mikvah lady, who has been looking on all along, will pronounce the immersion (or maybe the woman herself) "kosher."

Standing shoulder height in the water, the woman recites the blessing on immersion:

בָּרוּךְ אַתָּה יְיָ, אֱלֹהֵינוּ מֶלֶךְ הָעוֹלָם אֲשֶׁר קִדְּשָׁנוּ בְּמִצְוֹתָיו, וְצִוָּנוּ עַל הַטְבִילָה.

Baruch ata Adonai Elohainu melech ha'olam asher kidshanu b'mitzvotav v'tzivanu al hatvilah.

Blessed are You, Lord our God, Ruler of the universe, Who has sanctified us with His commandments and commanded us concerning the immersion.

Often a woman will follow this blessing with an additional brief prayer, the Yehi Ratzon (see p. 60). It is a prayer for restoration of the Temple, which really means a prayer for messianic times. Some women place a small headcovering (usually a white terry-cloth square) over their heads as they say the blessing. The mikvah lady hands it down to them after immersion. It has often seemed to me a little incongruous, to put it mildly, to cover the head when reciting the blessing, while all the rest of us is standing stark-naked in the shoulder-high water. But that is how many have been taught and continue to do it. God has seen, so to speak, stranger things than that.

After the blessing she dips completely underwater two more times. The mikvah lady again pronounces it "kosher." As the woman comes up the steps, the mikvah lady holds out the sheet for her and slips it over her shoulders. The mikvah lady then leaves or, if it's a semiprivate, she returns the woman to her bathing/dressing room, closes all the doors, and goes on to the next buzzer call.

The woman will dress, fix her hair, sit under the dryer, put on her makeup, and so forth. There are some high-class mikva'ot that have a free-lance hairdresser and manicurist in regular attendance.

There is a fee for using the mikvah. It ranges anywhere from four to fifteen dollars plus a tip, although some communities don't permit tips. The fee depends on whether private or semi-private facilities were used, and on the location of the mikvah. Newer mikvah, fancier neighborhood—more expensive. But the fee is not a rip-off. Even the fifteen-dollar mikva'ot are heavily subsidized by the community. And no one was ever barred from using a mikvah because of inability to pay.

When a woman leaves the mikvah, her husband might be waiting outside for her, parked discreetly away from the entrance; or she will get into her own car or into a cab whose company regularly services the mikvah. Some mikva'ot are in changing neighborhoods and their communities have hired guards at the front door which is, at any event, kept locked at all times. Somehow, a mikvah full of bathing women seems like a vulnerable place, so precautions are taken.

That procedure, in sum, is what a traditional Jewish woman does every month of her married life, except for when she is pregnant or reaches menopause. Why does she go? How does she feel about it?

TAHARAT HAMISHPACHAH AND ITS HUMAN DIMENSIONS

To the first question, that same old answer applies. It is a mitzvah, a Biblical one at that. God has commanded us to make ourselves a holy people, and this is one of the divine definitions of kedusha, holiness. We accept the commandment to observe Taharat Hamishpachah as we accept the whole yoke of mitzvot, and that, for the most part, is that. We do it, but that doesn't mean we have to love it every single month. It is all part of the discipline of being an Orthodox Jewish woman.

Or man, for that matter. For a woman could not undertake responsibility for niddah unilaterally. Without mutual consent and responsibility, the whole thing would be reduced to a test of wills each month, a contest in which all who win would eventually lose. A man, therefore, must not only agree, but must be willing to assume personal restraint.

Even with mutual consent and responsibility, even with full devotion and fidelity to Jewish law, taharat hamispachah turns out to be a wicked regimen, one that occasionally requires almost Herculean efforts, especially in this era of commercial sex overkill. Contemporary men and women are continually bombarded with sex fantasy material. Add to that the modern philosophy that everything-one-wants-one-may-have, and you have a formidable opponent to the laws of taharat hamishpachah. All of this is compounded by the fact that we are asked to resist suggestion and seduction in what would ordinarily seem to be a most legitimate arena—relations between husband and wife. Observing niddah is much harder than keeping Shabbat or kashrut; it is infinitely more difficult than fasting on Tisha B'Av, or asking forgiveness from enemies on Yom Kippur. There is hardly anything about being an Orthodox Jewish woman that has driven me to tears over the last two decades, but cleaning for Pesach is one and taharat hamishpachah, the other.

When I was fifteen, I overheard some women talking about a "tragedy." What had happened? A bride, whom they all knew, had badly fractured her leg water skiing while on her honeymoon. She would have to be in a cast for two or three months. A dense and shy fifteen-year-old, I could not figure out what the tragedy was, and I certainly wouldn't ask. But I was very puzzled. I had envisioned a romantic scene, an ethereal bride, now somewhat helpless. Her husband would kiss her cast every morning, noon, and evening, attend to her every need, his heart overflowing with love and compassion. What could be more tender, more beautiful? Why were these women clucking their tongues in sorrow, almost grief? It was only when I studied the laws of mikvah some two years later that I realized the bride and her new husband could have no sex until the cast came off. No mikvah, no sex. One fifth of their first year of marriage. A tragedy.

And yet, somehow we all manage. Niddah doesn't paralyze us, nor kill off our normal instincts for joy and pleasure. We take it in our stride, work around it, adjust ourselves to its demands, and then some. A tragedy? A hardship maybe, but not a tragedy. Certainly something a loving marriage could withstand, and perhaps be strengthened by.

Having mentioned all the difficulties, let me tell the other half: how these laws elevate us to a certain level of holiness in our most private lives, and how an ancient law addresses the modern condition. There are certain laws of the Torah, divine in origin though they are, that have undergone reinterpretation, toward stringency, toward leniency, toward atrophy. For a ritual as primitive and as difficult as the sex and blood taboo to be maintained, it must somehow hold inner meaning. And I believe it does. On many levels.

Despite my occasional grumblings, and my more frequent take-it-in-my-stride attitude, this mitzvah brings out a whole set of positive emotions in me. One, which I'm sure is not what tradition had in mind, is a sense of personal accomplishment. We've made it, we've succeeded in meeting the test, I'm quite proud of us. It's not a superiority I feel over others: it is a symbol to me that the human mind and soul—in fact, my mind and soul, his mind and soul—have some mastery over our human drives. Does that qualify for holiness? I have no idea.

A second impact on self is one of connections. At the mikvah I have an awareness, mostly unarticulated but ever present—of the millennia of Jewish women who observed these laws before me, women in every generation, and in every continent across the face of this earth, women to whom I feel inextricably linked because of our regular, private, determined mikvah-going habits. When the earliest press releases on the Masada discoveries appeared, it didn't surprise me in the least that the Masada mikvah was featured so prominently. The PR people, as well as the exploration team, knew what would engage the emotions of the Jewish reader. As I soak away in my private tub at the mikvah, I have that free-floating feeling that this is what Jewish women have done throughout the ages, and even the slick magazine I might be reading doesn't separate me from them. This is the essence of myself as a Jewish woman.

But it goes much beyond a woman's own experience as a Jew. I believe the laws address a human need; in fact, taharat hamishpachah serves a whole range of functions, each appropriate to the ebb and flow of an interpersonal relationship as it unfolds through time. Which is why I have suggested elsewhere—to the consternation of some in the Orthodox community—that Jewish couples living together as if in marriage, in a serious, sustained relationship, could also learn much from the laws of niddah and mikvah.

I should mention here first that taharat hamishpachah is useful when it comes to choosing a mate. How? It is a most reliable item on the compatibility scale. Of course there are no guarantees these days but, generally, mutual acceptance of these laws implies a like-minded commitment, a set of shared assumptions and a shared community, all of which correlate well with marital success.

What sorts of lessons do we take from this mitzvah? What impact does it have on love and sex?

Taharat hamishpachah implies that sex is a special part of marriage, but only a part. Early on, one learns that sex is not all there is to love, that not every newlywed spat can be settled in bed, that for almost half a month niddah requires of us to develop other, more difficult, more sophisticated modes of communication. A couple in love who observe niddah is forced to discover new techniques to express peaks of emotion; such a couple more readily understands the power of a glance, a word, a thoughtful gesture.

Moreover, because of the overall regulatory function of this law, a larger message about control quietly slips through—that sex is not something by which we reward or punish, control or manipulate the sexual partner. If sex is regulated by a force greater than the human parties involved, then it is less likely to be wielded, by men or women, as a human lever of power. Instead, it becomes a gift to enjoy and to give pleasure with, not to use.

Similarly, niddah generates a different sense of self for a woman in relation to her husband, a feeling of self-autonomy, of being her own person, of having a kind of control that is free of the need to manipulate and to control others. Some women can generate these feelings out of their own ego strength, and thanks to feminism, that is probably the case more now than ever before; but for those to whom autonomy is not innate or instinctive, niddah is a valuable aid.

Linked to this, but from a different angle, there is less likelihood of a woman being treated as a sex object—and that can happen in marriage, too. While this protection for a woman seems to be less necessary as society moves toward greater cognitive equality of men and women, nevertheless taharat hamishpachah generates a different male perception of women's sexuality, just as it does a woman about her own self.

But the laws have a positive sexual function as well, not only preventing abuse but promoting pleasure. How? By retaining a certain freshness to the sexual relationship and by synchronizing the needs and desires of the two partners, to the extent it is possible to do so.

In the Talmudic tractate on niddah, Rabbi Meir (second century) offers a romantic explanation: "so that a woman be as beloved to her husband throughout the marriage as she is to him as a new bride." Conversely, he states, without observance of niddah, "a man may become overly familiar with his wife and be repelled by her" (NIDDAH 31B). If we apply these comments to women as well as to men, they bespeak a real truth about sexual relationships: the well-documented, statistically verified, thoroughly analyzed, and loudly decried fact that interest in sex tends to fall sharply during the middle years of marriage. There are great periods of intense sex and periods of almost none.

While no one has documented this, I suspect there is more sustained and loving sex over the course of marriage among couples who observe these laws—and know they have to act before the boom is lowered again—than among couples who do not.

And on a different level, there has surely got to be a better meshing of male and female desire, within any given month, among couples who observe niddah, if only because of the shorter period of availability. Logically, there would seem to be less likelihood of rejection by one partner of another during a contracted period of sexual availability than in an open-ended one. In other words, by regulating the off times, it helps to synchronize the on times. In fact, the period of niddah, used properly, can heighten sexual anticipation—somewhat akin to an extended period of chaste foreplay. Not only is delayed gratification a healthy training for marriage in general, but also it heightens and sustains the sexual pleasure. Wanting is sometimes as pleasurable as having.

Finally, the laws of taharat hamishpachah have their referent on a much larger canvas of life, of marriage, of death and rebirth.

There are all kinds of rhythms in Jewish life—of nature, time, celebration, and history. Taharat hamishpachah also suggests a rhythm to life and to human sexuality. Not only is there a time for caution and a time for restraint, but there is also a time to bear children, and a time those options will be foreclosed. For a people whose very first commandment was to be fruitful and multiply, the fact that the end of niddah brings a woman into the peak of her fertility cycle is no mere coincidence. While I don't think it was intended that each month's egg be fertilized, certainly tradition intended that some of them be fertilized. More than for the purpose of swelling population ranks, which has always been a concern for the Jewish people, it was understood that the proper way for a family to constitute itself, to be healthy, to be maintained, and to have integrity is through the birth and nurture and love of children. Industrial societies have moved men away from primary family orientations. Feminism, to some extent, has moved women in the same direction as well. While I am appreciative of industrial society and am abundantly and irreversibly indebted to feminism, I cannot help but feel that the emphasis away from childbearing has gone too far. Taharat hamishpachah, then, tempers some of the new urgencies with its implied theme of the rhythm of life and the eternal values placed on childraising. The laws say, in effect: Have some perspective on life, on the totality of your life. Perhaps this is the right month to create new life. Perhaps next month . . .

Possibly the most important message of all that emerges from the laws of taharat hamishpachah is the way this very private mitzvah relates to contemporary assumptions about love and marriage. There is a profound idea embedded in the concept and structure of these laws, a kind of nuts-and-bolts attitude about human relationships that needs to be more widely expressed. It may sound unromantic, but it is surely more reality-oriented and more relevant than ever before.

It is clear to everyone that we live in a divorce culture today, a culture because it reinforces itself. Divorce is commonplace; serial marriages are no longer the exception; and oftentimes the honeymoon and the marriage finish at one and the same moment. One can walk away. It is much easier than working at the marriage; and, besides, there are really no sanctions against divorce in contemporary society.

What taharat hamishpachah is all about is exactly the opposite. It is about commitment, commitment to something beyond oneself and one's immediate needs, commitment to another person and to not taking that person for granted. And these laws are also about the realities of interpersonal relationships and the vagaries of love. Love, even the best of loves and the best of marriages, has its highs and lows. Marriage, the institution, allows for a certain maneuverability; one can feel emotionally distant for a time and then return to the center of feeling again without permanent damage. But marriage also requires that we continually work at it, and make a commitment to its longevity so that it doesn't collapse at the first sign of pain or anger or hurt. Sometimes it is only the commitment—call it will—that carries us through those rough times.

To the extent that ritual informs the human psyche, the laws of taharat hamishpachah speak to us about the power of willing something—not only to resist but to overcome and to persist, qualities without which no marriage could survive.

For everything I have said about mikvah and niddah, others might say the opposite, that it is an artificial barrier between two people who have a healthy sex drive; that it places undue strain on the relationship; that it engenders negative attitudes toward sex; that it puts down women; that it is an inflexible lock-step system not relevant and not geared to individual human needs; that it was designed to keep women breeding; that it stigmatizes menstruation. And I know there are problems even among those who observe and benefit from taharat hamishpachah—for example, the old, familiar, pick-a-fight-on-mikvah-night syndrome; or that one can abuse and manipulate the partner while being perfectly faithful to the laws; or worse, that one can actually use the stringency of taharat hamishpachah to his/her own ends; for example, a woman who refuses to go to the mikvah on time when it matters to her husband.

But for an observant Jew, the law is given. Rather than reject it, rather than merely adjust to it, we try to apply it to our lives in a manner that sharpens our identity, refines our marriages, and strengthens our community. For Orthodox Jews, then, niddah and mikvah are not outdated and mystical rituals. Instead, they are symbols and rites that connect us to holiness. Somehow, the laws were intended to make us more human in the way we construct our relationships and in the way we satisfy our basic sex drives, just as other laws are an attempt to make us more special in the way we eat, and the way we work and rest. Taharat hamishpachah is an integral part of the whole scheme of things: it is part of the larger picture of being an Orthodox Jew. There are no guarantees that any of it will work, but I think there is a good chance it might.

CHAPTER 4

DAILY PRAYER AND BLESSINGS

Prayer serves many functions, in fact, every function and its opposite:

It is a safety hatch when one is overcome by fear or dread, anger or need.

It calls forth a generosity of the human spirit. Prayer reminds us not to take totally for granted that which we all must presume as we go about our business—the gifts of life, health, love, and good fortune. If we constantly worried about these essentials, we would be paralyzed in our actions. If we took them for granted all the time, we would be ingrates, and most unprepared for the vagaries of life.

Prayer sometimes enables us to reach into our own souls, to see what it's like in there. The truth is that we can get by very well for long periods of time without this contact with our inner selves, but at some point it catches up.

Prayer is a sensation of community; but it is also a feeling of intense loneliness, and aloneness with God.

Prayer sometimes offers a few quiet moments to daydream, to wander without intrusions, to solve problems simply by reflecting on them. Rote can be pleasingly effortless, and it is the perfect cover for the mind or imagination to escape. Even in shul, where I revel in the crowd all around me, there are many moments where I savor my utter privacy. No one would dare interrupt me while I am looking into my siddur (prayer book).

Prayer adds routine and organization to life; it is also orientation away from everyday life, a momentary stepping out of time and of motion.

Prayer helps to put things into proper perspective and enables us to order our priorities in life.

Prayer is at times brazenness before God, at times humility.

Finally, prayer helps you maintain a belief in God when your faith undergoes its inevitable lapses. . . .

With all that, most people do not pray. Not because they wouldn't want or need these benefits of prayer, but because prayer does not come naturally to the human spirit. And it doesn't really make much of a difference whether one is male, female, affluent, poor, educated, unschooled, Westernized, premodern, or of any other characteristics we tend to scale positively or negatively to prayer. The larger truth is simply this: human beings must be taught to pray, just as they have to be taught a variety of other skills of feeling and communication. To be sure, spontaneity is to be admired and desired. But upon closer examination, the arguments for spontaneity are better in theory than in practice: most people do not pray.

One of the distinctive characteristics of Orthodox Jews is the regularity with which they pray each day. A Jew wakes up to prayer, and goes to sleep with prayer. The first two prayers a young child is taught are the Modeh Ani, which is recited immediately upon rising, and the Shema Yisrael, which is recited at bedtime. As he/she grows, a whole array of prayers fills the space between these two.

How did it come to be this way? The Jewish people were told: "And you shall love your God with all your heart" ((DEUT. 6:5). Also, "You shall serve the Lord your God with all your heart" (DEUT. 11:13). What is service of the heart? Prayer, say the Sages of the Talmud. Understanding that prayer doesn't come naturally, the Rabbis, over the course of two millennia, organized much of the prayer we have today—formal, fixed prayer, to be said at appropriate times throughout the day, or upon experiencing certain experiences of life, growth, or nature. Thus, Jewish prayer is daily prayer, three times a day minimum, recited at fixed times; also blessings for all occasions, shared community experiences, an awareness continually inserting itself into our everyday lives without waiting for our initiative. That is Jewish prayer.

Does it sound like service of the heart, this regimented routine? Not exactly. But having seen how it operates, I would say it beats all other ways of getting there.

Formal fixed-time prayer functions as a kind of checking-in operation—checking in with God, checking in with one's immediate community on a regular basis; in fact, checking in with the Jewish people in a way that goes far beyond the boundaries of time and space. Perhaps the real call to the synagogue for most Jews is the people Israel. There is something immensely satisfying in knowing that the words we recite are the very words recited at this moment by the Jews of Istanbul, or the Jews of Toledo a thousand years ago, of Rome two thousand years ago, of ancient Palestine three thousand years ago. And that is also why Hebrew will forever be the language of Jewish prayer, even though Jews will continue to take on the tongues of their adopted countries. The Rabbis understood that prayer makes for a powerful symbiotic relationship with community. The Talmud tells us that when one prays in the privacy of his or her own home, as many Jews do, he or she should time daily prayer to the set times of the minyan, the community prayer.

With routinely scheduled prayer, there is no need to get every last thought in each time, every iota of sincerity, depth of feeling, every pressing issue, every expansive expression of love and praise. You'll be back later in the day, or tomorrow morning, or tomorrow afternoon. There's always another opportunity to collect your innermost thoughts and set them before God.

Formal, fixed-time prayer helps us to organize our lives. It never ceases to amaze me that there are Jews who are otherwise tardy, absentminded, bordering on dysfunctional, yet who always manage to meet their obligations regarding morning, afternoon, and evening prayer.

Preformulated prayer is a boon to those unable to articulate or even be in touch with their own feelings. Actually, the language of Jewish prayer is simple, the syntax uncomplicated, the content well attuned to the existential needs of most ordinary mortals. Jewish prayer is lofty, but it is also earthy; and it doesn't require great mental gymnastics to be understood. The Rabbis went one step further. For those who were unable to read the prayers but felt the need or obligation to pray, the Rabbis instituted the shaliach tzibbur, one who would keep the prayers moving apace and who would repeat aloud the Amidah prayer for those incapable of reciting it silently on their own. The worshipers could be uplifted by reciting Amen to the vocalization of shaliach tzibbur.

Finally, regular, formal, fixed-time prayer serves the opposite function as well. Its routine can be understood as a vehicle, an outer shell, that can be filled randomly with the emotions of real prayer. When the heart is ready to open, it will not first have to invent the route—or the routine.

Its parallel lies in the tale of the clockmaker who lives in a Swiss village that is suddenly cut off from outside delivery of clock parts. Little by little, many fine old clocks of the town stop functioning. One clockmaker takes great pains with his most valuable clock, despite the ridicule of his friends who tell him he is wasting his time. Though it doesn't function, he oils it regularly, keeps it free of rust, and polishes it handsomely. When the missing parts are finally received, his clock alone is able to work.

Perhaps a better analogy is to the college student whose parents tell him to call home once a week. He might not have much to tell them, but he calls anyhow. When something does come up, it will be easier to spill it out.

The Rabbis tell us that it is within the formal structures of prayer that individualized prayers can and should be added. Ideally, every prayer should be a genuine encounter. The heart should overflow with strong feelings three times a day. Real prayer should have kavannah—devotional intent, being attuned to God, the whole self given over to God; "all of my bones" shall praise God, says the Psalmist (35:10). For all but a few, however, it just doesn't happen that way. But formal, fixed prayer increases the chances that it will happen occasionally.

In that respect, the Rabbis understood human nature much better than the prophets. I could never fully comprehend the verse in Isaiah where he speaks God's criticism of His children—

"they pray the fixed prayers but not with their whole hearts." Isaiah was human, too. What did he expect? But I suppose that is the nature of the prophetic voice—idealism untarnished by reality, a pure goal to strive for despite the difficulties.

And yet, Isaiah was right. One shouldn't be satisfied with routine. Indeed, there are many things one can do to increase the possibility of achieving heartfelt prayer:

1. Meditate a few moments before beginning prayer. Even sixty seconds can set the mind properly.

2. Try to conceive of the ultimate source of your prayers. In many synagogues, over the ark is engraved this phrase: "Know before Whom you stand." Jews of every age have known that they must make an effort to consider God as they pray, and to direct their prayers accordingly.

3. Understanding this, one should dress properly for prayer, even at home. That is why we first wash and dress, and then pray. One of the laws of tefillin (phylacteries) is that they may be worn only if the body is clean. I often remember Mr. Y., an elderly gentleman who was bedridden for years. Every morning he insisted on being dressed for Shacharit, after which he would take off his shirt and put his pajama jacket back on. You don't go to an audience with God in your pajamas or underwear.

Nor do we lounge about. When Goody was young, I periodically had to remind her not to daaven barefoot, not to put her feet up on the coffee table, not to flop down on the couch. I recall one morning when she was about ten and we were daavening at home on Shabbat during our summer vacation. She was stretched out on the sofa, siddur propped up on her chest. I told her to sit up nicely. She looked me straight in the eye and said, "I side with Shammai." In school the previous year, she had learned of the famous dispute between the two great sages Hillel and Shammai, concerning interpretation of the verse, "And you shall speak [of these words] when you lie down and when you rise up" (DEUT. 6:7). Hillel interpreted this to mean the Shema should be recited at bedtime in any posture, while Shammai interpreted the verse literally, that the Shema should be recited in the lying-down position. But, I told Goody as I laughed at her words, Shammai referred only to the Shema of bedtime, not 9:00 A.M. Shacharit. Over the years, she has come to under-

stand that prayer is to God, and that she must assume a respectful stance.

4. Periodically, once a year perhaps, read a book about Jewish
prayer. While most of them are academic in nature, they often
have a powerful effect on the spirit.

5. Pray with a minyan whenever possible. Oftentimes, the familiar melodies, the communal singing, the hum of the collective, carry the spirit far beyond the reach of the words alone.
Prayer is a mood and a feeling as much as it is a verse or an
idea.

6. Finally, if it is possible, study and pray with a master. There
is nothing quite like being in the presence of one whose heart
truly opens in prayer. You can easily distinguish between the
authentic petitioner and the perfunctory one. Somehow, you'll
just know.

ORGANIZATION

Daily prayer is structured along two lines:

1. Event-related prayer. These are prayers and blessings that
are recited in response to a particular act or experience, as it
occurs. For example, before or after eating, upon wearing a new
article of clothing, upon hearing news of someone's death; also,
the benedictions we recite just before performing a mitzvah,
such as blowing the shofar, lighting candles, performing a circumcision, reading the Purim Megilláh.

2. Fixed-time prayer of Shacharit (morning), Minchah (afternoon), and Maariv (evening). These are specific prayers, to be
recited in specific time slots. Once the time has passed, that
particular prayer can no longer be recited. While popular belief
has it that these three fixed-time prayers are substitutes for the
Temple sacrifices of Shacharit and Minchah, which could no
longer be offered after the Temple was destroyed in 70 C.E.,
history and archaeology teach us that the basic parts of these
prayers were instituted long before that. There are sources in
tradition which claim that Shacharit is derived from Abraham,
Minchah from Isaac, and Maariv from Jacob.

3. The content of prayer can be organized into distinct categories as well. The most common types are:

Tehillot—praises of God.
Tefillot—devotionals, reflections on human character and the role of the human being in this world.
Todot—prayers of gratitude.
Bakashot—requests, desires, personal and national needs.
B'rachot—benedictions, which alternately bless God and/or which state an intention to fulfill a mitzvah.

B'RACHOT—BLESSINGS

B'rachot come in three types:

Birchot nehenin—blessings for experiences of enjoyment.
Birchot ha'mitzvot—blessing for the privilege of performing a mitzvah.
Birchot hoda'ah—blessing of petition, praise, or thanksgiving. These latter blessings form a good part of the fixed-time liturgy, discussed below.

BIRCHOT NEHENIN

These particular blessings are among the most beautiful features of Judaism. What they imply is that we take absolutely nothing for granted. Appropriately recited, the birchot nehenin signify a never-ending awe and appreciation of nature, creation, health, life, creature comforts, and the incredible variety of distinct forms that make up life on earth. Inasmuch as these b'rachot are a direct response to the particular act or experience at hand, they serve to counterbalance whatever routine might creep into our formal, fixed-time prayers.

Each b'racha begins with these words:

בָּרוּךְ אַתָּה יְיָ, אֱלֹהֵינוּ מֶלֶךְ הָעוֹלָם,

Baruch ata Adonai Elohainu melech ha'olam . . .

Blessed are You, Lord our God, Ruler of the universe . . .

And concludes with its appropriate ending:

Food

For wine:

בּוֹרֵא פְּרִי הַגָּפֶן.

. . . *borai pri hagafen.*

. . . Who creates the fruit of the vine.

For bread:

הַמּוֹצִיא לֶחֶם מִן הָאָרֶץ.

. . . *hamotzi lechem min ha'aretz.*

. . . Who brings forth bread from the earth.

For fruit:

בּוֹרֵא פְּרִי הָעֵץ.

. . . *borai pre ha'eitz.*

. . . Who creates the fruit of the tree.

For vegetables:

בּוֹרֵא פְּרִי הָאֲדָמָה.

. . . *borai pre ha'adama.*

. . . Who brings forth fruit from the earth.

For cakes, cookies, crackers:

בּוֹרֵא מִינֵי מְזוֹנוֹת.

. . . *borai mineh m'zonot.*

. . . Who creates different varieties of sustenance.

For meat, fish, cheese, processed foods, and all liquids except wine. (This blessing is known as the sheh'hakol):

שֶׁהַכֹּל נִהְיֶה בִּדְבָרוֹ.

. . . *sheh'hakol ni'heyeh bidvaro.*

. . . through Whose word all things were called into being.

If an entire meal is to be eaten, the blessing over the bread suffices for all other foods at the meal. If no bread is eaten, the appropriate blessing is recited for the particular food.

The table is considered an altar. Thus, we not only show appreciation before we eat, but also, as the Torah instructs us (DEUT. 8:10), after we have eaten.

Bread, the staff of life, symbolizes a meal. Thus, the full version of Grace After Meals, the Birkat Hamazon is recited whenever bread has been eaten.

The first paragraph of the Birkat Hamazon is:

בָּרוּךְ אַתָּה יְיָ, אֱלֹהֵינוּ מֶלֶךְ הָעוֹלָם, הַזָּן אֶת־הָעוֹלָם כֻּלּוֹ בְּטוּבוֹ, בְּחֵן, בְּחֶסֶד וּבְרַחֲמִים. הוּא נוֹתֵן לֶחֶם לְכָל־ בָּשָׂר, כִּי לְעוֹלָם חַסְדּוֹ. וּבְטוּבוֹ הַגָּדוֹל, תָּמִיד לֹא חָסַר לָנוּ וְאַל יֶחְסַר לָנוּ מָזוֹן לְעוֹלָם וָעֶד. בַּעֲבוּר שְׁמוֹ הַגָּדוֹל, כִּי הוּא אֵל זָן וּמְפַרְנֵס לַכֹּל וּמֵיטִיב לַכֹּל וּמֵכִין מָזוֹן לְכָל בְּרִיּוֹתָיו אֲשֶׁר בָּרָא. בָּרוּךְ אַתָּה יְיָ, הַזָּן אֶת־ הַכֹּל.

Baruch ata Adonai Elohainu melech ha'olam hazan et haolam kulo b'tuvo b'cheyn, b'chesed u'vrachamim. Hu notain lechem l'chol basar kee leolam chasdo. Uvtuvo hagadol, tamid lo chasar lanu v'al yechsar lanu mazon leolam va'ed. Bavur shemo hagadol, kee hu el zan u'mfarness lacol umetiv lakol umechin mazon lechol bre'otav asher barah. Baruch ata Adonai hazan et hakol.

Blessed are You, Lord our God, Ruler of the universe, Who feeds the entire world with goodness, with grace, with kindness, and with mercy. You give food to all flesh, for Your kindness lasts forever. Because of Your great goodness, we have never lacked food; may it never fail us, for the sake of Your great name. For You are God Who nourishes and supports and does good for all. You provide food for all the creatures You have created. Blessed are You, O Lord, Who sustains everyone.

The full Birkat Hamazon includes additional themes, such as prayers for our general well-being, for the nation and the land, for Jerusalem restored, for the coming of the Messiah. The whole thing takes approximately three to five minutes to recite, depending on how much of it is sung aloud. It is the proper Jewish way to conclude a meal.

Most Orthodox Jews know the entire Grace by heart; nevertheless they recite it from a small Grace booklet, which is endearingly called the "bentscher" (from the Yiddish word *bentschen*, "to bless"). Bentschers are available in all sizes and forms, including a single laminated card that stays clean and can be stored neatly at the table. One of my inventions, developed partly in response to grumblings of "It's her turn to go get the bentschers," was to staple a wide piece of elastic, approximately six inches long, to the underside of the breakfast-room table at each person's place. To a weekday guest, who hasn't seen it before, our family looks like a bunch of poker players, as each person pulls out his/her laminated card from under the table just as we are ready to begin the bentschen (or benching, as we have Americanized the Yiddish).

If bread has not been eaten—and thus a meal has not formally been constituted—then specific blessings are recited, depending on the particular foods we have eaten. For example, after eating vegetables or certain fruits or any food over which the sheh'hakol blessing (see p. 145) was recited, we would say the following:

בָּרוּךְ אַתָּה יְיָ, אֱלֹהֵינוּ מֶלֶךְ הָעוֹלָם, בּוֹרֵא נְפָשׁוֹת רַבּוֹת
וְחֶסְרוֹנָן, עַל כָּל מַה שֶּׁבָּרָא לְהַחֲיוֹת בָּהֶם נֶפֶשׁ כָּל חָי.
בָּרוּךְ חֵי הָעוֹלָמִים.

Baruch ata Adonai Elohainu melech ha'olam borai ne'fashot rabot v'chesronan al kol mah sheh'barah le'ha'chayot bahem nefesh kol chai. Baruch chay ha'olamim.

Blessed are You, Lord our God, Ruler of the universe, creator of all life and its needs; for all the things He has created to sustain every living being. Blessed are You Who are the life of the universe.

After drinking wine, or eating any of the five "fruits" of the land of Israel (grapes, figs, pomegranates, olives, and dates) or any food other than bread that has been prepared from barley, rye, oats, wheat, or spelt, we recite the following blessing, known as the Ahl Ha'michya:

After cake or Holy Land fruits
(grapes, figs, pomegranates, olives and dates)

בָּרוּךְ אַתָּה יְיָ אֱלֹהֵינוּ מֶלֶךְ הָעוֹלָם,

Cake and wine	Cake	Fruit	Wine
עַל הַמִּחְיָה וְעַל	עַל הַמִּחְיָה	עַל הָעֵץ	עַל הַגֶּפֶן
הַכַּלְכָּלָה וְעַל הַגֶּפֶן	וְעַל	וְעַל פְּרִי	וְעַל פְּרִי
וְעַל פְּרִי הַגֶּפֶן,	הַכַּלְכָּלָה,	הָעֵץ,	הַגֶּפֶן,

וְעַל תְּנוּבַת הַשָּׂדֶה, וְעַל אֶרֶץ חֶמְדָּה טוֹבָה וּרְחָבָה שֶׁרָצִיתָ וְהִנְחַלְתָּ לַאֲבוֹתֵינוּ לֶאֱכֹל מִפִּרְיָה וְלִשְׂבֹּעַ מִטּוּבָהּ. רַחֶם־נָא, יְיָ אֱלֹהֵינוּ, עַל יִשְׂרָאֵל עַמֶּךָ, וְעַל יְרוּשָׁלַיִם עִירֶךָ, וְעַל צִיּוֹן מִשְׁכַּן כְּבוֹדֶךָ, וְעַל מִזְבְּחֶךָ וְעַל הֵיכָלֶךָ. וּבְנֵה יְרוּשָׁלַיִם עִיר הַקֹּדֶשׁ בִּמְהֵרָה בְיָמֵינוּ, וְהַעֲלֵנוּ לְתוֹכָהּ וְשַׂמְּחֵנוּ בְּבִנְיָנָהּ, וְנֹאכַל מִפִּרְיָהּ וְנִשְׂבַּע מִטּוּבָהּ, וּנְבָרֶכְךָ עָלֶיהָ בִּקְדֻשָּׁה וּבְטָהֳרָה.

On Sabbath:

רְצֵה וְהַחֲלִיצֵנוּ בְּיוֹם הַשַּׁבָּת הַזֶּה.

On Rosh Chodesh:

זָכְרֵנוּ לְטוֹבָה בְּיוֹם רֹאשׁ הַחֹדֶשׁ הַזֶּה.

On Rosh Hashanah:

זָכְרֵנוּ לְטוֹבָה בְּיוֹם הַזִּכָּרוֹן הַזֶּה.

On festivals:

שִׂמְּחֵנוּ בְּיוֹם חַג

Shemini Atzeret	Sukkot	Shavuot	Pesach
הַשְּׁמִינִי חַג הָעֲצֶרֶת	הַסֻּכּוֹת	הַשָּׁבֻעוֹת	הַמַּצוֹת

הַזֶּה. כִּי אַתָּה יְהוָֹה טוֹב וּמֵטִיב לַכֹּל, וְנוֹדֶה לְךָ עַל הָאָרֶץ

Cake and wine	Cake	Fruit	Wine
וְעַל הַמִּחְיָה וְעַל	וְעַל הַמִּחְיָה.	וְעַל הַפֵּרוֹת.	עַל פְּרִי הַגָּפֶן.
פְּרִי הַגָּפֶן. בָּרוּךְ	בָּרוּךְ אַתָּה	בָּרוּךְ אַתָּה	בָּרוּךְ אַתָּה
אַתָּה יְיָ עַל הָאָרֶץ	יְיָ, עַל	יְיָ, עַל	יְיָ עַל
וְעַל הַמִּחְיָה וְעַל	הָאָרֶץ וְעַל	הָאָרֶץ וְעַל	הָאָרֶץ וְעַל
פְּרִי הַגָּפֶן.	הַמִּחְיָה.	הַפֵּרוֹת.	פְּרִי הַגָּפֶן.

Blessed are You, Lord our God, Ruler of the universe . . .

(on wine)

. . . for the vine and the fruit of the vine,

(on fruit)

. . . for the trees and the fruit of the trees,

(on cake)
. . . for life-giving and sustaining food,
(on cake and wine)
. . . for life-giving and sustaining food and for the vine and the fruit of the vine,

and for the produce of the field and for the precious gold and spacious land that You desired to grant as a heritage to our forefathers, to eat from its fruit and be filled from its goodness.

Have mercy on us, Lord our God, on Israel Your people, Jerusalem Your city, Zion where Your glory rests, and on Your altar and Your Temple. And rebuild Jerusalem the holy city, speedily and in our day. Lead us up to her and let us rejoice in her building. And we shall eat of her fruit and be filled with her goodness. And we shall bless You for her in holiness and purity.

On Sabbath:	Strengthen us on this Sabbath day.
On Rosh Chodesh:	Remember us for good on this day of the new moon.
On Rosh Hashanah:	Remember us for good on this New Year.
On Pesach:	Let us rejoice on this Festival of Matzat.
On Shavuot:	Let us rejoice on this Festival of Weeks.
On Sukkot:	Let us rejoice on this Festival of Booths.
On Shemini Atzeret and Simchat Torah:	Let us rejoice on this Eighth Day Closing Festival.

For You, Lord, are good and You do good to all and we thank You for this land and . . .

(on wine)
. . . for the fruit of the vine.
Blessed are You, God, for the land and the fruit of the vine.
(on fruit)
. . . for the fruits.
Blessed are You, God, for the land and for the fruits.

(on cake)
. . . for the life-sustaining food.
Blessed are You, God, for the life-sustaining foods.
(on cake and wine)
. . . for the life-sustaining food and for the fruit of the vine.
Blessed are You, God, for the life-sustaining food and for the fruit of the vine.

Nature and Experience

There are many occasions other than eating that cause us to give thanks. We take note of the wonders of nature:

בָּרוּךְ אַתָּה יְיָ, אֱלֹהֵינוּ מֶלֶךְ הָעוֹלָם,

Baruch ata Adonai Elohainu melech ha'olam . . .

Blessed are You, Lord our God, Ruler of the universe . . .

On hearing thunder:

שֶׁכֹּחוֹ וּגְבוּרָתוֹ מָלֵא עוֹלָם.

. . . sheh'kocho u'gvurato maley olam.

. . . Whose might and power fill the world.

On seeing lightning:

עוֹשֶׂה מַעֲשֶׂה בְרֵאשִׁית.

. . . Oseh maaseh breshit.

. . . Who does the work of Creation.

On seeing a rainbow:

זוֹכֵר הַבְּרִית, נֶאֱמָן בִּבְרִיתוֹ וְקַיָּם בְּמַאֲמָרוֹ.

. . . *zochayr habrit v'ne'eman bivrito v'kayam b'ma'amaro.*

. . . Who remembers the Covenant, is faithful to the Covenant and keeps His word.

On seeing the sea for the first time in a long while:

שֶׁעָשָׂה אֶת הַיָּם הַגָּדוֹל.

. . . *sheh'asah et ha'yam ha'gadol.*

. . . Who has created the great sea.

On seeing beautiful trees or animals:

שֶׁכָּכָה לוֹ בְּעוֹלָמוֹ.

. . . *sheh'kacha lo be'olamo.*

. . . Who has such as these in His world.

On meeting a great Torah scholar:

שֶׁחָלַק מֵחָכְמָתוֹ לִירֵאָיו.

. . . *sheh'chalak mai'chach'mato li'rayahv.*

. . . Who has given of His wisdom to those who revere Him.

Or a person of great secular wisdom:

שֶׁנָּתַן מֵחָכְמָתוֹ לְבָשָׂר וָדָם.

. . . *sheh' natan mai'chach'mato levasar v'dam.*

. . . who has imparted His wisdom to flesh and blood.

On hearing good tidings:

הַטּוֹב וְהַמֵּטִיב.

. . . *hatov vehametiv.*

. . . Who is good and does good.

On hearing of someone's death:

יֹ דַּיַן הָאֱמֶת.

. . . *dayan ha'emet.*

. . . The true Judge.

. . . אֲשֶׁר יָצַר אֶת הָאָדָם בְּחָכְמָה, וּבָרָא בּוֹ נְקָבִים

נְקָבִים חֲלוּלִים חֲלוּלִים, גָּלוּי וְיָדוּעַ לִפְנֵי כִּסֵּא כְּבוֹדֶךָ

שֶׁאִם יִפָּתֵחַ אֶחָד מֵהֶם אוֹ יִסָּתֵם אֶחָד מֵהֶם, אִי אֶפְשָׁר

לְהִתְקַיֵּם וְלַעֲמֹד לְפָנֶיךָ. בָּרוּךְ אַתָּה יְהֹנָה רוֹפֵא כָל

בָּשָׂר וּמַפְלִיא לַעֲשׂוֹת.

. . . *Asher yatsar et ha'adam b'chochma, ubarah bo nekavim nekavim chalulim chalulim. Galu'ee veyadua lifney kisay kvodecha sheh'im Yepa'teh'ach echad mehem oh yesatem echad mehem, iy efshar lehitkay'em vla'amod lefanecha. Baruch Ata Adonai rofay kol basar umafli la'asot.*

. . . Who formed the human in wisdom and created in him a system of ducts and tubes. It is clear and known before Your glorious throne that if but one of these be opened or if one of these be closed, it would be impossible to exist in Your presence. Blessed are You, O Lord, Who heals all creatures and does wonders.

What a wonderful earthy religion. Nothing is taken for granted!

The Shehecheyanu blessing is recited on the occasion of a novel or happy event in one's life. It is often recited in conjunction with another b'racha appropriate to the particular experience. For example: on wearing a brand-new article of clothing, one would recite the regular blessing over clothing:

בָּרוּךְ אַתָּה יְיָ, אֱלֹהֵינוּ מֶלֶךְ הָעוֹלָם, מַלְבִּישׁ עֲרוּמִים.

Baruch ata Adonai Elohainu melech ha'olam malbish arumim.

Blessed are You, Lord our God, Ruler of the Universe, Who clothes the naked.

Immediately after, one recites the Shehecheyanu.

בָּרוּךְ אַתָּה יְיָ, אֱלֹהֵינוּ מֶלֶךְ הָעוֹלָם, שֶׁהֶחֱיָנוּ וְקִיְּמָנוּ וְהִגִּיעָנוּ לַזְּמַן הַזֶּה.

Baruch ata Adonai Elohainu melech ha'olam sheh'heh'cheh'yanu v'kiymanu v'higi'yanu lazman hazeh.

Blessed are You, Lord our God, Ruler of the universe, Who has granted us life and sustained us and brought us to this moment.

The Birkat Hagomel blessing is recited after having narrowly escaped danger, recovering from serious illness, or coming through safely after a long trip:

בָּרוּךְ אַתָּה יְיָ, אֱלֹהֵינוּ מֶלֶךְ הָעוֹלָם, הַגּוֹמֵל לְחַיָּבִים טוֹבוֹת, שֶׁגְּמָלַנִי כָּל טוֹב.

Baruch ata Adonai Elohainu melech ha'olam ha'gomel le'chayavim tovot sheh'g'malani kol tov.

Blessed are You, Lord our God, Ruler of the universe, Who grants favors to the undeserving, Who has granted me all kindness.

The Birkat Hagomel is generally recited in the presence of a minyan. All respond with:

שֶׁגְּמָלְךָ כָּל־טוֹב הוּא יִגְמָלְךָ כָּל־טוֹב. סֶלָה.

Sheh'g'malcha kol tov hu yigmalcha kol tov. Selah.

He who has granted you this goodness, may He continue to grant you all goodness. Selah.

Some people think that riding the New York subway warrants a Birkat Hagomel. In truth, however, there are many moments in our lives when we appreciate the narrow escapes, the close encounters. Sometimes it is only a small act of saving, but it could otherwise have been of large and serious consequences. Whenever someone recites the Birkat Hagomel in the synagogue, people always ask after his/her welfare.

On a lighter note: occasionally our children would ask what b'racha to make on this food or that. When they came home one day with a new brand of pseudo-potato chips and asked what b'racha it requires, I took one look at the ingredients, shuddered at all those chemicals, and pronounced my verdict—Birkat Hagomel! If they eat all that junk and live, it's a miracle!

Dire warnings notwithstanding, b'rachot are a serious business. Not only are we required to make the blessing as specific as possible to the food or experience or event, but also we are enjoined not to recite a blessing in vain. If one should begin a blessing and then be unable to complete it, he/she would not leave the words "Blessed be God" hanging in the air, which would mean using God's name in vain. The formula with which to complete it is,

$$\text{לַמְּדֵינִי חֻקֶּיךָ.}$$

Lamdeni chukecha.

which, when combined with the first three words of "Baruch ata Adonai," constitutes a verse from Psalms (119:12)—"Blessed are You, God, teach me Your statutes." Thus you've recited a verse from the Bible rather than an incomplete blessing.

BIRCHOT HA'MITZVOT

The second type of b'rachot—in contrast to the birchot nehenin described above—are those which we recite before performing a mitzvah. The first part of the phrase is,

בָּרוּךְ אַתָּה יְיָ, אֱלֹהֵינוּ מֶלֶךְ הָעוֹלָם אֲשֶׁר קִדְּשָׁנוּ
בְּמִצְוֹתָיו, וְצִוָּנוּ

*Baruch ata Adonai Elohainu melech ha'olam asher kidshanu
b'mitzvotav v'tzivanu . . .*

Blessed are You, Lord our God, Ruler of the universe, Who has
sanctified us with His commandments and commanded us . . .

לִקְבּוֹעַ מְזוּזָה.

likbo'ah mezuzah

. . . to affix a mezuzah (to a doorpost of a home).

לַעֲסֹק בְּדִבְרֵי תוֹרָה.

la'asok bedivrai Torah

. . . to busy ourselves with the study of Torah (each day).

עַל הַטְּבִילָה.

ahl hatevila

. . . on the immersion (in the mikvah, ritual bath).

עַל נְטִילַת יָדַיִם.

al netilat yadayim

. . . on washing the hands (upon arising and before eating).

לִקְרֹא אֶת הַהַלֵּל.

likro et ha'hallel

. . . to recite the Hallel (hymns of praise and thanksgiving).

לֵשֵׁב בַּסֻּכָּה.

leyshev ba'sukkah

. . . to dwell in the sukkah.

There are a host of such blessings, and they sanctify the act we are about to perform. To be sure, two thousand years of celebrating Jews would not allow these special occasions to go by with but a one-line b'racha. In many instances, brief prayers have been added on to embellish the ceremony. One should consult a siddur.

FIXED-TIME PRAYER

The structure of daily prayer—when one has time to consider it in sum—is like the unfolding of a beautiful flower, or the highlighting of a symphony. Each layer suits its proper moment or mood, as human beings move through the day.

Consider a moment the Birchot Hashachar, the morning blessings. Most likely, these were originally recited at different stages of the wake-up process, but were subsequently formalized into the Shacharit prayer. In the Birchot Hashachar (which are found at the beginning of the siddur), we thank God for the ability to wake up, to rub sleep from our eyes, to see, to eliminate waste, to wash ourselves, to stand up straight, to dress, to be strong, to be free, to be blessed with Torah.

Take this one, for example, the eleventh of the morning blessings:

בָּרוּךְ אַתָּה יְיָ, אֱלֹהֵינוּ מֶלֶךְ הָעוֹלָם, הַמֵּכִין מִצְעֲדֵי גָבֶר.

Blessed are You, Lord our God, Ruler of the universe, Who guides the steps of man.

Some might take that to be a statement about righteousness, but truly it is about balance. When was the last time any of us thought about the miracle of equilibrium, the ability to get off the bed in the morning and walk a straight line? It takes a few seconds until our balance is restored each morning, but it does come, and happily we can take it for granted all the rest of the day. As Jews, we are required to remember this gift a moment, and to praise God for it each morning.

Another of the Birchot Hashachar, one which has stirred a great deal of comment, is the blessing over sexual gender. Males recite it this way: "Blessed are You, Lord our God, Ruler of the universe, for not having created me a female."

In contrast, the female blessing, added to the liturgy in the fourteenth century (at least a thousand years after the male blessing had become part of the daily liturgy), is not at all sexist in tone: "Blessed are You, Lord our God, Ruler of the universe, Who has created me according to His will."

Some women and men object to the sexist tone of the male blessing. Nor is the sensitivity particular to this generation alone; there have been rabbis in our past who were conscious of the imbalance between male and female blessings. They explained the male blessing as intending no slur against women, but rather as recognition of the fact that men have been assigned more mitzvot to fulfill and are therefore more fortunate. Today, some few Orthodox males have quietly dropped the male blessing; others substitute for it the more general one of "creating me according to His Will." Conservative Jews have changed the language of the blessing to ". . . Who has created me in His image." Human sexuality and male/female distinctiveness being a good thing, I would hope that contemporary halachists would uphold the divine intention of gender distinction, and reformulate the blessings in a positive manner: ". . . for having created me a male/ . . . for having created me a female."

A male Jew wears the tallit and tefillin for morning prayer. The tallit, the prayer shawl with its four tzitzit, is customarily worn only by married men. A man removes his tallit from its tallit bag, holds the tallit with both hands, and recites the blessing. Then he wraps it around his shoulders—or over his head as some do. Men kiss the fringes of the tallit before reciting the blessing, a sign of their love for this mitzvah. The blessing recited upon donning the tallit is:

בָּרוּךְ אַתָּה יְיָ, אֱלֹהֵינוּ מֶלֶךְ הָעוֹלָם, אֲשֶׁר קִדְּשָׁנוּ
בְּמִצְוֹתָיו, וְצִוָּנוּ לְהִתְעַטֵף בַּצִיצִית.

*Baruch ata Adonai Elohainu melech ha'olam asher kidshanu
b'mitzvotav v'tzivanu l'hit-atef b'tzitzit.*

Blessed are You, Lord our God, Ruler of the universe, Who has
sanctified us with His commandments and commanded us to
wrap ourselves in the tzitzit.

The tefillin, phylacteries, as they are called, are worn only for
Shacharit. (See p. 275 for tefillin blessings.) Tefillin look like
nothing more than two small black cubes with black straps attached to each cube; but as ancient holy ritual objects, they carry
many layers of tradition. Their construction, their meaning, the
method of putting them on, the differences between the tefillin
shel rosh (head) and the tefillin shel yad (arm)—every detail is
rich in significance and attendant law. Inside each cube—which
is meticulously made of layers of parchment and then sealed and
lacquered—are scrolls of parchment on which are inscribed four
passages from the Torah: Exodus 13:1–10; 13:11–16; Deuteronomy 6:4–9; 11:13–21. Among other things, these include the
Shema and the verses that instruct us concerning tefillin.

The tefillin are a sign of the covenant, the mutual bond between God and the Jewish people. As I watch a man put on
tefillin, there are two things that are suggestive of this bond. One
is the wrapping process, the straps he pulls around his forehead
and the straps he wraps down his arm, as if he is wrapping up his
mind and his body to the service of God. Second are the words
from Hosea he recites as he binds the leather around his left
arm, the incredible statement of God's love for His people: "And
I shall betroth you to Me forever, And I shall betroth you to Me
in righteousness, justice, loving kindness, and compassion, And
I will betroth you to Me in faithfulness, And you shall know the
Lord" (Hos. 2:21–22).

One rabbinic tradition suggests that God, too, wears tefillin.
His tefillin contain parchments proclaiming the uniqueness of
His people.

From the experience of our three sons, I have come to understand tefillin as a powerful pedagogic device. From Bar Mitzvah on, a boy is required to wear tefillin. Tefillin add that tangible something that is needed to help bring a young boy into the imposing adult liturgical responsibilities that are now thrust upon him. Before they began to put on tefillin, our sons would occasionally miss a Shacharit here or there. Since then, they've not missed a day.

There are two foci to the Shacharit service: the Shema and the Shmoneh Esreh, the latter the silent benedictions. Around these two cores, much has been added. The service is structured as follows:

Birchot Hashachar, the morning blessings.
Pesukai Dezimra, passages taken mostly from Psalms, that serve
    as a kind of warm-up to the prayer.
Borchu, a call to communal worship, recited only in a minyan.
Blessings preceding the Shema thanking God for creating light
    and for giving us the Torah.
Shema Yisrael, the central affirmation of faith.
Blessing following the Shema, blessing God for redeeming the
    people of Israel.
Shmoneh Esreh, the eighteen benedictions (actually nineteen).
    These concern God's relationship to us; individual and communal requests such as for wisdom, health, survival, acceptance of all our prayers; expressions of gratitude; and a plea for peace.
Closing devotional prayers, including the Aleinu.

For Shabbat and holidays, additional prayers are added. On Mondays and Thursdays, part of the next week's Sabbath Torah portion is read. Whenever a portion of the Torah is read publicly, it is accompanied by aliyot and special blessings over the Torah.

Even on those days when the Torah is not read, the basic prayer service contains many quotes from the Torah. Particularly in Shacharit we find large excerpts, even whole paragraphs, from Torah and Talmud. Learning is a form of prayer; moreover, one is commanded to study Torah every day. For those who could not find another time, the Rabbis inserted these texts into the prayer service so as to enable people to fulfill the requirement of Talmud Torah, the daily study of Torah.

The Minchah service is much briefer than Shacharit. It includes the Shmoneh Esreh, but not the Shema. The Maariv, again, has both foci, with the accompanying prayers varied somewhat. Just as in Shacharit we take note of the day, so in Maariv we make special requests and offer words of gratitude that are related to the night. Unlike the Shmoneh Esreh of Shacharit and Minchah, the Shmoneh Esreh of Maariv is not repeated by the shaliach tzibbur, the prayer leader. It is dark out and people must hurry home.

Each of these three prayers must be said in its appropriate time slot. If one misses a prayer, it cannot be recited later. I find this fixed-time concept to be useful in ways the Rabbis never would have imagined. Moshe, also known around these parts as "the day sleeper," has over the years frustrated the efforts of nagging parents, first-period schoolteachers, waiting friends, not to mention numerous alarm clocks, flashing lights, blaring radios —until we finally discovered the key. A gentle whisper of, "Moshe, it's almost 'oh'ver z'man kriat Shema' " (the end time for saying the morning prayers), and miraculously, the body would stir.

A word about position and posture. Some prayers are recited sitting, some standing. The parts of the service that can be recited only in a minyan—such as Borchu, Kedusha (recited during the reader's repetition of the Shmoneh Esreh), Kaddish, and Torah ceremonies—are recited standing. So are other prayers that have an added measure of holiness to them. We also alternately stand and sit at set times to keep the momentum going.

The Shmoneh Esreh, the eighteen benedictions, is recited silently, standing, facing Jerusalem, toward the spot where the Holy Temple once stood. Before we begin the Shmoneh Esreh, we take three small steps backward, bow left, right, and center, and then take three steps forward again—to accentuate our standing in the presence of the Lord of the universe. When we conclude the Shmoneh Esreh, we similarly "bow out."

Jews never kneel, except at special moments of the Rosh Hashanah and Yom Kippur liturgies, as ancient Jews did in the Holy Temple on Yom Kippur. However, there are certain points in the liturgy where we do bend the knee and bow gently (or deeply for those less inhibited) from the waist.

Knowing where to stand or sit or bow comes from experience. Most prayer books do not instruct the petitioner at what points to stand or sit. The beginner would do well to take his/her siddur to someone knowledgeable to mark off the changes in posture.

A most remarkable thing about the prayer of Orthodox Jews is that every member of the congregation prays. There is no watching or waiting for someone else to do it. What the rabbi is required to pray so is the least of his congregants.

We begin the day with the Modeh Ani, giving thanks for the soul restored:

מוֹדֶה אֲנִי לְפָנֶיךָ, מֶלֶךְ חַי וְקַיָּם, שֶׁהֶחֱזַרְתָּ בִּי נִשְׁמָתִי
בְּחֶמְלָה; רַבָּה אֱמוּנָתֶךָ.

Modeh ani lefanecha, melech chai v'kayam, sheh'heh'ch'ehzarta be nishmati b'chemla. Rabbah emunatecha.

I give thanks to you, Ruler of life and everlasting, Who, in mercy, has returned my soul to me. Our trust in You is great.

We close our day with the Shema, affirming our belief in one God, our commitment to love God, fulfill the commandments, study the Torah, and pass on the chain of tradition:

שְׁמַע יִשְׂרָאֵל, יְיָ אֱלֹהֵינוּ יְיָ אֶחָד.

בָּרוּךְ שֵׁם כְּבוֹד מַלְכוּתוֹ לְעוֹלָם וָעֶד.

וְאָהַבְתָּ אֵת יְיָ אֱלֹהֶיךָ בְּכָל לְבָבְךָ וּבְכָל נַפְשְׁךָ וּבְכָל
מְאֹדֶךָ. וְהָיוּ הַדְּבָרִים הָאֵלֶּה, אֲשֶׁר אָנֹכִי מְצַוְּךָ הַיּוֹם, עַל
לְבָבֶךָ. וְשִׁנַּנְתָּם לְבָנֶיךָ, וְדִבַּרְתָּ בָּם בְּשִׁבְתְּךָ בְּבֵיתֶךָ,
וּבְלֶכְתְּךָ בַדֶּרֶךְ, וּבְשָׁכְבְּךָ וּבְקוּמֶךָ. וּקְשַׁרְתָּם לְאוֹת עַל
יָדֶךָ, וְהָיוּ לְטֹטָפֹת בֵּין עֵינֶיךָ. וּכְתַבְתָּם עַל מְזֻזוֹת בֵּיתֶךָ
וּבִשְׁעָרֶיךָ.

Shema yisrael, Adonai Elohainu Adonai ehad. Baruch shem k'vod malchuto l'olam va-ed. V'a-havta et Adonai Elohecha b'chol l'vavcha uv-chol naf-sh'cha uv-chol m'odecha. V'hayu hadvarim ha-aileh asher anochi m'tzav-cha ha-yom al l'vavecha, v'sheenan-tam l'vanecha v'dee-barta bam, b'sheev-t'cha b'vaitecha uv-lech-t'cha va-derech, uv-shach-b'cha uv'kumecha. Uk-shartam l'ot al yadecha, v'hayu l'totafot bayn aynecha uch-tavtam al mezuzot baytecha u-vish-arecha.

Hear, O Israel, the Lord our God, the Lord is One. And you shall love the Lord your God with all your heart, with all your soul, with all your might. And these words which I command you this day shall be on your heart. You shall teach them to your children, and you shall speak of them when you sit at home and when you go out on the road, when you lie down and when you rise up. And you shall bind them as a sign upon your arm and they shall be as frontlets [tefillin] between your eyes and you shall write them on the doorposts [mezuzot] of your house and on your gates.

Even those who have recited the Shema as part of the Maariv service will recite it again at bedtime; and certainly those who have not said the Maariv, such as most women and children, will recite the Shema before retiring.

One of the most precious moments of Jewish parents and children is the nighttime recitation of the Shema. Each night, as we put our young children to bed, the last thing we do is to sing this prayer with them, or to listen as they sing it aloud in our presence. Surely, it changes their lives; surely, it deepens the bond between parents and children.

WOMEN AND LITURGY

As I've said elsewhere in this book, no system is perfect. That is certainly true as regards women and liturgy. Indeed, this has been the most difficult chapter for me to write. On the one hand, I have described the specialness of Jewish prayer and the strength it brings to the individual; on the other, at many steps along the way, I have been tempted to add, "but not for women" or "women don't do this."

In Orthodox Judaism, prayer has tended to be a man's thing. What's more, although some have begun to probe the implications of different roles for men and women in liturgy, most feel rather comfortable with the status quo. Some of my best and deepest prayer experiences have come from watching the men in my family pray their daily prayers. When I walk into a darkened room, and find Moshe reciting the Maariv by heart, and with intense concentration, it moves me greatly. And I'm not sure why, but one of my morning thrills is to watch my husband put on tallit and tefillin. And in the album of my mind I hold scenes of Yitz and our boys daavening at the edge of a beach in Dahab, Sinai, with a group of Israeli soldiers he had just rounded up; or awakening in a hotel in Puerto Rico to find Yitz on the terrace daavening into the sunrise. For some reason these are all romantic memories for me; a mixture of faith and sexuality, and at times a sense of nearness to God.

By and large, Orthodox women do not seem to be much exercised about this relative lack of participation and performance. Most women take in stride the fact that this significant area of a Jew's life—daily prayer—is experienced only vicariously, if at all. Interestingly, the majority of women do recite the Sabbath and holiday prayers (which we are not formally obligated to do), but not weekday prayer (to which technically we are obligated). And for various reasons throughout our history, we have generally tended to consider ourselves devout, observant Jews, members in good standing, even without all that daily prayer.

Nor are women to be blamed for this lapse, for it is in great measure a function of conditioning and low communal expectations. Women are halachically exempt from certain time-bound positive commandments, and this exemption has had a domino effect on all aspects of women's prayer. Women are not counted in a prayer quorum; ten men make a minyan—not women. These are among the factors that have suppressed an instinct that does not develop or flower, as I said earlier, all by itself.

* * *

Prayer is a mystery to human beings. A thousand questions spring to mind. Is there a connection between ethics and prayer?

Between fortune and prayer? On the High Holidays, we often repeat the phrase, "Repentance, prayer, and righteousness remove the evil decree." Yet, who can know? Who can measure the efficacy of prayer, or the rewards of prayer?

In 1980, a study on longevity was done by medical researchers in Israel. They discovered that prayer in a daily minyan was significantly correlated to longer life and fewer heart attacks. Was it God's reward for this expression of faithfulness and love or was it, as the medical researchers speculated, not the content of prayer, but rather that in these few moments of community prayer each day, the supplicants could disengage and relax from wordly concerns and immediate pressures?

These are questions whose answers are not given to human documentation. There can be no definitive proofs of the efficacy of prayer.

However, one thing I do know: that prayer orients a person to life in a special way. Let me illustrate with a story about my father:

In 1973, my brother-in-law, age forty-three, recuperating from hepatitis, suffered a massive heart attack. Fortunately, it happened in New Orleans, twenty minutes from one of the best-equipped heart hospitals in the world, for by the time he reached that hospital his heart had stopped altogether. Several months later, he had recuperated sufficiently to undergo open-heart surgery—successful, but not without its painful aftereffects. During the next few years, my sister's family sustained other serious illnesses, and a robbery, and a fire which completely gutted their home and destroyed all of their belongings.

A year after the fire, one week before they were to move back into their rebuilt home, the fire department called them in the middle of the night to tell them that the house had burned down again.

My sister and I talked for a long while that morning, and in a moment of despair she said to me, "Somebody up there just doesn't like us." Feeling equally sour about what Life had served up to them those past five years, I said to her, "I know just what you mean, Judy. I was having the same thoughts myself."

Later that morning I spoke to my father, anticipating the worst, since my mother had reported to me earlier that he was crying during Shacharit. My father was subdued, but he was far from crushed. He said, "You know, all morning when I was daavening, I couldn't help thinking over and over again, Chasdei hashem ki lo tamnu *—Once again, they were saved. . . ."

* God's acts of loving-kindness never cease.

CHAPTER 5

PARENTING AND EDUCATION

Three women are sitting and chatting. The first one sighs a deep sigh. "Oy vey iz mier," she says. The others nod their heads and one replies in a drained voice, "I have no more strength left." The third one listens a moment, shakes her head from side to side, and says, "Tze, tze, tze." Suddenly the first one straightens her shoulders, turns to her companions, and says, "Now, my dears, we really must stop. We promised ourselves not to talk about the children today."

To be an Orthodox Jewish parent is at once the most difficult and the easiest task in the world.

Difficult, because there are so many additional responsibilities. Beyond feeding, clothing, sheltering, and training, beyond middle-class necessities such as play group, puppet shows, summer camps, braces, museum visits, piano lessons and a college degree—there is a vast normative system to be taught, Jewish identity to be transmitted, communal responsibility (yes, fifteen-year-olds understand that concept well) to be implanted, and the expectations of generations to be passed along.

Easy, because some of these clearly defined "extras" provide the structure and direction that parents need for parenting as much as children need for growing. Easy, because the "over and beyond" responsibilities help everything else fall into place. Easy, because faith and ritual, tradition and community are all very natural components of the process of growing up. Easy, because tradition confirms in a hundred ways what unadorned instinct knows—that children are our greatest blessing, our real wealth, our finest jewels. They are more precious to us than our own lives, and, feeling that way, we understand how to order our priorities. What some might consider sacrifice or burden is what a traditional Jew understands to be the natural way of parents and children.

What are the responsibilities of a parent?

The first obligation of Jewish parents to their children is to have them! To give them life. The very first commandment in the Torah is, "Be fruitful and multiply and fill the earth" (GEN. 1:28). Throughout history, Jews understand these words as blessing and not merely command. Many a Jewish conversation in history went like this: "How many children/grandchildren have you?" "Three/six/fifteen, *ken yirbu*" ("May the number be increased").

Even today, when alternate value systems often put "having children" pretty far down the list, or sometimes not on the list at all, most traditional Jewish families still put it at the top. To be sure, things have changed somewhat even among Orthodox Jews. Two decades ago, if a couple didn't have children by the second or third year of their marriage, friends and relatives would automatically assume the problem was a medical one. Recently, I overheard an Orthodox rebbetzin (rabbi's wife) say to her granddaughter sometime around the latter's second anniversary, "Don't rush things. You still have what to do with your life!" Twenty years ago, such a forthright bubbe would have asked her daughter, "Nu? Any good news from Rachel?" Yes, things have changed. Like other women, traditional Jewish women take advanced degrees, become professionally trained, delay childbearing. Still . . . an Orthodox family without children? Not if it could be otherwise.

The second obligation is that a child honors his/her parents. Honor, reverence, even fear (see LEV. 19:3): these are the underlying sentiments a child should feel and be guided by. But the obligation really falls on the parents, for who else can teach a child to respect and revere other than the parents themselves! Love comes naturally, but respect must be taught. Orthodox

Jews take the mitzvah of honoring one's parents with great seriousness.

When I was growing up, I remember my parents pulling out, at appropriate times, the catch phrase: kibbud av v'em (the honor of a father and mother). Those three words were more powerful than fifty speeches on the subject. If I stepped too far out of line in back talk, it was kibbud av v'em; when my father wanted us to do something special that was beyond the range of a child's obligations, he would say, "Who would like a mitzvah (of kibbud av v'em)?" The Talmud teaches us that honor is manifested in all sorts of little acts: Do not sit in a parent's seat; do not stand in his/her spot; do not speak in his/her place.

Kibbud av v'em extended to grandparents, of course, but somehow it rippled to include all adults. When my mother taught us, as young children, to give up a bus seat to an adult, it was not only for one who was elderly or frail; we were taught to stand for anyone who looked like an adult. Somehow, it fit into the context of showing deference to one's elders. I finally reached my own maturity when I became pregnant with our first child—and stopped giving up my seat to anyone who had one more wrinkle in his/her skin than I.

And, if kibbud av v'em included adults in general, it certainly applied to one's teachers. I remember a mock wedding our junior-high-school class staged. We showered confetti on the teacher as he walked into the classroom, for which he thundered at us, "You girls will lose your place in the world to come!" He knew whereof he spoke: that is the punishment reserved for those who fail to honor their parents, and by extension, their teachers. In our children's yeshiva high schools, this very day, all the students stand in respect as the rabbi-dean enters the room.

Kibbud av v'em sets the tone for the entire relationship between parents and children. Implicit in this is a concept of inequity, that is, a healthy distinction between parents and children. The Torah—and the tradition—never intended it to be a relationship of equals. While there were checks on parental exploitation of this imbalance, there was never any doubt as to who played what roles. The underlying principle of unequals has large and, I think, positive consequences for family relationships today where sometimes parents abdicate their responsibility too soon or too much. By saying "Honor your father and mother," and not "Love your parents," as it said "Love your God," the Torah in effect was saying to the Jewish parent: your primary responsibility is to be a parent and your secondary responsibility is to be a pal. This might not be true for every last parent and child, but it does hold true for most.

It's not always as easy as it sounds. Especially since we teach our children to think independently—beginning with the diaper crowd. Especially with bright children who know—almost instinctively—how to argue, cajole, and sometimes manipulate parents whom they love dearly and who love them even more. Orthodox Jewish parents are no different from other contemporary parents who are swept up in the constantly changing theories of child psychology. Despite the fact that we have come to understand a thing or two about structure and limits, we also feel torn between doing that which makes our beloved children feel happy, contented, and our pals—and doing the other which is often best for them. So the commandment that children "honor" is a helpful reminder all around that a bit of distance between parents and children can be quite sound.

I try not to use it as a crutch or a guilt trip, but I do find myself at times saying kibbud av v'em in one form or another. "Is that the way you show respect for your mother? father?" serves two functions: it corrects the immediate behavior and, without even bringing it up for debate, it reminds the children that there is a hierarchy here. Deep down, that sense of unequals makes them feel good about themselves; oddly enough, it gives them a sense of self. Even though our children—and most children—are very free-spirited by nature, nevertheless they like to know that there is a certain order to their lives, a structure within which they must function, a backdrop against which to test and define themselves.

Honor, fear, and reverence, then, are not only important structural components of a relationship whose natural base is love, they are also the optimal mode of discipline. For tradition cautions moderation in using physical force: "If you must hit, then hit only with a shoelace," sums it up quite well indeed (BAVA BATRA 21A). There was the recognition that sometimes a child needs physical force, but a parent should use it sparingly. Inequity does not mean indignity, honor does not mean a lack of mutual respect, and hierarchy does not mean a trampling of the spirit. Hardly ever does one hear of child abuse in a religious Jewish home. From the tradition we learn that even with the worst kind of child, the errant and wayward son who technically was subject to capital punishment (Jewish tradition informs us that there never actually was such a case), parents could not take punitive measures in their own hands. It became a matter of communal discipline.

When punishment is needed, Jewish parents use verbal reprimand and withdrawal of privileges. Still, sometimes . . . I remember when David, then six or seven, had done something very naughty; I gave him a good going-over—threats, criticism, punishments, the works. After a few minutes of my harangue, he interrupted, and in all seriousness asked, "Do you think you could just spank me instead?"

ADDITIONAL OBLIGATIONS

If kibbud av v'em is the tone of the relationship and its mode of discipline, what is the special substance?

The Talmud gives a very specific list of obligations of father to son: "to circumcise him, to redeem him, to teach him Torah, to find him a wife, to teach him a trade." And some say: "to teach him to swim so that he may save his life" (KIDDUSHIN 29A). If we adapt that set of obligations to the contemporary scene and adjust it to include obligations to daughters as well, it holds up pretty well in defining and describing an Orthodox Jewish parent today.

TO CIRCUMCISE HIM

Broadly defined, it means that parents must bring their children into the Covenant and teach them to live according to the mitzvot. They do this long before the age when children can voluntarily accept it for themselves. All that I have said earlier about Shabbat and kashrut and holidays is really about parents teaching children. What is the Passover seder if not a superb pedagogic device to make children feel that they are part of the great Jewish past?

The obligatory age of observing mitzvot is twelve/thirteen. But Orthodox parents don't wait till then. Just as we know that ethical values are communicated very early in life, so a Jewish parent teaches his/her child at an early age how to observe the rituals. Besides, it's much easier to instill when a child is young.

One scene I recall from long ago perfectly described the Talmudic dictum of teaching children mitzvot as soon as they begin to speak. I was walking through Jerusalem's Mea Shearim section when I spotted a young mother pushing a stroller. In the stroller was a beautiful child, but I could not determine its sex. The face was cherubic; the blond curls that framed the face would have been the envy of any female. But the child was also wearing this: a yarmulke (skullcap) that was tied under the chin with blue velvet ribbons. Was it a boy whose blond locks would be shorn when he reached age three (a tradition among some Jews) or was it a little girl? This was a time when not being able to tell gender was disorienting, so, to satisfy my curiosity I reversed direction and followed the young mother down the street. When she reached the kiosk she bought a cookie and said, "Here, Moishe." Obviously, it was a boy. Then, as she held the cookie out to him, she said, "Macht a brucheh," and this child who could barely talk repeated the blessing after her, syllable by syllable. But why the velvet bow under his chin? Because she wanted the yarmulke to stay on his head. Even at the age of two, it was to be as much a part of his life as was making a b'racha before putting a piece of food into his mouth. I could not remember how I had first learned the blessings, but at that moment, as I watched this mother, barely out of her teens herself, I suddenly knew. More than that. In that very same instant, I understood how I would do it some day with my own children.

TO REDEEM HIM

In a general way, this reminds parents that while we don't have to physically offer our firstborn up to be consecrated to the service of the Lord, we do raise them to love God, to worship, and to observe God's laws. That is why, at an early age, children are taught to pray and to speak of God unselfconsciously. That is why, too, children always feel welcome in an Orthodox synagogue, even if at times all they do is laugh in its halls or drift in and out of the sanctuary like free birds. Not only the firstborn, but all of our children, have some sixth sense that their lives are to be consecrated to the lifelong service of God.

TO TEACH HIM A TRADE

The Talmud says, "Teach your child a craft, for not to do so is to teach him to be a thief." At the heart of this parental obligation is a notion of self-sufficiency, that is, to help children make their own way in the world. The great Jewish emphasis on book learning, plus the multigenerational tradition of helping to establish one's children, is expressed in a strong commitment to general education and to professional training. My in-laws saved every bit of string and every paper bag; they read by the light of forty-watt bulbs; and never in their lives did they take a cab. But they put four children through the finest graduate schools in this country!

As the borscht circuit joke goes: What is a Jewish dropout? One without a Ph.D.

No sacrifice is too great to prepare a child to succeed on his/her own.

TO TEACH HIM TO SWIM

Why teach him to swim? Answer: for his life may depend upon it. Self-protection and self-sufficiency are at the heart of this obligation, too. Some time ago, as the teenagers in our community walked home at 11:00 P.M. Friday from an Oneg Shabbat gathering, they were set upon by a group of neighborhood toughs whose anti-Semitic clocks were ticked off by the sight of the boys' kipot. Some of the Jewish kids ran, scared, some got punched up, and the whole community was quite agitated. Next morning, in the synagogue, the rabbi did a most sensible thing:

he urged all the parents to enroll their children—male and female—in the karate class given in the shul gym each week. This is the contemporary equivalent of teaching one's child to swim —for his/her life may depend upon it.

TO FIND HIM A WIFE

"Taking a wife" for one's children can mean anything from an arranged marriage to encouraging one's children to marry. In between is a whole range of responses that indicate how serious Orthodox parents are about this obligation. For example, it is not all that uncommon for parents to support their children so they can marry in their early twenties, yet continue on with learning and/or professional studies, rather than waiting until they are able to support themselves. This is somewhat different from the European tradition where the most brilliant and promising yeshiva bocher would be chosen by the wealthiest householder for his daughter. The father-in-law would provide kest (support) so that his son-in-law could continue yeshiva studies while his daughter would begin to raise a family. Underlying both the American and the European response is the parental obligation to help their children marry.

Arranged marriages exist today only among a small group of the most traditional Jews. Modern Orthodox Jews date and select their own mates, but parents often do their best to see that their marriageable-age children have all the opportunities to meet other young people, ideally from the same background. Most Orthodox Jews do marry other Orthodox Jews, and this is by no means accidental. Parents have a great deal invested in the choice of mate; for a child to break with tradition because of marriage is a painful loss to a parent who wants to keep the chain going.

Some families with marriageable-age children go to the kosher hotels for Pesach or Sukkot for reasons over and above holiday celebration. . . . Likewise with choice of schools, vacation plans, and so forth. Before sending a college-age student off to an out-of-town college, parents will do a careful check of whether there is a supportive traditional community on campus or nearby.

TO TEACH HIM TORAH

The mitzvah of talmud Torah, daily study of Torah, is the most fundamental of all mitzvot—because it leads to all the others. For the habit of learning to take hold and last a lifetime, it must be inculcated early in life. Besides, if one is ever to master a significant part of the vast literature that awaits a Jewish mind, one had better start early. And persist.

That is why of all the obligations of parents to children, the one that is most distinctive about the Orthodox community is that of teaching a child Torah. Almost without exception, Orthodox Jewish children attend yeshiva day schools and high schools —no matter what the strain on family budget. People often base their choice of domicile more on the quality of the local yeshiva than on that of the local shul. Families who don't live in cities with Jewish schools will import a melamed (teacher, scholar) or send their children away at an early age. When my sisters and I and thirteen cousins grew up in Seattle, Washington, there was no day school (there are now two). So after public school each day we went to the Talmud Torah school, in which our parents were all actively involved. We studied Jewish subjects two hours a day, four days a week, and four hours on Sunday morning. It wasn't perfect, but it was quite enough to give us a solid background so that when my parents moved to New York we were able to enter our proper grade in yeshiva day school right off. All my male cousins, whose families stayed in Seattle, were sent East at the age of thirteen; and female cousins, for various reasons, including lack of dormitory space in the high-school years, came to New York at the age of seventeen, all in quest of a good yeshiva education.

There has been a tremendous growth of yeshiva day schools during the last two decades. Most yeshivot now have early-childhood programs, so that starting at age three a child is put into a learning-and-play environment that reinforces the life-style of the home. Until a decade ago, these were quite adequate as a holding pattern. In the last few years, however, as more and more traditional young mothers work or go to school, a vacuum has grown in terms of Jewish day care.

By kindergarten, most Orthodox children are established in

day school where they follow a dual program of secular and Jewish studies, a double load that lasts all the way up through high school and beyond. At the same time as they begin to learn to read English, they begin to learn Hebrew. Reading the prayer book, learning the Hebrew language, studying Torah, first the text alone, then later with Rashi commentary; also Jewish history, literature, ethics, laws, and customs, Talmud, the prophets, the commentaries, the codes, Jewish philosophy—this is the general pattern of studies as the children go through the system.

Finding good teachers is not easy because salaries are low; to some extent, however, this is not a totally negative selective factor because only someone who is very dedicated to Jewish education would choose the field in the first place.

In most Orthodox-affiliated high schools, the emphasis in Jewish studies is on Gemara (Talmudic study), sometimes to the exclusion of more rounded Jewish education. (The secular curriculum follows state requirements.) But that is to prepare the student for entering into higher-level studies and ultimately rabbinic training, where the whole focus is Talmud and halacha.

As is true of Orthodox homes, there are differences from one Orthodox school to another. Some schools teach matters of faith and history with some of their inherent complexities. Some schools group boys and girls in mixed classes, while others totally separate them at an early age. Some schools adopt a more modest dress code, such as long sleeves for the girls (at no school, however, even the most modern Orthodox, will you see girls wearing pants to school).

How to choose a day school or high school? Here are some ways of going about it:

1. Make a list of all the possible choices. It might be wider than you think.
2. Visit the most likely choices for a day.
3. Call parents whose judgment you trust. Make sure you don't rely on the judgment of one parent. Call several people until you begin to feel a consensus forming re the quality of the school, teaching, and administration; its religious ambiance; its attitude toward parental involvement.
4. Check out the first grade, fourth grade, and the eighth grade.

What is being covered in those grades? What skills have the children mastered?

5. Ask the school for a profile of the graduates of previous years. Unless some radical changes in administration have taken place, the character of the student body tends to be self-reinforcing.

6. Ask about homework policy. Some schools load homework on from day one. This can have differential effects, depending on the particular child and the family situation. It can help the child to learn faster, or create tension in a young child, or put an extra burden on parents, particularly where both parents work.

7. What is the daavening (praying) like?

8. Do boys and girls study together or separately?

9. What is the method of discipline?

10. What is the method of instruction, for example, open classroom, or a very formal structure?

11. Does the school have extracurricular activities?

12. What is the transportation situation?

13. Do older children mix with younger ones?

14. What is the extent of contact between siblings in school?

15. Does the school take telephone messages for students? Is there a public telephone for students to use?

16. What is the tuition, and how can it be paid?

17. What is the school's financial aid policy?

18. Is the school planning a move or an expansion in the near future?

19. Does the vacation schedule coincide with that of other members of the family?

20. How many undergraduates continue on with yeshiva education?

21. What is the acceptance at the various high schools/universities?

22. What is the relationship of the day school/high school to the local synagogues? Local rabbis?

23. What is the teacher turnover like; what is the ratio of new blood to seasoned teachers?

24. How are the subjects of the Holocaust and Israel taught? (You'd be surprised that some schools don't teach about them at all.)

25. To what extent is Jewish content integrated into the secular program? What portion of secular teachers also have a good Jewish background?
26. To what extent does the school place emphasis on midot, character building?

A trend among modern Orthodox parents is to send their children to high schools that are more traditional in practice and more to the right ideologically than they are, the theory being that a child generally picks up the values of the parents and will be more likely to relax or swing back from a more religiously intense environment than the other way around. Moreover, the negative social influences of modernity are less of a distraction in such schools. On the other hand, there always are a few youngsters who are more religiously sensitive and will take their values and practices from their rebbes rather than parents. The Talmud teaches that a parent may not inhibit a child on grounds of kibbud av v'em should the child become independently more religious than the parent.

What we have found in choosing is that no one thing works for every family, nor even for all the children of one family, particularly in high school. On the one hand, a Jewish parent is lucky to have choices. When I was of high-school age, there was only one yeshiva high school for girls serving three of the city's five boroughs, so I had to travel one and three quarter hours each way every day. On the other hand, choosing a yeshiva high school can be one of the toughest decisions a parent can make. Many factors come into play, not just the quality of teaching or the religious atmosphere, or the proximity to home. More than elementary school and more than college, the high-school peer group has a formative influence. The friendships one makes in high school are often active throughout one's adult life.

We chose one particular high school for our children. It had the right religious values, a student body who came from similar backgrounds, and a dean we respected and admired. Also, it was a five-minute walk from home and was not too large a school. But it didn't work for all five children. Two of them went through the school quite happily, and did well. One went through very unhappily, but received a superb education. Another went partway through, but somehow got turned off after the second year.

His rebellion took the form of not learning, so midway we switched him to another yeshiva high school, coed and reputedly less "frum" (religious). There he blossomed, became more religious in his practices and beliefs, and did very well in his studies. The fifth balked at our choice of high school for her, and chose her brother's coed yeshiva high school—and an hour trip each way. Since it was a high quality, well established school, headed by an exceptionally fine dean, we allowed her her choice. However, Yitz and I were of two minds regarding the principle of whether a child should be allowed to make the choice of high school, even within the acceptable range. After all the returns are in, ten or twenty years down the road, perhaps we'll know which were the right choices.

One difference between modern and right-wing Orthodox Jews is the emphasis on secular education. Right-wingers frown upon college, and their young adults spend the post-high-school years in yeshivot only, with no secular studies. Not so the modern Orthodox. In addition to the choice of a yeshiva college, such as Yeshiva University which is characterized by a dual track, many Orthodox college students attend universities that three decades ago would not at all have been considered. A kosher kitchen and Shabbat services at Oberlin or at Duke; next thing you know, they'll be having Yom Kippur services at Notre Dame! It's all part of the rising ethnicity in America, and the new unselfconsciousness of traditional Jews in this country.

In 1972, Yitz was instrumental in getting community support for a kosher eating house at Princeton, a project that was spurred on by the presence of several yeshiva boys in the hallowed halls of that WASPish school. But going to Princeton did not mean only a kosher kitchen. Little by little, first on the students' own initiative and later through the formal channels of the Hillel Foundation and the Princeton establishment, new Jewish learning opportunities were offered. Today, teaching a child Torah means a parent can pay a Harvard tuition and expect that institution and its quasi-affiliates to continue the Jewish education of his/her child.

Still, when all is said and done, teaching children Torah lies in the hands of the parents. To the extent that a parent sets this as a priority, a child will follow suit. Beyond finding the best

---

schools and the best teachers, there is the experience of parent teaching child Torah, one on one. "And you shall teach these things to your children" (DEUT. 6:7) was taken with great literalness. The Talmud adds, "He who teaches his grandchild Torah it is regarded as if the child had received it direct from Sinai." Our children study regularly with their grandfather and they take it quite for granted, but Yitz and I don't; and in later years, the children, too, will realize what a treasured thing learning with their grandfather is.

For most of our past, the singular emphasis was on father teaching son. But that is changing as young Jewish women increasingly are becoming better educated and fathers and mothers are equally able to teach their sons and daughters Torah. There are still large imbalances in the educational system as regards Talmudic studies, particularly in the intensity and length of years of study. But gradually these imbalances are being righted.

The image of parent learning Torah with child is one of the loveliest visions I can summon up. Many Orthodox parents set aside time every Shabbat to study with their children, and some also learn regularly during the week, too. Whenever I walk past Yitz studying with one of the children, as he frequently does, often into the midnight hours, I say silently, That's one of the reasons I married you. . . .

The story is told of Reb Chaim Brisker, the great Talmudist of the early twentieth century, who sent his son away for two years to learn in a famous yeshiva in another city. There was much excitement in the household on the day of the boy's return. The carriage pulled up, the young man stepped out. His father embraced him and said, "Come. Let us learn." For several hours, the father and son immersed themselves in the sea of Talmud. When they closed the large black volumes, they embraced again, and the father said, "Now, my son, how are you? Tell me . . ."

That is not how it happens in most ordinary families. Still, even in an ordinary Orthodox home the love of learning and the love of children are interwoven in remarkable fashion.

Another story: Both my father-in-law, of blessed memory, and my father can be characterized as Talmedei Chachamim, scholars of Torah and Talmud. Both spent their lives in daily study of

Talmud. Both completed the entire Shas (sixty-three tractates of the Talmud). One July 1, some years ago, we were about to leave for summer vacation with our five children, ages one through six. My father arose early that morning, took a subway from Far Rockaway at 6:30 A.M. so as to reach Riverdale by 8:30 to have a chance to say a last good-bye to his beloved grandchildren. He then had to travel back to Manhattan for a ten o'clock appointment. Three hours of traveling, just to get an extra hug from a small grandchild. My in-laws, too, were going to miss the children for two months, but they were not up to traveling, so we called them and said we'd come to Brooklyn before leaving for Massachusetts. My father-in-law, who loved each child more than his own life, said to Yitz, "Maybe you'll come alone, so we can learn a little." My father-in-law's passion for his grandchildren was no less than my father's; it was simply a different style of love, and peaks of emotion were often shared in puzzling through or mastering a piece of Gemara.

The obligations of a Jewish parent to a child are considerable: teaching respect, passing on ritual and tradition, preparing a child to be honorably self-sufficient, teaching Torah and ethics. All of that takes a lot of time, teaching, energy, contact, supervision, involvement, interference—and money. In the past, much of this was done by the Jewish mother. It was she who was responsible, for the most part, for the daily training and teaching; she who created an environment in which this learning and growing could take place; she who was generally available to pick up the pieces as Jewish children rushed through life, taking it all in, double time. Even day-school schedules, often eight hours plus, meant that the support systems had to be working well. Clean clothes, decent meals, a car pool to a distant school, a place to do homework and a parent to supervise and help, teachers to visit: all of these usually fell to the Jewish mother. An underlying premise of the yeshiva system is one of reciprocity: that a parent is able to supplement the schoolwork just as the school supplements the parent's task of teaching Torah.

A radical change is taking place in society today, with mothers no longer available on an open-ended basis. These social changes have affected the traditional community less than its more secular counterparts, but things are changing here, too. Orthodox Jewish women are still having children, but they also march to a different beat than did their mothers. By the time their children are in high school, most mothers have returned to school or to work. Even at the elementary level, 50 to 70 percent of the children in modern Orthodox day schools have working mothers. The only real difference seems to be at the preschool level, where most of the traditional mothers are still having babies and doing full-time mothering. But even there, and certainly for elementary and high school, administrators now consider the special needs of children with two working parents: there is no parent available for a class trip or a sukkah-hopping program, or a special school performance, or an assist with a tough homework assignment. We have only begun to estimate the impact upon children of coming home to an empty house or of trying to get the attention of a preoccupied mother. Jewish mothers helped a good deal in the past. Only now that a vacuum has been created is there recognition of how much went into the Jewish mother's role. It remains to be seen what toll this takes on the young, on the size and spacing of families; what compensations families will come up with and to what extent will Orthodox Jewish fathers pick up some of the slack. Perhaps the pendulum wiill swing back, as it did at the turn of the century, to full-time mothering for women who could afford it.

To return for a moment to kibbud av v'em: the lesson must be taught well, for it has to last a lifetime, through the life of middle-aged children. No one denies that there are at times large dilemmas and forced choices. There are many pulls on middle-aged children: their own spouses and children, the demands of career, community, the needs of self, and the needs of parents growing older day by day. Still, the tradition insists that we balance the claims of our parents upon us, even as we become adults and greatly independent of them. That is why the fifth commandment, "Honor thy father and thy mother," addresses the human being as "child" rather than "parent," even though the initial responsibility of teaching respect falls to the parent. We remain the children of our parents all our lives, and the commandment to honor them is binding all that while.

The majority of Orthodox Jews I know have surpassed their parents in education, achievement, and status. Yet they do not consider themselves to have surpassed their parents as human beings. They have not forgotten the merit of their parents, the acts of loving-kindness in their youth, the love that builds and mellows over a lifetime. That is not to say that one cannot separate fully, even at times to confront parents, and certainly to become independent. But unlike contemporary culture, where oftentimes parents are cast off as children become adults, Judaism says you don't have to be exactly like your parents, but you must maintain a lifelong respect for them.

The Talmud has numerous stories of how adult children honor their parents. My children know the story of Dama by heart: whenever they wake me up from an afternoon's nap without due cause, I repeat the story of Dama to them. Dama and his father, Netina, were dealers in precious jewels. One afternoon a buyer came to purchase a stone that would have netted Dama a huge profit, six hundred thousand gold coins. But Dama passed up this once-in-a-lifetime opportunity. Out of respect for his father, he refused to remove the key to the safe that was under his father's pillow, for risk of waking his father. For that act of extreme honor and sensitivity, Dama was rewarded. The Rabbis say the following year the calf that was to be used for the red heifer in the Temple ceremony was chosen and purchased from Dama's flock. . . .

The story of Rabbi Tarfon is another case in point. Rabbi Tarfon would crouch on the floor and make himself into a footstool so that his mother could reach her bed, which was otherwise too high for her. The law doesn't require such extreme acts of love and honor: it is merely suggesting a model of respect for parents that was given by those who were themselves esteemed and rich and famous.

Financial support and responsibility for elderly parents are clearly spelled out in the Talmud and in later codes of Jewish law. There are no two ways about it. One should feed, clothe, warm, and lead his/her parents in and out, and it must all be done with love, and not grudgingly. In general, halacha is an ecologically sound system, and that goes for a recycling of the nurturing process as well.

Orthodox Jewish couples—both partners—accept it as a given. Rarely, if ever, does one hear of an argument between husband and wife over the support of the spouses' parents. Middle-aged children will often take their parents into their own homes, or have them live nearby. Or, if elderly parents go into nursing homes, they will not be abandoned there. When I see women in the community taking their mothers to luncheons which they themselves would not otherwise go to, or men taking their fathers to the morning minyan, it always gives me pause for thought.

HEBREW ETHICAL WILLS

Today, most people write wills to leave their worldly goods. No responsible parent would leave the matter to the state. But worldly goods are not the most important possession we can leave behind us. Jewish tradition recognized that moral example and personal values are a more significant legacy and, therefore, the custom of writing Hebrew ethical wills developed.

Not a single one among us can be sure we will have an opportunity to say to our children all that we wish to say. When a child reaches Bar or Bat Mitzvah or marries and the parent's heart is full of emotion and pride, and we understand our priorities in life with a special clarity, that seems as good a time as any to write an ethical will. Once you have done it, you will revise it many times, hopefully over the next sixty to eighty years. To some extent, changes in circumstance—yours and your children's—will affect the content and emphases of your legacy.

There is no standard form to a Hebrew ethical will, and thus there is great personal leeway. Though entitled "Hebrew," an ethical will can be written in any language. In it, you should discuss those things that are closest to your heart, as well as what you have learned about the eternal values of life. Try to think of what would make you proud of your children as mature adults and as members of the Jewish community. You should mention whatever virtues are important to you, and not be worried that you are imposing impossible demands on your children. This is, after all, a legacy and not a commandment. It serves as a direction for their lives, not an order. Nor should you be worried that something that is important to you is objectively trivial and therefore not of sufficient weight to be included in a will of this nature. In some of the classical Hebrew ethical wills of the medieval period, we find that parents admonished their children to be strict about personal cleanliness or to be impeccable about their sexual behavior or not to gossip.

A man I knew wrote an ethical will to his children after his second daughter had married. He died some fifty years after he wrote the first will, and he changed it a few times, leaving three or four older versions in his safe-deposit box. His children commented that four things had never changed: "If I die before Mama, call her every day, and visit her once a week. She always took care of you. . . ." "Give one tenth of your earnings to tzedakah. This will be more of a hardship to you the wealthier you become, but you'll manage. . . ." "Observe Shabbos, and teach your own children to do the same. This is what kept our family so close. . . ." "Try to give other people the benefit of the doubt. . . ."

Writing an ethical will is not an easy thing to do, in part because it forces you to confront and understand your own values in life. However, you should not be intimidated at putting it all down on paper. The most important ethical legacy is the living example you have given them all your life. This will only serve to confirm.

Earlier, I said being a traditional Jewish parent is both the hardest and the easiest thing in the world. But I didn't say this: it also is the best.

CHAPTER • 6

DRESS

All his life, Shloime Mazel was a good Jew—devout, learned, careful of every little detail of the law, and more serious about it than most.

As he neared sixty-five, he began to realize that life would not go on forever. "Before I go," he said to his pious wife, "let me have a taste of this world—for just one week." So he took his money out of the shochtim pension fund, shaved his beard for the interim, discarded his long, black frock-coat in favor of a dapper sports jacket, tilted a fedora over his black velvet yarmulke, packed a suitcase of kosher salamis, and, feeling much like a stranger in his own skin, flew off to Las Vegas.

Alas, on his very first day there, in pursuit of 'this-worldliness,' he stepped off a curb and was hit by a car. Lying there in pain in the Las Vegas gutter, Shloime cried out, "Ribono Shel Olam, Master of the universe, what have I done that is so terrible? All my life I have served You faithfully, never neglecting any of Your mitzvot. All I wanted was one week in Las Vegas, one week to see what the world is like. Why have You punished me?" Suddenly, a Voice boomed overhead: "OH, MY HEAVENS! Shloime, IS IT YOU? I AM SO SORRY! I DIDN'T RECOGNIZE YOU!" *

By and large, a modern Orthodox Jew can physically blend

* Courtesy, Rabbi Joshua Shmidman, Montreal, Canada.

into the general community, in Las Vegas as in New York as in Dallas. The men are generally clean-shaven and do not wear earlocks. (However, they use only electric razors; Leviticus 21:5 prohibits applying a razor directly to the face.) They wear three-piece suits and sports clothes quite like other American men. The women are up to the latest in fashion. But there are differences—among Orthodox Jews and also between the most liberal Orthodox Jews and the non-Orthodox. The differences lie in the virtue of modesty.

Modesty is, of course, relative. Still, I would characterize Orthodox Jewish dress as modern but modest. For example, modern Orthodox teenagers, both male and female, wear the universal uniform—jeans—but not skintight ones, and not to their yeshiva schools. Young women will wear bathing suits, but not the teeniest bikinis; generally, a woman will head for the one-piece rack. When skirts were mini, Orthodox women wore them, but not the shortest ones. In fact, hemline inches could be significantly correlated to identity positions along the Orthodox continuum. At a fashionable Orthodox wedding, you won't find strapless or décolleté dresses except on an unknowing outsider. Some Orthodox women wear slacks, but others consider it "male gender attire" and would not wear such. Those women who do wear pants would never wear them to shul. Many modern Orthodox women wear sleeveless clothes, but never to shul; and some would never wear anything cut above their elbows. A woman from the Chasidic or right-wing sectarian community would never wear a short-sleeved dress, but she might wear a modest one-piece bathing suit at a Catskill hotel. An American Orthodox woman would not think of entering the shul without stockings, even in the summer heat, but her right-wing counterpart in Israel wouldn't hesitate to come to prayer in sandal-shod bare feet.

So the lines are drawn like a crazy quilt. Perhaps in no other area is there as much diversity among Orthodox Jews. The same holds true for married women covering their hair. Some women wear wigs; some, hats; some, scarves; some, nothing at all, except for when they light candles or go to shul. There are some families where the mother doesn't cover her hair and the married daughter does. There are differences even among those who wear hats or scarves. Some wear them all the time, some only when they go out of their own homes.

In my community, the Modern Orthodox, most of the women of my generation do not cover their hair. But it is also true that the numbers of younger women who cover their hair at marriage has increased over the past generation.

There are two associations with regard to women's head covering. One is that it is a sign of dignity; the other, that exposed hair is a sign of licentiousness. Each of these associations reflects the difference in rabbinic understanding of the Biblical law of the unfaithful wife. A married woman, charged with infidelity, was required to undergo an ordeal of bitter waters, during which the priest uncovered the woman's head.

From this law, and from other sources, it was commonly understood that proper Jewish women of the past went about with their hair covered, most likely with shawls or head veils. By the sixteenth century, Jewish women had begun to wear wigs, although not without a good deal of halachic controversy over the matter. In late medieval times, the custom arose in certain Chasidic communities for brides to shave their heads before covering them with a tichel, a head scarf. In the nineteenth century, as traditional Jews moved out of the ghetto, many of them began to follow general practice of leaving the hair uncovered. Others continued to wear wigs as an alternate way of maintaining modesty, yet look attractive.

Which brings us to a third commonly held understanding of why women cover the hair—that a married woman should not make herself attractive to anyone other than her husband. The assumption is that a wig is less attractive than one's own sensuous locks. But the wigs today are so beautiful that the "dowdy theory" is more rhetoric than real. Everyone knew this, which is why the majority of rabbis opposed wigs from the start. But happily asceticism is not a formidable characteristic of Judaism, so the women won out.

A little insider gossip. On the right are those who criticize the bareheaded married woman as being impious, errant. On the left are those who say that wigs are more attractive than most natural heads of hair and therefore the spirit of the law is being violated even as its letter is being kept. In my community, the modern

Orthodox, most of the women of my generation do not cover their hair except for shul and candlelighting. For my part, it does not bother me in the least to hear a beautiful wig-coiffed woman explain to me that a Jewish woman covers her hair so that she be less attractive to other men. A little inconsistency never hurt anyone; a little vanity is a sign of health; and there are occasions when the letter of the law, as one interprets law, is more appropriate to the human condition than the spirit of the law.

BLESSING NEW CLOTHES

Whatever it is that we wear, we are taught not to take it for granted. Upon dressing each morning, a Jew recites this blessing:

בָּרוּךְ אַתָּה יְיָ, אֱלֹהֵינוּ מֶלֶךְ הָעוֹלָם, מַלְבִּישׁ עֲרוּמִּים.

Baruch ata Adonai Elohainu melech ha'olam malbish arumim.

Blessed are You, Lord our God, Ruler of the universe, Who clothes the naked.

This is one of the Shacharit blessings; it was originally intended to be recited, as were the other morning blessings, at its appropriate moment—that is, when getting dressed. Gradually, however, all the morning blessings were grouped together as part of the formal prayer; thus, sometimes we tend to lose sight of the fact that we indeed thank God for clothing as we thank Him for food and shelter and for life restored each day.

The Malbish Arumim blessing is also recited when one wears a new article of clothing for the very first time. Like all firsts, we add a Shehecheyanu, thanking God for bringing us to this special moment (see p. 153). The only exception to this is when we buy shoes of leather. As on Yom Kippur, when we wear no leather on a day that we ask for life, similarly all the year through we refrain from reciting a blessing on the wearing of new shoes. Though, happily, we can put it out of our minds every day, at the moment of its newness we are reminded that leather shoes, after all, represent life that no longer exists.

SHATNEZ: THE LAW OF MIXED KINDS

Other than modesty, which is given wide latitude in interpretation, there is only one other restriction on clothing for a Jew. That is the law of *shatnez*. Shatnez is the Biblical injunction against wearing a garment made of a mixture of wool and linen. This is one of the laws of the Torah for which no reason is given, but rabbis throughout the ages have attempted to give their own explanations. The most logical ones refer back to Genesis in which each animal is described as being created "according to its own kind." In other words, there is a certain distinctiveness of species which must be preserved. The laws of mixed kinds, therefore, are meant to remind us not to violate this ecological integrity of nature. So even when we fling ourselves with abandon upon the racks of Barney's or Bloomingdale's, the laws of the Torah ad'dress' us there.

There are certain synagogues and independent laboratories which test garments for shatnez; that is, a shatnez expert will take apart the lapel of a woolen suit and test the interlining for linen. As in all other thou shalt nots, this law of shatnez is binding upon men and women alike.

TZITZIT

To some extent, the issue of "Jewish dress" is more relevant to men than to women. Only males are obligated to fulfill the mitzvah of tzitzit, the wearing of the ritual fringes.

The tzitzit garment is also known as a *tallit katan* (a small tallit) or *arba kanfot* (four corners). "Four corners" refers to the fact that the Bible requires the strings to be attached only to a garment that has four corners. As clothing changed and garments no longer had four corners, a special rectangular garment with four corners was created to be worn under the clothes so that males would carry this reminder with them all the time.

The difference between tzitzit (tallit katan) and a regular tallit is that the latter is a prayer shawl worn only at prayer time, while a pair of tzitzit (that is, one garment) is worn all through the day. Why day and not night? Find the clue in the Biblical passage quoted on page 190, or the answer on page 192.

To the uninitiated, tzitzit look like nothing more than strings. And so it is the amazing power of a religion to transform strings into something of much greater meaning. My favorite translation of tzitzit came from Moshe.

One summer, on a sandlot in Gloucester, Moshe was playing baseball with a group of boys from town, none of them Jewish. As he ran around the field, his tzitzit strings began to fly out from under his T-shirt. After the game, as the boys were finishing up and getting ready to leave, one of the townies asked Moshe, "What are those strings hanging out of your shirt?" Moshe, then fourteen, thought for a moment, grinned, and said, "Those are my soul threads."

The origin of those "soul threads" is Biblical: "And God spoke to Moses, saying, "Speak to the children of Israel and say it to them so that they shall make for themselves tzitzit on the corners of their garments throughout their generations . . . And you [the children of Israel] shall see them and shall remember all of the commandments of the Lord and observe them so that you do not go after your own heart and your own eyes to go lusting after them. So that you will remember to observe all of my commandments and become holy unto your God" (NUM. 15:37–40).

Very simple, very direct. The purpose of tzitzit, then, is to remind the wearer that he is commanded to live according to a special set of values. Like tefillin, tzitzit are a sign of the Covenant between God and the Jewish people.

Before donning the tzitzit in the morning, a man recites this blessing:

בָּרוּךְ אַתָּה יְיָ, אֱלֹהֵינוּ מֶלֶךְ הָעוֹלָם, אֲשֶׁר קִדְּשָׁנוּ בְּמִצְוֹתָיו, וְצִוָּנוּ עַל מִצְוַת צִיצִית.

Baruch ata Adonai Elohainu melech ha'olam asher kidshanu b'mitzvotav v'tzivanu al mitzvat tzitzit.

Blessed are You, Lord our God, Ruler of the universe, Who has sanctified us with His commandments and commanded us concerning the mitzvah of tzitzit.

This is what a pair of tzitzit looks like (one garment is called a pair):

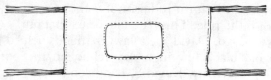

The garment is white, and generally made of cotton or poly-ester, although it can be made of any kosher material, in other words, not shatnez. (There ought to be a market for woolen tzitzit among energy-minded Jews in northern winter climes, but so far none exists.) The fringes are either white cotton, or white wool. The Biblical command was to use strings of sky-blue wool, a color that was used in the original Sanctuary; since we do not know what shade it was, the mitzvah is fulfilled with all-white fringes. Tzitzit can be purchased in a Jewish religious articles store or from the synagogue sexton. The fringes will be tied just so, as in the tallit, and there is a good deal of numerical symbol-ism in the manner of tying. The tzitzit garment is worn over an undershirt and under the regular shirt. In the religious neigh-borhoods in Israel, something very practical is sold, which I have yet to find in America: tzitzit undershirts. The bottom side seams of a regular undershirt are cut in a small inverted U to make a four-cornered garment through which the tzitzit fringes are looped and tied.

In contrast to the tallit, which is worn only by married men, tzitzit are worn by males of all ages. Long before the mandatory age—thirteen for all adult mitzvot—young boys begin wearing them. We started our sons on tzitzit when they were about four years old. If it is daytime, you can pretty safely bet that the fellow at the next desk wearing a kepah is also wearing tzitzit. But don't put a whole lot of money on it, because there are some few Jews who wear a kepah and not tzitzit. They consider themselves as having fulfilled the mitzvah of tzitzit through donning the prayer shawl for morning prayers. The blessing recited upon donning tallit is slightly different from the blessing over tzitzit. (See p. 158)

To say that the tzitzit garment is characteristically worn by

Orthodox Jewish males does not mean that individuals in other denominations don't wear them. However, in Conservative, Reconstructionist, or Reform Judaism, it is the exception, while in Orthodoxy it is the rule. This true tale bears that out:

Several years ago, David S., a lawyer friend, helped place an eleven-year-old black Jew in a day school in the borough of Queens, New York City. David S. had been active in an organization called Hatza'ad Harishon (The First Step), whose purpose was to help integrate America's black Jews, of whom there are a very small number, into Jewish community life. The child had formerly attended an Orthodox yeshiva in the Bronx, but now the family had moved to Forest Hills; the closest school was a Conservative day school. After a week, our friend called a colleague of his whose child attended the same school. In reply to David's question, the colleague said, yes, the new boy had been nicely received; in fact his son had come home after the first day and told his father all about the new student, adding, "And you know, Dad, we went to gym together and I learned something else about black kids. They wear strings under their shirts."

Clue: The Torah says, "And you shall see them." By daylight, it was possible to see them, but not by the dark of the night. Therefore, the rabbis ruled that the mitzvah of tzitzit is only by day.

Taking this one step further, there are those who have interpreted "And you shall see them" as meaning that they should be obvious to all, which is why some loop their tzitzit fringes through a belt loop or leave them hanging outside their clothes, so that they will be highly visible to all.

Women do not wear tzitzit. There is slight discussion of this issue in rabbinic literature; the conclusion is that women are exempt. The same reason given above with regard to fixed-time prayer applies here: women are exempt from time-bound positive commandments. Since tzitzit must be worn by day and not by night, the Rabbis placed it in the category of time-bound commandments. That categorization seems a bit overdrawn, I would say, but it achieved their general goal of distinguishing between male and female in certain mitzvot and of levying fewer distinctive ritual responsibilities on women. As a result, tzitzit came to be generally associated with a man's clothing. So, Orthodox women do not wear them. In the most authoritative medieval code of Jewish law, the *Shulchan Aruch*, we read, "A woman should not wear tzitzit because she should not try to outdo her husband" (THE LAWS OF TZITZIT 17:2). What does that mean to men and women of these times?

KEPAH

The kepah is another story altogether. Not Biblical in origin, not even Talmudic, it has taken on a whole life of its own. Most non-Orthodox Jews wear a kepah at prayer, but Orthodox Jews wear it all the time—indoors, outdoors, at work, on the campus, in the bank, and so forth. I even spotted one behind a desk recently in the bureaucratic labyrinths of New York's City Hall. Like a woman who sets her rings on the night table before retiring, and puts them on when she arises, so a man does his kepah. No matter what he does during the day (except perhaps nap or shower or swim), it hardly comes off his head.

But it wasn't always that way. I have observed the transformation of kepah, even in my own lifetime. Barely a generation ago, hardly any Jews wore one in the street. "Be a Jew in the home, be a man in the street" was the unspoken maxim. A hat or a cap? Yes. In fact, that was how you could smoke out an Orthodox Jew in a summer crowd. But what about proper etiquette? Orthodox Jews were also reasonably well-mannered, and that meant removing one's hat in the public indoors—an elevator, the theater, the public library, a college classroom. I remember, as a young girl, the time my father took me along to the Fort Lewis army base in Washington State to visit my twin uncles who were then U.S. marines. My father removed his hat without replacing it, as he always did, with his black rayon, slightly bepurpled yarmulke. I have never before seen him bareheaded and it startled me.

Gradually, I came to understand that inside public office buildings or places of business, my father and all of Seattle's Orthodox Jews did not wear their yarmulkes. But they weren't necessarily changing their stripes, either.

In the fifties, young men on dates, including Orthodox rabbinic students and ordained rabbis, were much less casual about wearing a kepah in public than their sons are today. I recall the various maneuverings by means of which they would try to be inconspicuous, yet remain faithful to Jewish law, such as slipping on a kepah in an ice-cream parlor to recite the blessing, then removing it while eating, or waiting until the theater darkened before putting it on. It wasn't that wearing a kepah was distasteful or disagreeable to them or presented a problem on ideological grounds; it was simply the social burden of being different, of sticking out in a crowd. In the fifties Orthodox Jews, like everyone else, wanted to look like the Pepsi generation: wearing a kepah just didn't jive.

It wasn't only the wearer who was affected by this "with it" psychology. My husband-to-be, ahead of his time in many things, wore his kepah all the time. With some retrospective shame, I remember the great discomfort I felt on our very first date, when he wore it through the entire Broadway musical *Silk Stockings*. Even though it was he and not I who was wearing the kepah, I was extremely self-conscious, and while I knew it wasn't right to ask him to "hide his religion," as I told my sister later, I sure as anything wished he would remove it so I could relax and enjoy myself. But today, wearing the kepah has become so perfectly natural. It is a sign of membership in a particular community, a sign of a singular commitment, and to the extent that it commands any special attention, it generally is one of respect, not derision.

The metamorphosis of the kepah in Orthodoxy reflects many things: the growing ethnicity in America, the general comeback of Orthodoxy after its decline in the thirties and forties, the influence of the post-Holocaust European immigration, the increasing Holocaust consciousness among Jews in general, Israel's Six Day War in 1967 and its freeing of young American Jews from the ghetto mentality of their parents, and the increasing desire for ritual and for overt expressions of identity and commitment.

Of late, the kepah has also become the symbol of the new social initiative of young women. Young women, some starting at age thirteen, crochet kipot (plural) for their boyfriends (as well as their fathers and brothers). I even know of one mother who felt bad for her fifteen-year-old son, the only boy in the crowd who didn't have a kepah crocheted by a female friend. So she quietly commissioned a white kepah with a border of green hearts and had it sent to him "from a secret admirer." The mother probably spoiled it for him for life: the boy, now twenty-one, is still fantasizing that some Jewish femme fatale will come up to him in a crowded room and disclose herself.

How is it that the kepah has become such a sensitive social and cultural barometer? The answer lies in the nonspecificity of the original laws, which has allowed great leeway in interpreting "covering the head." Earlier, I said its source wasn't to be found in the Talmud but that is only partly true. The Talmud does discuss headcovering, as a sign of piety and reverence, but it doesn't mandate a hat, kaffiah, or any other headdress popular in the Middle East at that moment in history. Even the word *kepah* (which means "dome") is a very late invention. By the end of the Middle Ages, the legal codes fleshed out a bit more the laws of covering one's head; still, nothing about the sizes, shapes, and exact laws of kepah wearing. As late as the eighteenth century, Elijah Gaon the great sage of Vilna, in his commentary on the *Shulchan Aruch*, assumes that headcovering is worn regularly only in synagogues.

Today, however, it has become firm and fast a mark of the Orthodox community. Even battle lines have been drawn around the kepah. For example, the large, black velvet yarmulke crowd looks down critically upon the small, finely crocheted, colorful kipot. I would venture to say that the large black yarmulkes signify Chasidic and right-wing Orthodoxy while the crocheted ones are a sign of the modern Orthodox Jew. A year ago, in the Dear Abby column of Jewish law (Dear Rabby??) of a right-wing, English-language Jewish newspaper, a young man wrote, explaining his plight: as part of a professional commitment, he was required to view a contemporary film being shown in the public theaters. Inasmuch as movies were off limits in his religious circle, he asked whether he should wear his yarmulke as always or remove it so as not to shed disgrace on his community. The answer: he should not go about bareheaded. Instead, he should substitute a crocheted kepah when going to the movies.

Internecine politics aside, the kepah takes on large overtones of identity and community. Sometimes, one must pay a price, for a kepah is like waving a red flag before a violent anti-Semite. Many Jewish youth have been beaten up for wearing one, and some street-wise Jews have learned to camouflage kipot when traveling in unsafe territory.

But there are also compensations; for example, on the coldest day of the year, we were to pick up J.J. at Madison Square Garden. We were fifteen minutes late, and I was upset at the thought of hatless J.J. standing there with his ears and toes freezing off. When he got into the car, I apologized. He said, "Oh, no, I was fine. Some nice man let me wait in his car." In a millisecond, all the weirdos of New York marched through my mind, and I began to chastise J.J. "Don't you know by now never to get into a stranger's car, even at your age?" "Oh, Ema," * said J.J., combining laughter and exasperation, as only a teenager talking to his mother can, "the man saw my kepah and called out my name [his Hebrew name is crocheted into the design] and asked me if I wanted to wait in a warm car. . . ."

When I see a kepah-hatted young man in a place where I expect to see none, such as driving a Greyhound bus out of Pittsburgh, the music hall at Oberlin College in Ohio, or at a lonely bus stop in the northeast Bronx, I feel a great sense of camaraderie. I am not in the habit of picking up strange men, but immediately I go over and strike up a conversation. We're part of the same family.

But it's not only family; nor is it only community and shared values. It's expectation. Underneath that crocheted kepah I expect to find something as beautiful as pure gold and as fine as the finest silk. A kepah says to me something about its wearer that we all long to say with a measure of surety about another human being—that there is a special person here, with decency, a good heart, a pureness of soul, and high ethical standards.

But that, too, is not all. The kepah has a kind of circular effect. Not only does its wearer bring to the kepah a whole set of values, rituals, and ethical precepts; it also places upon him an immediate sense of responsibility. In that respect, the kepah achieves what the tzitzit was intended to achieve: to remind the wearer that he must act in a manner that befits the kepah. We call this

---

* Hebrew for mother.

Kiddush Hashem (sanctification of God's name)—by living a certain way we give testimony to God's teachings.

THE CHAI AND THE JEWISH STAR

The chai and the Jewish star (Magen David) are worn increasingly by Jews all over the world. Neither has its origin in tradition, but they carry much of the symbolism of the tzitzit and kepah. In effect, these symbols say, "I am a Jew, a member of the covenantal people, and I'm proud of my identity." They also say to another Jew, "Here I am." Clearly, a chai or Magen David is a statement of membership in the community. Every Magen David is a witness to the existence of the Jewish people, and therefore, to the existence of God. You might think you're just wearing a piece of jewelry, but in fact you are giving testimony. And who knows but that in a millennium or two, these symbols will be described as "ancient, hallowed tradition. . . ."

CHAPTER • 7

SPEECH

In contrast to the handful of regulations regarding dress, there is a plethora of rules concerning speech. The laws about honesty, authenticity, and integrity of speech are at least as extensive as, say, the laws of kashrut.

And this is exactly as it should be, for speech is the primary medium of human interaction. If eyes are mirrors of the soul, then speech is the echo of character. Speech is not the whole of human ethics, but it is a good part. So a plethora of laws about speech is perfectly in order.

A Jew is forbidden to insult, shame, defame, embarrass, or slander another person. The Hebrew for gossip—*lashon hara*—literally means "the evil tongue." Lashon hara includes not only the speaker of evil, but also the hearer of evil; the theory is that the consumer, the one who listens to gossip/slander and thereby creates the market for it, is as guilty as the purveyor of the rotten goods. The Rabbis went so far as to disallow praise of a third person before his enemies. They understood quite rightly that it would provoke negative comments.

The Talmud paints a most graphic picture: deceiving is equated to stealing; insulting is analogous to killing. How so? When a person is insulted, he/she blanches. It is as if the culprit has drawn blood from his victim's face.

A Jew is forbidden to curse, utter profanity, swear falsely, or lie. Bearing false witness is a sin, but no more so than holding back from bearing true witness. A Jew who has witnessed evil may not say, "I don't want to get involved."

The spoken word must be authentic. We may not say one thing and mean another. Insincere flattery is worse than no flattery at all. The promise of a gift that one knows beforehand will not be accepted is a travesty.

It is only in the context of authenticity and appropriateness that one can understand the strict line the Rabbis toed on blessings. Not only must every blessing be specific to the object for which we bless God, but one may not recite a blessing that is not required. There are all sorts of halachot about what to do if an inauthentic blessing has been begun or completed. But why such rabbinic stringency on this issue? What's the difference if we make one more blessing? So what if we don't eat the fruit? Does it really matter to God? Why were the Rabbis so concerned to protect the Almighty from a superfluous blessing? One reason is that we are forbidden to take God's name in vain. But equally important, we are taught not to make utterances that are not authentic and not appropriate to the norms and expectations of community. The sensitivity and caution we exercise when we speak to God are applied to all manner of speech.

A word should be as good as an oath. No, it should be better than an oath; oaths and personal vows were strongly discouraged by the Rabbis. ("Let your yes be a yes and your no be a no" was not original to Christianity.) A Jew may not go back on his/her word. Every Jewish child grows up with tales of "trustworthies," ethical heroes whose word or handshake was more reliable than any document signed in blood or witnessed in a court of law. "Be faithful to what issues from your lips," says the Torah.

But Torah and tradition didn't stop there. What is it that leads to inauthentic, debased, or evil speech? An impious heart. Therewith the commandments of the heart:

Do not harbor resentment.
Do not be overcome with jealousy.
Do not seek revenge.
Do not bear a grudge.
Do not hate your brother in your heart.

What an incredible Torah! A commandment not to harbor a grudge. Not surprising, the laws of speech—and of the heart—like the laws of eating and of sex, are part of the holiness code.

But! Can human beings live by it? Who has not felt a tide of resentment rise within? Who has not been momentarily consumed by jealousy, nursed a grudge, relieved hostility with a well-placed barb, idled in a moment's delicious gossip? Besides, many of these ill feelings are altogether normal. A human being with no anger, no envy, no pride, no hurt is a saint—and saints come few and far between. Surely it is easier to live within the parameters of kashrut than it is to live by the Biblical and rabbinic definition of holiness of speech and purity of emotion.

Some very large questions arise then. Given the general adherence to halacha on the part of the Orthodox Jewish community, how does an Orthodox Jew relate to these laws? Are the laws concerning speech reduced to guidelines, while the laws about sex are immutable and inviolable? Is it true about some Jews—that what goes into the mouth has become an exact science, and what comes out a random matter? If a little gossip, envy, resentment, and false flattery are perfectly normal responses of normal human beings, what could the Torah possibly have had in mind when it said, "Thou shalt not harbor a grudge"? Can human beings master those emotions?

And finally. Are traditional Jews really any different in matters of speech? Do they gossip less? Do they tell fewer white lies? Are they truer to their word? Is the speech of their teenagers less peppered with profanities?

Many of these questions must remain open-ended; one can offer neither harsh indictment nor pious self-congratulations, for both would be false. And both would be true. Global answers obviously are not the key. Perhaps one should not even ask some of these questions. Perhaps we should leave the murky areas alone, and simply consider the laws in a vacuum. Yet, having asked . . .

Clearly, the Torah intended to elevate individual and community to a certain level of holiness, or at least a notch or two above the ordinary. Yes, the law says to us, it is possible to control speech and, to some extent, master feelings. Yes, it is possible to take oneself in hand and give special direction to the skills of communication. At the very least, hostile behavior must be held in check.

The Rabbis were quite realistic in their interpretation of these laws of the Torah. They understood normal human passions very well. Therefore, they defined commandments of the heart in terms of overt action. Okay, so you can't flush hatred or envy out of your heart. But you can control how it is spent. For example, not to harbor a grudge meant something like this in the Talmud: if you ask to borrow from your neighbor and he refuses, but the next day he comes and asks to borrow your ax, you must lend it to him (for otherwise that would be revenge), and you may not say, "Here, take it, because I'm not like you who did not lend to me . . ." (YOMA 23A). The Rabbis also understood that actions bring the heart around and not the reverse. . . .

Underlying much of halacha, although not always explicit, are notions of self-discipline and sublimation. In this respect, Judaism runs counter to the psychology of "let it all hang out": let hostile emotions be expressed as freely as loving ones. Judaism would say, if you hate your neighbor, or your brother, you just better well keep it in check; you may not say everything is permitted. Many years ago, a well-known singer-actress, who was then on her way up, was interviewed by a popular magazine. She told the interviewer how she couldn't stand her mother and her sister, how frumpy and stupid they were. I was then a student of psychology, a recent graduate of adolescence, and not unaware of the somewhat universal elements of mother-daughter friction. But this! In print! A million readers! I felt pained for her mother. Although I'm certain this star has become more judicious in her interviews and I'm sure she supports her mother and sister in regal style, as I listen to her sing, I somehow cannot entirely forget that old association.

As in all things that we do as individuals rather than in concert, the law speaks more forcefully to some than to others. Some Jews have made a personal crusade of extreme watchfulness of their own speech, taking the laws of speech as law. At the other extreme are those who spend half their days in malicious gossip or outright deceit. It is simply a fact that individuals will locate themselves at every single point along the speech-holiness continuum.

Still, I believe there are some differences in the community as a whole. Given that Orthodox Jews experience the same range of human passions, loves, hates, tender spots, and weaknesses, the modal response of the community nevertheless is to be more rather than less sensitive to speech—to matters of honesty, authenticity, and goodwill. While it is difficult to know always what people really feel inside, what comes out is measurable, quantifiable, and quite open to comparison. Judging overt speech, yes, the communal center of gravity is shifted closer to the holiness pole than would be the case for any random group of people. This should be true for any highly structured religious community. Or looking at it another way—for the most part, Orthodox Jews are probably not much different from other decent, well-intentioned, goodwilled people; what is significant is that most of the community's members fall into these categories. This distinctiveness shows up in four ways:

1. Relative ratio of "good" speech to "bad" speech
2. Awareness
3. Guilt
4. Determination

Note similarity of 2, 3, and 4 to the processes of teshuvah (see p. 312).

1. How often is our speech debased or vulgar; how often do evil thoughts and words get the best of us; what percentage of oral energy is expended in deceit, lies, slander; how often do we engage in mean speech? I would submit: for the Orthodox community as a whole, less often than ordinary.

2. To what extent do we observe our speech patterns? The Biblical commandment "Watch what issues from your lips" is generally translated as "Keep your word," but it also means, literally, "Watch, monitor, observe, be aware of your own speech." Sometimes I have that sensation, in the midst of telling a white lie, or listening with full attention to a piece of gossip, that there is a part of me standing outside of myself, standing on the sidelines so to speak, monitoring this fault of character. Even as I rationalize away a lie, or an insult, I still know what I'm really doing. When I tell the children to answer the phone and say I'm not home, I am aware that I am teaching them a dishon-

est mode of response. It doesn't matter that I can rationalize this as less insulting to the caller than to have them say, "I am sorry, my mother is busy right now." I know I am teaching them weakness and not strength.

3. If we are unable to overcome the passion for inflicting pain through the use of words, at least we do not delude or defend ourselves. We know we are guilty. We understand that gossip and lies not only hurt another but are essentially evil.

4. We make some determination—sometimes once a year, sometimes continuously—to improve on the quality of stuff that issues from our lips.

How is the message about more pure speech reinforced and what makes it work?

One answer is the power of the sources. There is barely any traditional text, ancient or modern, that doesn't deal with the theme of purity of speech. If one read nothing more than the Torah each year, chapter by chapter, the message would come pounding through. Three times a day, in the closing prayer of the Shmoneh Esreh, we say, "My God, guard my tongue from speaking evil and my lips from speaking falsehood. Let my soul be silent to those who curse me . . ." (But it works two ways. In the same prayer we also ask, "As for those who plot evil against me, thwart their efforts and frustrate their intentions.") Even if only once a month or once a season that prayer makes a dent in the armor around the heart, that is something!

Jews had self-improvement books centuries before they hit the best-seller lists. What we tend to look upon as pious literature was really the articulation of a "pull-your-ethical-self-up-by-your-bootstraps" approach to life. And much of it worked.

A classic text which has had an impact on the life of every Jew who studies it, and which is taught in most yeshiva high schools, is one devoted entirely to the subject of the evil and false tongue. Its author was Rabbi Yisrael Meir Hakohen, also known as the Chofetz Chayyim. He was a nineteenth-century halachist who wanted to set forth the laws of human speech in as consistent a manner as the laws of Shabbat. Whenever I meet someone who tells me he/she is studying that book, I know that he/she is in the process of transformation.

I came to know this work, *Shemirat Halashon (The Speech*

Watch), at a relatively young age, when I was a student in junior high school. Some friends and I were party to an episode that left its painful mark for several years thereafter. There was a girl in our class who wanted to be in our clique. We didn't respond to her overtures, we didn't bring her in, we didn't include her in our sorties. Let her run with another pack, we said. Only, there wasn't another pack. It was a small school. Five in the clique meant there were another four outside of it, but not enough to pull together like the insider group. Came September of eighth grade, and the girl didn't show up. Her mother told the principal, who told us more than once, that she didn't return to our yeshiva because of the way our clique had mistreated her. In later years, I began to think that might not have been all there was to it, but for the long meanwhile I would periodically smart with shame whenever I would remember her. At any rate, our principal assigned us a few pages to study in this special book. It was well beyond our level, so he taught it to us himself. In those few pages, it seemed as if the Chofetz Chayyim had been watching us the whole year, describing every action of this clique of thirteen-year-olds.

A second answer is the power of models. Not just distant models or historical figures to whom the later commentators have attached saintly characteristics, but rather immediate and very available human models. I never heard my parents use a profane word. Nor did I hear them gossip, slander, or curse anybody. Very occasionally, my mother would try out a bit of harmless gossip, but my father gave no satisfaction. If anything, he would defend, so there was never any mileage nor anything an impressionable child could sink her teeth into. Nor did my husband hear his parents gossip or use mean speech. Thus, when we married and had our own family, we simply didn't gossip in front of the children.

It's not that we don't talk about people in front of the children. Of course we do. But there is a real difference between news and gossip, and though it may be hard to define this difference, it is quickly learned. When Deborah, who is friendly to everyone, comes home and reports that on the avenue she met so-and-so and he/she "is such a nice person," I know I've succeeded in some small measure—for I don't particularly care for so-and-so. When our children report some misdeed at school, and we ask,

"Who did it?" and they refuse to tell on the grounds that it would be lashon hara, we know that even though the underlying reason might well be peer solidarity, nevertheless it signifies that they are beginning to make distinctions in their own speech.

Third is the frontal approach, parents directly instructing their children. Example alone is not sufficient, for the example set by peers is often more compelling. Forthright intervention and discipline are often required.

As each of our lovely, well-bred children entered yeshiva high school, for example, their vocabularies suddenly enlarged to include words that were unprintable barely a decade ago. We told them this kind of language was neither clever nor cool, as they might think it to be. It was—vulgar. Even though some of their nice friends might speak that way, it was still vulgar, no matter who used that language, and it was unacceptable to us under any circumstance. To their argument that these words don't mean anything, we would counter with, "There are other ways to express anger and disgust." We would say, "This is not how a member of an Orthodox Jewish family speaks; it is not nice for a yeshiva bocher; it is a sign of poor breeding, undignified . . ." Finally, I would pull out the last stop, which Yitz would never permit me to use, but which I used on the qt because it was so effective: "It is unbefitting a son/daughter of Rabbi Greenberg. . . ."

My brother-in-law used a different tack with his daughter, when she began to pepper her speech with f's and b's. She also happened to be studying Hebrew at the time. Her father said to her, "Look, Judy, you're going to have to make a choice. You can't use the same mouth to speak both the holy tongue and foul language." Her mother tried a different tack, "All his life," she said of her deceased father, "Grandpa spoke only words of Torah or Talmud. He loved you so much and was so proud of you. For the granddaughter of Rabbi Eliahu Chaim to debase her speech in this manner . . ."

Something similar must be going on in other traditional homes. I began to realize that the friends whom I remember as setting a poor example for David and J.J. a year or two back have also cleaned up their language. The frontal approach, I suspect, is quite widely used.

Community must surely reinforce values learned through

family. To confirm my feeling that there is a difference in quality of speech among Orthodox Jews, I donned my most unscientific hat and placed myself on two consecutive afternoons of the week in two different pizza parlors in the same neighborhood: one kosher, closed on the Sabbath, and generally catering to the yeshiva crowd; the other a regular pizza joint. "Reading" my newspaper, sipping a Coke, and sort of blending into the background as the neighborhood young people came in after school, I listened.

I heard what I thought I would hear. Clearly, the language of adolescents who inhabit a kosher pizza parlor is less vulgar and easier on the ears of an adult than the language of their less-traditional counterparts. And while vulgarities of speech might mean nothing at all to its utterer—as one would conclude simply by noting its frequency—nevertheless it is disconcerting.

Speech is not only a sign of character; for a Jew, it is also a symbol of faithfulness, a human response to the divine calling to be holy, to be part of a holy community.

Holiness of speech is not merely what we refrain from saying. Holiness is not silence or curtailing communication. The ascetics (nezirim), who took upon themselves vows of silence, were never significant models in Jewish tradition.

Holiness also means what you do in general with the gift of speech. If we are to spend less energy on lies, deceits, insults, and vulgarities, how do we fill the time? Tradition teaches that whenever three persons gather together they should speak some words of Torah. Similarly, at a meal, where conversation is as important as food, there should be some words of Torah—a dvar Torah (although the Rabbis said that, for health reasons, people should not talk while there is food in their mouths). Some families do have a dvar Torah regularly at mealtime. Some do so at Shabbat meals; others, at organizational meetings, luncheons, and dinners.

Speech is a reflection of faith in another way. Many Orthodox Jews, when talking about the future or about their current or past situation, will include such phrases as, "thank God" ("Baruch Hashem"), "with the help of God" ("B'Ezrat Hashem"), and "God willing" ("Im Yirtzeh Hashem"). The familiar "Baruch Hashem," thank God, is often used by itself as shorthand answer to the questions, "How are you?" or "How is the family?" Not merely pious platitudes, they are profound reflections of the spiritual baggage a person carries around all the time in the innermost recesses of his or her soul: somehow we know that everything is in the hands of God, that healthy children are a gift, and good fortune comes because God wills it, that there are a thousand hitches that could foul up the trip we plan four months hence, that we get through every day by virtue of miracles. It is not pessimism or fear—it is realism and faith—and it comes through in a mere turn of speech.

Recently, a professor, an Orthodox Jew who generally tends to have a critical eye, commented to me how disgusted he was when he overheard the men standing at the back of his shul one Shabbat morning, discussing whether digital watches were okay to wear on Shabbat. "Ugh!" he said. "They're so legalistic and petty." "Would it be better," I asked him, "if they were discussing this one's divorce (gossip), or that one's greed (slander), or the stock market (inappropriate in shul on Shabbat)?" Of course, Orthodox Jews discuss those things, too, but to leaven it with conversation of a halachic nature, to deflect from the passion for gossip or the consuming nature of envy is not bad at all.

To an extent, that back-of-the-shul scene points up how it all hangs together. Not only the thou shalt nots regarding speech, but everything else in the Torah, has bearing on speech and ethics. For each person, the ritual expression, the concern with halacha, the construction of holiness in so many areas of life have impact on so private and personal a matter as speech. Once again, we find it to be a system of vast, deep, and intricate interconnections.

CHAPTER 8

MEZUZAH: SYMBOL OF A JEWISH HOUSEHOLD

A Jewish household is created by the people who live in it—by the way they act, the things they do and don't do, the beliefs they hold. To a great extent, a Jewish way of life is a portable faith: you can take it with you anywhere you go. This is true for Shabbat, kashrut, Taharat Hamishpachah, daily prayer, and study of Torah.

It is generally accepted that Judaism as a religion is more oriented to holiness of time than holiness of place. There are many occasions we sanctify, but very few places we call holy.

Is that the whole truth? Not at all, for the very place in which we live, our permanent residence, is sanctified. This is achieved through a very concrete ritual, through the mitzvah of mezuzah.

Mezuzah is of Biblical origin and therefore carries great weight. "And you shall inscribe them on the doorposts (mezuzot) of your house and on your gates" (DEUT. 6:9, 11:20). What is to be inscribed? Divine instruction is very clear: "The words that I tell you this day": that you shall love your God, believe only in Him, keep His commandments, and pass all of this on to your children.

Thus, a mezuzah has come to refer also to the parchment, or klaf, on which the verses of the Torah are inscribed (DEUT. 6:4–

9; 11:13–21). Mezuzah refers as well to the case or container in which the parchment is enclosed. A mezuzah serves two functions: every time you enter or leave, the mezuzah reminds you that you have a covenant with God; second, the mezuzah serves as a symbol to everyone else that this particular dwelling is constituted as a Jewish household, operating by a special set of rules, rituals, and beliefs.

Before describing the ritual of affixing a mezuzah, let us examine some of its attendant laws:

The klaf must be hand-lettered by a kosher scribe—one who is observant of halacha and who qualifies for the task. The case or container, on the other hand, has no special requirements. It can be purchased or homemade; it can be of any size or shape or material. The scroll is rolled up from left to right so that when it is unrolled the first words appear first. The scroll is inserted into the container but should not be permanently sealed because twice in seven years the parchment should be opened and inspected to see if any of the letters have faded or become damaged.

A mezuzah should be fixed to the doorpost of every living space in the house, not just the entrance door. Any room that has two doorposts and an overhead lintel requires a mezuzah. There is some difference of opinion as to whether an arched opening with no door and no posts require a mezuzah, so one should check with a rabbi. Bathrooms, closets, laundry room, boiler room, and so forth, however, do not require a mezuzah.

The mezuzah should be put up as soon as possible after moving in, and not later than thirty days. A temporary residence, that is, a place we reside in for less than thirty days, doesn't require a mezuzah; nor does an office or place of business. A dormitory room, which a student considers a home away from home, should have a mezuzah.

When a family moves it should not remove its mezuzot from the doorpost if it knows that another Jewish family will be moving in subsequently. (If the case is a valuable one, one can substitute another case, but the klaf should remain.) If one knows that a Gentile family is to follow in that place of abode, the mezuzot should be removed, lest they be considered useless and thrown away.

The mezuzah is affixed to the right side of the door as one enters a room. In other words, if your door swings open from hallway into bedroom, the mezuzah would be nailed to the right-hand doorpost as you face the bedroom from the hall. This is so no matter whether the doorknob is on the right- or left-hand side. It should be placed at the lower part of the top third of the doorpost, which is generally about eyeball height for a six-foot-tall person. It is affixed at a slant, with the lower part of the container toward you as you face the right doorpost. A mezuzah contains God's name and therefore great pains are taken to see that it doesn't fall. The case must be securely attached at top and bottom rather than hanging by a nail from the top of the mezuzah. If the doorpost is too narrow to affix the mezuzah on a slant, it can be attached vertically, but still must be nailed or glued at top and bottom.

Women are equally obligated in the mitzvah of mezuzah and can perform this mitzvah for the entire household. If children are old enough to understand and to perform this mitzvah, it is a nice idea to have them put up the mezuzah on the doorpost of their bedroom.

The ritual for affixing a mezuzah is very brief and very simple, especially so considering its enduring nature.

Mezuzah in hand, one recites this blessing:

בָּרוּךְ אַתָּה יְיָ, אֱלֹהֵינוּ מֶלֶךְ הָעוֹלָם אֲשֶׁר

קִדְּשָׁנוּ בְּמִצְוֹתָיו, וְצִוָּנוּ לִקְבּוֹעַ מְזוּזָה.

Baruch ata Adonai Elohainu melech ha-olam asher kidshanu b'mitzvotav v'tzivanu likboa mezuzah.

Blessed are You, Lord our God, Ruler of the universe, who has sanctified us with His commandments and commanded us to affix a mezuzah.

All those standing about answer Amen.

Immediately, the mezuzah is nailed or glued to the right doorpost.

That's it—a thirty-second ritual that lasts the lifetime of tenure in that place. . . .

A newly married couple will do this upon moving into their apartment. I'm not sure what the origin or meaning of carrying the bride over the threshold is, but this is at least its Jewish equivalent. To the new couple it says, we are building a Jewish home together.

CHANUKAT HABAYIT

You don't have to get married to put up a mezuzah. It can be done anytime there is a doorpost without one.

Often, when a family moves into a new house, it will celebrate the event with family and friends. The celebration, of which the central part is the ceremony of the mezuzah, is known as a *chanukat habayit*, which means "dedication of the house."

The reader will notice the same word is used for dedicating a house as was used for dedicating the Holy Temple after the Maccabean victory.

Since the mezuzah ceremony is so simple, many people expand it by adding special readings, a dvar Torah, singing and dancing, and—always an accompaniment of a mitzvah that marks another milestone in life—a nice repast.

One final word about the symbolic status of a mezuzah. The parchment is inscribed on only one side. On its reverse side, only one word appears, Shaddai, one of the names used for God. When the scroll is rolled properly, the Shaddai is facing the eye. The letters of Shaddai, shin, daled, yod are also the initials of the phrase *shomer delatot yisrael*, the Guardian of the doors of Israel.

Partly as a result of this lettering, partly because some people naturally tend toward superstitition, the mezuzah sometimes has been accorded the status of amulet, a magical charm. Not only in medieval cultures but even in our day, some would attribute or explain misfortune as linked to the lack of kosher mezuzot.

A mezuzah is not meant to be a protective device, nor lack thereof a source of direct punishment. A mezuzah is a sign and reminder of the Covenant, of our love and commitment and our willingness to create a Jewish household. That, in itself, is sufficient!

PART TWO

Special
Stages
of Life

CHAPTER 9

MARRIAGE

It always has been that way. In Jewish tradition, one who doesn't marry is considered an incomplete person. Marriage, not celibacy, is the higher form of existence. Sex outside of marriage is forbidden, while sex within marriage is seen as a positive human expression, not only for procreation but also for pleasure. Marriage is considered a sanctification. It is no coincidence that the word for marriage, kiddushin, is derived from the root word, kadosh, holiness. One partner, set aside, consecrated to the other.

What about the 1980s, when a singles or divorce life-style is more common than not? What about today, when no group is insulated from broader cultural values? Still, traditional Jews remain avowedly committed to marriage. Happily, singles and divorced persons are no longer considered pariahs as they once were in the traditional community. Happily, too, they nevertheless remain the exceptions.

Many factors come into play: traditional notions of marriage are but one part of a much larger system of traditional values; ritual and rite, keyed to celebration in units of family, naturally reinforce the desire to marry; and, perhaps most of all, the taboos on premarital sex help push young people with healthy drives toward finding a proper mate and marrying. In consequence, while the average marriage age for women in America has advanced several years during the past decade, Orthodox women still tend to marry in their early twenties.

Given a strong commitment to marriage, for our children and ourselves, there are a hundred things we can do to broaden the circle of friends of similar backgrounds from which to seek a suitable mate: schools, camps, and tours sponsored by Orthodox Jewish organizations; spending the Jewish holidays at a hotel that caters to a clientele with shared values; asking friends and relatives of all ages to suggest possible dates/mates; arranging blind dates and parties. In other words, while it is all quite low-key and discreet, the dating game is a purposeful endeavor with the goal of marriage clearly in mind. There is no embarrassment, for it is a mitzvah not only to marry but also to make a match.

The Midrash tells of a Roman matron who asked Rabbi Jose bar Halafta, a defender of the faith, what his God had been doing since the six days of creation. The rabbi replied that God had been busy as a matchmaker, spending time finding appropriate life mates for His earthly creatures. The Roman woman replied derisively, "That is His occupation? Why, I can match thousands in an hour." She lined up one thousand of her female slaves and one thousand of her male slaves and married them to one another. The next day, they returned to her with all sorts of wounds, bruises, and broken bones. Not one was satisfied with the mate she had chosen for him or her. Graciously, she called for Rabbi Jose bar Halafta and said to him, "Indeed your Torah is true and beautiful." Rabbi Jose bar Halafta said, "Though it looks easy to make a match, even for God it is as difficult as splitting the Red Sea."

Most modern Orthodox choose their own mates, but the shadchan (matchmaker) is beginning to have a bit of a comeback. Shadchanim were widely used to arrange marriages in Europe and have long been used by Chasidic and more traditional Jews in this country. Nowadays, some of them are beginning to update the trade to meet the needs of modern youth. What with society so highly atomized, the services of a good shadchan are at least as good as a good computer dating service. No one says you have to marry the shadchan's first choice! The point of it all is that if a community is committed to the idea of marriage for its young, it will find a way.

THE ENGAGEMENT PERIOD

Engagement used to be formalized by t'naim, the signing of a legal document which stipulated certain conditions: that the two parties were obligated to keep their commitment of marriage, the financial resources or possessions each party would bring to the marriage, the responsibilities of each family to the other, and the penalties to be paid were either side to break off the engagement. Breaking t'naim was considered a disgraceful act by the initiator, and a humiliation to the rejected party. Through time, as modern values won out and romantic choice became the more dominant motive, t'naim were postponed until right before the wedding ceremony. In effect, t'naim became a mere formality. Nowadays, if an Orthodox couple breaks an engagement, it's like any other informal civil act. There are no community sanctions. Despite what they say about girls and diamonds, the ring is always returned.

The engagement period is the time for the mechutanim, the in-laws, to meet each other to plan the wedding and discuss the financial responsibilities of each. It used to be widely held, and largely still is, that the bride's family absorbs all the cost of the wedding except for liquor, flowers, and the photographer. This was based on the premise that the husband (and his family) would be supporting the newlyweds' household for the rest of their lives. What with women working and sharing the breadwinning roles until children arrive, and often afterward, and with both husband and wife being supported by both families through school, some parents have begun to divide the wedding costs more evenly. Whatever arrangements are made, parents are generally careful to settle things amicably so as not to put undue stress on the new couple, or, as it is widely referred to in Jewish circles, not to "fashter the simcha" (take the joy out of the occasion).

Choosing a wedding date must not only mesh with the desires of the couple, their parents, the rabbi who will perform the ceremony, the availability of the synagogue or wedding hall, and the caterer's schedule; it must also satisfy two other criteria. One is easy to determine: the dates of the Jewish calendar when weddings are permitted. Weddings are not permitted during Sefirat

Ha'Omer—the period of quasi mourning between Passover and Shavuot—in memory of the Hadrianic persecutions of Palestinian Jews in the second century. The major exception within this seven-week stretch is Lag B'Omer, the thirty-third day of the Omer on which the persecutions ceased. Lag B'Omer is a popular wedding day. Israel Independence Day and Jerusalem Reunification Day, which fall in this period, have been accepted by the Israeli rabbinate and by some in the American Orthodox rabbinate as festive days which also break the period of quasi mourning and during which weddings are permitted. Weddings may also be held on the three days prior to Shavuot. Weddings are not permitted during the three weeks leading up to Tisha B'Av, which is a period of mourning for the destruction of the Temple in 586 B.C.E. and 70 C.E.

Fortunately, that leaves most of June, plus all the other days of the year, except, of course, Shabbat, holidays, and fast days. There is a tradition to hold the wedding on a Tuesday, if possible, because it is considered a day of good fortune. Of that day in the creation cycle, God said of His work not once but twice, "And it was good" (GEN. 1:10,12).

The second criterion in finding a date has to do with a woman's menses. Given the fact that an Orthodox woman is likely to be a virgin at marriage, the rupture of the hymen will make her a niddah: four days count for blood flow (a dispensation from the usual minimum of five) plus seven white days during which husband and wife must separate sexually. Thus, a young couple will try to time their marriage toward the end of her monthly cycle, just before the onset of menstruation; otherwise, she will be niddah twice consecutively in one month, which isn't the most pleasant way to start one's married life. Most Orthodox women keep some track of their periods before setting a wedding date. It doesn't have to be discussed with the entire world, but a couple will arrive at a convenient date and everyone will work around it.

A Jewish wedding consists of a religious ceremony followed by a seudat mitzvah. A seudat mitzvah, sometimes translated as a religious feast, is a festive meal with which we celebrate the performance of certain mitzvot, such as Brit, Bar or Bat Mitzvah, completing a tractate of Talmud, and, of course, a wedding.

No special foods are required, except that it must begin with the blessing over bread and conclude with the Birkat Hamazon, the Grace.

The ceremony can take place anywhere, the seudat mitzvah can be formal, informal, catered, homemade, simple or lavish, so there is great leeway. Lists of kosher caterers and wedding halls, Jewish party planners, music bands, calligraphers, and printers are all available through synagogues, the national Jewish organizations, how-to books, and best of all, through the grapevine.

Invitations are always sent out in Hebrew and English, including the Hebrew date and the Hebrew names. Whether or not the costs are shared, the invitation goes out in the name of both parents: Estelle and Benjamin Schwartz and Dr. Chaim and Sarah Gold take pleasure in inviting you to the marriage of their children, Dena and Daniel . . .

The ketubah, the marriage contract, should be secured in advance of the wedding. It is filled in just prior to the ceremony. A standard ketubah form can be purchased in a religious articles store or can be drawn by hand. The ketubah is an ancient legal document, dating back to the second or third century B.C.E. This marriage contract is read aloud at the ceremony and is presented by the groom to his bride under the wedding canopy.

In medieval Europe, it was the custom among wealthy Jews to commission a special hand-lettered, illuminated ketubah. This has become the vogue again today. Many couples commission a ketubah or do it themselves if they have artistic ability. An illuminated ketubah is often given as a gift from friends. Unlike most other religious documents, such as mezuzah or Torah scroll, the ketubah need not be written by a scribe, nor on parchment. The standard text can be written well before the wedding date, but the details of date, place, and name are left blank to be filled in immediately prior to the ceremony. After the ceremony, these ketubot often are framed as works of art in the newlyweds' home. Since Jewish law requires that a husband and wife not live together unless they have their ketubah, and since it would be a little awkward to take along a thirty-by-forty-inch ketubah under glass when they go off to Aruba, many couples also have prepared a smaller, commercially printed ketubah for travel purposes, which is often kept in the suitcase to avoid last-minute searches.

During the engagement period, some couples prepare a special chuppah for their wedding. The chuppah is a canopy, under which they will be married (and if specially made for them will probably later adorn the walls of their bedroom). The bride's family often purchases a tallit for the groom, and that can also serve as the chuppah, held aloft on four poles or handheld staves. The bride will often buy or make for him a tallit bag as well. Beautiful hand-woven taleitim (plural) are available from special weavers. If she is handy, the bride might also crochet a special kepah for her husband just for the wedding. All of these items take on dual meaning as religious articles and as gifts of love.

Sometime before the wedding, the young couple will visit the rabbi for a chat. Even if he knows them, he will nevertheless ascertain (1) that they were born of Jewish mothers or converted according to halacha, (2) if either were previously divorced, that a proper Jewish divorce had been arranged. The rabbi will also determine that they do not fall into other categories of forbidden marriages according to Jewish law. For example: a Kohen may not marry a divorcée or proselyte; a woman who has committed adultery and has been divorced may not marry the adulterer; a woman may not marry less than three months after the death of, or divorce from her husband, so that there may be no question of paternity. These can be painful situations. In such cases, an Orthodox rabbi will not sanction the marriage. If the partners are committed to traditional Judaism, they will not marry. Other Jews might likely seek a rabbi from one of the liberal denominations or will marry in a civil ceremony.

The rabbi will also discuss the details of setting up a kosher home, observing mikvah, Shabbat, birth control, and the like. The more sensitive rabbis will also engage the couple in a discussion of what marriage should be like, what their expectations of each other are, and how to commit themselves to each other so that the inevitable impasses do not become overwhelming hurdles. One of the problems of having a family member or a close friend officiate at a wedding is that he cannot always discuss these things in a way that an outsider can without embarrassment.

ONE WEEK TO GO

Before the wedding day, three things take place: the ufruf of the groom, the mikvah immersion of the bride, and the week-long prewedding separation from each other.

The ufruf, calling up the groom to the Torah for an aliyah, takes place on the Shabbat before the wedding. Some grooms read the portion of their aliyah as well. Oftentimes, as soon as the groom completes the Torah blessings, friends and relatives from the women's section will shower him with candy, or nuts and raisins wrapped in small packages tied with white ribbon. In many synagogues, the congregation will sing a mazel-tov song after his aliyah. The ufruf is sometimes held a week earlier than the last Shabbat before the wedding. This is done for convenience or so that the bride can also attend the ufruf. If it is to be held on the Shabbat immediately preceding the wedding—during the period of separation of bride and groom—her parents might attend the ufruf, but she will spend a quiet Shabbat at home, attended by siblings and/or close friends.

A few days before the marriage, the bride goes to the mikvah, attended by her mother. Sephardic Jews make a party out of it, but with Ashkenazim it is strictly a quiet mother-daughter affair. A bride-to-be can go to the mikvah during the day; however, a special appointment must be made, for the mikvah is not ordinarily open in the daytime.

A week before the wedding, the couple will take leave of each other. They will not see each other until the badeken, the veil ceremony that takes place right before the processional. But that doesn't mean they can't talk to each other, which they do, to the delight of Ma Bell and the chagrin of siblings. However, because of the physical separation, little matters like Wasserman tests and a marriage license cannot be left for the last week.

Orthodox Jews occasionally have things like prewedding "stag parties." In fact, our rabbi's son, a premed student who married recently, had this stag party: a group of his friends gathered at one of their homes. They brought with them a few bottles of sweet red wine, over which they made a *siyyum*: that is to say, in honor of his marriage, the groom had timed his private daily study so as to complete a tractate of the Talmud just before the wedding day. He read the last few lines of the text, and then recited Kiddush over the wine. There were none of the lewd or macho jokes that are typically associated with stag parties, which tend to bring out the very worst in otherwise decent people. Traditional Judaism might have real problems with male/female hierarchies, but stag parties, with their sexist vulgarities, are not one of them.

THE WEDDING DAY

On the day of the wedding, the bride and groom fast until after the ceremony is over, unless it is Rosh Chodesh, when fasting is not permitted. Fasting enters a note of solemnity and seriousness amid the gaiety and joy. If the wedding is held in the evening, both bride and groom recite Yom Kippur Viddui (confessional) earlier at Minchah services. If the wedding is an afternoon wedding, they recite it privately before the ceremony. Symbolically, their past life and sins are overcome and they are forgiven as on Yom Kippur. Thus, one is supposed to enter marriage in a state of purity, sinlessness, and absolution. Of course, fasting and Viddui remind the bride and groom that they are at the threshold of a new life.

The wedding consists of three parts: preceremony rituals, the ceremony itself, the seudat mitzvah. Since there are several preceremony rituals, most traditional weddings begin with a smorgasbord to keep the guests busy until ceremony time. However, I have been to weddings where the order is reversed—first the ceremony, then the smorgasbord, and then the sit-down dinner. In this instance, the principals who are involved in the preliminary rituals are asked to come an hour before the invitation specifies. Shortly, I will explain the rationale for doing it this way.

For the preceremony rituals: the chattan (groom) and the kallah (bride) are ensconced in separate rooms up until the ceremony itself. At the chattan's tish (table) several things take place:

The t'naim, the prenuptial contract, is signed by the fathers of the bride and groom. T'naim are largely vestigial, since the essence of t'naim was to ensure that the wedding take place at a future date. Nevertheless, the custom has persisted among many.

The ketubah, the marriage contract, is then completed. The names of bride and groom, the date and place of the wedding, are filled in. The ketubah spells out the contractual responsibilities of bride and groom to each other. For example, the groom is obligated to provide her with food, clothing, shelter, and sexual satisfaction. She, in turn, accepts to love and honor and care for him.

On the theory that love is fine, but that love and noodles are even better, there is a financial stipulation in the ketubah of two hundred zuzim, an ancient coin of some value. In other words, in event of the dissolution of the marriage through death or divorce, the wife is guaranteed a fixed settlement, a sum that is above the poverty level. It means that she will continue to live comfortably with all her needs taken care of and will never be destitute nor have to resort to the public dole. Inasmuch as in all civil matters Jews follow the principle of "the law of the land is the law," this particular financial clause carries less weight in America, since divorce laws in many states mandate equal division of the estate. Nevertheless, it is well to remember that in Jewish tradition the husband's decent and proper obligations to his wife extend long past the life of the marriage.

The ketubah is not signed by either bride or groom; it is signed by two male witnesses, observant Jews who are not immediately related to either bride or groom. If a small "portable" ketubah is also to be drawn, this is the time to do it, while the same witnesses are present. If a ketubah is later lost, it must be redrawn and rewitnessed. A couple may not live together without a ketubah. (This later drawn document is called a ketubah de'irkesah.)

Kabbalat kinyan (the acceptance of contractual obligations). Since marriage is also a formal legal transaction, the rabbi, representing the bride's interests, will hold out a handkerchief to the chattan, who takes hold of one end. The rabbi explains, publicly, that this symbolizes the groom's acceptance to be bound by the conditions of the ketubah.

The Dvar Torah is one of the more humorous customs at the tish. The chattan prepares a Dvar Torah (a brief discourse on a religious text) in honor of the occasion. But his friends heckle him periodically by breaking into song, so that, although he tries, he never quite gets through.

The bride's Dvar Torah. A new custom that has arisen in very recent years and is still quite rare is the Dvar Torah given by the bride. It is symbolic both of the better education of Jewish women in modern times and of the more active role of women in communal settings. Unlike what goes on at the chattan's tish, the bride's Dvar Torah is not interrupted. This takes place in the bride's room. At one wedding I attended, the Dvar Torah was given by the bride's sister, who is teacher of Talmud.

One of the singularly romantic moments at an Orthodox wedding is the badeken. Before the ceremony is to begin, the bride is ushered out of her room, attended by the female members of the bridal party, and is seated in a special bride's seat, usually at the end of the reception hall where the guests are gathered. The female members of her party stand about her. The groom enters, accompanied by all the men who participated in his tish, many of whom sing and dance as they accompany him to his bride. This is the first moment the bride and groom have seen each other in a week. If they are not too shy at the moment, they will say a few words to each other. Mostly, their eyes meet, and the groom gently draws the veil over his bride's face. Family and friends look on, and the rabbi recites the Biblical blessing, "Oh, my sister, may you become a multitude of thousands." It sounds more poetic in Hebrew. One fairly widespread custom among modern Orthodox Jews is for the father and the father-in-law to bless the bride and kiss her "keppele" (on the forehead) right after the groom has drawn the veil over her. The whole thing is indescribably sweet. People who cry for joy at weddings often cry at the badeken, too. There are several attributed origins to badeken. One, that the groom should look at her and she at him to make sure they know what they are getting, unlike Jacob, who was promised Rachel and was given Leah, hidden demurely behind the veil. (Although if the groom changes his mind, there's not much he can do at that moment with his father-in-law in tow.) A second origin is that Rebekah veiled herself upon seeing Isaac, and so Jewish brides throughout the ages wear a veil during the marriage ceremony.

Immediately after the badeken, the groom and his party leave, again ushered by a group of friends who sing and dance him out of the room. All the guests then move toward the wedding hall, while the bridal party prepares for the processional.

PROCESSIONAL AND CEREMONY

The first one under the chuppah is the rabbi. If a cantor has been asked to participate, he, too, will enter before the wedding party. At times the rabbi and the cantor walk down the aisle; at others, they simply materialize under the chuppah and wait for the wedding party to arrive. The rabbi will check to make sure there are two Kiddush cups and wine which will be used during the ceremony.

In traditional Jewish weddings, grandparents generally walk down the aisle first. Usually, a seat is reserved for them in the first row so that they do not have to stand throughout the entire ceremony. Sometimes, the ring bearer comes down the aisle, singing a Hebrew song, such as "How goodly are thy tents, O Jacob, thy dwelling places, Israel." More often, it is the cantor who will sing this prayer as he walks down the aisle. Bridesmaids, ushers, maid and matron of honor, best man—these generally are all part of the entourage at a modern Orthodox wedding, each walking down the aisle to the accompaniment of a different melody the bride and groom have chosen for them.

There is a good deal of flexibility in the processional, but there are also certain basic minimum practices which are universally followed. The bride and groom do not walk down the aisle together. Each is accompanied to the chuppah by his/her parents. The groom's party enters first, and the last to enter are the bride and her parents. The parents remain standing at the sides of the chuppah throughout the entire ceremony. Of all the things that surprise non-Jews at a Jewish wedding, the presence of parents alongside the couple is the most unexpected of all. This is because of its contrast to the bride and groom standing alone at the "altar." Often, at a traditional wedding, sisters and brothers also will stand at the chuppah. To me, it beautifully symbolizes the fact that bride and groom do not marry in a void, nor will they build their future home or shared life in isolation, but rather each comes with the whole baggage of parents and siblings and sometimes close friends up there, too, who will lend stability and strength to this marriage.

As the groom walks down the aisle, the cantor sings an appropriate song welcoming him. Reaching the chuppah, he dons a kittel as he waits for his bride. The kittel is the white garment worn on Yom Kippur, symbolizing purity, forgiveness, and a clean slate. (Immediately after the ceremony, before he leaves the wedding hall with his bride, he removes the kittel.) In families where one or both parents of the new couple is no longer alive, a candle may be carried down the aisle in memory of the departed. It used to be that the memorial prayer for the dead, the El Maleh Rachamim, was chanted as the surviving member of the family walked down the aisle. The Rabbis decreed that this was too morbid a note to inject into a happy ceremony, and thus at times it is recited beforehand in the presence of the rabbi; the candle carried down the aisle is but a visual reminder. Many survivors of the Holocaust carry candles down the aisle at the weddings of their children, in memory of all the members of the extended family who would have been here on this day. . . .

Even if you're from the "groom's side," the excitement mounts as the bride enters, her parents' arms linked through hers. The last part of the processional at a traditional wedding is the bride's encirclement of the groom. When she reaches the chuppah, an unusual ritual ensues, practiced almost exclusively these days by Orthodox Jews. With her mother and mother-in-law following her, carrying the train of her gown, she encircles the groom. Seven times she encircles him, envelops him. Some modern people tend to think of this as sexist, but to me it has always seemed a most wonderfully sexy ritual, as if she were wrapping him up in the train of her gown to take him home with her. The number seven comes not from the seven wedding blessings, as one would imagine, but from the number of times in the Torah where it is written, "And when a man takes a wife." After the seventh revolution, she takes her place at his right. No symbolism here; this is simply to make it easier for him in a few moments to slip the ring onto the index finger of her right hand.

Now the couple stand side by side, under the chuppah, facing the rabbi. The chuppah symbolizes the new home of the bride and groom. It used to be that weddings took place under the stars, out in the open. Many weddings still do. In fact, some wedding halls are constructed with a removable skylight above the wedding platform. Why did couples marry under the stars? Hint, hint: so that they should multiply like stars in the sky. Out in the open, the symbolism of the chuppah as their home was more apparent. Nevertheless, the chuppah is always used whether one marries indoors or out; it is one of the essential elements in the halachic regulations of marriage.

The ceremony under the chuppah is about to begin. There are three parts to the ceremony, all very brief. First, the Birchot Erusin, the two betrothal blessings. The rabbi, who serves as mesader kiddushin, the marriage facilitator, will recite these two blessings over a cup of wine from which not he but the bride and groom will each take a sip. Usually, the rabbi hands the cup to the groom's father who raises it to his son's lips. The father then gives it to his wife, who lifts her daughter-in-law's veil for a moment and brings the cup to her lips.

Next comes the core ritual of a marriage ceremony: the giving of the ring and recitation of the marriage formula. The rabbi will call up two preselected witnesses, again two ritually observant males who are not related to the bride or groom. In the presence of the two witnesses, the rabbi asks the groom if the ring belongs to him. If it is an heirloom, the groom is also required to have made a token purchase so that it is legally his. The ring must be one solid piece, without any precious stones. This was instituted in order to avoid any deceit, lest the bride be misled about the worth of the ring, possibly mistaking colored glass for precious stones. As the witnesses look on, the groom places the ring on the index finger of her right hand, and recites the ancient nine-word formula:

הֲרֵי אַתְּ מְקֻדֶּשֶׁת לִי בְּטַבַּעַת זוּ כְּדָת מֹשֶׁה וְיִשְׂרָאֵל.

Harai at mekudeshet lee, b'ta'ba'at zu, k'dat Mosheh v'Yisrael.

Be sanctified (betrothed) to me with this ring in accordance with the law of Moses and Israel.

Even though the groom knows the formula by heart, he follows the rabbi, who says it aloud, two or three words at a time. There were some (there still are) who could not memorize this formula, and in order not to embarrass them, all grooms, learned and otherwise, were required to repeat it after the rabbi.

Now the ketubah is read in its original Aramaic. Either the

rabbi will read it, or another guest is given the honor. Often a brief English translation is read after the Aramaic text is completed. One very recent innovation is to have a woman read the ketubah. There is no other part of the ceremony that a woman can perform; according to Orthodox interpretation of halacha she cannot recite the blessings, nor serve as a witness. Although some would be loath to admit it and others reluctant to permit it, reading the ketubah is not expressly forbidden to women. Thus, in an attempt to redress imbalances in female "public" ceremonial roles, a prominent Orthodox rabbi has permitted women to read the ketubah.

After it has been read, the ketubah is handed to the groom, who gives it to the bride to keep. The legal part of the ceremony is completed. At this point, the rabbi will often say a few words to the bride and groom.

Traditional Judaism does not include a double-ring ceremony. Most Orthodox couples are satisfied with the ceremony as is, and save the groom's ring for later. However, where the bride wants to give him a ring under the chuppah, she will generally do this after the reading of the ketubah, but without reciting the ancient marriage formula. Another option: if the bride wishes to make an oral declaration as she gives him the ring, she will recite selected verses from the Bible to him, and he will respond to her in kind. An Orthodox rabbi will integrate this into the ceremony in a manner that does not confuse it with the traditional marriage ritual.

Most rabbis, however, will not permit the bride to recite the traditional marriage formula under the chuppah. Yet, I know of an Orthodox wedding where the bride, an ardent feminist with strong feelings about the matter, wanted to recite the traditional marriage formula. The rabbi's Solomonic solution, which satisfied her well, was to explain that "by traditional ruling, the act of consecration was accomplished through the husband's recitation of the formula several moments ago. The bride now wishes to give her husband a ring, and say the formula as a statement of her commitment, and in the hope that Jewish tradition will grow to incorporate this act in the legal structure of the ceremony."

The third and closing part of the ceremony is the cluster of seven additional blessings of marriage, the Birchot Nissuin, which are also called Sheva (seven) B'rachot. These, too, are recited over a cup of wine. These blessings, however, are quite separate from the earlier ones. In order to make the distinction very clear, a separate wine goblet is used.

The honor of reciting a b'racha is given to different guests, each of whom is called in turn to the chuppah. Each holds the cup of wine as he recites the blessing. After the Sheva B'rachot are completed, the rabbi hands the cup of wine, this time to the bride's father, who raises it to the groom's lips, and then the mother of the bride raises her daughter's veil and brings the wine to her to sip.

The ceremony is over. But before we can all shout out mazel tov to the new couple and their families, we must intrude reality and memory for an instant. In the last of the seven blessings, we asked God to restore the sounds of joy and gladness, the sounds of bride and groom to Zion and Jerusalem. It has reminded us that the Temple was destroyed, that the world is not yet wholly redeemed, that our own happiness cannot be complete until Zion and Jerusalem are secure. As a symbol of that ancient shattering and the as-yet unredeemed world, a glass is wrapped in a napkin and placed on the floor where the groom shatters it with a well placed stomp.

There. We have remembered and it is done! Now, our joy returns. Everyone calls out with full voice, "Mazel tov! Mazel tov!" Orthodox couples generally don't kiss each other under the chuppah (although some do), but before they leave they hug their parents, and new in-laws. As they turn to go back down the aisle, they are ushered out by a host of young men who have rushed forward and who link arms in rows of fours and fives to sing and dance their way backward out of the wedding hall, escorting the happy couple to the yichud chamber, for a few moments of precious privacy.

Yichud is the time immediately following the ceremony when the bride and groom can break their fast and spend a few moments in complete privacy. There are even two witnesses posted at the door to ensure their privacy. Yichud has two associations: (1) In Biblical times, the bride and groom would have their first intercourse immediately after marriage, and the bride would bring forth tokens of her virginity—the sheet with bloodstains—

which her family would then display as a badge of honor. Primitive? Well, at least it's not done any longer. (2) According to Jewish law, there were three ways to get married: with money (ring), with a legal document, and with intercourse. The latter way was rejected by the Rabbis as not being a legitimate mode of marrying. Nevertheless, with yichud, the couple secreted alone, the ceremony symbolically incorporates all three modes. Yichud finalizes the halachic requirements of a Jewish marriage.

After yichud, the couple participates with all their guests in the seudat mitzvah. However, since they were separated right up until the ceremony, no photographs could be taken of them together and with their respective families other than the moment of badeken and, of course, the ceremony itself. Add the eighteen minutes for yichud, which even a photographer may not violate, and you begin to understand why some couples do not rejoin their guests at the dinner for almost an hour after they have walked back down the aisle.

Photographers can be somewhat overbearing in their attempts to do their job. Moreover, the family wants those posed wedding pictures. Yet, it seems rude to stay away from the wedding-dinner guests for so long. There are three compromises possible:

1. Stipulate that a photographer has fifteen minutes to take the most essential formal poses of the couple and their families, and the rest he must capture in candid photos.
2. Skip the formal poses altogether. The best wedding pictures I ever saw of a traditional Jewish wedding were taken by an Italian photographer who took only candid shots. The pictures were his wedding gift to his friends. (Of course, the fact that professionally he was a Time-Life photographer didn't hurt. . . .)
3. Schedule the wedding with the ceremony first, smorgasbord reception next, during which there is ample time for yichud and a photography session, before the dinner even begins.

At most Orthodox weddings, there is a minimum of social dancing and more likely none at all, and a maximum of Chasidic and Israeli dancing, which centers around the bride and groom. All the guests are enjoined to rejoice with the bride and groom, who dance in thier respective female/male circles. Several times during the reception, they will be seated in the center of the dancing circle, or carried aloft in chairs, while their friends clap and sing around them. Each year, the dances become more elaborate, and now the popular thing is for friends to dance in costume, to put on skits, to compose grammen (rhymed lyrics about the couple). At a recent wedding, two yeshiva boys danced in fedoras that were aflame (alcohol). "When it began to get hot, we removed them." A couple of friends donned magician's costumes and performed tricks in the center as others danced around, and the bride and groom looked on. One could even stand on the sidelines, and feast one's eyes and laugh every moment. The musicians play a big part in helping the spirit along. They must know or be instructed what music to play, when, how loud, and how long; thus, the choice of musicians is an important one.

The dinner closes with a special Grace that includes the repetition of the Sheva B'rachot. Again, individuals are given the special honor of reciting the blessings.

A Jewish wedding is part religious ceremony, part party. Thus, the rules regarding separation of the sexes (the guests) are quite complex, and open to variation. In certain Chasidic and "black hat" circles, everything is separate—the prewedding reception, the seating at the ceremony, the dinner, even the bride's and groom's dinner tables. A friend of mine once reported tongue in cheek of such a wedding, "Everything was so separate—the bride and groom got married on different nights."

In the modern Orthodox weddings, men and women mingle comfortably at the preceremony reception and are seated together at the formal dinner. At about half the weddings of modern Orthodox that I've attended during the last decade, men and women were seated separately during the ceremony, as they are in shul. Twenty years ago, that wasn't the case. That the whole community has shifted to the right is visible in these fine details.

A traditional Jewish wedding is a delightful, joyous beginning to another bayit ne'eman, a faithful household in Israel. And just to make sure it gets under way properly, the custom among Orthodox Jews is to continue the celebration for a full week of Sheva B'rachot at the homes of family and friends.

Each evening (or afternoon) a dinner is given in honor of the couple. Often, friends who could not be invited to the wedding are invited to one of the Sheva B'rachot dinners. People understand that the high cost of caterers and the multiple family and friendship circles we all have make it impossible to invite everyone to the wedding. Sheva B'rachot, then, are a way of saying we want you to share in some part of our joy. One does not take insult (hopefully) to be invited to Sheva B'rachot, even though he/she was not invited to the wedding.

Sheva B'rachot are filled with singing, words of Torah, and general rejoicing. The special wedding Grace with its Sheva B'rachot, seven blessings, is recited each night, which is why these affairs are called Sheva B'rachot. A minyan is required for reciting the Sheva B'rachot.

But Sheva B'rachot are not a hard-and-fast rule. Some couples have two or three Sheva B'rachot in their honor. Some leave immediately for a honeymoon, where pulling together a minyan is not possible. The flexibility is designed to meet the needs of the new couple. Let's hope life will treat them that way.

CHAPTER 10

BIRTH

Of this community it can be said: the vital signs are good!

The very first commandment/blessing in the Torah is: be fruitful and multiply. It used to be, among most Jews, that fairly soon after a man and a woman married they would begin a family. A year or two later if there were no signs of pregnancy, relatives and friends would begin to wonder, and sometimes to ask, "Is everything okay?"

Nowadays, Jewish women do a lot of other things after they marry; often they decide not to have children for a long while. And some decide never. The birthrate for American Jews is 1.5 children per family, the lowest ever in this country, lower than the national birthrate of 1.8. Moreover, because of the drain-away factors of assimilation and intermarriage, the replacement level for Jews has been determined to be at 2.3 children per family, slightly higher than the general replacement level of 2.1. The gloom-and-doomers predict that American Jews will be out of business by the year 2100.

All of that falls very hard on the ears of an Orthodox Jew. It seems so remote, so out of touch with internal realities. Among the Orthodox, high value is placed on having children. At better than replacement levels. In our shul, for example, which seems to be bursting at the seams with life, the median number of children per family is three. As I look around every Shabbat at those young couples, with their offspring decked out in Shabbat finery, a hundred babes perched on their mothers' laps, or held in their fathers' arms, I sense that there is a very powerful peer-reinforcing factor operating here. Even those who postpone children because of careers are caught up in it. It becomes simply a matter of time.

PREGNANCY

There is nothing quite like a first pregnancy: the excitement until you know for sure; feeling growth and movement; the breathing and pushing classes; buying new maternity clothes; the joy of "telling and showing"; the gradual realization that this is the beginning of your own family; taking time to read those books about pregnancy, child care, and "how to give your child a superior mind"; and, finally, treasuring those last few months of privacy, knowing that soon there will be no more spontaneous 6:00 P.M. decisions to drop everything and go out for a dinner and a show. But if you're a member of an Orthodox community, there is something else, too: knowing that everyone approves and admires and thinks that you are doing the most absolutely perfect, clever, wise, and wonderful thing in the world.

CHOOSING AN OBSTETRICIAN

If you life in a city where there are many choices, then finding a good obstetrician can mean several things:

1. A doctor who will be encouraging in the kind of delivery you prefer (two decades ago, doctors discouraged natural childbirth and some would refuse to take the "naturals" as patients. Some obstetricians still have a strong bias in favor of full anesthesia).

2. A doctor associated with a good hospital, one that accommodates your particular needs (husband in labor and delivery rooms, visiting schedules as you like them, early release for home, and so forth).

3. Inquiring whether the hospital allows in-hospital circumcision to be performed by a qualified mohel in case the need should arise (for example, after Cesarean section, when mother and child are kept in the hospital past eight days). The Union of

Orthodox Jewish Congregations publishes a list of such hospitals in New York City. In any given town, the rabbi can put you in touch with a mohel who will know which hospitals permit ritual circumcision.

4. Most hospitals in large cities serve kosher food packages or will carefully accommodate a kosher diet. It is to your advantage to have "kosher diet" noted on your hospital application form before and not after delivery.

As the delivery date approaches, there is much to do. Many couples, especially with a first child, follow the custom of purchasing a layette and nursery furniture, but not having anything delivered until after a healthy, normal birth has taken place. I should add that this is custom and not law, and therefore there are those who, having every reasonable hope that things will turn out fine, go right ahead and outfit a nursery weeks before due date.

In packing a bag for the hospital, remember to put in a siddur (prayer book), a small chumash (Bible), a set of inexpensive travel candlesticks, Shabbat candles, matches, and a small bottle of wine—just in case recovery time comes out during Shabbat. (Do not put in a silver Kiddush cup, as chances are, in a large hospital, it will not be there for Shabbat morning's Kiddush.)

SHABBAT AND GIVING BIRTH

There is a one-in-seven chance that you will go into labor on Shabbat, which will require calling the doctor, traveling to the hospital, paying for a cab, and being registered. Whatever must be done may be done, but there are ways to do it that are more in keeping with the spirit of Shabbat. One is the principle of shinui, doing something with a different touch so as to symbolize that, despite our actions, we are aware it is Shabbat. For example, dialing the phone with the left hand to call the doctor, if we are right-handed. A friend used to prepare his "hospital hat" each time his wife began her ninth month. Under the grosgrain trim, he placed several folded dollars, enough to cover cab fare and tip to the hospital, so that he wouldn't have to go to his wallet, or receive change from the cabbie. If there are other children, a Shabbat contingency plan should be worked out with neighbors; you can't call your mother and tell her to drive over and fetch the kids.

DELIVERY

Interestingly, there is no special ritual or blessing for women that marks the act of giving birth. (Could it be that if men had been giving birth all these centuries, some fantastic ritual would have developed by now?) Whatever, it has become a time to savor the miracle in a very personal, individual, and intimate way. Some follow the tradition of reciting after birth the blessing on hearing good tidings:

בָּרוּךְ אַתָּה יְיָ, אֱלֹהֵינוּ מֶלֶךְ הָעוֹלָם, הַטּוֹב וְהַמֵּטִיב.

Baruch ata Adonai Elohainu melech ha'olam hatov vehametiv.

Blessed are You, Lord our God, Ruler of the universe Who is good and does good.

After a safe delivery, the husband-father will recite the Birkat Hagomel for his wife the next time he goes to pray with a minyan. Some women recite this at the Brit. Birkat Hagomel is a blessing of thanks for saving a person from potential danger. It is a reminder that an easy, safe, and successful childbirth is not to be taken for granted.

בָּרוּךְ אַתָּה יְיָ, אֱלֹהֵינוּ מֶלֶךְ הָעוֹלָם, הַגּוֹמֵל לְחַיָּבִים
טוֹבוֹת, שֶׁגְּמָלַנִי כָּל טוֹב.

Baruch ata Adonai Elohainu melech ha'olam ha'go'mel le'chayavim tovot sheh'g'malani kol tov.

Blessed are You, Lord our God, Ruler of the universe, Who metes out goodness to the undeserving and Who has dealt kindly with me.

NAMING

Finding a name and giving a name are two different things. "Finding" a name is a personal and private affair, the process of deciding what the Hebrew name will be, whether the English name shall simply be an Anglicized version of the Hebrew (for example, Dah'veed in Hebrew and David in English) or a distinct English name altogether.

"Giving" the name, on the other hand, is a public act, a community event. Males are named at the Brit; females, in shul, when the father is called up to the Torah, and/or at the Simchat Habat (see p. 248). The custom is not to announce the name (except to family insiders) until the formal ceremony. That is why Orthodox Jews will hardly ever ask each other, "What are you going to name the baby?" If asked, one will probably answer, "We haven't decided yet." Some couples prefer not to give the English name to birth registry personnel until after the Hebrew name has been given in the formal Jewish ceremony, just in case there are any last-minute changes. Countless Jewish children have had their original birth certificates drafted with something like Baby Boy Goldberg, which is then amended a week or two later.

Finding a name can be more anxiety-producing than giving birth. Of course, it doesn't have to be decided upon until minutes before the Brit or the formal naming ceremony for girls. But since there are approximately four thousand names to eliminate, it is wise to start early. That way, you'll be left with only three names to wrestle with as the mohel and your mother-in-law walk in the door. There are several books on the market for finding Jewish names and a good English equivalent. For finding a Biblical name, scanning the English index of Hebrew Scriptures will be more than adequate. Yiddish names are having a comeback, albeit a minor one.

Since the rebirth of the State of Israel, there has been a trend among Diaspora Jews to give their children modern Hebrew names, such as Shira, Adina, Yonina (for girls), or Eitan, Roni, Ami (for boys). Modern Hebrew names are used more widely for females, because so many male names can be chosen from throughout the twenty-four books of the Bible, while relatively few female names have come down through the literature.

Traditional Jews tend to give their children Hebrew Biblical names. Some, however, depart from the standard Anglicized version and try to match only the first letter corresponding to the Jewish name (for example, Binyamin—Bruce). But they are careful not to give their children English names that have a Christian resonance to them, in contrast to secular Jews who wouldn't hesitate to give names such as Peter Mark or Christopher Scott (probably named after a grandfather Chaim Beryl). And yet, it does vary: My cousin's four children are all civilly named Jonny, Kathy, Billy, and Bonnie—all fine yeshiva students, all properly observant of halacha. Kathy has more Jewishness in her little finger than does a doctor I know who was given the rich Jewish name Mordecai and who hasn't been to a synagogue in over forty years.

There are two different customs in choosing a namesake. The Ashkenazim usually name a child after a deceased relative, while the Sephardim name a child in honor of an esteemed or beloved living relative, although not a parent. Even Sephardic Jews shy away from the Thomas Tuttle III syndrome.

Unless there is a special relative one knew personally before his/her death, or unless there is a Biblical or Hebrew name one is especially fond of, the best thing to do is to consult with parents and grandparents. Often we begin to find out more about our family trees as we begin to search for names for our progeny. This seems an appropriate moment to connect to the past.

Our preference for our own children was to give them Biblical names. Common or not (I counted twelve David Greenbergs in the Manhattan phone book when David was born), we wanted to avoid a large gap between the English and Hebrew names. But we also wanted to honor the memory of immediate past members of our families. Since most Jews throughout history have felt the same way, we had no problem in finding just what we wanted. Each child has a beautiful Biblical name and also knows about the specialness of the family member whose name he/she carries.

But things don't always run so smoothly. Our first child was born while we were in Gloucester, Massachusetts, for a summer vacation. He was born during the Three Weeks (see p. 471). The Haftorah reading of that particular Shabbat happened to be Yitz's favorite: Jeremiah's prophecy of the return to the land of Israel, a prophecy all the more poignant because it was sounded in the very throes of destruction, devastation, and exile. Jeremy, as the Anglicized version, was a favorite name of mine. We also wanted to name our son after my uncle Heshie, whose Hebrew name was Tzvi Hirsch. Uncle Heshie, zichrono livracha, was a tzaddik who had been killed in Jerusalem eight years earlier at age thirty-six. A terrorist's bullet pierced him as he sat in his home late one evening, poring over a page of the Talmud. He died as he had lived, studying Torah. Uncle Heshie had left behind a wife and five children. My cousins were all quite young, at least fifteen years away from having children of their own to carry his name.

So Jeremy Tzvi the name would be. For once in our lives, we had planned ahead, settled the issue, and gave no more thought to the matter.

On the eighth day, my father-in-law arrived from New York, an hour before the Brit was to begin. When he heard the names, he became terribly distraught. "About what?" we asked. "These are two beautiful Jewish names." He was upset because we were naming the baby after two persons who had died in unnatural circumstances, one of whom died very young. But we had already become attached to the names, had already associated them with our eight-day-old son, and had no contingency plans. My sister Judy, wise in all things, took me aside and said, "You'll have more children, but you have only one father-in-law. . . ." So we named him Moshe Tzvi, Moshe—after my saintly grandfather who had lived to a ripe old age. My father-in-law was very happy. And we never regretted the change for a moment. (But we did keep Jeremy Moshe on his birth certificate.)

You don't always have to choose the name of a deceased relative. My cousins Marv and Shirley named their second son Yonatan after their friend Yoni Netanyahu, a hero who fell in the raid on Entebbe. Every so often, when I think of little Yonatan, I remember Entebbe. So will Yonatan, when he grows older and people ask him after whom he was named.

A hero complex never hurt a Jewish child. When Yitz used to put the children to sleep, he would tell them stories about their Biblical namesakes. And then some. There was Moshe Rabbeinu, Moshe the Deliverer, Moshe the Lawgiver. There was also Moshe, Super Jew; Moshe, Master Hero, who could outdo any feat thought up by the editors of Marvel Comics. One night, as I was putting Moshe to sleep and continuing with the story, I casually asked, "And who saved the Jews and took them out of Egypt?" Moshe, who was then three, pointed his little index finger at his own chest, and in wide-eyed seriousness and pride said, "I did."

The full Jewish name, used in religious documents and ceremonies, goes something like this: Abraham ben (son of) Mordecai, or Sarah bat (daughter of) Mordecai rather than Abraham Strauss or Sarah Strauss. If the father is of priestly or levitical descent, that, too, is included: Abraham ben Mordecai Ha-Kohen or Esther bat Moshe Ha-Levi. In reciting the prayer for help and saving (the me'sheh'bay'rach) the mother's name is used: Abraham ben Miriam or Sarah bat Miriam.

In most Orthodox synagogues and ceremonies, the full formal name continues to include only the father's. However, winds of change are in the air. At the Simchat Habat ceremonies (see p. 248) the child is named after both mother and father: for example, Tamar bat Mordecai Ve Miriam. And at a Brit I attended recently, the infant was formally named with both father's and mother's name. It seems only just. . . .

SHALOM ZACHAR

Another custom that many Orthodox Jews observe is the Shalom Zachar, which literally means greeting the male. On the Friday night (leil shabbat) that precedes the Brit, friends and relatives in the community are invited to celebrate the great event of a new child. Fruit, cake, and beverages are served. I can't locate its origin, but moist, salted and peppered chick-peas (nahit) are a familiar treat at a Shalom Zachar. There is much singing; the rabbi and/or learned guests and relatives will deliver a dvar Torah. Often the Shalom Zachar is held in the home of the new parents, but sometimes it is the grandparents who host the informal gathering. Occasionally, if the number of invited guests is large, it is held in the shul social hall after dinner.

SHALOM NEKEVAH

In recent years, as community consciousness has risen, many Jews have a similar Friday-night celebration for the birth of a daughter. It is called either Shalom Nekevah (greeting the female) or Shalom Bat (greeting the daughter). It is a new custom and one that is rapidly taking hold.

BRIT MILAH

Judaism is a very practical religion, but it certainly does allow for moments of high drama. A Brit is one such moment.

Brit (or Bris, as Ashkenazim pronounce it) means a covenant, a mutual pledge. The history of the Jewish people is really the history of the covenant with God, a promise of each to the other to be faithful unto eternity. Shabbat is one primary symbol of this covenantal relationship. Brit Milah—covenant of circumcision—is another:

> This is My covenant that ye shall observe between Me and your children and their offspring that follow. Circumcise every male and you shall circumcise the flesh of your foreskin, and it shall be a sign of the covenant between Me and you. A son of eight days you shall circumcise, each male unto the generations.
> —GENESIS 17:10–12

The clearest understanding I ever had of what a Brit is all about came from a friend who called us from Maryland the night before David's Brit to tell us he was sorry he wouldn't be able to come: "Tell your little son for me tomorrow," he said, "that his loss is our gain."

The Brit must be held on the eighth day after birth, no matter whether that comes out on a Shabbat or a holiday, no matter who can or cannot be present. This past year, the chazzan of our synagogue, who is also a seasoned mohel now performing second-generation circumcisions, had to perform two of them on Yom Kippur. This he did during the recess between Minchah and Ne'ilah (closing service).

The only reason to postpone a Brit is if the doctor feels the infant's health warrants postponement. As soon as the infant is well enough, the Brit should be rescheduled without delay, although not for Shabbat or a holiday. Brit, a medical procedure as well as a religious rite, takes precedence over Shabbat or holiday (when nonemergency medical procedures are proscribed) only if it is performed on the eighth day. Once the eighth day has passed, it is proper to wait another day or two until sacred time, with its ban on work, has ended.

CHOOSING A MOHEL

According to Jewish law, the obligation to circumcise the son falls upon his father. Since most fathers are not trained to carry out this skilled procedure, a father was permitted by halacha to appoint a stand-in, who happens to be the *mohel*, the circumciser. Thus, the father will not "hire" the mohel; he will invite him to be his stand-in. Being a stand-in, however, does not mean that a mohel doesn't have set fees which he will discuss forthrightly. After all, this is his faith but it is also his livelihood. Currently, the standard fee in New York City is one hundred and fifty dollars plus travel expenses; but the new father should feel free to ask.

Only a mohel may stand in, not a doctor or surgeon. A mohel must be personally pious, observant of Jewish law, and carefully trained in the laws of Brit Milah. The certification of mohelim (plural) requires that they also must be rigorously trained in surgical hygiene. There are some doctors who are licensed mohelim, and have trained for this apart from their medical education.

Each mohel may have a different style, but as a rule, they are deft, quick, and expert at their profession. Not only do they perform this minor surgery, but they simultaneously perform the religious ceremony, coordinating each part of it with the other. If asked, a mohel will also explain the different parts of the ceremony to the invited guests, some of whom may never before have attended a Brit Milah. A thoughtful mohel will also explain beforehand to first-time parents (and to second- and third-timers as well, since one forgets easily) exactly what he will be doing, what the child feels, and what to expect in terms of the healing process. Generally, there is no need for follow-up; however, a mohel should be prepared to respond as often as the parents feel they need him.

Most mohelim use the clamp, either the Magen or Gomco clamp, designed especially for ritual circumcision. The healing is almost instantaneous; the foreskin is sealed by the pressure of the clamp and, thus, the major source of bleeding is sealed. If the mohel has done his job well, the child heals normally, and there should be no need for the mohel to return. However, some mohelim use a surgical knife which is equally safe, but which requires dressing the wound and then professionally removing the dressing the next day. A mohel who uses a knife routinely returns the following day to complete his task. While both methods are halachically permissible, new parents might have a preference for a particular method of circumcision and should not hesitate to ask.

Another question to ask beforehand is the mohel's attitude toward the presence of women at the Brit. It used to be—and in some circles still is—considered inappropriate for women, including the mother herself, to be present in the room when circumcision took place. This was legitimated in an age when women were thought to be light-headed, fragile, and would therefore faint just from imagining what the mohel was doing across the room. In most Brit ceremonies today, however, women are present, the mother is part of it, and no one looks askance if the father pales and weaves as he stands near the mohel looking on.

The best way to find a good mohel is to ask friends or to call the rabbi for several names. As soon as a baby boy is born, the parents should immediately contact a mohel, since there are not all that many of them and, in some seasons, they are in heavy demand.

Before putting prospective clients on his calendar, a mohel will always ask at what hour the baby was born. Sometimes, people forget that the Jewish day starts at night. Circumcision takes place eight days from the day of birth. If the baby was born on Monday after dark, the Brit would take place on Tuesday of the following week.

Generally, the mohel will bring along with him everything that is needed for the medical procedures. Still, there are a few things the parents must do:

1. Invite the guests. Well, not exactly. Traditionally, we don't formally invite guests to a Brit. We inform them. Why? Because participating in a Brit Milah is a mitzvah. If one is invited to perform a mitzvah, one may not decline. But we all know that there are some friends who simply will not be able to drop everything on a few days' notice. So the invitation generally goes like this: the new father calls and says, "Mazel tov! Ruthie gave birth

244 • *How to Run a Traditional Jewish Household*

to a boy yesterday, and the Brit will be next Monday morning at Beth Shalom at eight thirty A.M." And the recipient of the phone call will know that he/she has been invited. Although a Brit can take place with only a father, mohel, and infant present, it is preferable to perform the mitzvah in the presence of a minyan. Since Orthodox Jews count only men in a minyan, at least ten men are "informed." Increasingly, women are informed and do attend Brit ceremonies in equal numbers.

2. Designating the honors. The primary honor is that of *sondek*, equivalent to a godfather. Generally, one of the grandfathers is asked to be the sondek. The sondek holds the infant while the mohel performs circumcision. It is considered a great honor to be invited to the sondek. Since there is only one sondek and, hopefully, two sets of grandparents present, a wise couple will casually mention to the other grandfather that next time. . . .

The other honorees are these:

The *kvatterin*, the woman who takes the baby from the mother, carries it in, and gives it to the

kvatter, the man who brings the baby to the

kiseh shel eliahu, the man who is called by the title of the chair on which he is seated. A special chair is designated as the seat of Elijah, the prophet who is associated in Jewish tradition with Brit and with protection of little children.

The chair set aside for Elijah doesn't need any special preparation. It can be any regular chair, designated on the spot for this special purpose. (In many European synagogues of previous centuries, there was a special chair that was called kiseh shel eliahu, which was used only for the purpose of a Brit ceremony; synagogues of today do not have such chairs.)

The man who is honored with kiseh shel eliahu holds the baby while special prayers are recited and then he gives the baby to the sondek, and the circumcision begins. After the ceremony, either the original kvatterin can take the baby out or another woman can be given the honor.

3. If the Brit is going to be performed in a synagogue, the service can be followed in a regular siddur, of which there will be more than enough. If the Brit will be at home, it is a thoughtful gesture to have enough copies of the service available so that guests can follow.

4. Preparing the seudat mitzvah. As with so many other mitz-vot, we celebrate with a feast. A religious feast does not mean a six-course meal. It means breaking bread together in celebration of performance of a mitzvah. Since the Brit is usually held in the morning, the religious feast is light fare. Very often it consists of bagels, cream cheese, lox, fish salads, and fresh vegetables. If a Brit takes place during the Nine Days (see p. 472), it is customary to hold it in the late morning or early afternoon, and serve a meat meal, which otherwise could not be eaten during the Nine Days. A Brit meal can be simple or lavish, prepared by the new parents, family, friends, or a caterer. There should be enough booklets of the Grace After Meals for every guest to follow, since a special Grace is recited at the seudat mitzvah of a Brit. If a Brit falls on a fast day, there is, of course, no seudah.

5. Some families have a small crocheted kepah prepared for the baby to wear at his Brit ceremony. First-time teenage aunts are very good at speedily whipping up these little creations.

BRIT CEREMONY

The ceremony itself is very brief—fifteen minutes at most. When the kvatterin enters with the infant, the mohel calls out, "Baruch haba" ("Blessed be he who comes in"). Everyone present rises and remains standing throughout. The kvatterin transfers baby to kvatter. The mohel takes the baby from the kvatter and calls out his intention to fulfill the mitzvah of Brit Milah. Next, he takes the baby to the kiseh shel eliahu, who holds him for a minute as the mohel recites a brief prayer. All those assembled respond. The mohel then takes the baby from the kiseh shel eliahu, gives him to the sondek, and the circumcision begins.

The actual law is to perform the Brit while the child is being held on the sondek's lap (al ha-bircaim, on the knees). Very often, however, the mohel prefers to work at a table, so the sondek will stand or sit on a stool in such a way that his knees touch the bottom of the table, while his hands hold the infant on the table as the mohel does his work.

Mohelim have a good reason for working on a table—the son-dek! Our mohel always uses a table. Many years ago, he was preparing to perform a Brit on little Chaim Gross when Chaim's uncle, a thirty-year-old rabbi and psychologist who was honored with sondek, said to him, "Why don't you do it the right way, on the lap and not on the table?" Said Reverend Martin Horowitz, the mohel, "Because it's safer for the baby this way. What would happen if the sondek would faint and drop the baby?!" Said the uncle, "Well, I guess you've got a point there." So the uncle/sondek/rabbi/psychologist stood at the table holding little Chaim. And in the middle of the circumcision, he passed right out.

There are three central points to the circumcision: a blessing preceding the act, the act itself, and a blessing following. The mohel recites:

Blessed are You, Lord our God, Ruler of the universe, Who commanded us regarding circumcision.

In the next instant, he actually removes the foreskin, making sure that at least one drop of blood is drawn from the wound.

Immediately, the father recites:

בָּרוּךְ אַתָּה יְיָ, אֱלֹהֵינוּ מֶלֶךְ הָעוֹלָם אֲשֶׁר קִדְּשָׁנוּ בְּמִצְוֹתָיו, וְצִוָּנוּ לְהַכְנִיסוֹ בִּבְרִיתוֹ שֶׁל אַבְרָהָם אָבִינוּ.

Baruch ata Adonai Elohainu melech ha'olam asher kidshanu b'mitzvotav v'tzivanu l'hakhniso bivrito shel Avraham avinu.

Blessed are You, Lord our God, Ruler of the universe, Who has sanctified us with His commandments and commanded us to bring him (the child) into the Covenant of our father Abraham.

Everyone present answers Amen and calls out:

כְּשֵׁם שֶׁנִּכְנַס לַבְּרִית, כֵּן יִכָּנֵס לְתוֹרָה וּלְחֻפָּה וּלְמַעֲשִׂים טוֹבִים.

K'shem sheh'nichnas labrit, ken yikanes l'Torah, u'le'chupah u'l'maasim tovim.

Just as he entered the Covenant, so may he enter into a study of Torah, into marriage, and into the performance of good deeds.

Meanwhile, the mohel applies a surgical ointment, diapers the infant and places him in his father's hands. The mohel takes a cup of wine and says the blessing over wine. Then he recites the final prayer in which he announces:

Let his name be called in Israel _____, the son of _____ .

The baby usually cries after circumcision, so as the mohel sings out his final prayer, he touches a bit of sweet wine to the lips of the infant who immediately ceases crying and begins to suck his lip in search of more of that good stuff.

What is the role of the mother at the Brit? She is a kimpatur, a woman recovering from childbirth. Great attention, deference, and love are showered upon her. In an intangible sort of way, infant, husband, sondek, and mohel notwithstanding, she is the center of this universe.

If the Brit is performed in a synagogue, the mother will walk in with the kvatterin. Most likely she will take a seat that has been set aside in the front row for her. Some mothers go up to the bimah and stand alongside their husbands. If the Brit is performed at home, her role is even more flexible. Some recite their own prayers or readings during the ceremony.

Most Orthodox women, however, continue to play a low-key role. Jewish law requires the father to recite the circumcision blessings, which seems to suit most women who have a sense of accomplishing this marvelous feat and tend not to want to be "up front" during the circumcision ceremony. Perhaps it's the power of conditioning, but somehow, it all seems to be quite balanced and sweet, a kind of natural division of functions. On the other hand, when women participate fully in the Simchat Habat ceremonies, that, too, seems just right.

The ceremony is followed by the seudat mitzvah, at which there is a brief speech, or two or three, by the new father, the grandfather or grandmother, the rabbi, and occasionally, the mother. The father usually tells something about the person after whom the child was named. There is often some singing and the meal ends with a special Grace for a Brit Milah.

HATAFAT DAM BRIT

If the baby was circumcised in a hospital before the eighth day, he must nevertheless undergo a symbolic circumcision in order for it to be considered a real Brit and not merely a medical procedure. This ceremony takes place on the eighth day and is called Hatafat Dam Brit—"shedding the blood of the Covenant." The procedure is very simple. A pinprick brings a drop of blood from the skin of the glans. (This drop of blood will normally result during the actual circumcision on the eighth day.) The proper blessings are then recited, and a seudat mitzvah follows. If an older child is being converted to Judaism and has already undergone a medical circumcision, a Hatafat Dam Brit is performed as part of his conversion.

SIMCHAT HABAT

Of this community, it must also be said: there has long been a gender-skewed appreciation of new life. Until this past decade, the birth of a baby girl went relatively unnoticed by tradition, unmarked by community. Most baby girls in Jewish history have been named during the course of a regular synagogue service when the father is called up for an aliyah and offers the me'sheh'bay'rach blessing.

The me'sheh'bay'rach blessing in which a female is named is:

He Who blessed our fathers Abraham, Isaac, and Jacob, Moses and Aaron, David and Solomon, may He bless the mother _____ and her newborn daughter, whose name in Israel shall be called _____. May they raise her for the marriage canopy and for a life of good deeds, and let us say Amen.

Occasionally the mother would be present in the synagogue, but usually not. All who were paying attention would wish the new father a mazel-tov and that, for the most part, was that!

Not any longer. The wisdom of marking so personal an event within the framework of community has finally begun to impress itself on all of us. Girls do not need to undergo circumcision, but that doesn't mean their entry into the world, and from there into the covenant between God and Israel, must remain a private affair. In all sectors of the Orthodox community there are now celebrations for infant girls that simply didn't exist a generation ago. For these innovations, we must thank our more liberal co-religionists.

The ceremony is so new that there is no standard procedure, not even a single name by which it goes. Simchat Habat (the rejoicing of the daughter), is most widely used. There is also Brit Kedusha (the covenant of holiness), Brit Sarah (who entered into the covenant along with Abraham; this title was used for a ceremony prepared by a couple who named their daughter Sarah), Brit Nerot (in which candles are used).

The Simchat Habat ceremonies usually follow these outlines:

1. Carrying in the baby ceremoniously, with someone singing a prayer welcoming her. Generally, the carry-in honor is given to one grandmother and holding the baby throughout the ceremony is given to the other one.
2. Reciting the Birkat Hagomel and the Shehecheyanu blessings. The mother or mother and father recite these blessings.
3. A special prayer naming her with her Jewish name. Some use the traditional me'sheh'bay'rach that is used in the synagogue for naming girls. Others use the naming prayer in the Brit altered appropriately for females. Still others formulate their own naming prayers.
4. After her name is given, the guests respond: "Just as she has been entered into the Covenant, let her enter a life of Torah, marriage canopy, and good deeds." (Recall the traditional prayer for girls omitted the part about Torah.)
5. In some ceremonies, Biblical readings are interspersed throughout.
6. Often a guest or one of the parents delivers a brief speech on this special occasion.
7. The baby is blessed with the priestly blessing.
8. And the ceremony concludes with the blessing over wine, followed by the meal.

As one can see, the ceremony for girls closely follows the covenant ceremony for boys. The Jewish Women's Resource center in New York City publishes a pamphlet describing several Simchat Habat ceremonies. As has happened many times before, it will take a few decades before it will become standardized and formalized. Or it could happen next year: the publisher of a traditional siddur might select one ceremony and include it in his siddur—and it would henceforth become fixed for all time. Meanwhile, however, since nothing has been fixed as yet, the time of celebrating is also flexible. Some parents celebrate a week or two after the birth, others wait until the baby is a month old —and can write and deliver her own speech.

ADOPTION

The Brit for an adopted child whose natural mother is not Jewish is a bit different. Or, to be more accurate, the procedures are quite the same, but the prayers and blessings are not. The circumcision is specifically designated for the purpose of conversion. But conversion is completed only by ritual immersion. Since immersion in a ritual bath cannot possibly take place that day (that is, until the penis heals), the conversion is incomplete, and the child is still not considered a Jew. Therefore, his full Hebrew name will not be given at a Brit. As soon as ritual immersion takes place, the Jewish name is given. If the child had been previously circumcised as a medical procedure, the Hatafat Dam Brit ceremony is performed. Since there is no need to wait for healing, the ritual immersion can take place immediately following the drawing of a drop of blood from the skin of the glans. In this instance conversion and naming are done at the same time.

Similarly, a girl born to a non-Jewish mother is not named until after her ritual immersion. A Simchat Habat might immediately follow a conversion, but does not precede it.

All of this, by the way, applies to children of an intermarriage where the mother has not yet been converted to Judaism.

As it should be, an adopted child is given the name of its adoptive parent (for example, Aharon ben Moshe for an aliyah or Aharon ben Rivkah for a me'sheh'bay'rach). However, levitical or priestly descent is not passed on to an adopted child.

PIDYON HABEN

The ceremony of the firstborn son is also of Biblical origin:

And God spoke further to Moses, saying: Consecrate to Me every firstborn man and beast. The first issue of every womb among the children of Israel is Mine.

—Exodus 13:1–2

Consecration to the service of God was a gift, a special privilege, all the more so in contrast to the lot of firstborn Egyptians at the time of the Exodus, who were killed by the tenth plague.

In time, however, the Jews sinned by fashioning the golden calf. The consecration privilege of the firstborn was taken from the Israelites as a whole, and was given only to the tribe of Levites, who had refrained from idol worship:

Now I take the Levites instead of every firstborn among the children of Israel.

—Numbers 8:18

In particular, the privilege and responsibility for maintaining the Sanctuary was given to the descendants of Aaron, the High Priest. Thus it was that the firstborn male of an Israelite had to be redeemed by paying symbolic ransom to a priest rather than to a general Levite. Even the price of redemption was fixed in the Bible:

The firstborn . . . from a month old shall you redeem . . . Their redemption money shall be the value of five shekels of silver.

—Numbers 18:15–16

So! Every firstborn who is male, born of his mother's womb, must be redeemed from a Kohen (a Jew of priestly descent) who has replaced him in the divine service. There is no need for a Pidyon Haben if:

1. The first issue of the womb is a girl.
2. Either father or mother are of Kohen or Levi lineage (since they are dedicated to the service anyway).

3. The birth was Cesarean (it didn't issue from the womb).
4. If the mother previously miscarried a fetus that was more than three months old. If the previous miscarriage occurred some time between the fortieth day and three months, then the Pidyon Haben is required for this son; however, the blessings recited by the father are omitted.

The ceremony takes place on the thirty-first day after the birth. If the thirty-first is Shabbat, or a holiday, Pidyon Haben is postponed until a day later.

A Pidyon Haben is generally held at home. A table is set with a cup of wine. The mother carries the baby in on a pillow set on a large tray. The father, standing in front of the table, takes the baby on his pillow and places pillow with baby on the table between himself and the Kohen.

The father faces the Kohen and says:

"This is my firstborn son, the first issue of his mother's womb, that God has commanded me to redeem . . . for five shekels."

The Kohen asks:

"Which would you prefer? To give me the child, or to redeem him?"

The father answers (usually):

"To redeem him."

Then, holding the five shekels in his hand, the father recites the blessing:

בָּרוּךְ אַתָּה יְיָ, אֱלֹהֵינוּ מֶלֶךְ הָעוֹלָם אֲשֶׁר קִדְּשָׁנוּ בְּמִצְוֹתָיו, וְצִוָּנוּ עַל פִּדְיוֹן הַבֵּן.

Baruch ata Adonai Elohainu melech ha'olam asher kidshanu b'mitzvotav v'tzivanu al pidyon haben.

Blessed are You, Lord our God, Ruler of the universe, Who has commanded us regarding the redemption of the firstborn son."

He also recites the Shehecheyanu.

Then he hands the money to the Kohen, who waves it over the child's head, saying:

"This money is in place of that . . . May the child grow to a life of Torah and fear of heaven. May it be God's will that as he has entered into the redemption of the firstborn, so may he enter into a life of Torah, marriage, and good deeds."

The Kohen then puts the money down, places his hands over the child's head, and recites the priestly blessing. Next, he takes the cup of wine, recites the blessing, and the seudat mitzvah (what else!) can then begin.

Today most priests return the money to the parents as a gift for the child. Often, five silver dollars are used, or, more recently, five special silver coins struck by the Israeli government specifically for the Pidyon Haben ceremony.

The Pidyon Haben service can be found in most any siddur, or in special booklets printed with the Brit and Pidyon Haben ceremonies.

In some Jewish circles there is a move to celebrate Pidyon Habat, an equivalent ceremony for girls that expresses the parent's joy and gratitude for this first child. This has not caught on among the Orthodox, in part because these same sentiments (themes) are generally expressed at the Simchat Habat celebration, and because the idea of redeeming a girl from priestly function—which females never served—seems even more remote and vestigial than redeeming a boy, for whom it is, nevertheless, a mitzvah d'oraita, a Biblical commandment.

Socially, a Pidyon Haben has certain advantages over a Brit. You can schedule it with better advance notice, the mother is stronger and the baby less fragile, and the party can be scheduled for evening or daytime of the thirty-first day. On the other hand, one party per infant seems quite sufficient; after the high of a Brit, the Pidyon Haben always seems anticlimactic. Still, I like it because I am the wife of the Kohen who usually performs the ceremony. If the kid is real cute, I urge my husband to refuse the money and run with the kid. But some men just don't listen.

More than at a wedding, more than at a funeral, I find myself swept away with emotion at a Brit or Simchat Habat. Sometimes, it is the sense of history and past that rushes over me. At a Brit, memory bridges to consciousness: this is what Jews have been doing ever since that very first encounter between the nomad Abraham and the Creator of the Universe!

Sometimes, it is recalling what trials Jews have gone through in one era or another to have children and to circumcise their sons. Oftentimes, Brit Milah was the first thing an enemy would forbid; yet Jews would do it upon pain of death. Sometimes the joy is tinged with a moment's panic—the fear that every male Jew who carries the mark of circumcision in his flesh can be singled out on an instant's notice. Sometimes, a Brit forces me to remember that during the Holocaust, Jewish girls could risk being runners from the ghetto, while Jewish boys could not; boys had to fear the Nazi order, "Pull down your pants!"

Sometimes, at a Simchat Habat, I think to myself it will take a century until we will have built up layers of associations with the covenanting ritual of newborn females. And an instant later, I think how fortunate I am to be present at its historic beginnings.

But most of all, the feeling that surges through me, as it does through everyone present at a Brit or Simchat Habat, is the celebration of new life. New life not only for the immediate family, whose joy and love and tenderness we share, but new life for every one of us there, and for every other member of the covenanted community whose ranks this special child has now entered and enlarged. We celebrate the birth of a Jew, a precious immediate symbol of our promise, our continuity, our future, our strength. This, we know, is a child of all of us.

I'm not exactly sure how tradition and community personalize the commandment: "Be fruitful and multiply." But I know it happens. I'm not sure why Orthodox Jews still consider children to be the greatest blessing in their lives, when much else in life competes for our time and attention. But I know it is so. For this shared value alone—for not letting me lose perspective of what really counts in life, what is really important as I order my priorities—for this alone . . .

CHAPTER 11

ABORTION AND BIRTH CONTROL

Abortion

Abortion is a complex issue. Throughout the centuries, rabbis have recognized it as such. They did not give flat, simplistic rulings, but rather often made fine distinctions that are so necessary in dealing with the complexities of human life. Many rabbinic opinions regarding abortion have been registered in the vast halachic literature, so that we have before us legal precedents that range from very strict to very lenient.

In the opinion of most authorities, abortion is not considered killing. The view is derived in part from the laws concerning accidental abortion: if a man accidentally injures a pregnant woman and causes her fetus to be aborted, he must pay only damages (Exod. 21:22). (Note there that the damages are paid to the father of the fetus and not the mother.) At any rate, there is no substantial rabbinic discussion of abortion as murder. This can be sharply contrasted with the antiabortion arguments abounding today.

The general rule is that abortion is not permitted except under special circumstances:

If a woman suffers a hard [that is, protracted, life-endangering] childbirth, we are to dissect the child in her womb and bring it out piece by piece, for her life takes precedence over its life. If the greater part of the child has emerged, we may not touch it, for we are not permitted to take one life for another.

—MISHNAH OHALOT 7:6

In case of danger to the mother's life, an abortion can be—must be—performed, even up to the last moment before birth. In consequence of the focus centered on the life of the mother, there hardly appears in rabbinic literature an explicit debate on the right to life of the fetus. In fact, the Mishnah makes it clear that fetal life is not the same as newborn life.

What constitutes threat to a mother's life? Here, the opinions range from actual, imminent threat to her life at the one end, and a threat to her health at the other. The lenient interpretation of threat to health includes psychological stress or other factors significantly affecting her mental health. Interestingly, Jewish law doesn't require testimony and proof from experts. According to some authorities, her own assessment is sufficient. Thus it can be said that abortion on demand is not permitted, but in cases where carrying to term would aggravate a stressful condition or would place the mother in a situation where she could not cope, some authorities would interpret the law to permit an abortion. Other rabbis forbid abortion even when there is a strong chance of the child being born with serious birth defects, as in the thalidomide cases, and even where parents have tested positively as Tay-Sachs carriers.

In the responsa, the interpretation of threat to a mother's health has been broadened to include the health of other family members. For example, an abortion was ruled permissible where the pregnant mother would have been no longer able to continue nursing an older child, endangering its health.

In situations where the mother's actual life is not at stake, timing has something to do with the halachich rulings. Within the first forty days of pregnancy, the fetus is technically considered as water, that is, not fully formed; certain of the rabbinic rulings on abortion reflect that fact. Moreover, some rabbis make a distinction between a fetus in the first three months and the period following.

Timing happens to be one of the complicating factors in the

Tay-Sachs controversy. One in thirty Ashkenazi Jews carries Tay-Sachs genes, a very high percentage, which is why Tay-Sachs is often considered a Jewish genetic disease. Therefore, Jewish couples about to be married are routinely encouraged to be tested for Tay-Sachs. If both husband and wife are carriers, there is 1 chance in 3600 that a child will carry the dread disease in which the body begins to decay at birth and the child inexorably dies at age four or five. Amniocentesis, which cannot be performed until the fourth month, can detect the presence of Tay-Sachs genes in the fetus. Certain rabbis discourage Tay-Sachs testing and amniocentesis for fear it might lead to an abortion, and a relatively late one at that. At the other pole are rabbis who interpret a genetically impaired fetus as valid reason for an abortion, because of the severe mental and emotional stress it can place on the mother.

Rabbis do not give dispensations. They give interpretive decisions. A couple is required to consult with their rabbi as to whether halacha does or does not permit abortion in this particular situation. Thus, the traditional position is such that it gives neither a blanket veto on abortion nor unfettered license to a woman to decide what to do with her own body. The answer for an Orthodox Jew lies somewhere between these two poles. This allows community norms to be brought to bear on this most personal decision.

Yes, Orthodox women have had abortions. Because of the community's dread of abortion, however, great care is taken not to become pregnant by chance, after the desired number of children have been born. Abortion is a sensitive and private subject, and it is difficult to say whether Orthodox women who terminate a pregnancy do or do not consult with a rabbi. I know some women who did. And some who didn't.

Birth Control

Although it would seem to be self-contradictory, the contraceptive laws of Judaism seek to establish the primacy of human regeneration. At the same time, these laws acknowledge that sex drives are healthy, natural, pleasurable—and not for procreation only. In practice, then, Jewish law permits interference with natural conception, but circumscribes the method and the timing.

One can construct a positive theology of contraception: the basic principle is that the two most sacred human acts are to love and to create new life. Both of these should come together in the act of conception. But if a man and a woman were to create life each time they made love, this might well destroy love. On the other hand, contraception unlimited might lead to an inner orientation that is selfish, self-centered, and dehumanizing. To bridge the gap, then, laws of limited contraception were formulated. The laws balance the tensions between freedom and control, individual conscience and group norms, sublime principles and mundane realities. It is a practical approach, yet it does not overlook the spark of divinity that inheres in human life's creative processes. In other words, an exquisite dialectic operates here.

The laws themselves are derived from an interplay of three Biblical principles:

1. The mitzvah of pru urevu (GEN. 1:28)—be fruitful and multiply—is perhaps the most significant factor in limiting the use of birth control. Strange as it may seem, this mitzvah, the Rabbis explained, devolves upon man and not woman. (A host of sociological interpretations and Scriptural pegs are offered, but none of these totally satisfy modern sensibilities.) Nevertheless, it must be added that an alternate view does attribute to women a shared role in this mitzvah; at the very least, they enable their husbands to fulfill it. Moreover, another commandment of procreation—lashevet, to settle the earth with human life—is equally incumbent upon women and men.

What did all this mean in real life? What did it have to do with the sex life of normal human beings? Unlimited procreation? Of course not! Certainly there was an awareness that human beings must curb their breeding functions and could not simply go on multiplying without concern for the consequences. Absolute and strict interpretation of pru urevu would result in life that would be disorderly, the health and strength of women sapped, the needs of the individual treated with insensitivity. Accordingly, the Rabbis defined a bare minimum for pru urevu. The school of the great sage Hillel (first century) held that one girl and one boy were the minimum for fulfilling this mitzvah; this view was preferred over alternate minimums such as two boys or two girls and two boys. The idea was that, at the very least, human beings should replace themselves. Not to do so was not merely reprehensible, it was an outright sin. Cosmic significance was attached to the mitzvah of pru urevu: "He who does not engage in procreation it is as if he has diminished the image of God in the world."

2. On the other hand, procreation was not all there was to sex. The Biblical principle of onah (EXOD. 21:10) establishes women's rights to sexual pleasure. Sex as a woman's right and a man's responsibility? An uncommon thought! Yet there it was, a fundamental of Judaism some three thousand years before anyone heard of D. H. Lawrence or the sexual revolution.

Broader implications of onah are that marital relations are independent of generativity. If this is so, then birth control must be an appropriate condition of married life. Consider that a normal woman ovulates and produces an egg every month for about forty years of her life; consider, too, the end of niddah coincides with the peak of fertility. The only contraceptive solutions would be to curb sex or to interfere with the generative process. One might say that onah, the principle of sexual pleasure, served to eliminate rhythm as an option.

3. A third principle is that of hash'cha'tat zerah, the law forbidding improper emission of seed (semen). One source of this law is the story of Onan, who was destroyed by God because of his grave sin of "wasting his seed" on the earth. Every time he would have intercourse with his widowed and childless sister-in-law, whom he had been required to marry in order to carry on the family name, he would withdraw just before ejaculation (GEN. 38:8–10). From this story, as well as from the commandment of pru urevu, the law prohibiting coitus interruptus was derived. By extension, so was the prohibition against any other mechanical device that impeded normal intercourse. Under certain circumstances of health, however, mechanical impediments —the moch—were permitted, and thus the whole question of mechanical impediments became relativized.

But hash'cha'tat zerah was interpreted more broadly than onanism or wasting seed. Indirectly, the second interpretation was linked to the principle of onah, marital pleasure. Thus, any form of intercourse that impeded the fullest pleasure of the sex act was forbidden. The male and female sex organs were optimally to be in direct and fullest contact.

These three broad factors, plus the ever-present overarching considerations of health, were the bases of countless rabbinic decisions over the years. The question generally wasn't whether birth control is or isn't permitted. It is. The real questions centered on whether a particular type of birth control device was permissible or preferable, and under what circumstances was that so. While it would be impossible here to give every difference of opinion, along with its circumstances, we can draw some general conclusions:

Under what circumstances is birth control permitted?

1. Technically, a couple is not permitted to use birth control until they have met the minimum requirements of pru urevu. Since this was the naturally accepted thing for women to do— that is, marry and begin their families immediately—questions of practicing birth control right after marriage, except for reasons of health, were hardly ever asked.

2. However, there are legitimate questions of spacing of children, family planning, and so forth. In several responsa, we learn that contraception is permitted as long as a couple intends to have children at some point or other in their married lives. These particular rabbinic decisions are relevant to the modern Orthodox, many of whose young married women are not having babies as soon as they marry, but rather are completing their educations or establishing themselves in careers. In all honesty, it must be said, that we do not find in the sources justification for contraception based on pure convenience, priority of career, or financial considerations. Formally, these are not sufficient reasons for delaying a family. What has happened, then, is that many Orthodox couples use the lenient interpretations of birth control as a base upon which to construct their own decisions about timing. Couples are aware, in light of the law, that it is preferable to begin their families earlier rather than wait extensively. Contemporary Orthodox women on the whole do begin their families

sooner than their more secular counterparts. Whether it is law or community that affects their decision is hard to say. For many Jews living in the post-Holocaust era, there is a special desire to affirm life in the most real way—by having children.

WHICH METHOD MAY BE USED?

Some methods are forbidden outright, others are ranked in terms of preference. All of the statements below are general conclusions. One must consult a rabbi for definitive answers.

Sterilization

Permanent sterilization is considered mutilation. For this reason, as well as for its negation of pru urevu, it is forbidden outright. Sterilization by means of oral contraceptives (known as the kos shel ikkarim, the cup of roots) was forbidden by some Rabbis because it was thought to be permanent, yet was permitted by others because it was understood to be temporary. Sterilization of the male is forbidden under any circumstance.

Tying the fallopian tubes

This is at times permitted, because it does not impede intercourse, nor is it permanent, since the tubes can be surgically reconnected.

Rhythm

Since rhythm-combined-with-niddeh would mean abstaining from sex altogether it is usually forbidden on grounds of onah.

Coitus interruptus

Onanism notwithstanding, coitus interruptus is sometimes permitted when insemination would otherwise present a possible health hazard for the woman.

The condom

Condoms are not permitted, as they interfere with normal intercourse. "And he shall cleave unto his wife and they shall become one flesh" (GEN. 2:24). Moreover, condoms restrict the male; since the mitzvah of pru urevu is upon him, all forms of male contraception are inherently objectionable. And third, the condom prevents his seed from being deposited in the vaginal canal, and therefore makes intercourse more unnatural.

The diaphragm

Until the pill was discovered, the diaphragm was probably the most widely used contraceptive device among traditional Jews. It does not interfere with normal intercourse; all it does is close the entrance to the uterus, thus preventing passage of sperm to the egg. It does not kill the sperm, but rather allows it to die naturally. Some authorities still object on the grounds that it is a mechanical barrier, but even these sources find it less objectionable because it operates on the woman.

Spermicides

These are permitted by some authorities but rejected by others on the grounds that the seed is chemically destroyed. The majority of those who compare spermicide to diaphragm find diaphragm less objectionable. The douche, which doesn't kill the sperm, is less objectionable, but is ruled out by several rabbis on the grounds that it doesn't work, and therefore to rely on it might cause impregnation when it should be avoided for health reasons.

IUD

This is somewhat controversial because scientists are still not sure whether it causes an abortion of the egg after it is fertilized, or whether it simply prevents the egg from being fertilized. In recent years, medical evidence seems to be leaning toward the former, that is, that it prevents implantation of the fertilized egg.

If this should become definitively established, those who have ruled in favor of the IUD would probably shift their ruling, since aborting a fertilized egg is a much more serious objection than preventing fertilization of an egg.

The pill

This or other oral contraceptives which do not *permanently* alter a woman's fecundity is permitted to women (but not to men because of pru urevu). Most rabbinic authorities see the oral contraceptive as the preferred method, for it does not interfere in any way with natural intercourse. It allows the seed to travel along its natural path without being destroyed.

The pill, however, has two problems: one is that it can cause bleeding which would render a woman niddah almost the entire month. Second, as we discover increasingly with every passing year, the pill can have negative side effects which may not show up for years, but which can adversely affect children born to anovulant pill users. Many Jewish women who formerly relied on the pill have now returned to other methods which they deem safer to their own and to their future children's health.

In sum, everything is forbidden and everything is permitted. The Rabbis, past and present, dealt with the issue at great length, trying to bridge the gap between the ideal and the real. Family size and spacing, health, the claims of community, history, and tradition, the intimate needs of the couple, the specific timing and methods of birth control, the far-reaching implications of creating life or curtailing it—a hundred factors come into play in every contraceptive decision. And that is exactly as it should be.

CHAPTER 12

BAR MITZVAH—
BAT MITZVAH

With or without fanfare, when a boy reaches thirteen, and a girl reaches twelve, he/she becomes Bar or Bat Mitzvah, an adult in the eyes of Jewish law, responsible for the full range of mitzvot. It is an involuntary step, as is all growth. In one sense, then, Bar or Bat Mitzvah can be understood as the involuntary act of growing into Jewish maturity.

Twelve- and thirteen-year-olds, however, are quite capable of making voluntary responses, so the celebration of Bar and Bat Mitzvah, essentially, is the celebration of the joyous acceptance of this responsibility.

Now, let us look at it from another angle. One of the special qualities of Judaism is that nothing is taken for granted. Not a thing—not biological growth, nor physical sensations, nor events in nature, nor emotional stages—goes by unnoticed. This extraordinary quality of acute awareness and celebration always applied in greater measure to male experiences and stages of growth. But under the impact of new values for women, the imbalance is being corrected.

The fact that a young man at thirteen became fully responsible for observing the commandments of the Torah and was simultaneously conferred with full rights as an adult Jew made it only logical that a rite of passage connected to the Torah should develop. Thus, the core of the ceremony was an aliyah to the Torah at which a thirteen-year-old recited the Torah blessings.

This symbolized his commitment to Torah, his voluntary acceptance of the covenant, and his full rights as an adult Jew.

From the perspective of what a thirteen-year-old is all about, it was a brilliant puberty rite, a simple yet profound ritual that caught a child-man at this important transition stage in his life and focused his energies in a particular direction—of Torah, synagogue, mitzvot, community, and faith. . . .

Bar Mitzvah

CELEBRATION

The term "Bar Mitzvah" is used interchangeably to refer to the celebrant or to the celebration. It is a noun, not a verb, and though people often do say, "David was Bar Mitzvahed," this usage is nevertheless incorrect.

To celebrate the event of Bar Mitzvah, all one needs, besides a thirteen-year-old boy, is a day on which the Torah is read in a minyan, prearrangement for him to be called up for an aliyah, and a seudat mitzvah in honor of that event.

The Torah is read at morning services every Monday, Thursday, Shabbat and holidays. It is also read each Rosh Chodesh, the first day of a new Hebrew month. Although the Torah is read on fast days, with accompanying aliyot, for obvious reasons a Bar Mitzvah is not celebrated at that time. Theoretically, a boy could be called up for his first aliyah during Shabbat or holiday Minchah (afternoon services), for the Torah is read at that time too; but this is very rarely done.

In these times, most families celebrate the Bar Mitzvah on Shabbat. However, in previous generations a Monday or Thursday Bar Mitzvah was quite common. Millions of Jewish boys throughout history have celebrated the event simply by having an aliyah in shul on Monday or Thursday morning, followed by a slightly more elaborate breakfast or lunch at home.

SELECTING THE DATE

The celebration should be held as soon as possible after the thirteenth birthday, according to the Hebrew calendar. Originally, Jewish manhood was defined by the development of secondary sexual characteristics such as the growth of pubic hair. Rather than check each individual for physical signs, the age of thirteen years and one day was chosen as the standard day. As soon as the child is born, one can know what his Torah portion will be simply by consulting a comprehensive (hundred-year) Hebrew calendar. If the Bar Mitzvah is to be celebrated on Shabbat, the date should be reserved on the shul calendar many months in advance. Some synagogues have a policy not to schedule two Bar Mitzvah celebrants on the same day.

Although formal celebration might not be scheduled for the week of his birthday, it is customary to call up the young man for an aliyah at the first Torah reading after his thirteenth Hebrew birthday plus one day. In many yeshiva day schools, he is called up for his first aliyah on Monday or Thursday at the school morning minyan, to which his family has been invited.

THE SYNAGOGUE

Because the essence of the ceremony is so simple—reciting the Torah blessings—it allows great flexibility in embellishing it. For example, on a Shabbat Bar Mitzvah in an Orthodox congregation, a boy might very well lead the Friday-night services. On Shabbat morning, he might lead the entire service, or perhaps only Shacharit. He will generally read the entire Torah portion, and the Haftorah, although some choose to read only the verses of their aliyah. In smaller congregations, he may be permitted to give a dvar Torah before Mussaf, the additional service for Sabbath.

THE ALIYAH

The Maftir, the eighth and final pair of Torah blessings, is the aliyah traditionally reserved for a Shabbat Bar Mitzvah; this is so even if he has read the entire Torah reading before he gets to his aliyah. The aliyah blessings are as follows:

בָּרְכוּ אֶת יְיָ הַמְבֹרָךְ.

Congregation responds:

בָּרוּךְ יְיָ הַמְבֹרָךְ לְעוֹלָם וָעֶד.

He repeats the response and continues:

בָּרוּךְ אַתָּה יְיָ, אֱלֹהֵינוּ מֶלֶךְ הָעוֹלָם, אֲשֶׁר בָּחַר בָּנוּ מִכָּל הָעַמִּים, וְנָתַן לָנוּ אֶת־תּוֹרָתוֹ. בָּרוּךְ אַתָּה יְיָ, נוֹתֵן הַתּוֹרָה.

Barchu et Adonai hamvorach. Baruch Adonai hamvorach l'olam va-ed.

Baruch ata Adonai Elohainu melech ha'olam asher bachar banu mikol ha-amim, v'natan lanu et torato. Baruch ata Adonai, notain hatorah.

Bless the Lord Who is blessed. Blessed be the Lord Who is blessed forever and ever.

Blessed are You, Lord our God, Ruler of the universe, Who has chosen us from among all peoples by giving us Your Torah.

Blessed are You, Lord, giver of the Torah.

Just before he recites these blessings he will kiss the Torah. He does not actually lean over and kiss it. Instead, with the fringes of the tallit (prayer shawl) between his fingers, he touches the spot where the reading paused, then brings the tallit fringes to his lips to kiss.

Immediately after the Torah portion is read, he will again kiss the spot where the reading concluded, and recite this blessing:

בָּרוּךְ אַתָּה יְיָ, אֱלֹהֵינוּ מֶלֶךְ הָעוֹלָם, אֲשֶׁר נָתַן לָנוּ תּוֹרַת אֱמֶת, וְחַיֵּי עוֹלָם נָטַע בְּתוֹכֵנוּ. בָּרוּךְ אַתָּה יְיָ, נוֹתֵן הַתּוֹרָה.

Baruch ata Adonai Elohainu melech ha'olam asher natan lanu torat emet, v'chayai olam nata b'tochainu. Baruch ata Adonai, notain hatorah.

Blessed are You, Lord our God, Ruler of the universe, Who has given us Your Torah of truth and thereby planted among us life eternal. Blessed are You, O Lord, giver of the Torah.

BARUCH SHEH'P'TARANI

Immediately after his final blessing, the boy's father will recite these words:

Baruch sheh'p'tarani Me'ansho shel zeh.

Blessed be He Who has released me from the responsibilities [punishment] of this child.

It sounds harsh, but in fact it has no bearing whatsoever on the next ten years of the parent-child relationship, high-school education, college tuitions, discipline, health and welfare, and so forth. What it really symbolizes is that the Bar Mitzvah has now reached Jewish maturity and is independently responsible for his own action or inaction. The blessing lends a sense of closure to the involuntary cycle that began with the Brit. Now the young man must make his own determination to carry on the ways of his forebears. As soon as the father recites the blessing, in many synagogues the congregation will sing a mazel-tov song.

HONORING THE GUESTS

Other aliyot are usually distributed to members of the family and their special guests. In larger synagogues, a certain number of aliyot are reserved for the celebrating family. In smaller synagogues, oftentimes all of the aliyot and indeed all of the synagogue honors, such as leading the services and giving the guest sermon, are at the discretion of the Bar Mitzvah family.

Two examples of the ability of Jewish law to accommodate personal needs: sometimes there are not enough aliyot to go around. On one Shabbat there might be two Bar Mitzvah celebrations, a groom's ufruf ("calling up" for an aliyah the day before his wedding), a new baby born, an ill person to pray for, or someone's near escape from an accident, all of which warrant an individual aliyah. Moreover, the first two aliyot are reserved exclusively for Kohen and Levi. These aliyot cannot be given to an Israelite if a Kohen or Levi is present. In order to "free up" the first two aliyot, those who are of priestly or levitical descent will step into the vestibule for a brief moment while the sexton calls up an Israelite, "in place of" a Kohen or Levi.

On occasion, hosafot are added. These are additions to the regular seven aliyot. A pause is made in between one of the latter aliyot, and an additional person is called up to recite the Torah blessings. Many congregations, however, prefer not to do this, because then the Torah readings and the service drag on too long. Where there is an urgency to honor additional guests or family members, however, it can be and has been done.

In most synagogues, the rabbi's sermon follows the Torah reading. At the end of the sermon, the rabbi will call up the Bar Mitzvah boy to say a few words directly to him. It can be a bit uncomfortable or awkward for a thirteen-year-old; parents can help by reviewing with him where to put his hands, eyes, feet— all of which seem to feel unconnected to his body at that moment of full public view. As a friend replied to her jittery son, trying to relax him when he asked where he should put his feet, "Just walk them over and set them down near the rabbi and then let the rest of your body settle on them to hold them steady."

After services, the family will often host a Kiddush in the shul social hall, to which members of the congregation may be invited. The Bar Mitzvah boy usually recites the Kiddush blessing for all the guests. The Kiddush reception can be simple or lavish depending on the inclination of the family and the size of the congregation. For some families, the Kiddush will suffice as the seudat mitzvah. Where that is so, challah should be provided in order to recite the hamotzi and to conclude with the Grace which formally symbolize a meal.

An ounce of prevention: Although most Bar Mitzvah boys are well bred and quite mature, it doesn't hurt to take sixty seconds before the big day to remind a young man how to shake hands, look directly at well-wishers, accept graciously the hugs and kisses of loving relatives, and remain accessible until all the guests have left. Also, that he should not remove his jacket at the Kiddush, not play with soda-pop bottles in the corner of the room as his less mature friends might tempt him to do, nor to roll his eyes if someone says "I was at your Brit."

SEUDAT MITZVAH

As with most other happy events, we celebrate with a religious feast. At the seudat mitzvah, the boy will lead in the hamotzi and in the mezuman, the quorum that convenes the Grace After Meals. He will most likely recite his Dvar Torah at the seudat mitzvah rather than in the synagogue. If the space and setting allow, there will be speeches, dancing, and singing. Some families and friends prepare a skit and write grammen (rhymed lyrics) about the Bar Mitzvah boy.

THE DVAR TORAH

Most Bar Mitzvah boys are expected to prepare some words of Torah with commentaries or a discussion of a Talmudic passage. Occasionally this is delivered during services, but more often it is part of the seudah. The boy is usually asked to work on it himself, but he often needs some help from parents, rabbi, and/ or teachers. In the more right-wing yeshivot and Chasidic communities, the tradition is to have the boy memorize and recite a complex and sometimes abstruse Talmudic discussion, complete with post-Talmudic commentaries and arguments on the fine points of the law. Sometimes the boy really understands, sometimes not. However, one cannot really say that this is less meaningful than a speech prepared on one's own; at the very least, it is a symbol of his commitment to be familiar with the sources and the methods of learning. Simply to memorize such a speech is an accomplishment and an important statement in this rite of passage.

HOW TO CELEBRATE

The seudat mitzvah, like the synagogue ritual, allows for great flexibility. It can range from simple to elaborate as one's taste and finances allow. Happily, the trend these days, even with catered affairs, is toward the simple. I haven't been to an ice-duck Bar Mitzvah in at least a decade. People do keep in mind that a Bar Mitzvah is not a wedding, and they scale it down accordingly. One should have a clear notion of simplicity before setting out to negotiate with a caterer. Party planners, the cooks at the local yeshiva, kosher take-home food places, a talented amateur cook in the neighborhood who is on the verge of striking out professionally—there are many resources to call upon.

LOGISTICS

The advantage of a Shabbat or holiday celebration is that there is a special aura about marking an event in holy time, and with one's full community. The disadvantage for Orthodox Jews is that a family and friends who are not within walking distance must arrive before Shabbat and stay until it has ended. Many people cannot leave their homes for the entire Shabbat. More-over, for the host family, it means providing lodgings and several meals for a large crowd.

There are numerous ways to get around the "distant guests" problem:

1. Schedule the Bar Mitzvah for Shabbat morning, with a Kid-dush or luncheon following services and then
2. Host an open house—with staggered times if it's a small house and a large crowd—on a Sunday for guests who couldn't come for Shabbat. In winter, when Shabbat ends early, Sat-urday night is also a good time for an open house.
3. Host a catered brunch or dinner on Sunday following Sha-charit or Minchah services. Even though the boy had his aliyah on Shabbat, the fact that he leads the prayers allows guests to feel that they are participating in his religious ma-turation and not just a party.
4. Schedule the Bar Mitzvah for a Sunday Rosh Chodesh or a weekday holiday when the Torah is read.
5. Combine several of the above. I have been to numerous Labor Day (Monday morning) or Thanksgiving Day (Thurs-

day morning) Bar Mitzvah celebrations which were "second affairs," with the boy leading the weekday services and reading a new Torah portion just as he had done several days earlier for Shabbat services and the previous week's Torah reading. It wasn't just a rerun; on the contrary, it symbolized that the boy had mastered two sets of skills.

Other alternatives: Some people take all their guests to a hotel for Shabbat; some families celebrate the Bar Mitzvah in Israel at the Western Wall or Masada with whichever extended family and friends happen to be in Israel at the time.

PREPARATION

Preparation for a Bar Mitzvah really begins when the child is born. Everything we do with our children is to teach them not only to become "mentschen," mature, decent human beings, but also to take upon themselves, bit by bit, step by step, an entire way of life known as ohl mitzvot, the yoke of the commandments. "Yoke" often carries with it a negative connotation, so let us think of it as the mantle of mitzvot, as is symbolized by the tallit on the shoulders of the thirteen-year-old, a child, who takes on as an adult a broad and deep range of commandments for which he has been training for as long as he can remember. Like all things in life, the event takes on significance in direct proportion to the preparations for it.

THE PRE-BAR MITZVAH YEAR

Nevertheless, like a symphony, Bar Mitzvah reaches a crescendo in a series of last-minute or final-year moments of intensity. The year before the Bar Mitzvah is something quite special. During that year, a boy will begin to learn the how-to of many Jewish rituals.

He will begin to learn the prayer services sufficiently well so that he can lead a minyan. This is generally taught in his school, where he will learn by trial and error by being given a chance to lead the school minyan.

LEARNING TRUP (CANTILLATIONS)

If a Bar Mitzvah boy is to read the entire Torah portion, it is well to secure a good teacher a year in advance of the date, for it is not that easy a task to master. There are many fine teachers—including some women—who specialize in teaching trup, the Torah cantillations. Synagogue cantors and sextons also have much experience and enjoy the opportunity. If a parent has the skills, the time, and the right chemistry, there is nothing better. I know of one woman, an excellent Torah reader herself, who helped her son with his trup lessons. Many boys are aided by the use of tapes that are prepared specially with their parshah.

The Bar Mitzvah boy will surely be practicing around the house for many hours. A month or so before his "debut," the practicing will intensify. By the time each of our sons reached his Bar Mitzvah day, his siblings and some of his closest friends, knew most of his Torah reading by heart.

One word of advice to parents: if the child doesn't seem to be picking up the melody, seems tone deaf, and makes the same errors week after week, stay calm. Children learn at different rates. All of our children were prepared for Bar or Bat Mitzvah by their father. He taught the three boys to read trup. Moshe learned his portion in three weeks, and then hardly practiced the whole year long. David learned evenly and at a steady pace; a month before his Bar Mitzvah, we switched the date to one week later, so he had to learn an entirely new portion, which he did with great calm. J.J. studied for several months, with little progress; just when his father was secretly convinced that J.J. had cantillation dyslexia, he got his whole act together and outperformed our wildest dreams for him. Not one mistake. . . .

A week before the Bar Mitzvah, a boy will read the first part of his Torah portion, without an aliyah, at Minchah on Shabbat afternoon. It is kind of a tryout for him. So, too, at the Monday- and Thursday-morning minyan. By the time the next Shabbat comes he will have developed some public presence. Even so, if there is time during the week prior to the actual Bar Mitzvah, it doesn't hurt to have a full dress rehearsal at the synagogue where he can read from the bimah (the platform) and practice leading the prayers, just as he will be doing before a full house on the coming Shabbat. If he is to give a Dvar Torah in shul, that, too.

TEFILLIN

More important for a boy than learning to read the Torah with cantillations, more important than the seudat mitzvah, more important than anything else connected with his Bar Mitzvah is his introduction to tefillin, phylacteries. As an adult Jew, he will be required to wear tefillin daily, one for the hand and one for the head. "And you shall bind them as a sign upon your hand and they shall serve as a symbol between your eyes" (DEUT. 6:8). Tefillin are worn on weekdays, while reciting the Shacharit prayers.

In outward appearance, tefillin are two sealed black boxes with long, black leather straps attached. Inside each box (bayit) is a tightly rolled parchment on which a scribe has painstakingly and finely written four Biblical pericopes: Exodus 13:1–10; 13:11–16; Deuteronomy 6:4–9; 11:13–21.

Because of the exactness with which they are written, sealed, painted black, positioned on arm and head, straps wound around hand and fingers, the way they are removed and placed in their protective box, tefillin possess a mystique that goes beyond the contents of the four passages inscribed within. It is all part of the magic that engages and absorbs a young, impressionable boy.

Unless tefillin are ordered long distance, such as from Israel, fathers will generally take their sons to buy tefillin together, and teach them how to put them on. To be given the tefillin of a beloved deceased grandfather is especially meaningful to a young boy.

For educational purposes, a boy will begin to put on tefillin before he reaches Jewish maturity. Our sons all started approximately two months before the Bar Mitzvah day. Sephardic Jews make a special celebration out of this day, called Yom Tefillin. They take the child to the synagogue, or to the Western Wall in Jerusalem, and there he puts on tefillin under the watchful company of family and friends. Afterward they make a special party to celebrate. Among Ashkenazim, it is a less formal and more private affair. One especially moving memory is of my husband teaching J.J. to put on tefillin, and discussing with him what tefillin are all about. The amateur photographer in this family lurked about the corners of the room, as inconspicuously as possible so as not to distract from the quietly wonderful happening, and recorded the whole thing for posterity. I highly recommend it.

If there is no one at home who puts on tefillin, it can be taught by anyone in shul or school or learned from a book. There are a number of books available that explain how to put on tefillin.

Two special blessings are recited when donning the tefillin. The first is recited just before the tefillin shel yad (arm) are fastened to the arm:

בָּרוּךְ אַתָּה יְיָ, אֱלֹהֵינוּ מֶלֶךְ הָעוֹלָם אֲשֶׁר קִדְּשָׁנוּ בְּמִצְוֹתָיו, וְצִוָּנוּ לְהָנִיחַ תְּפִלִּין.

Baruch ata Adonai Elohainu melech ha'olam asher kidshanu b'mitzvotav v'tzivanu l'hanee-ach tefillin.

Blessed are You, Lord our God, Ruler of the universe, Who has sanctified us with His commandments and commanded us to put on tefillin.

The second is recited when the tefillin shel rosh (head) are placed on the head:

בָּרוּךְ אַתָּה יְיָ, אֱלֹהֵינוּ מָלֶךְ הָעוֹלָם, אֲשֶׁר קִדְּשָׁנוּ בְּמִצְוֹתָיו, וְצִוָּנוּ עַל מִצְוַת תְּפִלִּין.

Baruch ata Adonai Elohainu melech ha'olam asher kidshanu b'mitzvotav v'tzivanu al mitzvat tefillin.

Blessed are You, Lord our God, Ruler of the universe, Who has sanctified us with His commandments and commanded us concerning the mitzvah of tefillin.

The Rabbis were not sure whether this second blessing was proper, since both phylacteries make up one composite mitzvah.

So they added the formula that is recited in case a superfluous blessing has just been made:

בָּרוּךְ שֵׁם כְּבוֹד מַלְכוּתוֹ לְעוֹלָם וָעֶד.

Baruch shem kvod malchuto l'olam va-ed.

Blessed be He Whose glorious majesty is forever and ever.

Ritual has its own power, the power of habit. Once a youth begins to wear tefillin, in all likelihood he will continue to wear them every day for the rest of his life. But not on Shabbat, holidays, Tisha B'Av morning, or as an onen (one who grieves the loss of an immediate relative who has not yet been buried). The reason tefillin are worn only on weekdays is that they are considered a sign of the covenant; inasmuch as Shabbat and holidays are also signs, tefillin were considered superfluous.

Tefillin are kept in a special bag, which can be purchased or handmade. Tefillin should be periodically inspected by a professional scribe, at least two times every seven years. Even though the parchment is sealed inside the box, which is then placed in another protective box, which is then stored in its own bag, the parchment can somehow become damaged: a letter can fade and must be reinscribed, or the straps may need to be reblackened.

TALLIT

A boy who is a Kohen, and who will henceforth don a tallit several times a year to offer the priestly blessing, will buy a special tallit for the Bar Mitzvah. Unlike tefillin, however, purchasing a tallit is not absolutely essential. In most Orthodox communities, a tallit is worn only by married men. Other than the Bar Mitzvah day, and occasionally coming up for an aliyah or leading the service, an unmarried man will not wear a tallit for prayer.

Bat Mitzvah

Although some of the above can be applied to females as well, the plain truth is that girls were short-changed as tradition developed, without taking them seriously in many areas of Jewish life. Never mind that women are the carriers of the faith (that is, a Jew is one born to a Jewish mother); most of synagogue life, liturgy, and Torah study were closed off to them. For example, tradition offers no equivalent for females to the powerful liturgical stimulus of tefillin.

But the good news is that times are changing, including a communal awareness of Jewish female adulthood. Bat Mitzvah was introduced by Reconstructionists, later taken up by Reform, and then Conservative Jews. Only in the last decade have the Orthodox begun to integrate Bat Mitzvah celebration as part of community norms. When I became Bat Mitzvah, the only thing that was special about that day was my awareness that from then on I would have to fast a full day on Tisha B'Av and Yom Kippur. True, in some Orthodox communities, Bat Mitzvah still goes by unnoticed. But in most—modern as well as the more traditional —there is an active recognition of a twelve-year-old girl becoming Bat Mitzvah. In many synagogues, shaleshudos, the third meal, taken between Minchah and Maariv services on Shabbat afternoon, has become the accepted time for celebrating a young woman's entry into Jewish adulthood. Often, it will entail a dvar Torah, prepared by the Bat Mitzvah girl, and a speech by the rabbi, and perhaps another by her father. In modern Orthodox day schools, the girl gives a Dvar Torah at the morning minyan.

The process of tradition and change is inherently slow, but it is inexorable. In the last five years, there have been several "revolutionary" Bat Mitzvah celebrations. Revolutionary because they were never before done in history, revolutionary because they set the tone and serve as a model for others. One was a Sunday-morning Rosh Chodesh Bat Mitzvah in which the women and men guests prayed at two separate minyanim. At the women's service the Bat Mitzvah girl led the prayers and read her parshah. The four aliyot were given to women who had never before in their lives had an aliyah, including an Orthodox grandmother of sixty-eight. With the exception of tefillin, the preparations of the Bat Mitzvah girl during the preceding year were similar to that of any Bar Mitzvah boy.

The second Bat Mitzvah was even more extraordinary, in that it took place on Shabbat morning, again at a women's minyan. The young woman read the entire Torah portion and the Haftorah with perfect cantillation. All of the aliyot were given to women; the mother of the Bat Mitzvah girl led the Mussaf prayers. Her father, uncle, and brother sat behind the mechitza.

The way I see it, this is a transition generation. Currently, for most families who celebrate the Bat Mitzvah of their daughter, the feast is fuller than the religious ceremony. Nevertheless, that imbalance will be righted in due time. The combination of women's learning, the models from society all around us, and the ripple effect of religious celebration in the liberal Jewish denominations are slowly taking root in the Orthodox community at this time in history.

Surely it will not happen overnight, but rather in a series of "clicks." Several years ago, Deborah, then fifteen, was talking to a twelve-year-old guest, trying to make him feel at home. He mentioned he was studying for his Bar Mitzvah. "What is your parshah?" asked Deborah. "Kedoshim" (in Leviticus), he answered. "Oh, that was my parshah, too." There was a pause. "What do you mean?" the boy asked. "Girls don't have a parshah from the Torah, only boys do!" But then Deborah went on to explain to him how she prepared to become a Bat Mitzvah. He looked at her for a long time, his fertile mind opening up to engage a brand-new idea.

I do not know how history will record, a hundred years from now, the celebration of women coming under the mantle of mitzvot. I do know, however, that what is now inviolate as regards a boy of thirteen did not even exist a thousand years ago.

And community plays a powerful role. Deborah had to prepare her Bat Mitzvah speech by herself. Given her native intelligence and excellent study habits, we knew she would produce an original and wise speech, which she did. But at twelve, Deborah was also extremely shy, painfully shy. I could not imagine that she would stand and speak even before her classmates, much less before a number of adult family and friends. Yet, like a million Bar Mitzvah boys through history, that is exactly what she did, and with perfect poise despite a heart that surely must have been fluttering wildly. She rose to the occasion. I know that if it had not been expected of her by the "community" she would never have done it. And if more had been expected of her, she would have done that, too.

Some Practical Suggestions

INVITATIONS

A Bar or Bat Mitzvah is not a casual event. Therefore, invitations should be sent out in advance or telephoned with sufficient lead time. They should always be printed in Hebrew and in English. In addition to pertinent information an invitation might include a suitable phrase from the Torah: (1) from the parshah to be read; (2) if the child has a Biblical name, from some passage related to his namesake; (3) a special Biblical phrase particularly appropriate to him/her; (4) or using one's "pasuk." Most Jewish names have a pasuk, a verse from Scriptures. The first and last letters of the pasuk are the same as the first and last letters of the name. For example, David is Dirshu Hashem Ve'uzo, Bakshu Panav tami*d*, which means "Seek God and His strength, and forever search for His face." The verse for Natan is from Proverbs 20:27: "*N*er hashem nishmat adam chofes kol chadrei bahte*n*," "The human spirit is the lamp of the Lord illuminating the inner emotions."

The pasuk can be found in a siddur right after the Shmoneh Esreh of the daily shacharit, or a rabbi can find it handily. As with other parts of tradition, women were overlooked. Thus, the appropriate pasuk for a female name will not be found in the siddur. However, a rabbi can help with this, or it can be a special project for the family to find a pasuk in Scriptures for the Bat Mitzvah girl's name.

To avoid postmortems, make out the invitation list well in advance. Address the envelopes and sit on them for a week or two. We all have to make choices, and sometimes these come out differently on a different day. It is better to aggravate over it in advance rather than spend nine months following the bar mitzvah "working through" one's mistake. I know.

SYNAGOGUE DECORUM

If the Bar or Bat Mitzvah is going to be held in shul on Shabbat, and the invitation will be sent to people who are not Sabbath-observant, a printed card should be enclosed explaining the customs of the community. That ends up to be less embarrassing all around. The card can read something like this: "We wish to share with you some of the customs observed in our synagogue: cars are not driven to the synagogue on the Sabbath, women do not carry pocketbooks; men wear kipot on their heads (these are available at the entrance to the sanctuary); married women cover their heads as well—a hat is advised; dress is always modest in taste; packages are not brought to the synagogue on the Sabbath."

Many synagogue offices will print up such a note under their own letterhead. Some synagogues already have standard decorum cards printed, which are available just for the asking.

TZEDAKAH

Many families make a contribution to the synagogue and to the school on the occasion of their child's Bar or Bat Mitzvah. These, after all, are the institutions without which it would have been infinitely more difficult to have brought the child to this day. In addition, it is appropriate to encourage the young celebrant, who often receives monetary gifts, to contribute one tenth, a tithe, to charities of his or her own selection. It is a mitzvah, an act of gratitude, and a good habit that should be taught at an early age.

DECORATING THE SYNAGOGUE

It is a lovely touch to decorate the shul with flowers, plants, or some other greenery for the occasion.

GIFTS

Some people like to give money as a gift for all occasions. Others like to give gifts they know the child will particularly enjoy (such as a microscope for the budding scientist). Still others prefer to give gifts that have a Jewish touch. In this latter category are sefarim (books of Jewish learning), other books of Jewish interest, tallit and tefillin bag (for boys), etrog box, Kiddush cup, Shabbat candlesticks (for girls), subscription to a Jewish publication, besamim box, mezuzah, or Chanukah menorah.

RECORD KEEPING

Keep a notebook with lists of who has been invited for Shabbat, for Sunday, for both, table arrangements, countdown details. Go over the list of invitees with the young celebrant so that he/ she will at least recognize second cousins Helen and Lily when they appear. Also, enter the addresses so that when it comes time to write a thank-you note, the young person will have no excuse that the address cannot be found. Jewish maturity is "Torah im Derech Eretz," which is translated as "Torah plus good manners."

Bar Mitzvah is a wonderful event. The extended family comes together for a happy occasion; it is a celebration that ties in community, synagogue, Torah, and family; you don't have the guest list of future in-laws to cope with; and the morning after, you can take the child home with you. And in addition to all of that, it is a symbol of everything we put into our children. On the way to J.J.'s second Bar Mitzvah celebration, we were doing our usual thing: reviewing details last minute to see what we had missed. It was a Sunday-afternoon affair, and we scheduled it in the synagogue so that we could use the sanctuary for Minchah before the dinner. But we hadn't determined who would lead the prayers. Without much forethought, we turned to the spiffily dressed Bar Mitzvah boy wedged between us on the front seat of the car. "Do you want to daaven Minchah for the amud [lead the prayers]?" "Okay," said J.J., and then we moved on to another detail. It was only later, as I sat in the red-carpeted synagogue and listened for the first time in my life to J.J. orchestrate the Minchah prayers, knowing just when to read aloud, knowing just when to wait for the congregation to respond, that I began to realize what we had taken for granted. I thought to myself that every penny we spent on his education was worth it, just for that moment alone.

Whichever way a family celebrates, Bar or Bat Mitzvah is an important day in the life of a young Jew. And it doesn't end with that day. It remains alive in the memory, a focal point of one's adult life. A young person will associate a particular portion of the Torah with his or her coming of age. More than that, it becomes his or her parshah for life. Many a Bar Mitzvah boy is called up for an aliyah and reads his parshah every year thereafter.

A parent will continue to educate his/her children and remind them of their responsibilities as a Jew. But the task is made that much easier because the young person knows from this day on what tradition and community expect of him/her.

Torah and mitzvot. What an incredible rite of passage!

CHAPTER 13

DIVORCE

From ancient times onward, Judaism permitted divorce. However, tradition always understood divorce to be a last resort. "Even the altar sheds tears when a man divorces his wife," the Talmud teaches us.

Although permitted, divorce was never commonplace in Jewish society. Today, no group is completely safe from the ravages of a contemporary divorce culture ("It's okay, everyone's doing it"); nevertheless, Orthodox Jews, like members of other traditionalist communities, seem to enjoy a measure of insularity. In my own synagogue for example, with 350 member families, there has been a total of approximately ten divorces during the last decade. In a random sample of other traditional synagogues in and around New York City, the rates are well below the norm.

Nevertheless, divorce among traditional Jews does exist, and will continue to be a reality, for even marriages made in heaven can fail. That being so, Jewish law is most specific about how a divorce must be effected. Just as the marriage is formed according to the laws of Moses and Israel, so must it be dissolved in that manner. Without a Jewish divorce, a man and woman are still considered married even if they have already secured a civil divorce.

A Jewish divorce goes something like this: after all attempts at reconciliation have failed, and the husband and wife have either been granted a civil divorce or have mutually agreed to seek one, they arrange to appear before a bet din, a Jewish court of law. The bet din consists of three rabbis, each of whom is an expert in the intricate laws of gittin, Jewish divorce. Since Jewish divorce is not a decree of the court but rather a transaction between two parties, various authorities maintain that a single expert suffices. (The prevalent custom in America is to require only one rabbi.) In either case, a sofer (scribe) and two male witnesses must also be present. The wife will often bring along a friend to help her get through the trying time; so will the husband. The appointment with the bet din or officiating rabbi can be scheduled by one's own rabbi, lawyer, or by the parties themselves.

The essence of a Jewish divorce is the giving of the get, the writ of divorce. The man gives the writ of divorce to the woman, who accepts it, in the presence of two witnesses. It is not an adversary proceeding; no reasons are given, no fault finding, no financial arrangements are made at this time. All of that was taken care of at some previous time, including prior attempts on the part of the bet din to effect a reconciliation or, barring that, an agreeable financial settlement. Despite all that, it is neither a simple nor easy matter.

First the scribe must write the writ of divorce. Before he begins the actual writing, however, he makes a formal gift of his materials to the husband, who must authorize the writing of the get on his behalf. The husband lifts the writing materials and offers them back to the sofer, saying, "I give you this paper, ink, and pen and all the writing material, and I instruct you to write for me a get to divorce my wife." The sofer hand-letters the get, filling in the details such as the names of the two parties, the city, the time, and the standard text of the writ of divorce in which the husband attests to divorcing his wife and setting her free to marry any other man. It generally takes an hour for the scribe to write the get in Hebrew lettering, during which time the man and woman to be divorced usually wait in separate rooms.

After the sofer finishes his writing task, he and the witnesses make a distinguishing mark on the get. The witnesses read the document and affix their signatures to it. One of the three rabbis of the bet din will then ask the following questions:

To the sofer: "Is this the get you have written?" "Is there any special mark by which you can identify it?" "Did the husband tell you to write the get?" "Were the witnesses present, at least during the time you wrote the first line?"

To the witnesses: "Did you hear the husband order the sofer to write a get for his wife?" "Is this your signature?" "Did the husband tell you to sign it?" Then the get is read again.

To the husband: "Do you give this get of your own free will?" "Did you perhaps make a statement you may have forgotten that might cancel all other statements you made?"

To the wife: "Do you accept this get of your own free will?" "Have you made any statement or vow that would compel you to accept this get against your will?" "Have you made any statement that would nullify the get?"

To those present: "If there is anyone who wishes to protest, let him do so now."

The husband then calls upon the witnesses to witness the delivery of the get. The rabbi tells the wife to remove all the jewelry from her hands, and to hold her hands together with the palms open, facing upward, so as to receive the get. The sofer folds the get and hands it to the rabbi. The rabbi hands it to the husband who, with both hands, drops it into the palms of his wife. He says, "This is your get, and with it you are divorced from me from this time henceforth, so that you are free to become the wife of any man." The wife holds up her hands with the get in them, walks a few paces, and returns. She hands the get to the rabbi, who reads it again with the witnesses who are asked once more to identify the get and signatures. The rabbi pronounces an ancient ban against those who try to invalidate a get after it has been transferred. Then the four corners of the get are torn, so that it cannot be used again. It is placed in the files of the bet din for safekeeping, and the rabbis give each party a shtar piturin, a document of release, stating that the get from X to Y is effective, and each is now free to remarry.

If either of the parties cannot, or desires not, to be present, he/she can appoint an agent to stand in. The husband must place the get which he authorized and which was written for him by the sofer in the hands of the agent, who proceeds to deliver the get to the woman or her agent on a day that is specified in the get. The laws of agency are quite complex, which is why the rabbis of the bet din prefer both parties to be present. Nevertheless, agents for the principals are used whenever necessary.

No divorce, no matter how amicable, is pleasant. Even in the best of situations, it is a quiet but profound trauma for the individuals involved. To some extent, a Jewish divorce action, with its routine, methodical procedures and its absence of interpersonal negotiations helps to keep the tensions low. In addition to being the Jewish way of becoming divorced, the get proceedings also lend a note of closure to the relationship, speeding up the process of psychological closure as well. With all that, there are three problems of inequity in traditional Jewish divorce law.

One is the case of the recalcitrant husband who, for reasons of spite or blackmail, withholds the get from his wife, and thereby does not release her to marry or even date other men; for until she has the get in her hand, she is considered his wife and cannot maintain an intimate relationship with another man.

Second, if the husband disappears and his whereabouts are not known, or, if he is presumed dead but his death has not been verified, his wife is unable to secure a release from him in the form of a get, and she remains, therefore, an aguna, a woman "anchored" to an absentee husband. Although the rabbis try very hard to resolve cases of aguna and generally find a means of doing so, sometimes the proceedings can drag on interminably and there is always some extra measure of distress or humiliation involved.

Both of these problems grow out of the fact that it is only the man who may write and deliver the get. And if none is forthcoming, a woman is relatively powerless to coerce.

And third, largely because of the potential abuse of women in this law, the other more liberal segments of the community have formulated their own procedures, which tend to divide the community further.

In sum, this is the time when an ancient Jewish law must and will undergo a measure of reinterpretation so that those women faithful to halacha will not find themselves disadvantaged in family law.

CHAPTER 14

DEATH AND MOURNING

Mendel knew he was about to die. He had laid to rest so many of his cronies from the shul that he could read the signs. He asks his elderly wife to call for a priest. He wants to convert and be given the Last Rites. "What!" she shrieks. "A pious Jew like you, whose whole life was yiddishkeit? Are you meshugga?" "No," he replies, "but why should another one of us die?"

No matter what, each one of us will die, and just as there is a way to live as a Jew, there is a way to die and be buried as a Jew. There is a spare dignity to Jewish death rituals, an earthiness and a healthy realism about death, that are coupled with honor for the dead. In fact, the principle of k'vod hamet, the honor of the dead, is the yardstick applied to many of the laws concerning death, burial, and mourning. If it doesn't meet the test of k'vod hamet, it doesn't fly.

But more than that, the Jewish way of death contains within its strictures an abiding sensitivity to the living—the survivor, the bereaved, the mourner, the grief-stricken. There are two things in particular about Judaism that no other religion offers quite so uniquely. One is the traditional Shabbat; the other— shivah, a seven-day period of mourning when friends and relatives converge on the bereaved to console/distract/exhaust/ numb/feed/comfort/listen/remember/cry/laugh/retell/or simply sit mute and share the silence and the pain.

EUTHANASIA AND LIFE MACHINES

Before one can talk about death, one must say a word about dying. Jewish law forbids anything that would hasten the death of a terminally ill person, but neither does it require postponing death by artificial means. Can one pull the plug? Some authorities say yes, some say no.

VISITING THE SICK

The mitzvah of bikkur cholim, visiting the sick, carries great weight in Jewish tradition. The Rabbis tell us it is a mitzvah the observance of which ensures us a place in the world to come.

VIDDUI

If a dying person has his faculties about him, he—or she—should recite the final Viddui (confession). Although someone attending the ill might feel an inner constraint and an awkwardness, the law nevertheless suggests that that person encourage the dying patient to recite the Viddui. There are several versions of the Viddui, of differing lengths, and all are found in the standard siddur. A moderate-length Viddui goes like this:

I acknowledge before You, God, and God of my fathers, that my recovery or my death are in Your hands. May it be Your will to heal me with a full healing. Yet, if I should die, let my death be an atonement for all my sins and transgressions and evil deeds that I have committed before You. Allow me a share in the Garden of Eden, and make me worthy of a place in the world to come that is reserved for the righteous.

At the final moment, before life gives out, a Jew recites the Shema.

FUNERAL AND BURIAL PRACTICES

When death occurs, the first thing the family does is to call either the rabbi or another of the synagogue functionaries. The synagogue is prepared to take over and see to many of the details. This is what will be done:

The funeral parlor will be contacted to arrange for transfer of the body to its premises, and to set the time of the funeral. Burial must be on the same or the next day, in accordance with the principle of k'vod hamet: it is considered a humiliation of the dead to leave the corpse unburied any longer than absolutely necessary. Only if there are special extenuating circumstances, such as an immediate relative coming in from overseas, or there is not enough time for burial to take place before Shabbat or a holiday, may it be postponed another day.

A well-organized congregation will often make a standard arrangement with the morticians, so that the family need not go immediately to the funeral parlor to sign a contract and choose a casket. In most instances, however, this task does fall to the immediate family. Jewish law mandates a simple pine casket. A Jew faithful to halacha is thus relieved of the morbid task of choosing this style casket over that one.

The Chevra Kadisha (the sacred burial society) must be alerted. Three or four members of the Chevra will assemble at the funeral parlor to perform the preburial purification of the body (taharah). What is their holy task? They wash the body thoroughly with warm water, from head to foot, including all orifices; they turn it from side to side to wash it, but, as a sign of respect, never with its face down. After the washing, they dress the body in tachrichim, a simple white linen or cotton shroud (again, it is kept simple and uniform in order to avoid distinguishing between rich and poor and embarrassing the latter). If a man wore a tallit regularly during his lifetime, he is buried with it. The custom is to render it defective by cutting off one of its fringes. If a person suffered a loss of blood—such as in an injury or an accident—and the blood soaked through into his clothing, he is buried without taharah in those same clothes, because the blood of a person is considered as holy as his life and deserves proper burial.

Most synagogues have their own Chevra Kadisha group, one for males and one for females, each with a dozen or so volunteer members who alternate taharah assignments. It never ceases to amaze me who serves on the Chevra Kadisha. In our synagogue, on the men's Chevra, there is a busy millionaire. On the women's Chevra, there is a stunningly chic young woman, in her mid-thirties, always strikingly dressed, always coiffed, manicured, and made up to perfection. Who in the world would guess that every few weeks she spends a morning or an afternoon washing and dressing a withered, decaying, dead body? She doesn't love it, but she feels it's her responsibility. I'm grateful she feels that way, because I could never do it, and someone has to.

The body is placed in its plain, wooden casket to await the funeral and burial. Judaism forbids cremation and embalming. Once the body is placed in a casket, it remains closed. The custom of making up the body with cosmetics and placing it on view—as some Jews practice today—is a Christian custom and is clearly forbidden by Jewish law.

Shemira is a ritual that grows out of the principle of k'vod hamet: the body may not be left alone from the moment of death until the moment of burial. Either the family, the synagogue, or the funeral parlor will arrange to have someone in attendance in the room with the body every moment. That person, called the shomer, passes the time reciting Tehillim (Psalms).

Why a hasty burial? Why a simple coffin and plain shrouds? Couldn't one just as easily interpret k'vod hamet to be the very opposite of these pared-down forms?

Judaism teaches us two profound lessons. One is that life and death are absolutely distinct. When life is over, it is over. Once I attended a wake; I continually heard people say, "My, he looks so good! He looks so alive!" While Judaism is not suggesting that one ought to say, "My, he looks so dead," it recognizes that life is over and one ought to be returned to the earth as quickly as possible. The body is only the shell of the full human being that once was. It does not do justice to the person to parade the shell no matter how dressed up or cosmetized.

The second lesson is that neither an ostentatious funeral nor designer coffins nor lying in state nor any of the accouterments of status we seek in our lifetime are of ultimate value. It is death that restores that relative perspective. There is only one form of honor that is central to Jewish mourning rituals—that people who were related to the dead person through ties of love and of family come in person to escort and to bury the dead and to comfort the mourners. That is why we do not hire professionals to do these tasks. The ultimate honor one can bestow on the dead is acknowledgment that he or she lived a life interrelated with others and these others care enough to pay tribute in person.

The Funeral

In many funeral parlors, the family sits in an anteroom prior to the funeral, while friends come in to pay their respects. This is not absolutely necessary, and a mourner who is not up to it can request not to have visitors prior to the funeral.

Immediately before the funeral begins, kriah takes place. Kriah, making a tear in the garment of the mourner(s), is a symbol of the torn and broken heart. While all mourn the death of a relative or friend, "mourner" technically refers to the seven immediate relatives: spouse, mother, father, daughter, son, sister, brother. Generally the rabbi, or whoever is officiating at the funeral, will make a tear in the garment. The blessing recited at the time of kriah is:

בָּרוּךְ אַתָּה יְיָ, אֱלֹהֵינוּ מֶלֶךְ הָעוֹלָם, דַּיַּן הָאֱמֶת.

Baruch ata Adonai Elohainu melech ha'olam dayan ha'emet.

Blessed are You, Lord our God, Ruler of the universe, the true Judge.

A shortened form of this blessing is recited by anyone upon witnessing or learning of a death:

בָּרוּךְ דַּיָן אֱמֶת.

Baruch dayan emet.

Blessed be the one true Judge.

Jewish funerals are very simple. They begin with a recitation from Psalms, which is followed by a eulogy and the chanting of the El Maleh Rachamim, the memorial prayer. Partly as a result of the factorylike business of funeral parlors, and partly because of the simplicity of Jewish law in these matters, a funeral rarely takes more than half an hour. The casket is carried or wheeled out of the room by members of the Chevra Kadisha (even if the deceased is a woman and the women's Chevra did the taharah, still the men's Chevra ushers the casket out). The mourners follow behind the casket. Those assembled respectfully stand in their places and wait to leave until all the family mourners have filed out. For those who go to the funeral but not to the cemetery, the custom is to walk behind the hearse for several yards as it leaves for the burial grounds. This is in fulfillment of the mitzvah of levayat hamet, escorting the dead.

A Kohen, a Jew of priestly descent, is not permitted to enter a funeral parlor, or any other interior space where the dead body rests, except in cases where the dead person is one of seven immediate relatives. Thus, a Kohen who is a close friend or distant relative will often be found standing outside the funeral parlor, paying his respects that way, for he can come no closer. Similarly, a Kohen will never enter a cemetery, except for the burial of immediate family members.

THE CEMETERY

At the gates of the cemetery, the coffin is removed and carried by several people to the grave. The custom is to stop seven times along the way, reciting Psalm 91. After the coffin has been lowered into the grave, members of the family or close friends throw a few handfuls of earth over the coffin. Psalm 91 is read again, and the El Maleh Rachamim is also recited. After the burial service, the nonfamily members present form two lines, and the family mourners pass between them while the others recite the traditional condolence formula:

הַמָּקוֹם יְנַחֵם אֶתְכֶם בְּתוֹךְ שְׁאָר אֲבֵלֵי צִיּוֹן וִירוּשָׁלָיִם.

Hamakom y'nachem etchem b'toch sh'ar availai tziyon vee'yerushalayim.

May God comfort you among all the mourners of Zion and Jerusalem.

Before leaving the cemetery, each person washes his/her hands as a symbolic cleansing.

According to Jewish law, suicides were not permitted burial in the regular Jewish cemetery, but instead were confined to a corner immediately outside of it. Nowadays, the law takes into account that a suicide is not a criminal but a victim, and is buried with full honors accorded the Jewish dead.

Shiva

Immediately after the funeral, the family goes home, preferably to the home of the deceased, to begin the period of shiva. The seven close relatives are obligated to observe this mourning period.

There are many laws and customs that define this shiva period: The first meal, upon return from the cemetery, is called the seudat havra'ah, the meal that begins the process of healing and repair. This meal is prepared and served by friends or neighbors. It usually includes round foods, such as eggs, which are a symbol of life and hope, and also of the wheel of fate in which life and death are in an endless circle with each other.

All the mirrors in the house of a mourner are covered with white sheets or are "smoked" with a soapy film. A special shiva memorial candle is lit. It burns through the entire seven days. The mourners sit on low stools, wear no leather on their feet, do not shave, have haircuts, or wear cosmetics. Nor do they have sex during the shiva period. A daily shower is permitted, but not a luxurious bath. Mourners wear the garment with the kriah throughout the shiva period, although this can be washed and dried overnight for hygienic reasons.

The mourners do not leave the place of shiva, neither day nor night, unless some of them must go home to sleep. It is preferable for families to sit shiva together. It is amazing how many family reconciliations have taken place during shiva.

Beginning with the shiva period, the mourners recite the Kaddish three times each day. Kaddish can be recited only in the presence of a minyan. Since mourners do not leave the place of shiva for a full week, a minyan must come to them each morning for Shacharit and each evening for Minchah and Maariv. Most communities are sufficiently well organized to ensure a quorum for each service, but even so, there are the inevitable 7:00 A.M. phone calls in search of a tenth man.

A Torah scroll may be placed in the house of the mourners, where it will be read as usual on Monday and Thursday mornings, and oftentimes at Shabbat Minchah service. The laws of transporting a Torah scroll, however, are quite complex, so this custom may vary from community to community. Some consider it a lack of respect to move the Torah from its permanent resting place to a temporary location. Therefore, in some communities, the Torah will not be provided at all, or it will be provided only when there is a minimum of three separate readings during the shiva.

If Shabbat intervenes, the mourners go to the synagogue for prayer services. The custom is for the mourners to wait in the vestibule, outside the sanctuary, until the congregation has sung the Lecha Dodi prayer. Then, the mourners enter the sanctuary, and the congregation greets them with the consolation prayer:

הַמָּקוֹם יְנַחֵם אֶתְכֶם בְּתוֹךְ שְׁאָר אֲבֵלֵי צִיּוֹן וִירוּשָׁלָיִם.

Hamakom y'nachem etchem b'toch sh'ar availai tziyon vee'yerushalayim.

If intersected by a Jewish holiday, shiva will be terminated before it runs its full course. For example, if shiva begins on Tuesday, and the festival of Sukkot begins on Wednesday eve, the mourners sit shiva only two days, for the holidays conclude shiva no matter when it had begun. On the other hand, if burial takes place during Chol Hamoed, shiva will not begin until after the entire holiday has ended. To compress this period somewhat, the last day of the holiday, the rabbinic second day, counts as the first day of shiva. Such a situation—delay of shiva—might be emotionally difficult, but the principle is perfectly consistent: there is no mourning during holidays. Contain your public grief a few days, said the Rabbis. And, somehow, people manage to do just that.

VISITORS

It is a mitzvah to visit people who are sitting shiva. When one enters or leaves, one does not give the usual greetings. In fact, there is no greeting at all. It seems awkward to come in and not be able to say, Hello, how are you? or to shake a hand, but that is the accepted custom and thus to do otherwise is the awkward manner. Another custom, which makes it easier for the visitor, is to wait until she/he is spoken to by the mourner. Many people, however, do not observe this strictly and whoever begins to talk first does so. What to talk about? About the deceased, about other members of either family, about what has happened in the community in the last day or so, about anything at all. Sometimes a mourner wants simply to be distracted. Survivors of the Holocaust who sit shiva are often reminded of that time and those people in their lives. A visitor should encourage them to talk and should feel it an honor to be able to hear their testimony.

People do not telephone a mourner during shiva, nor do mourners make or accept telephone calls unless it is something quite urgent. An exception is often made when family members are far away and can be in touch only by telephone. Although some visitors mean well, it is in poor taste to take flowers, candy, or gifts to the home of a Jewish mourner. The way to honor the dead and console the living is to give charity to a righteous cause in memory of the deceased.

Where there is only one person sitting shiva at a residence, members of the community often will organize shifts so that the mourner will not be left alone for long periods of time. In general, during the shiva period, friends and family come in to prepare and serve the meals to the mourners.

A visitor should not expect to be served. However, people do come from long distances to pay a shiva call and need to be refreshed. In some homes, a large automatic coffee urn is set up with hot cups nearby, so that a traveler can help himself to a cup of coffee without having to be served by the mourner. That is perfectly in order.

The last day of shiva is barely a half day. Often it ends before noon. The custom is for the rabbi or another close friend to escort the mourner for the first walk outdoors.

In addition to consoling the bereaved, shiva offers something at least as important to the consoler, what I would call living models of holiness. Recently, my husband and I made two shiva calls, each to a woman who was sitting shiva for her mother. The first, Elissa S., a native Californian, had brought her aging parents to New York to live nearby during these last few years. In the course of a conversation, she mentioned how grateful she was that her mother had been released from the hospital two weeks before she died, presumably to die at home. "It was so good to have her here at home these last few weeks. I had a chance to tell her how much I loved her, and what a wonderful mother she was to me all my life. . . ."

The second woman we visited was a survivor. Bertha K. told stories of the incredible daring with which her mother had rescued the family, literally, from the hands of the Nazis. Her mother had a low visa number, and could have left Germany several times, but she would not leave nor would she rest until she secured a visa and passage for her husband and daughter. They were so poor when they came to this country that for several years they lived in a tiny, one-room apartment with no facilities, but her mother always sang and told her stories to make her happy and hopeful. Moments later, an elderly woman, a friend of her mother's, entered to pay her respects. She had not heard our earlier conversation but straightaway she commented on what a wonderful daughter Bertha had been, how she took care of her mother every single day, and how she always brought good cheer to her mother, how devoted she was to her mother all her life, what a wonderful son-in-law her husband had been. The mourner answered, "I never did enough for her. She gave me life and happiness, not once but a thousand times." The novelists who caricature Jewish mothers are not the only voices to be heard.

SHLOSHIM

Formal mourning tapers off gradually, corresponding rather directly to the natural responses of a human being. For indeed, time and distance from an event of great loss do heal, though one never imagines at the moment that grief and pain will recede. After shiva concludes, the mourner goes about his/her daily business but observes shloshim, the thirty-day period following burial. During the shloshim, no weddings or parties with song, and no musical events or dances, are held or attended. Some people do not shave until the end of the shloshim as well.

KADDISH

If a parent has died, this period of mourning (avelut) is extended for twelve months. The avel (mourner) recites Kaddish, the memorial prayer, three times a day, every day, in the presence of a minyan. Kaddish is an example of the healing that goes on through the gentle and loving ties of a supportive community.

In Orthodox circles, Kaddish is said only by a male, as traditional law requires. Thus, if a woman's mother died, and there were no male descendants of the deceased, then the bereaved's husband might take on the responsibility to recite Kaddish. Or, she might engage a Kaddish zahger (a Kaddish sayer), often donating to a yeshiva at whose daily minyan someone would recite Kaddish in memory of her mother every day for eleven months. In the last decade, however, I have known several women who assumed the formidable responsibility of saying Kaddish regularly for a deceased parent. It did not matter to them whether they were or were not counted as part of the minyan. In most instances, they gradually came to be warmly accepted as a presence, if not a legal entity in the eyes of the Jewish law.

YAHRZEIT

The yahrzeit is another ritual that helps a human being confront and accept the finality of death. On the first anniversary of the death, and each year thereafter, a yahrzeit candle is lit in the home. It burns for a full day (which begins the night before). On the day of the yahrzeit each year, the mourner is called upon to lead the three prayer services, beginning with Maariv. On the Shabbat before the yahrzeit, the memorial prayer, El Maleh Rachamim, is chanted in the synagogue. The custom in most synagogues is to recite the El Maleh at Minchah on Shabbat afternoon, immediately following the Torah reading, in commemoration of all those whose yahrzeit will fall during the coming week.

Yahrzeit is many things. It is a moment of focused memories, of longing, even of pain, though the years have flown by. But with that also comes a firmer appreciation of what was and a renewed insight into what life is all about. Can yahrzeit actually accomplish all that? Yes, if one wills it.

PART THREE

Celebration
and
Remembering

CHAPTER 15

JEWISH RHYTHM

Not only are there many links between nature and the Jewish calendar, there are many parallel lessons to be drawn as well. For example, nature teaches us a thing or two about human vulnerability. Oh, we might resist such notions, we might cling to comforting images of self-sufficiency, but nature's lesson penetrates nevertheless. What the mind does not organize, what the lips do not form, the heart understands. Else why would its beat quicken as we cross a patch of ice or feel the momentary tug of undertow?

Another lesson of nature is one of hope, of optimism about what the next season will bring. The consistency of the rhythms of nature affords us promise, if not actual security. Life unfolds, new life comes; and with it comes new spirit and new hope.

Somehow, we all manage to hold in mind these two lessons— vulnerability and hope—in perfect tension. Without this dual orientation to life we would be neither humble nor confident. Nor human.

So it is with the Jewish calendar. There is an old saw—"a Jew's calendar is his catechism." One could, in fact, teach all of Jewish history and dogma through the Jewish calendar, and it would be quite an exhaustive lesson at that.

But the old saw tells only half the story, especially for a Jew who lives the Jewish calendar with every fiber of being. The calendar is much more than catechism. It is the orientation of the whole self. In the process of internalizing the Jewish calendar, one inevitably engages the Jewish past and experiences the Jewish present; but simultaneously, one also becomes mindful of the Jewish future. The Jewish holidays—their meanings and memories—affect not only the way we recall and reflect upon history, but the way we understand life, including such things as a Jew's vulnerability and a Jew's hope.

Without this dual perception, without juggling these contradictory images, a Jew could not live in the real world. The Jewish calendar teaches us to have optimism; it also reminds us of how close to the edge we have always lived.

Another similarity exists between the Jewish calendar and the unfolding of nature—the sense of rhythm. There is an organic flow of the Jewish seasons, of this holiday to the next. On Purim, one thinks about Passover, on Rosh Hashanah, Sukkot. The psychic rhythm of a Jew's life is tied to the holidays, the festivals, the feasts, the fasts, and Shabbat.

I came to understand and appreciate this rhythmic quality of the Jewish calendar in an odd manner. It happened during the course of writing this book. Throwing myself into the subject of Rosh Hashanah after Chanukah or writing about Passover before Purim were strange sensations indeed. I would awake mornings feeling thoroughly discombobulated. I found I had to keep switching gears between the real me, living the immediate Jewish calendar, and the other me, immersed in writing about a distant part of it. It was like having Jewish jet lag. I did not realize to what extent I had internalized the Jewish calendar, the rhythm of Jewish life, the ebb and flow of the special and the ordinary. It was in my blood, not just in my mind. So many years of celebrating the Jewish calendar had done this thing to me, this extraordinary thing.

THE ANNUAL CALENDAR

The Jewish calendar is a lunar calendar, with twelve lunar months and 354 days per year. Each lunar month consists of 29½ days. Since we cannot switch months midday, certain Hebrew months have twenty-nine days while others have thirty.

In order for the lunar calendar holidays to be synchronized with the proper seasons they celebrate—for example, Passover as a spring festival—a leap year is added every few years. In every nineteen-year cycle there are seven leap years: the third, sixth, eighth, eleventh, fourteenth, seventeenth, and nineteenth years. (That is why your Hebrew and Gregorian birth dates will coincide every nineteen years of your life, no matter into what part of the cycle you were born.)

The Jewish leap year, however, is not like the Gregorian leap year, when one day is added on to February's end. A Jewish leap year adds on an entire month to close the gap between 354 (lunar) and 365 (solar) days per year. Since the month of Adar (approximately February–March) is the last month of the year, it was given the honors: we have Adar I and Adar II, which assures us that the holidays will be celebrated in proper season.

With the exception of Heshvan, the eighth month of the year, every single month of the twelve lunar months has some sort of special day or special observance. Some are connected to the harvest, others to the plantings, but more than their links to agriculture and nature are their connections to history, to faith, and to peoplehood.

The names of the months are not Hebrew but Babylonian. An important Jewish community lived in Babylonia at the time the calendar was fixed. The Bible refers to the holidays only by the order of the months and not by the Babylonian names, which were ascribed much after the canonization of the Torah. For example, the Torah gives the date of Yom Kippur as the tenth day of the seventh month; the date of Pesach is the fifteenth day of the first month.

The month of Heshvan sometimes goes by the name Mar Heshvan. There is a special explanation for this: the Hebrew word Mar has two meanings: bitter and mister. One tradition has it that because Heshvan contains no holiday or special observance, it has a taste of bitterness to it. Another more endearing tradition is that the Rabbis felt sorry for the month of Heshvan, with its lack of any special day, and therefore, to puff it up a bit and to give it some honor, they called it Mister Heshvan.

In addition to all of the special dates, there are twelve or sometimes thirteen other special days. The twelve holidays, or thir-

The Months and Their Special Days

Order of the Mos	Name of Month	Holiday Date	Hebrew Name of Feast, Fast, or Special Observance	Meaning	Approximate Time of Year Celebrated	Origin
1st	Nissan	15–22	Pesach	Passover, the celebration of the Exodus; the festival of freedom.	April	Biblical
1st	Nissan	16-Nissan–Sivan 5	Sefirat Ha'Omer	The seven-week count of the Omer, the barley harvest	April–June	Biblical
1st	Nissan	27	Yom Hashoah	Holocaust Remembrance Day	April–May	Modern
2nd	Iyar	4	Yom Hazikaron	Israel Memorial Day	April–May	Modern
2nd	Iyar	5	Yom Ha'Atzmaut	Israel Independence Day	April–May	Modern
2nd	Iyar	18	Lag B'Omer	The thirty-third day of the Omer count	May	Rabbinic
2nd	Iyar	28	Yom Yerushalayim	Jerusalem Reunification Day	May	Modern
3rd	Sivan	6–7	Shavuot	Feast of Weeks; celebrates the giving of the Torah	May–June	Biblical
4th	Tammuz	17	Shivah Asar B"Tammuz	The seventeenth of Tammuz, a fast commemorating the penetration of the walls of Jerusalem preceding the Churban (the destruction of the Temple)	July	Rabbinic

	Month	Day	Name	Description	Gregorian	Category
5th	Av	9	Tisha B'Av	The ninth day of Av; a fast commemorating the Churban, the destruction of the Holy Temple in 586 B.C.E. and in 70 C.E.	July–August	Rabbinic
6th	Elul	1–29	Teshuvah	Repentance	August	Rabbinic
7th	Tishrei	1–2	Rosh Hashanah	The first day of the New Year	September	Biblical
7th	Tishrei	3	Tzom Gedaliah	Fast day commemorating the assassination of Judean governor Gedaliah, 585 B.C.E.	September	Rabbinic
7th	Tishrei	10	Yom Kippur	Day of Atonement	September–October	Biblical
7th	Tishrei	15–22	Sukkot	Festival of Booths	September–October	Biblical
7th	Tishrei	22	Shemini Atzeret	The Eighth Day of Solemn Assembly	October	Biblical
7th	Tishrei	23	Simchat Torah	Rejoicing of the Torah	October	Medieval
8th	Heshvan	—	—	—	—	—
9th	Kislev	25	Chanukah	Feast of Lights, rededication of the Temple, 165 B.C.E.	December	Rabbinic
10th	Tevet	10	Asarah B'Tevet	The tenth of Tevet, a fast commemorating laying siege to Jerusalem, leading to the Churban	January	Rabbinic
11th	Sh'vat	15	Tu B'Shvat	The New Year of the Trees	January–February	Rabbinic
12th	Adar I	13	Ta'anit Esther	The fast of Esther	February–March	Rabbinic
12th	Adar II	14	Purim	Feast of Lots; deliverance from destruction in Persia; fifth century B.C.E.	February–March	Rabbinic

teen if it is a leap year, are called Rosh Chodesh, the first day of the new month. And, of course, there is the holy Shabbat which comes every seventh day.

These special days in the calendar do not all carry the same weight. Some of them are of Biblical origin—therefore, a special significance is attached to them. These are Shabbat, Rosh Hashanah, Yom Kippur; also, the three festivals Pesach, Shavuot, and Sukkot, and the holiday of Shemini Atzeret; also the special days of Rosh Chodesh. The holidays of rabbinic origin are Chanukah and Purim; also of rabbinic origin are five fast days: Tzom Gedaliah, Asarah B'Tevet, Shivah Asar B'Tammuz, Tisha B'Av (all four connected to the Churban, the destruction of the Temple), and Ta'anit Esther. In the Talmud, we also find Tu B'Shvat, the New Year of the Trees, and Lag B'Omer, the thirty-third day of the counting of the Omer, during which the Hadrianic persecutions miraculously ceased.

There is one more commemoration, rabbinic in origin, which I have not listed on the calendar, nor do I deal with it below. It is Birkat Ha'chamah, the day of special blessing over the sun. This day comes only once every twenty-eight years, when the sun completes its grand cycle through the heavens (as viewed from earth) and returns to its original position at the time of creation. The last time it came was in spring 1981; by the time it comes around again, those of us alive will all have passed the year 2000. The central core around which an entire liturgy has been constructed is the blessing:

Blessed are You, Lord our God, Ruler of the universe, Who does the work of creation.

Birkat Ha'chamah, celebrated at dawn, captures the magic and awe of God's creation, and expresses the most profound appreciation of nature.

Contemporary Jews live in extraordinary times, epoch-making times. Events have occurred in our times that are equivalent in mystery and majesty to the events of Biblical and rabbinic eras: the tragic Holocaust, the rebirth of Israel as a Jewish nation-state, the reunification of Jerusalem, events so new and so awesome that the community has barely begun to formalize, ritualize, and sacralize them. The generations who make history are never the ones who encapsulate it. That task falls to those for whom there is a comfortable distance from the event itself. One can predict that a century from now the special days marking these events will be as sacred a part of the Jewish calendar as the most sacred days in our long history. It will take volumes for historians and sociologists of the twenty-first century to describe the ways our great-grandchildren will prepare for, celebrate, commemorate, retell, and reenact those events that our generation actually lived through. Meanwhile, the process is just beginning. These days are Yom Hashoah, Holocaust Remembrance Day; Yom Ha'Atzmaut, Israel Independence Day; also Yom Yerushalayim, Jerusalem Reunification Day; and Yom Hazikaron, Israel Memorial Day for those fallen in the struggle for the Third Commonwealth of Israel.

A JEWISH TIME LINE

Since all of our holidays, with the exception of Rosh Hashanah and Yom Kippur, are all connected to special events in history, a Jewish time line is offered below for quick reference. Although Jews count by a traditional calendar, which places us currently in the year 5743, events in Jewish history are also dated according to the world calendar which, by convention, dates everything in relation to the birth of Jesus. However, rather than use the Christian referents of B.C. and A.D., Jews use the letters B.C.E. (Before the Common Era) and C.E. (Common Era).

B.C.E. (Before the Common Era)

Year	Historical Event or Personality	Holiday
Ca. 1750	Abraham	
Ca. 1250	Moses, the Exodus from Egypt, Revelation, wandering in the desert	Sukkot, Pesach, and Shavuot
Ca. 1000	King Solomon builds the first Holy Temple in Jerusalem	
586	Babylonians destroy the Temple	Tisha B'Av
522	The second Temple is rebuilt	
Ca. 460	The Jews of Persia are saved. (Although there is much controversy over the historicity of Purim, this dating is the most widely held.)	Purim
165	Rededication of the second temple under the Maccabees	Chanukah

C.E. (Common Era)

Year	Historical Event or Personality	Holiday
70	Romans destroy the second Temple	Tisha B'Av
Ca. 135	The Bar Kochba revolt	Lag B'Omer
Ca. 500	The main redaction of the Babylonian Talmud	
11th–12th century	Rashi and the exegetical schools	
1096	The First Crusades in Christian Europe	
1100–1200	Maimonides and the Spanish–Jewish philosophers	
1492	Spanish Inquisition	
1648	Major pogroms in Eastern Europe	
1740	Rise of Chasidism	
1880s	Beginnings of modern Zionism	
1933–45	The Holocaust of European Jewry	Yom HaShoah
1948	Israel independence—the beginning of the Third Jewish Commonwealth	Yom Ha'Atzmaut Yom Hazikaron
1967	The Reunification of Jerusalem	Yom Yerushalayim

CHAPTER 16

ELUL, THE MONTH OF REPENTANCE

Elul. You don't just run headlong into repentance and renewal —you warm up to it. You get yourself in the proper mood. You try it on for size. You reflect. Rosh Hashanah and Yom Kippur without Elul would be like a symphony without an overture, a championship fight without training, a trial without prearraignment.

THE SHOFAR

From the very first day of Elul and all through the month, the shofar—a wind instrument made from a ram's horn—is sounded in the synagogue. This takes place each morning after Shacharit. But never on Shabbat, when instruments are forbidden. And never on the last day of Elul, so as to set apart the preparatory shofar of Elul days from the real thing—the Biblical commandment to sound the shofar on Rosh Hashanah.

The shofar blasts in Elul are the same as for Rosh Hashanah itself:

1. Tekiah—one solid blast, between five and ten seconds long.
2. Shevarim—a broken sound, three bleeps, altogether equaling the length of one tekiah. A melancholy tradition has it that this sounds like a broken heart.

3. Teruah—an alarm sound, nine rapid-fire bleeps, again approximately the length of a tekiah. (If shevarim is a broken heart, this is a weeping one.)

It is amazing what a piercing sound this little instrument brings forth. But it takes much practice. I remember one Elul in Jerusalem; all during the month, and at all times of the day, as I walked through the streets, I could hear the sounds of shofar coming from the open windows—people practicing and perfecting their shofar-blowing skills.

A shofar can be purchased at a Hebrew bookstore in a Jewish neighborhood. Like all religious objects, the price ranges from low to astronomical. A few years ago I happened to be in a Jewish bookstore in the Boro Park section of Brooklyn, during Elul. You could feel the spirit of Rosh Hashanah all around. In one corner were two men and a woman looking through machzorim—the holiday prayer books. At the counter was a woman, with five or six small children, purchasing new tzitzit in sizes two, three, four, and five. In another corner, four young boys were trying out the different shofarot (plural). In front of the mirror, which was affixed to the center column of the store, was a pimply-faced, twenty-year-old Chasid trying on different black velvet yarmulkes, tilting each one back a bit there, straightening it a touch here, looking himself over in the mirror with all the interest and vanity of a woman trying on a new hat at Saks Fifth Avenue. I was caught up in the mood myself. Impulsively, I decided to purchase a shofar as a Rosh Hashanah gift for my husband. As I tried out one for sound, a young man immediately came over and offered to help. He put down the shofar I had used and tried a few others. Then, when he got back to mine, he discreetly put his handkerchief around the mouthpiece and blew into the hole. It had the best sound. "That one," I said. He smiled. I suspect he was grateful that he would not have to keep track of that particular shofar any longer, the one that had been touched by a woman's lips. The price: twenty-two dollars.

Anyone can make a shofar that will cost nothing but time. Ask your kosher butcher to get a ram's horn for you (ask all year long and you might get it on time). Boil it in a metal pail for a long while, five or six hours, depending on the size. Then pull out the cartilage with long tweezers or a dull scissors. After the shofar has dried thoroughly, saw off the hollow tip and enlarge the blowhole with an electric drill. Sand it if you want it smooth, carve it to decorate, but don't paint it. A shofar must be in its natural state. It also makes a lovely ritual art object all year long. We have two over our mantel.

The shofar reminds us of many things:

It summons up the image of Isaac, bound and waiting to be sacrificed. In his place a ram was slaughtered so that Isaac could live to father Jacob who fathered Levi who fathered . . .

The shofar recalls the experience of Revelation. The sound of the shofar accompanied Revelation at Sinai. In 1976, Yom Kippur in New York started out as it usually does, a glorious Indian summer day. As we reached the shofarot part of the service, the part that commemorates Revelation, the sky became overcast. Suddenly, as the congregation waited in silence to hear the shofar, the sky outside darkened. In a moment, a fierce lightning storm was upon us. There was the shofar, there were the peals of thunder: the shofar, the lightning, the thunder, the shofar. We had just read of the smoke, the flames, and thunder, followed by "And the sound of the shofar grew louder and louder . . ." (EXOD. 19:19). One could almost feel oneself transported back in time, waiting with the crowd at the base of Mount Sinai.

The shofar was sounded to herald the Jubilee. As such, it represents the sweet sound of freedom for slaves who were set free, and for poor people whose original land was restored to them in the Jubilee year.

The shofar, Maimonides tells us, is a warning, a reminder, an alarm clock—to wake up from our deep sleep. Marriages can fall into a slumber, relationships with children and parents and friends can stagnate, our personal ethics can become lax. The shofar reminds us to shake ourselves awake, to fight routinization, to look into our own deeds, to regret our mistakes, to repent, to resolve anew, to reverse errant directions our lives may have taken. Nothing, says the shofar, is irrevocable.

SELICHOT

After the last Shabbat in Elul, and up until Yom Kippur, Selichot are recited every day, except for Shabbat. Selichot are prayers for forgiveness; we ask God to forgive us, to have mercy on us, to grant us favors. And in between each prayer, we recite the thirteen attributes of a merciful God (EXOD. 34:6–7). If you should happen to check your Bible and don't find thirteen attributes in those passages, it's because the Rabbis did a little fancy footwork. They omitted the last two Hebrew words of verse 7: "and he will not wipe out all the punishment," thereby changing the meaning to "he will wipe out all punishment." Rabbinic license—because the Rabbis believed in and hoped for God's unconditional love.

The Selichot are recited before Shacharit. One must arise very early to arrive in time for the Selichot minyan. In most shuls, Selichot start between 6:00 and 6:30 A.M. (except for the last day before Yom Kippur, when Selichot are longer and therefore start a bit earlier). Selichot services take approximately forty-five minutes. They can also be recited at home; however, certain parts, such as the refrain of God's merciful attributes, can be recited only in the minyan.

While the daily Selichot services are generally attended only by men, the first Selichot service has become a community-wide event. It takes place shortly after midnight, on the last Saturday night before Rosh Hashanah. It has become a custom on this night for the rabbi to address the congregation on a topic related to teshuvah (repentance), and for the cantor to lead the special service. Men, women, teenagers with their dates, and even some younger children fill the shul with their bodies and souls in the late, late hours of the night.

TESHUVAH (REPENTANCE)

One is supposed to do teshuvah—repentance—all year long. For most of us unsaintly types, that's not altogether realistic; however, set at a special time, it is a task we are compelled to undertake. Not only do we take stock, but we become altogether serious about the issue of forgiveness. In order to be forgiven by God for whatever small and large slights, abuse, exploitation, pain, harm, dishonesty, insults, loss of temper, and gossip we have inflicted on another, we are required to ask forgiveness of that person straightaway. If we don't do that first, all the prayers in the world will not wipe it away. It is difficult to bring oneself to do it, although once one makes up one's mind to act, the rest is relatively easy. I would rather kasher a hundred chickens, or clean a hundred rooms for Pesach, than have to go to certain people and tell them I now apologize for this or that wrong, when I don't even want to admit that I was wrong in the first place.

Over the years I've tended to fulfill this obligation somewhat perfunctorily. Right before Yom Kippur, I ask forgiveness from the people whom I love most dearly, whom I haven't really wronged, who haven't wronged me—my husband and my children. With few exceptions, that's about as far as I've gone. Like most decent people, I do try not to abuse or exploit or hurt others, at least not wittingly. Yet I know there have been many occasions when I should have asked forgiveness, but had too much pride.

Similarly, Elul is the time to start thinking about forgiving others. I am not quite the one to talk about this. Some years ago, not all that far back that the pain has yet eased, a petty tyrant in a position of administrative power exploited that power and made my life miserable. Each year before Yom Kippur, I am confronted with the realization that I still can't find it in my heart to forgive him. Fortunately for me, he's never asked. Were he to do so, I'd be forced to genuinely forgive and forget the whole incident. Meanwhile, petty tyrants and their petty victims notwithstanding, one should try to be openhearted. It takes time, both to drum up the nerve to ask forgiveness and to muster the will to grant it. One must start in Elul.

Let me present a more positive example of teshuvah. Traditional Judaism is oriented to practice. As such, we learn from our peers as well as from the masters. I learned about teshuvah from a junior-high-school classmate of three decades ago. In fact, I never think of teshuvah without thinking of Dena G. We were friends, but there was a little envy there. When we graduated, I was accorded honors; it came back to me that Dena had been saying it was only because my father was chairman of the board of education of our yeshiva. I was pretty angry when I first heard it, but then came graduation, and summer, and a new school, and the thing was long since forgotten. Elul came and went, as did Rosh Hashanah, the Ten Days of Repentance, and then Yom Kippur. Big new things were happening in my life, and I wasn't really into issues of life and death, renewal, repentance and forgiveness. It touched me only peripherally. After Mussaf on Yom Kippur, the shul had almost emptied out. I saw

Dena approaching from the other side of shul. I noticed she had been crying, something that only middle-aged and older women did in shul during the Netaneh Tokef prayer, but never a stunningly beautiful, blue-eyed, fourteen-year-old friend. I couldn't imagine that she was coming toward me. Without ever saying specifically what she had in mind, she asked if I would forgive her for whatever she had done to hurt me. "Of course," I said, telling her that she hadn't done anything at all to hurt me. (I had completely forgotten the graduation business and only remembered it a day or two later as I tried to understand what had moved her to this genuine religious expression.) She started to cry again, and, moved by her spirit, I cried, too. If I ever forgive that petty tyrant, it will be not because of his merit, but because of hers.

New Year's Greetings

Starting from the beginning of Elul, although some people start even earlier, it's customary to wish people a good year—Leshanah Tovah. The image is one of God keeping records. If God inserts you in the Book of Life, that means you're going to make it for another year, so the greeting is:

לְשָׁנָה טוֹבָה תִכָּתֵבוּ וְתֵחָתֵמוּ.

Leshanah tovah tikatevu vetehatemu.
May you (plural) be inscribed and sealed for a good year.

To be grammatically correct, the greeting is "Leshanah Tovah Tikatev Vetahatem" when addressing one man, or "Leshanah tovah tikatevi vetehatemi" when addressing one woman. Or a briefer form, which is gender correct for all situations and which means essentially the same thing, is "Ketivah Ve'Chatimah Tovah." People respond by saying, "Gam Atem," which simply means, "The same to you."

These greetings are said through Rosh Hashanah, but immediately after, we switch to another form of greeting. In that little switch lies a subtle nuance of traditional Judaism: according to rabbinic tradition, there are three steps to getting into the Book of Life—inscribing, sealing, and final irrevocable sealing. Sealing takes place on Yom Kippur and final sealing comes ten days later on Hoshana Rabbah (the sixth day of the Sukkot cycle). Also according to tradition, righteous people are inscribed for a good year on Rosh Hashanah day. Only borderline people are kept hanging until Yom Kippur. So we treat each person as if he/she were righteous. Therefore, after Rosh Hashanah, we no longer say, "May you be inscribed . . ." Instead we say, "G'mar Chatimah Tovah," or a shorter version, "G'mar Tov," "May a good sealing complete (your good inscription)." This greeting is used up until Hoshana Rabbah, when the heavenly court closes session. Although all this is custom and myth, with no hard-core halacha involved, this fine-tune variation in greetings affects the sales practices of a card store in a traditional Jewish neighborhood. Right after Rosh Hashanah, the cards whose printed message carries the word "inscribed" go on sale at half price, while the ones that say "sealed" continue to sell at full price until the eve of Yom Kippur.

It has become an "American" custom to send Rosh Hashanah cards to friends, neighbors, and relatives. It makes sense, when people live far away, but less so when many of your friends and neighbors are people you'll be seeing in person in shul at least a dozen times within the Elul-Tishrei complex. As a result, in the last few years many Orthodox synagogues have begun to use the synagogue bulletin to send greetings on behalf of Family A, Family B, and so forth to all their friends in the community. In this manner, families A and B support the synagogue instead of the U.S. Postal Service. There are still enough distant relatives and friends to keep the card makers, card shops, and Uncle Sam in business. . . .

THE MACHZOR

Elul is a good time to purchase a machzor, a special prayer book for Rosh Hashanah and Yom Kippur. Carrying is permissible on Rosh Hashanah (unless it falls on Shabbat in a place where there is no eruv). Even though most synagogues offer machzorim, it is a nice custom to buy and keep one's own machzor for use every Rosh Hashanah—and for Yom Kippur where it can be carried to shul within an eruv. I use the one my grandfather gave to me when I was nineteen. In its frontispiece my mother inscribed all the Hebrew and English birth dates of all the members of my family. When I married I added a name. Again, when each child was born. The inside cover of a machzor is an excellent place to begin a family tree.

VISITING THE CEMETERY

During Elul, many people visit the graves of their loved ones. It is part of the mood of the holiday that connects one to past and future, to life and death. There are special prayers in the siddur that are recited at graveside, so many people will take along a siddur or machzor; but others go and take with them simply their memories and emotions. . . .

SYNAGOGUE RESERVATIONS

In many congregations, annual membership dues include reserved seats for Rosh Hashanah and Yom Kippur services. In other communities, however, seats are sold separately. Elul is the time to purchase seats.

One Yom Kippur, a young man came to the synagogue to visit his father. He didn't have a ticket and the usher wouldn't let him in. The young man explained to the usher that he wasn't intending to stay, all he wanted to do was wish his father a good year. The usher thought it over for a moment, his decency overriding his suspicion. "Okay," he said, "you can go in, but don't let me catch you praying!"

There are people who complain about having to "buy" seats to pray. Those are the "unreconstructed idealists" who also undoubtedly believe that a synagogue should be available to everyone at all times, but who are not interested enough to participate in its administration and upkeep nor clever enough to have figured out who would finance these services. Many congregations generously open their doors to such people free of charge, for no one wants to say, "Don't let me catch you praying!" But it is not these "idealists" who have the right to complain. . . .

CHAPTER 17

ROSH HASHANAH AND YOM KIPPUR

Yamim Noraim—Days of Awe

Rosh Hashanah and Yom Kippur, together with the intermediate Days of Repentance, form a unit. That unit is often referred to as the High Holy Days. I don't know who first coined it, but it somehow sounds like High Church to me. Orthodox Jews usually refer to the unit as Rosh Hashanah–Yom Kippur, all in one breath, or as the Yamim Noraim, which means Days of Awe (or literally, Awesome Days).

This unit is also called the Ten Days of Repentance—Aseret Yemai Teshuvah—which includes Rosh Hashanah, Yom Kippur, plus the seven days in between. The Selichot prayers are the formal requirements of those in-between days; the whole tone is one of repentance, requests for forgiveness, and turning oneself around—the same as for the two holy days themselves.

Rosh Hashanah: Two Equals One

I said, "two holy days," referring to Rosh Hashanah and Yom Kippur, when I should have said three, for Rosh Hashanah is two days long—the first and second days of the month of Tishrei. But unlike the second day of the festivals, which is considered to be auxiliary to the first and is celebrated only in the Diaspora, the second day of Rosh Hashanah is considered as part of one extended day and is observed in Israel as well.

This deserves an explanation. In ancient times, each new month was proclaimed by the high court in Jerusalem. How did they know when the month began? Through the testimony of witnesses whose task it was to sight the sliver of new moon and then speed back to the court with their testimony.

Now the moon reappears after a twenty-nine-and-a-half-day cycle. But the witnesses did not always spot it in time to return to the court only on the thirtieth day and, accordingly, the new month was proclaimed for the next day. Thus, some months lasted twenty-nine days, others, thirty. Since the actual cycle is twenty-nine and a half days, it generally averaged out.

The crucial question, however, was on what day the holidays of that month would fall. It was important for communities far and wide to know the first day of the new month, so as to celebrate the Biblical holiday on its proper day.

Once the high court decreed the new month, it sent out the announcement via an intricate signal system. When the signal system broke down, messengers were sent. However, there were certain communities in the Diaspora too distant for messengers to arrive before the fifteenth day of the new month, when the festivals of Sukkot and Pesach were to begin. Therefore, to be sure of celebrating the proper day, they observed as sacred the fifteenth day after the twenty-ninth day of the previous month and the fifteenth day after the thirtieth day of the previous month. This insured that no matter which day the new month began, the people would be observing the proper sacred day of the holiday. Since labor is prohibited on the last day of the holiday as well as the first, those days were also doubled. Hence, in the Diaspora, the first and last sacred days of the festivals are doubled, while in Israel they continue to be celebrated as single sacred days. For example, one seder in Israel and two in America.

Rosh Hashanah, however, is a different story. Unlike other festivals that begin later in the month, Rosh Hashanah begins on the first day of the month Tishrei. In Temple times, the messengers would occasionally arrive late in the afternoon with the belated information that the moon had been sighted earlier. This meant that the wrong sacrifice had been brought for that day. To avoid any such problem, the Rabbis decreed that Rosh Hashanah be observed on both possible days of the new month, in the Holy Land as well as the Diaspora. The two days of Rosh Hashanah, said the Rabbis, are one long day.

The setting of the additional sacred days is discussed at length in the Talmud, for an important decision had to be made. By the end of the fourth century, the calendar was firmly fixed according to mathematical and astronomical calculations. There was no longer a functional value in maintaining the second day as sacred. Nevertheless, the Rabbis decided in favor of keeping it. They, like Jews in our times, treasured the traditions they inherited. Accordingly, they saw fit to fix forever the second day, which by then had accumulated centuries of holiness. Similarly, the two days of Rosh Hashanah in Israel, which had an even earlier precedent. Thus, fifteen centuries later, both first and second days are sacred to us, this one by divine decree and that one by Rabbinic enactment.

HATARAT NEDARIM

One of the unique rituals of erev Rosh Hashanah is hatarat nedarim, the release of one's vows. But first, a brief word about women and ritual.

Everything I have described in this book I have experienced in one way or another—either doing it myself or observing others. Except for hatarat nedarim. In fact, until two years ago, I never even knew this ritual still existed, or that the men in my life perform it every single year. I was under the impression that hatarat nedarim was phased out long ago.

Coming to this knowledge late evoked two responses in me: one was an appreciation of the spiritually rich life of men in the Orthodox synagogue; the other, a realization that learning by doing is the only sure guarantee of knowing. And that, I believe, is the strongest possible argument one can advance for full participation of women in ritual.

In shul, immediately following the morning Shacharit, men gather in groups of four. Three men constitute a bet din, a Jewish court of law, and the fourth asks for release from self-imposed religious obligations that he may have forgotten. The men then switch roles, until every male adult over thirteen has had his vows annulled. It takes about a minute for a man to recite the formula, and for the three judges to grant annulment. The assumption is that, during the year, he may have unwittingly made a religious resolution which he has not kept. More than that, hatarat nedarim serves as a generalized reminder to us to watch our words.

In traditional Judaism, men only may constitute a Jewish court of law, which is why hatarat nedarim fell to men.

PREPARATION

Inasmuch as there is great emphasis on preparation of the spirit and the soul, there is less emphasis on the specific, detailed physical preparations for the holiday. But there is some.

One should clean the house, as one would for any holiday, and prepare a fine meal for the evening and noontime on both days (no need for a third meal, as on Shabbat). The table is set much as it is for Shabbat, with candles, wine, and two challot. A dish of honey is always placed on the table for Rosh Hashanah.

On Rosh Hashanah the rules for cooking differ from those of Shabbat. On Rosh Hashanah, as on the three festivals, cooking is permitted, as long as the foods being cooked are for that day's meals, and as long as one does not kindle or extinguish a flame. In other words, a fire can be drawn from an existing fire, but a fresh match cannot be struck. If there is a steadily burning pilot light on a stove, then, according to some authorities it is permissible to turn the burner on and off, the theory being that the flame expands from the pilot and reduces back to it, and no new fire is kindled or extinguished. Some people leave a candle burning, and fire can be taken from that. (That is also why smoking is permitted on the holiday. You will often see, in the shul lobby, people light a cigarette from someone else's cigarette or from a candle that has been strategically placed.) However, neither the candle nor the flame drawn from another, nor the cigarette, may be put out; it must be allowed to burn itself out.

Many people, even with pilot lights, keep the stove burner on straight through, enlarging or decreasing its flame as need be, without actually turning it on and off during the two days; and where there is no pilot light, this is how it must be done. However, even though cooking is permitted, in most Orthodox homes the greater part of the cooking is done beforehand, so as not to spend the holiday in the kitchen.

ERUV TAVSHILIN

On occasion, Rosh Hashanah and the sacred festival days will fall on Thursday and Friday, backed right up to Shabbat. But one may not cook on Shabbat, nor cook on the second day of the holiday for any other day. So in order to be able to prepare on Friday for Shabbat, another kind of eruv is prepared. This one is called *eruv tavshilin*, an eruv of cooked foods. This is a symbolic meal, just as the eruv of boundaries is a symbolic wall. We hard-boil an egg and set it on a plate alongside a square of matzah or a roll and say over it the following words:

בָּרוּךְ אַתָּה יְיָ, אֱלֹהֵינוּ מֶלֶךְ הָעוֹלָם אֲשֶׁר קִדְּשָׁנוּ בְּמִצְוֹתָיו, וְצִוָּנוּ, עַל מִצְוַת עֵירוּב.

Baruch ata Adonai Elohainu melech ha'olam asher kidshanu b'mitzvotav v'tzivanu al mitzvat eruv.

Blessed are You, Lord our God, Ruler of the universe, Who has sanctified us with His commandments and commanded us concerning the mitzvah of eruv.

Following that blessing, we recite a formula in Aramaic, the language of the Talmud:

בְּדֵין עֵרוּבָא יְהֵא שָׁרֵא לָנָא לְמֵיפָא וּלְבַשָּׁלָא וּלְאַטְמָנָא, וּלְאַדְלָקָא שְׁרָגָא, וּלְמֶעְבַּד כָּל צָרְכָנָא מִיּוֹמָא טָבָא לְשַׁבְּתָא, לָנוּ וּלְכָל הַדָּרִים בָּעִיר הַזֹּאת.

By means of this eruv may we be permitted to bake, cook, keep dishes warm, light Sabbath lights, and prepare during the festival all we need for the Sabbath—we and all the inhabitants of this city.

It is as if we had already done the cooking for Shabbat in advance and any further cooking is considered insignificant. This symbolic meal will be kept intact until the Sabbath. The rabbi of the community will generally make an eruv tavshilin, keeping the entire community in mind. However, in most homes, the wife or husband will do it as well. By means of this legal formula, we are permitted to cook on the holiday the foods that will be eaten on Shabbat. A sham? No. By means of this legal fiction, halacha manages to reconcile two valid conflicting claims.

SPECIAL FOODS

Among the special foods for Rosh Hashanah are round challot, instead of the usual long braided ones. These symbolize the continuous and, hopefully, unending cycle of life. Often raisins are added as an extra touch of sweetness for the sweet year. Honey cakes and nullent, a syrupy honey pastry with dried fruit and maraschino cherries, are baked for Rosh Hashanah. Fresh apples are set aside for a special honey-dipping ceremony at the table.

In addition, many households observe the following food customs: the head of a fish is cooked for the first course. Why? "May you be a head instead of a tail"; tzimmes, a sweet carrot dish, because carrots in Yiddish are called *merin*, but merin also means increase as in "May you increase" (fortune and children).

NEW CLOTHING

One wears new clothes on Rosh Hashanah, which never hurt anyone's holiday pleasure. It is a day of spirit and soul, but in no way is it dreary. On the contrary, it is a day of sweetness and optimism. The special prayers for new clothing are recited (see p. 188).

CELEBRATION

Before candlelighting, parents bless their children for a good year. This blessing can take the form of the Shabbat blessing (p. 65) and/or it can have its special personalized accretions at this special time of year.

CANDLELIGHTING

Candlelighting by the woman (or women) of the household is recited over the same number of candles that one usually lights for Shabbat. The blessing, however, is a bit different. This blessing is also recited for candlelighting of the three festivals:

בָּרוּךְ אַתָּה יְיָ, אֱלֹהֵינוּ מֶלֶךְ הָעוֹלָם, אֲשֶׁר קִדְּשָׁנוּ בְּמִצְוֹתָיו, וְצִוָּנוּ לְהַדְלִיק נֵר שֶׁל (שַׁבָּת וְשֶׁל) יוֹם טוֹב.

Baruch ata Adonai Elohainu melech ha'olam asher kidshanu b'mitzvotav v'tzivanu l'hadlik ner shel (shabbat v'shel) yom tov.

Blessed are You, Lord our God, Ruler of the universe, Who has sanctified us with His commandments and has commanded us concerning the lighting of (the Sabbath and) the holiday candles.

On both nights of Rosh Hashanah, as on the first and second days of the festivals, at candlelighting we add a second blessing: the Shehecheyanu:

בָּרוּךְ אַתָּה יְיָ, אֱלֹהֵינוּ מֶלֶךְ הָעוֹלָם, שֶׁהֶחֱיָנוּ וְקִיְּמָנוּ וְהִגִּיעָנוּ לַזְּמַן הַזֶּה.

Baruch ata Adonai Elohainu melech ha'olam sheh'heh'cheyanu vekiye'manu vehigi'ya'nu lazman hazeh.

Blessed be the Lord our God, Ruler of the universe, Who has given us life, and sustained us, and has brought us to this day.

The Yehi Ratzon prayer (see p. 60) may also be recited, as well as any other individual prayer a woman wishes to add.

Unlike Shabbat, one may light the candles after the start of the holiday. However, the flame must be taken from an existing flame, such as the stove pilot. It is proper to light candles before the holiday starts. On the second night, however, the candles may not be lit until an hour after sunset, or until three stars have appeared, signifying the end of the first day. The reason, you will recall, is that one may not do anything on day one that is intended for the next day.

THE MEAL

After Maariv is completed, we are ready to eat. A special Rosh Hashanah Kiddush, which can be found in a siddur or machzor is recited. Kiddush is followed by ritual handwashing and ha-motzi. A number of food rituals have been developed to express hopes for a good new year. For example, immediately after the hamotzi, we dip the challah into honey instead of salt. We dip a slice of apple into the honey and say:

יְהִי רָצוֹן שֶׁתְּחַדֵּשׁ עָלֵינוּ שָׁנָה טוֹבָה וּמְתוּקָה.

Yehi ratzon she-t'hadesh alenu shanah tovah um'tukah.

May it be the Lord's will to renew for us a year that will be good and sweet.

In our family, as in many others, this honey ritual with challah is continued for three weeks right through the holiday of Sukkot.

If a fish head has been prepared, the head of household will taste a bit and pass it around to whoever wants to partake. (Usually, one fish head is cooked for the entire group; it would look somewhat ghoulish to have twenty fish eyes staring up at you from around the table.) Then all say:

May it be Thy will that we be the head and not the tail.

At dinner, we spend a few minutes reviewing with our children the order of the morrow's service, so that they get a sense of its organization. Much of it they already know, having studied it in school the previous weeks.

THEMES AND LITURGY

Rosh Hashanah is referred to in the Bible as the day of remembrance (of creation). Tradition has it, by way of detailed calculation, that Rosh Hashanah is the anniversary of creation. The Torah refers to it also as Yom Teruah, the day of shofar sounding, and the Rabbis called it Yom Hadin, the day of judgment. You can see how it has taken on all three meanings—the renewal of life, the shofar, Judgment Day.

On Rosh Hashanah morning, the Shacharit service begins very early. Most Orthodox services begin sometime between 7:00 and 8:00 A.M., and conclude by 12:30 or 1:00 P.M.

The Shacharit service starts with the chazzan calling out in a very loud voice: HA'MELECH—THE KING, as if to announce the entry of the King, seated on His throne in the heavenly court.

One of the special features of Shacharit is the Avinu Malkenu prayer, Our Father, Our King. The first Avinu Malkenu is a confession. We clap our right hand over our left breast as a sign of remorse and guilt and say, "Our Father, we have sinned before You." Having made that blanket confession, we proceed with a series of Avinu Malkenu prayers, which are simple, direct, and earthy pleas for God's saving grace.

TORAH READING

The Torah portion tells the tale of the binding of Isaac. One tradition suggests that Isaac was conceived on Rosh Hashanah. Most sources, however, connect this reading to the shofar, the horn of a ram, the animal that was sacrificed at the last minute as substitute for Isaac. Thus, as a kind of mercy plea before God, we summon up the readiness to sacrifice which Jews have shown in every generation.

Some scholars believe that the liturgical use of Isaac's binding was intended to provide a Jewish equivalent to the Christian sacrificial mystery story. Christians claim that through the Crucifixion, humanity is forgiven. Jews claim that sacrifices made by human beings in the course of their lives are sufficient. Starting with Abraham, the first Jew, the sacrifices of the living constitute a fund of merit upon which all Jews can draw.

The prophetic portion for the first day tells the story of Hannah, a barren woman, who prayed for a child. Her prayers were answered and her son, Samuel, grew to become a great prophet in Israel. (See Book of Samuel, Chapter 1.) According to tradition, on Rosh Hashanah all things are remembered and our prayers are answered. Interestingly, Hannah's prayer, recited in this prophetic portion, became the model for prayer: Hannah prayed silently; thus, the Rabbis determined that the central prayer of the service be a silent one. So although women are not formally counted as members of the spiritual congregation, the prayer of a woman is the classic paradigm for Jewish prayer.

The Rosh Hashanah readings are suffused with the themes of a mother's love. In addition to stories of Sarah and Hannah, we read of Rachel's love for her descendants. The Haftorah reading for the second day of Rosh Hashanah is from Jeremiah, chapter 31, with the promise of redemption and return to the land. In its most moving passage, the prophet envisions Rachel weeping and mourning for her exiled children, the people of Israel. She weeps until God finally yields to her tears and promises to restore the Jews to the land of Israel.

THE BLOWING OF THE SHOFAR

Before the Torah is returned to the ark, the shofar is sounded (thirty blasts). Shortly thereafter, during Mussaf, we hear the shofar again; ten blasts accompany each of the three sections of Mussaf: (1) Malchuyot, the kingship section, celebrating God's rule over the world; (2) Zichronot, remembering the good deeds of our ancestors; and (3) Shofarot, the sounds of Revelation and Redemption. And before the service is altogether finished, another forty sounds are emitted (so the very latecomers will hear it). This totals one hundred shofar sounds, which is the most widespread tradition in Orthodox synagogues today.

A good shofar blower is worth his weight in gold. I can take a weak sermon, I can cope with an off key chazzan, but I find I get knots in my stomach if the shofar blower fails. I always feel sorry for his wife and his children. Shofar blowing is a real skill, the temperature has to be just so, the humidity, the pursing of the lips, the force of breath . . . It is a special combination that only a seasoned shofar blower can put together successfully. On the other hand, a good shofar blower can lift the entire congregation.

One tradition has it that the shofar was originally sounded during Shacharit, the morning service. During the persecutions when a hostile Diaspora government proscribed sounding the shofar, spies were stationed in synagogues to report any breach. So the Jews switched the shofar blowing to Mussaf. Why did the spies leave after Shacharit? They just don't make spies like they used to.

If one is confined to the home, or to a hospital, some member of the community will come to blow the shofar, for it is a mitzvah, an obligation, for one to hear the shofar blown. All it takes to arrange this "private blowing" is a phone call to the shul a day or two before Rosh Hashanah.

MUSSAF

Easily the most moving prayer of Rosh Hashanah Mussaf—and of the entire day's liturgy, for that matter—is the Netaneh Tokef. It's not true that only older women cry or sigh in shul. Whatever it is that people carry heavily in their hearts comes right to the surface with this prayer. Partly its content, partly the tragic story of its composer, partly the cathexis the prayer has taken on for a dozen centuries since it was written, partly that your neighbor wipes his/her eyes. . . .

"The great shofar is sounded. A still small voice is heard. Even the angels are frightened . . . the day of judgment is here . . . Who shall live and who shall die? Who shall have a full life-span, who shall not . . . Who shall find rest and who shall be restless? . . . Who shall be free from sorrow and who shall be tormented? . . . Who shall be raised up and who shall be humbled? . . . Who shall be rich and who shall be poor? But Redemption, Prayer, and Good Deeds lift the harsh decree . . .

"As for man, he comes from dust and shall return to dust . . .

At the cost of life, he earns his bread. Man is like . . . withering grass . . . a fading flower, a passing shadow . . ."

Powerful, sobering images, even if you're riding high.

Jewish lore tells us that the author, Kolonymos Ben Meshulam, a scholar-poet of a family of scholar-poets, and a leader of the Jewish community of Mainz, Germany in the eleventh century, was called in by the officers of the German court and was offered a choice: convert or die. In fear, and thinking to mollify them temporarily, he said, "Let me consider it for three days." No sooner had the words left his mouth, than he regretted it. Sick at heart with what he felt to be great weakness and failure at that moment—to even suggest for an instant that he would consider conversion instead of martyrdom—he returned three days later and requested martyrdom. They cut off his arms and legs. He was carried into the synagogue on a stretcher, and before he expired from his bleeding wounds, he recited the Netaneh Tokef. Poor, poor Kolonymos. The hearts of thousands upon thousands of Jews in every corner of the world, in every year since his death, have gone out to Kolonymos, hearts that fill with pride and grief as they think about this humble, towering keeper-of-the-faith. These are the kinds of things Jews think about as they sit/stand in shul a long, long Rosh Hashanah morning, and hope and pray that next year they and their families will be healthier, smarter, richer, happier, alive . . .

TASHLICH

In the afternoon, between Minchah and Maariv, the ritual of *Tashlich* takes place. Tashlich, which means literally "and you shall cast," is one of those ceremonies that, if I saw someone else doing it, I would say, "superstition," but when we do it, I say, "symbolism." Orthodox, and some Conservative and Reform Jewish congregations as well, go to the water's edge or to where a live body of water is within sight. Standing there they recite a prayer, and symbolically throw their sins into the water. Among other prayers, we recite the last three verses of Micah which include the passage, "And You will cast [Ve'Tashlich] all the sins into the depths of the sea" (7:19).

Why the sea? (1) Water is a purifier. (2) In the expansive sea, there's no danger of our sins being dredged up again. (3) Fish don't gossip. They'll know but they won't tell. Were the Rabbis serious when they offered this third interpretation? I don't know.

When I was a teenager, my family lived near the shores of the Atlantic Ocean. We used to put a few bits of bread into our pockets as we left for Tashlich, and then throw these into the ocean after saying the Tashlich prayer. Now Jews don't really believe we can throw away our sins just by emptying our pockets, or making a tossing gesture. Tashlich is simply one more symbol to generate a desire within all of us to rid ourselves of sinful ways and to ask God to forgive us if we have done wrong.

Tashlich, like many religious ceremonies, serves a strong social function. This was not the original intent, but it is one of the important by-products. In dense Jewish communities, such as New York's Boro Park, Flatbush, and Kew Gardens, the water's edges are filled with young people saying Tashlich and then getting to other important business, that is, meeting socially. I am sure there must be several dozen Tashlich couples every year, which is perhaps one of the nicest things one can say about a religious ritual.

If the first day of Rosh Hashanah comes out on Shabbat, we have Tashlich the second day. One other thing about Rosh Hashanah coinciding with Shabbat: we do not blow the shofar.

THE SECOND HALF

The second day of Rosh Hashanah—or rather the second part of the extended day—still has its own ritual candlelighting, Kiddush, hamotzi, festive meal, prayer service, and so forth. The Rabbis took the blessings and the mention of God's name very seriously; they did not want these to become light and easy matters. So an important principle was laid down: no superfluous blessings. But there was some ambivalence over saying Shehecheyanu on the second night at candlelighting and then again at Kiddush. Was Rosh Hashanah two days, or wasn't it? Should they, or shouldn't they? Only God knows for sure. So the rabbinic resolution was to introduce a new substance altogether, to cover all bets. For women who lit the candles, the recommendation was that she wear a new article of clothing the second night of Rosh Hashanah. For Kiddush, they suggested a brand-new fruit, one that is somewhat unusual or new, and would not have been eaten that season. If Rosh Hashanah was one long day (over which the Shehecheyanu had been recited the previous night), Shehecheyanu would apply to the new dress or fruit. If, on the other hand, Rosh Hashanah was actually two days, the Shehecheyanu would appropriately apply to candle-lighting and Kiddush of the second day. God may, so to speak, take His choice.

Rosh Hashanah is concluded with the Havdalah service for festivals.

THE FAST OF GEDALIAH

Even though we have eaten very well all during Rosh Hashanah, and barely feel like eating dinner after the holiday is over, members of an Orthodox household will nevertheless sit down to a very late repast. Light, perhaps, but late. The reason for this is to prepare for the fast that begins at dawn the next morning. Tzom Gedaliah, the fast of Gedaliah, commemorates his tragic death in the sixth century B.C.E. Gedaliah was a governor of Judea who was murdered by misguided fellow citizens. With his death, the last Jewish community living in Israel after the destruction of the first Holy Temple was dispersed. In mourning over the exile, the Rabbis decreed that the day be a public fast. So, today, many Orthodox Jews fast in his memory.

In our house, it has become a decadent but loving custom for mother to take meals to the younger ones on a tray in bed at around midnight: a bowl of cream of mushroom soup, hot spaghetti, cheese, and a banana malted. There's absolutely no religious symbolism to these foods. It's just that I imagine these to be stick-to-the-ribs food, to help them get through the next day a bit easier.

TEN DAYS OF REPENTANCE

In addition to Selichot, on these intermediate days, it is also time to tidy up the loose ends of repentance. There are four steps to repentance, a matter of learning the four Rs:

Recognition of having done wrong.

Regret.

Resolution not to repeat.

Restraining oneself in the face of the same temptation or opportunity that previously led to wrongdoing. This fourth and final step can be taken, of course, only as the situation presents itself.

For those who didn't make good use of the month of Elul, the Ten Days of Repentance are like a crash program.

SHABBAT SHUVA

Shabbat between Rosh Hashanah and Yom Kippur is called Shabbat Shuva, the Sabbath of Return. It's customary for the rabbi not to give a sermon (at least, not a full-scale one) in the morning, but to save all his energy for a major presentation in the afternoon, to show his most learned and scholarly stuff. It used to be that in Europe, the rabbi spoke only twice a year—once on Passover and once on Shabbat Shuva. The rabbi studied all year instead of giving sermons. Now in this single discourse the congregation would see how much he had accomplished in six months of learning.

The story goes that in a good-sized shtetl in Poland there was a rabbi who was a very great scholar. It was his custom to give a three-hour discourse on the most esoteric Talmudic point. The sooner the congregation lost him, the more proud of him they were, for it showed his scholarship had outdistanced theirs during the half year.

One year it happened that the president of the congregation was out of town on Shabbat Shuva. When he returned, he apologized to the rabbi for his absence. The rabbi immediately offered to repeat his discourse. "Oh, no, Rabbi, I'm not worthy," said the tired president. "Ah, but you are most worthy," said the innocent rabbi, and proceeded to repeat his learned discourse. After two hours, the president interrupted. "But, Rabbi," he said, "tell me, what difference does it make?" The rabbi was stunned. "My dear fellow, you are no doubt referring to an objection to my point raised by great scholars. I left it out of my discourse because I thought people could never follow this. No one ever asked such a brilliant question before!" The rabbi then commented for an extra hour on this fine point that had been raised. After the hour, the president again said, "Tell me, Rabbi, what is the difference?" The rabbi gasped. "My God! I never knew what a fine mind you had! Surely you must be referring to the complex Talmudic issue of Rabbi Ploni Almoni." And the rabbi proceeded in exquisite detail to respond further to the president's question. An hour later, the president interrupted again. "Rabbi, please tell me, what is the difference?" The rabbi looked a little bewildered. "Mr. President," he said, "the first time I understood your question to be the brilliant question posed by our sages. The second time, you asked an important detail posed by yet another scholar. But tell me, I am confused; I don't understand your question this third time." The president said, "Rabbi, all I was trying to say was, what is the difference if you talk to me or you talk to the wall?"

Of course, despite all this abstruseness, congregations were moved to repentance. Today, on the other hand, despite brilliant, persuasive talks from highly skilled rabbis who speak weekly, few people change their lives and are "born again." The conclusion is that it is not the rabbi-speaker who moves the congregation. It is the congregation which creates and absorbs the rabbi's impact. But a day such as Shabbat Shuva provides the opportunity for this to happen.

Yom Kippur

Of all the holidays, Yom Kippur is probably the most widely known and most widely observed in the Jewish calendar. Non-Jews, who might know nothing else about Judaism, know about Yom Kippur. Several years ago, in the spring, I was in Sam Goody's record shop in Yonkers, New York, with Moshe who was wearing his kepah as always. Three Irish-looking teenagers were coming from the opposite direction. As they passed Moshe and saw his kepah, they said, "Yon Kipper," and laughed.

Yom Kippur is certainly the most solemn day of the year, but it is not sad or even somber. It took a long while for me to understand that distinction. Yom Kippur, in the life of a person who enjoys life and good health, can be a hopeful day despite the fast and abstinence. There are moments of pensiveness, of reflection, remorse, guilt, and fear, but why should there also not be an optimism that God will bless us with good? Even for those who have suffered, the proper mood is one of life overcoming death, hope overcoming despair, forgiveness overcoming rancor, good overcoming evil. The thought of starting with a clean slate, or of having an opportunity to continue to build up one's life, can be exhilarating.

EREV YOM KIPPUR PREPARATIONS

An erev Yom Kippur custom, observed only by males, is a visit to the mikvah for ritual immersion. In Temple times, men would immerse themselves in the mikvah with some frequency. However, after the Temple was destroyed in the year 70 C.E., the need to be ritually pure for access to the Temple no longer obtained. Thus, men no longer went to the mikvah to purify themselves. On erev Yom Kippur, however, when there is a desire to come into the holy day with as much purity as possible, some males do go to the mikvah.

Unlike most holidays, when Minchah and Maariv are back to back, Minchah of erev Yom Kippur has its own special slot. Attended mostly by males, it is different from the usual weekday Minchah in that the Viddui, the confessions of sins, is recited. Also unlike a weekday Minchah, men and boys come attired in their holiday clothes.

KAPPAROT

Kapparot is a strange custom by any stretch of the modern imagination, or medieval imagination, for that matter; some medieval scholars labeled kapparot "magical" or "Amorite" (pagan ways, a bad label in Jewish scholarly circles). However, the kapparot ritual is so far out that it's in!

Here's what you will see in a very traditional neighborhood: the father will bring home a live rooster, or hen, or chicken, or he will take his family to the local chicken market or kosher butcher. Bird in hand, he will twirl it three times over the head of each member of the family, saying the following: "This is in exchange for you. This is in place of you. This is your atonement. This rooster (chicken, or whatever) will go to its death, but you will go on to a good and long life and to peace." Afterward, the least squeamish child in the family will run off with the live bird to the shochet, who slaughters it ritually and gives it to the poor as tzedakah (charity).

The word *kapparot* comes from the same root as Kippur— "atonement." The animal symbolically atones for the individual, just as the ancient Yom Kippur scapegoat sacrifice atoned for all the community.

People also do kapparot with live fish. In our home we do kapparot with money, which is dedicated to charity. (There are no roosters around, and I don't think I'd want a live carp swimming in the bathtub until we needed it.) Meanwhile, like many Orthodox Jews, we twirl a few bills over the head of each child and each other, while reciting the appropriate formula. During our prefast dinner, we determine the charities to which we shall contribute the money.

Holiday themes have a way of cropping up all year long: In the spring of 1981, we were robbed. In the middle of an afternoon, Evil shattered our glass and entered the quiet of our home. It violated our sanctuary, rifled our belongings, stole our valuables, and, hours later, quite likely discarded our mementos—or, as Goody cried that night: "I can't bear the thought that right now someone is throwing away my memories."

What did our friends say as part of their commiseration and consolation? "Let it be for a kapparah," similar to the ritual of kapparot. It is as if we were using up whatever bad credit was on the ledger, thereby tipping the scales of beneficence, security, rescue, and protection in our favor.

While I'm not so sure it consoled me, I knew it was well-intentioned. And while it may sound like superstitious behavior, it's not terribly different from the way modern urbanites tend to think about themselves in relation to crime and victimization statistics, the underlying assumption of this one being chance, and that one being the divine order of things.

WHITE CLOTHING

Yom Kippur clothing is special and should be prepared in advance. The theme is white, symbolizing purity and innocence. Most Orthodox men wear a kittel, which must be pulled out of the bottom drawer for washing and ironing: or, a kittel can be purchased in a religious articles store. The kittel is a white robe, made of cotton or a fabric mixture; it is worn over one's regular suit. White kipot are worn by men and boys and are usually supplied by the shul. For young boys, who won't wear anything but the hand-crocheted kind, and who don't have a friend to speedily crochet one the week before, it is advisable to plan ahead. Women generally wear white or beige clothing during Yom Kippur, particularly the first evening. It is a custom not to wear gold because of its association with the golden calf, one of the moments of great apostasy of the Jewish people. When one's life is hanging in the balance of judgment, this is no time to summon up those kinds of memories.

A PREFAST MEAL

Unlike any other holiday, the Yom Kippur meal is eaten before candlelighting, for once candles are lit, the fast begins. There is no Kiddush for the prefast meal, which begins with the hamotzi recited over round challot, whose thick slices we dip in honey. Although this is a mitzvah meal (that is, one is *required* to eat before the fast), no special dishes are designated. However, like most mitzvah meals, it is traditional to serve meat or poultry. Most people stay away from heavily spiced food, for these would cause thirst, which cannot be slaked during the fast, even by a single sip of water. We have also found, in recent years, that eating moderately makes it easier to fast than trying to eat for two days. Chicken soup with kreplach is a popular feature at the prefast meal. I recall one erev Yom Kippur returning home from City College on a city bus when it seemed to me that all of New York was scented with the aroma of chicken soup.

LAST-MINUTE DETAILS AND YAHRZEIT CANDLES

Meals should be scheduled early enough to allow time for everyone to finish dressing, brush teeth, drink lots of water; also to ask forgiveness, bless the children, light the candles, and walk to shul. Many Jews light a yahrzeit candle in memory of a deceased member of the immediate family.

The erev Yom Kippur blessing of the children is a poignant moment. Even parents who don't regularly bless the children on Shabbat, do so on erev Yom Kippur. Many give the regular Shabbat blessing, adding to it the priestly blessing, plus a special wish that the children be sealed in the Book of Life and Happiness. Children, too, are vulnerable to the vagaries of life, and at this time of year we become sensitive to what we take for granted all year long—normal, healthy, happy children.

In addition to blessing them, Yitz and I also ask the children and each other forgiveness for being too hard, too soft, insensitive, losing tempers, inattentive—whatever a parent and spouse are likely to have done during the year. We promise to try harder, to be more aware, more understanding. Our children do the same to us, and to each other. Several years ago, our oldest son Moshe, then fifteen, with a genuinely religious spirit underneath all that adolescent cool, said to me quietly, "I hope you'll forgive me for anything I did wrong to you, and anything you *think* I did wrong to you." In his own inimitable way, he was trying to cover all his bets without giving up everything. I wondered what specifically he had in mind.

CANDLES

The candlelight blessing is unique to Yom Kippur:

בָּרוּךְ אַתָּה יְיָ, אֱלֹהֵינוּ מֶלֶךְ הָעוֹלָם, אֲשֶׁר קִדְּשָׁנוּ בְּמִצְוֹתָיו, וְצִוָּנוּ לְהַדְלִיק נֵר שֶׁל יוֹם הַכִּפּוּרִים.

Baruch ata Adonai Elohainu melech ha'olam asher kidshanu b'mitzvotav v'tzivanu lehadlik ner shel yom hakippurim.

Blessed are You, Lord our God, Ruler of the universe, Who has sanctified us with His commandments and has commanded us to light the candles of Yom Kippur.

This is followed by the Shehecheyanu.

If you live in a Jewish neighborhood, the walk to shul after candlelighting is one of the unique pleasures of this day: seeing all those families going in all directions on their way to their respective shuls, many walking through the streets in their white robes and sneakers, the old and the young, the regulars and those who come only this night; there is a great feeling of the unity of the Jewish people. The walk to shul is a religious experience in itself.

PROHIBITIONS

Why sneakers? In addition to the prohibition against eating and drinking, there are several other prohibitions: washing, anointing, wearing leather shoes and sexual intercourse. The Torah tells us: "On the tenth day of the seventh month you shall afflict your souls." Like eating, these are bodily pleasures that gladden the soul. Forbidding them would constitute a deprivation, which is how the Rabbis interpreted "afflicting" the soul.

But still, why sneakers, which are more comfortable than shoes? Two reasons:

1. In ancient times, leather shoes were—and still are—a symbol of comfort and support.
2. When one is asking for life, it would be callous to come shod in leather, which represents the ended life of an animal.

Anointing is not common in these times, but applying makeup is. Thus, many women will apply makeup before the fast, but will not reapply it once it has worn off.

Washing means washing the body. Except for ritual hand-washing of the Kohanim before they give the priestly blessing, and except for washing hands after elimination or removing eye film with a moist hand, all other washing is forbidden. On Yom Kippur we come to realize what we take for granted all year long.

Sex. Pleasure, said the Rabbis, so wait until another night.

Yom Kippur is also called Shabbat Shabbaton, the ultimate of Sabbaths. Thus, in addition to the five special Yom Kippur prohibitions, all restrictions that apply to Shabbat also apply to Yom Kippur.

IN SHUL

On Yom Kippur, there is a whiteness in the shul that sets it apart from any other day of the year. Not only do most people wear white, but even the shul "wears" white. The regular ark curtains have been removed and special white ones for Yom Kippur now cover the ark. A white covering is draped over the chazzan's reading table as well. Another startling thing to see on Yom Kippur evening: every man wears a tallit. Other than this night, the prayer shawl is worn only by day. Moreover, many men have a special white-on-white tallit which they use only on Yom Kippur. All this is what meets the eye upon entering shul.

EVENING SERVICES

The Maariv service opens with Kol Nidre. What Netaneh Tokef is to Rosh Hashanah, Kol Nidre is to Yom Kippur. In this prayer, which is recited three times by chazzan and congregation responsively, we ask to be absolved from all vows that we might take during the course of the coming year. This doesn't mean business promises or ethical resolutions; it means religious vows. This prayer harks back to those times in our history when Jews were denied the freedom to practice Judaism and were forced to take formal religious vows of Christianity. Somehow, the words don't apply as much to Jews of today who enjoy full rights to live openly as Jews, but Jews carry a lot of baggage, and the memory of persecutions of previous generations, plus the soul-stirring melody for Kol Nidre, binds the congregation together and puts one immediately into the spirit of Yom Kippur.

One of the features of the evening service—and repeated throughout the Yom Kippur services the next day—is the confession of sins. The confession comes in many forms in the liturgy, some of which are quoted directly from the Talmud. But the heart of the confessional is the Al Chet ("For the sin of . . ."), a litany of forty-four sins, all ethical in nature. We clap our breast in contrition as we recite each one.

The framers of the liturgy considered human sensibilities and used the plural form instead of the singular for the Al Chet. Thus we say, "For the sin which *we* have committed before You in the hardening of the heart," ". . . with the utterance of the lips," ". . . out of haughtiness," ". . . out of a lewd eye."

By reciting the sins in plural form, the sinner does not feel isolated; the righteous person need apply directly to himself/herself only those sins that are appropriate; and the community recognizes that the group must assume some responsibility for the acts of individuals.

Without false modesty, I consider myself to be generally decent and good. Yet, almost every sin applies to me. How can that be? I wonder. I rationalize that these are very normal, very common, very human, and in many instances very mild sins. Nevertheless, the confessional jogs my memory and gives me great pause, and, when I am truly open to it, I resolve anew to act more ethically in the coming year. Many years ago, I resolved not to gossip, and while one can't live without at least a little gossip, I think I have been able to keep it somewhat under control. On Yom Kippur a few years ago, I resolved never to tell a white lie (except, I made sure to add, to an editor, like, "Tomorrow you'll have it"). While there are still many situations where a white lie is kinder, or easier, I have become more conscious of telling them. As for controlling evil thoughts, I just can't. Not yet. But one of these years, I shall work on that a bit harder. The Yom Kippur liturgy makes us realize how slipshod we can be in our ethical responsibilities, particularly in sins of the tongue.

Yom Kippur Maariv generally ends at 9:00 or 9:30 P.M. There are no prescriptions for behavior following the evening service. However, the proscriptions set the mood. Jews walk home to a quiet house, talk quietly, think, and try to stay in the spirit of Yom Kippur until retiring, without such distractions as the latest novel. There's plenty of time for that. Mostly, folks go to bed early in order to have the energy to carry through the next day.

MORNING SERVICES

One of the prominent themes in the Yom Kippur Mussaf is the Avodah, the Temple worship service in which the High Priest played a major role. Both liturgy and Torah readings center on the High Priest's activity on Yom Kippur, events filled with high drama, pomp, ceremony, and awe. Clearly, that was *the* moment of mysterium tremendum in ancient times. And we read it in exquisite detail.

The Haftorah reading is clearly appropriate to the overall theme of ethical behavior. Through the prophet Isaiah (57:14–58), God reminds the people that rituals such as fasting are for the end purpose of removing wickedness, freeing the oppressed, and feeding the hungry. They are not an end in themselves.

The chazzan works harder on Yom Kippur than any other day of the year—and on an empty stomach and dry mouth, no less. Yom Kippur services are longer than any other service, which is fine, because there's no festive meal to rush home to. In most Orthodox shuls, Shacharit and Mussaf services go on until midafternoon, with but an hour or two of recess until Minchah.

AFTERNOON SERVICES

Unlike the morning Torah readings, the Minchah Torah portions seem to have nothing to do with Yom Kippur whatsoever. Forbidden sexual perversions, incestuous relationships, and their punishments? What could be the connection? But these are signs of moral decay. The lack of morality will destroy the fabric of society. Since the shul is packed on Yom Kippur, this is as good a time as any to sound these warnings.

But there's another tradition concerning this Torah reading that is even more interesting. It seems that during the Second Temple period, the afternoon of Yom Kippur was an official courting time in Jerusalem. The young women would go out, all wearing white linen or cotton garments of a very plain style, so that no one could tell who was rich and who was poor; and the men would come to look for a life mate. Thus, this Torah reading which legitimated sex only in its proper context.

On no other day but Yom Kippur is there a Haftorah reading in the afternoon. The entire Book of Jonah is read. The story of

Jonah and the whale is replete with themes of sin, repentance, forgiveness, and God's dominion over this earth—all solid Yom Kippur themes.

THE CLOSING PRAYERS

The fifth and closing service on Yom Kippur is called Ne'ilah (the other four being Maariv, Shacharit, Mussaf, and Minchah). Ne'ilah means closing up—the closing of the gates through which our prayers have entered. Ne'ilah also means sealing; the Ten Days of Repentance are over, and the divine decree is given its final seal.

Throughout the Ne'ilah service, the ark is kept open, to symbolize the open gates of prayer. Although everyone has fasted all day, almost the entire congregation stands throughout this last service. Even people who had begun to wilt earlier somehow manage to revive themselves for this last special thrust of prayer. Like most climaxes of life, there is a special tension, an almost palpable excitement that runs through the congregation. The prayers are quite beautiful. They are final pleas for mercy and blessing.

The last ten minutes of Ne'ilah are the climax of the climax. Avinu Malkenu, which we have recited every day since Rosh Hashanah, is recited for the last time. The Shema Yisrael, "Hear, O Israel, the Lord our God, the Lord is One," is recited in full congregational voice. After this, the Baruch Shem K'vod, "Praised be His name Whose glorious kingdom is forever and ever," is recited three times by the chazzan and congregation. And finally, the last declaration, "The Lord is God" is recited, almost shouted out, seven times. After the seventh repetition there is a long, final blast of the shofar. As we often do at moments of intense feeling, we link ourselves to Zion and Jerusalem. Yom Kippur concludes with the congregational cry of *Lishanah ha'ba'ah be'yerushalayim*, "Next year in Jerusalem."

The congregation has been together a full day through many peaks of emotion. There is much hugging and kissing and well-wishing. A very hasty Maariv is convened up front, while others begin to leave. In a few moments, the synagogue will be empty, everyone on the way home to break the fast and to begin preparations for Sukkot, which is only four days off.

CHAPTER 18

SUKKOT, SHEMINI ATZERET, SIMCHAT TORAH

Sukkot

Of this I am convinced: the Jews were the original show-and-tell people.

Some years ago, a Christian student of mine in a basic Judaism course raised her hand in class one October morning. "Around the corner from us [in St. Margaret's parish] lives a Jewish family. Every September, they build this odd structure in front of their house. They eat there, and it seems as if they also sleep there. Why do they do that?" I thought for a moment and, in the best one-liner I could find, admittedly borrowed from Pesach, I said, "So you should ask."

I come from a long line of Sukkot-celebrating families. Yet our sukkah and those of our friends and relatives have always been backyard affairs, not "public" ones. Nevertheless, her question made me realize it is not only for third-generation American Catholics to ask, but for Jews of all ages and in every generation.

The sukkah (booth) has two referents, one in history and one in nature. Both are given in the Torah:

1. The sukkah is a reminder to all generations that God re-

deemed the people of Israel from Egypt. Like a loving, caring parent, He caused them to live temporarily in booths that sheltered them from the elements. We commemorate that saving grace by living in booths for seven days.

2. After the summer harvest, there is great cause for joy and gratitude. How did a nation express those feelings? Through a festival of ingathering, a celebration that the harvest is in, a holiday of rejoicing, a seven-day feast of booths. But why booths? During the harvest, where every moment counted, the farmers lived in booths at the edge of the field, so as not to have to travel back and forth to their homes.

Thus, for the last three thousand years, Jews have built booths. While only a relatively small number of Jews actually sleep in the sukkah, most Orthodox Jews take all of their meals for the entire holiday in these fragile, temporary houses. And we love it. Not only because we are commanded to feel joy during this festival, but because it is so pleasant, so different, so exotic, so laden with memories.

PREPARATION

Building a sukkah can be as enjoyable as sitting in it. One is not supposed to begin building before Yom Kippur. However, if there's a Shabbat in between or if it's an elaborate sukkah that would not otherwise be ready on time, one can begin to get the frame together but not to complete the greater part of it until after Yom Kippur.

Ideally, the sukkah should be built as a joint family project. However, if mutual scheduling isn't possible, every member of the family should contribute at least some little part toward its completion.

A sukkah must have a minimum of three sides. The sides can even be the walls of the house, as long as there is no regular fixed roof protruding over the sukkah area. Some families build family rooms or closed-in porches with removable roofs that can be lifted off at Sukkot time. The walls can be made of anything —four-by-eights, old doors (the real McCoy), fiberglass, and, the most common and easiest to assemble, aluminum poles for a frame with "canvas walls" hung all around.

The most beautiful sukkah I ever saw belonged to an Oriental carpet dealer in Jerusalem. On metal frames, he had hung four "walls" of Persian carpets and had placed another Shiraz down on the floor. How he could be so sure it wouldn't rain was a puzzlement to me, but it seems it never rains in the Holy Land during Sukkot. When I said to him and his wife, "Aren't you worried? Even though the sukkah is built on a fourth-floor terrace, there are such things as cat burglars around." No, they said, they weren't worried. Their three teenage sons and a cousin had been sleeping in the sukkah for years. A skinny cat burglar who might scale that wall would be no match for them. "All we have to do is make sure the boys don't drink too much wine at night . . ."

If there's no canvas around, and no Persian carpets, then quilts or comforters make wonderful side walls. They give a thick and cozy feeling and can be easily hung from plastic curtain rings sewed to one edge at eight-inch intervals. The rings are then suspended from S-shaped hooks looped over the top of the frame. Almost any fabric that is strong enough to withstand a moderate wind can be used as walls in this manner.

A sukkah must be solid, but not too solid. It is supposed to remind us of human vulnerability and of the fact that we are all in God's shelter. Which is why a permanent sukkah—closed-in porch type—doesn't really seem like a sukkah to a Jew who grew up with the old four-by-eights.

Several years ago, when Yitz was a congregational rabbi, we had the first night's meal in the shul's sukkah, with a hundred people. It was a very windy night. After the first course, my husband decided to move the crowd inside because of the powerful winds. We looked like a group of refugees as we sadly trudged out of our beautiful sukkah with our dishes and cutlery in hand. Ten minutes after we had set ourselves up in the social hall and had just begun to resume our meal, we heard the sounds of a terrible crash: the shul's sukkah had completely collapsed. All that wood and glass windows and bamboo poles and evergreen and decorations, all in one huge rubble heap. There were gasps of horror and a long moment of silence as people pondered fearfully what might have been. Yitz rose, and broke the silence by saying, "Well, at least we know it was a kosher sukkah. . . ."

The next morning in shul, he recited the Birkat Hagomel (giving thanks for escaping danger—see p. 153) for all those who were in the shul sukkah and for other families around town whose own booths had also collapsed.

Whereas the walls can be made of anything at all, the roof cannot. The roof, known as the s'chach, is what makes the sukkah a sukkah. The roof is the last thing to go up. The s'chach must be of a natural product, in its natural state. Anything that grows out of the ground (except for fruit-tree branches) and that has been severed from its source is permissible. In other words, an overhanging tree would not qualify for a kosher sukkah, but branches cut from a tree would. Steel bars, which are not a product of nature, may not be used. We use long bamboo poles, laid crosswise, six inches apart, and on top of that we lay evergreen branches which cover the entire roof. A sukkah must have more shade than sun, yet allow a view of the stars to come through, and the bamboo-evergreen combination is perfect. It also has a wonderful fresh smell. Bamboo poles can be purchased in a Jewish neighborhood, right before Sukkot. Wooden slats or one-by-twos are also permitted as a base upon which to rest the real s'chach: hemlock, pine, and tall rushes that grow near marsh ponds are excellent. Branches of trees are okay, except that after a few days they dry and wither and look more like death than the spirit of life. By the seventh day, the hemlock begins to fall into the soup, spawning the usual Socrates puns, but hemlock and pine still manage to look fresh up until the very last.

Some people prepare a plastic cover that can be drawn across the top in case of rain; the sukkah is unusable when it rains, so it doesn't matter if one covers the top temporarily. These plastic tops, however, have to be tipped slightly, otherwise huge pockets of rain gather in the middle of the sukkah top, and if the rain is heavy, the water can pull the plastic top right through and make a huge mess. At best, the one who removes the plastic after the rain gets all wet. In our sukkah we prefer to cover the table and chairs with plastic drop cloths in event of rain. The rug underneath also stays dry, the canvas walls dry out quickly, and the sukkah is ready for use as soon as the drop cloth is removed.

Persian carpets notwithstanding, a sukkah looks as good as its decorating job. Sukkah posters, paper decorations, a wall of Rosh

Hashanah cards—and for the top, hanging decorations, fruits strung on string, gourds, paper chains, cranberry chains, glass medallions—whatever one can imaginatively use that would hold out for seven days, for one is not permitted to "build" (re-decorate the sukkah) after the holiday has begun. Another custom is to hang on the walls pictures or signs with the names of the Ushpizzin, the Jewish forefathers whom we formally invite, one each day, into our sukkah: Abraham, Isaac, Jacob, Joseph, Moses, Aaron, and David. Until a decade ago, no one even asked why foremothers were also not invited. Technology and community have not yet caught up with ideology. I still haven't seen an Ushpizzin sign with Sarah, Rebecca, Rachel, and Leah, but that doesn't mean it won't happen in the future, nor that families cannot make these signs on their own.

A floor covering adds immensely to the comfort and appearance. Indoor-outdoor carpet, a tatami mat, or an abandoned remnant from a carpet cleaning store—something with low pile that can be swept after each meal, for vacuuming is not permitted on the first and last two days of Sukkot. A table and chairs for eating, a small side table to make serving easier if there's room for it, an electric light rigged up to the top, covered with a Japanese paper lantern or a clip-on lampshade and voila! Something out of the past has come alive once again.

LULAV AND ETROG

The second important ritual object of the holiday Sukkot is the lulav etrog, which must be purchased and assembled in advance.

The lulav is the branch of the date palm tree. When we say lulav, we really mean the palm branch with its two sidekicks: the hadas, three short branches of myrtle leaves, and the aravah, two branches of the willow of the brook.

An etrog is a citron. It looks like a lemon, but it smells different, tastes different, and has a pitom, the pistil, without which the etrog would not be kosher.

Why these four kinds—lulav, etrog, hadas, and aravah? Because the Bible specifies, "On the first day [of Sukkot] you shall take the product of the hadar (citron), the palm, the myrtle, and the willow" (LEV. 23:40). But why were these four kinds chosen to be a symbol of thanksgiving and rejoicing after the harvest? There is no answer from the Torah, so oral tradition filled in where written one left off. Each of the four kinds is unique. The etrog has "taste" and "smell," that is, it can be used as a food and has a wonderful fragrance. The date palm has no smell, but gives delicious fruit; the myrtle has the sweet scent but no nourishment; and the willow has neither.

By analogy, the Rabbis extended these qualities to human beings. Taste becomes wisdom, smell becomes goodness. Some people have both, some have one, and so forth; together, they make up a whole society. I never quite went for that mixed metaphor, "He's a peach of a guy," and "He's an etrog of a guy" appeals to me even less. Nevertheless, the idea that the community is made up of all types, not just saintly types, is a powerful one. Each type is precious, each person is of value; without one or the other the community would not be whole—that was a basic humanitarian theme of the Rabbis.

Choosing a lulav and etrog is an art. The lulav must be green (that is, fresh) and its ribs must come to a point at the top. They should be tight, and not spreading apart and hanging out all over. The etrog must be yellow and its skin must be free of any blemishes. A perfect etrog is truly a thing of beauty.

Some Jews spend hours at selecting a set, although others do it in fifteen minutes, and yet others simply order it by phone or mail through the synagogue shamash or the local day school. Purchasing a lulav and etrog, or standing in a corner watching the show, can be a unique experience. People examine the ribs to see if they are tight or if there's a palm missing (unkosher); they sniff the etrog and examine it for blemishes, handling it gently all the while; if one breaks the pitom, it's the same as breaking a china dish in Macy's. One of my favorite scenes is of a Chasid looking over an etrog skin with his diamond dealer's magnifying eyepiece.

During the last few years, there have been lots of complaints about the high cost of etrogim (plural). I saw an etrog in our shul one year whose purchaser, David K., paid two hundred dollars for it. It was quite beautiful, but not ten times more beautiful than our children's, for seventeen dollars apiece. The market for etrogim dies at 3:00 P.M. erev Sukkot; some people stick it out until that hour, then pick up a perfect etrog (always with a lulav) for five or ten dollars. But as of this writing, even well in advance, a nice kosher etrog and lulav can be bought for fifteen to twenty dollars.

A word here about the high cost of Jewish living in general. And another word about a quality we call hiddur mitzvah: enhancing and beautifying a mitzvah. It costs money to be an Orthodox Jew—to educate one's children, to eat nice foods for Shabbat, to dress well for the holidays, to buy kosher meat, to purchase ritual objects, to support a synagogue, and to give charity. And yet, there is hardly anything that cannot be done, properly and with taste, at a price that anyone can afford. Second, if something is precious to you then you organize your priorities differently. Of course it costs a great deal to educate our children according to Jewish tradition. But this, we feel, is the very best use of our hard-earned money; it is infinitely better than a ski vacation or a new car.

Some people in shul said of David's two-hundred-dollar etrog, "What a rip-off." Others said, "What a jewel!" Others, "What a sucker he is!" And others, "What a generous man." I'll vote with the latter. No one forced him to buy such an etrog. An intelligent man, he knows perfectly well he can pick one up more cheaply.

But the combination of wanting the best and the most beautiful with which to perform a mitzvah, and knowing that the person who sells the etrog to him spends his life and earns his living by making things like a lulav and etrog available, makes David K. feel better about spending two hundred dollars on the etrog than on a key ring at Gucci's.

Nor does an Orthodox Jew always have to spend money. He or she can spend time and effort, ingenuity and love. After the Persian carpet, my second favorite sukkah is ours, a metal and canvas arrangement that we've had for ten years. Several years ago, the canvas began to look shabby. Deborah, then fifteen, took some fabric remnants from the attic, and, with a box of straight pins, and unadulterated talent, she draped and folded and pinned and created something that looks like it came right out of the Arabian nights.

One could write a sociology of religion thesis based on lulav and etrog. I consider myself a transition woman, growing up in a time of transition from prefeminist to postfeminist values. I am also a transitional Orthodox Jew, in the sense that I see the flowering of Orthodox Judaism in my lifetime. I see it in many little signs, lulav and etrog among them. Not only do more people buy lulav and etrog than ever before, but Jews display them openly, without self-consciousness. When I was younger, I remember men would carry their lulav and etrog through the streets, to shul, under wraps, in a long, thin, nondescript brown paper bag, or under their jackets. Now they carry them without camouflage and with great pride.

It used to be that only the male head of household would buy a set, and all the males in the family over thirteen would take turns using that lulav and etrog in the synagogue; the women would recite the lulav blessing each morning at home. Women, according to the Rabbis, were not originally obligated. However, they took it upon themselves, with increasing diligence, and now the mitzvah is theirs for life.

As Jews became more affluent, they began to buy several sets per family, including sets for children and for female members of the family. Older children often order their own sets through their yeshiva schools or youth organizations. There's a whole new industry of small-size lulavim (plural) for pint-size Jews, who march around shul with their fathers for the lulav processional. (A parent, however, should supervise their use. Several years ago, I arrived at shul just in time to break up a fierce lulav duel raging on the shul lawn between a six- and a seven-year-old.) And one sees something in this decade that was never seen in previous generations, even though the numbers are still small; women and girls take their own lulav and etrog to shul to use ritually during the service.

Thus, the lulav and etrog are subtle but potent indicators of the growth in observance of ritual, the expansion of women's public religious expression, the economic betterment of traditional Jews of this era, and the increased pride of American Jews in their faith and rituals.

ASSEMBLING A LULAV

Although the four parts are purchased together, they are not assembled. The reason for that is we usually buy them several days before Sukkot, and want to keep them as fresh as possible.

So we put the palm into a jar of water, and we wrap the hadas and aravah in a damp paper towel and then in aluminum foil and place them in the refrigerator. On the day preceding Sukkot, we assemble the lulav properly and leave it assembled throughout the holiday. The etrog, too, must be refrigerated to keep fresh.

To assemble a lulav: With its spine toward you, slip the lulav into the woven palm holder (you receive this when you purchase the lulav). It will rest one third of the way up the lulav. Then insert the hadas into the tube opening to the right and the aravah into the tube opening to the left of the palm.

The woven palm holder should hold everything close so that the hadas and aravah touch the sides of the lulav. If not, work it with your fingers so that they do touch.

The woven palm holder will enable you to hold the palm, myrtle, and willow in one hand, with each in its proper position, and leave your other hand free for holding the etrog, as you will need to do in reciting the blessing over lulav each morning of Sukkot.

DRESS

One of the obligations for joy, the Rabbis tell us, is that women buy new clothes for the holiday. (The actual phrasing is that the husband is required to purchase nice clothing for his wife.) Although this mitzvah is given specifically in relation to joy on Sukkot, it applies as well to all other holidays. Of course, we shop only because it's a mitzvah. . . .

FOOD PREPARATION

Sukkot is one of the three pilgrimage festivals, the other two being Pesach and Shavuot. Unlike Shavuot, which lasts two days, Sukkot and Pesach last eight days in the Diaspora. But not all of the eight days have the same sacred weight. The first two and the last two are considered more sacred than the intermediate days.

Work is not permitted on the sacred festival days. However,

any work that pertains to preparing food to be eaten on the holiday may be done, as long as one does not light a fire anew. If the second day of the festival is Friday, we prepare the eruv tavshilin (see p. 321).

Sukkot is a holiday for entertaining, particularly for inviting guests who don't have a sukkah. Unless one wants to spend the entire holiday preparing and serving, it is wise to cook as much as possible beforehand. The planning and logistics of meals can mean the difference between rejoicing and feeling like a caterer. What to strive for are meals that can be brought out all at once, yet kept piping hot in a cool sukkah. This is a bit difficult, but with good planning it is altogether possible.

Some helpful hints in setting up, preparing, and serving:

1. Use disposable goods. Although holiday celebration calls for use of our finest utensils, items such as pretty paper plates can become part of the sukkah beauty.
2. Keep a two-tiered table in the sukkah for serving and storing: the lower tier for keeping an extra supply of paper goods, bentschers (Grace books), challah cover, salt and pepper shakers, relishes, and condiments; the upper tier for bringing in salads and desserts.
3. Foods that have little waste are excellent for Sukkot, such as casseroles, holuptches (cabbage stuffed with beef or with rice for veggies—see p. 494), beef Bourguignon, boned chicken breasts, and kugels. I always serve the first tsholent of the season on Sukkot.
4. Use trays to bring out several items at a time, both in setting up and serving. Before the meal begins, put hot food into covered casserole dishes, place on a tray, and cover with a towel or small blanket, and rest it on the kitchen counter. When it's time for that course, all one has to do is remove the insulating blanket and carry the tray out.
5. If it's cold, the best part of the meal can be hot soup. Serve it from a soup tureen, ladled at the table, family-style, or serve hot broth in Styrofoam cups or bowls that are covered with plastic wrap until they reach the sukkah. Often one has to dispense with certain indoor graces, such as waiting until everyone gets his/her soup before the first one served can

begin. Serving soup to fifteen people in an autumn sukkah means that if the first one waits for the last, he/she will have lukewarm soup.

6. The one exception to foods that have little waste is turkey. Some families now serve turkey for Sukkot. It's an example of how an American custom is fused with an ancient Jewish one. Sukkot is a thanksgiving holiday, and since as Americans we associate that poor bird with giving thanks, a turkey is often served for one meal of Sukkot.

7. Bring out foods such as dessert and cold fresh salads before the meal begins. The fewer times one has to dash into the house, the more pleasant it will be for everyone.

8. Some people set up a Salton hot-tray in the sukkah, timed to a Shabbos clock. I think it's a little risky, in the event of rain; however, there are people who have done it for years and say no harm done.

CELEBRATION

The Torah tells us to celebrate Sukkot for seven days, beginning the fifteenth day of the seventh month (Tishrei). Diaspora Jews add a day to the festivals (see p. 318).

But Sukkot is a strange holiday; it doesn't end when it ends. It goes right into another day, a day that is distinct and yet also part of Sukkot. This is called Shemini Atzeret, the Eighth Day of Solemn Assembly. And in the Diaspora, that day is followed by another day of great joy—Simchat Torah, the rejoicing of the Torah. Thus, the calendar looks like this:

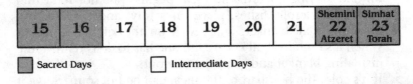

CANDLELIGHTING

Candles are lit in the sukkah. It takes an extra minute to find a safe spot—safe from wind and safe from fire. It is important to do this, because there's so much flammable material around, and there is no one minding the candles for at least an hour, until shul services are over. The blessing over the candles is:

בָּרוּךְ אַתָּה יְיָ, אֱלֹהֵינוּ מֶלֶךְ הָעוֹלָם, אֲשֶׁר קִדְּשָׁנוּ בְּמִצְוֹתָיו, וְצִוָּנוּ לְהַדְלִיק נֵר שֶׁל (שַׁבָּת וְשֶׁל) יוֹם טוֹב.

Baruch ata Adonai Elohainu melech haolam asher kidshanu b'mitzvotav v'tzivanu (Shabbat v'shel) Yomtov.

Blessed are You, Lord our God, Ruler of the universe, Who has sanctified us with His commandments and has commanded us to light (the Sabbath and) the holiday candles.

On the first two nights and the last two nights, the Shehecheyanu blessing is added:

בָּרוּךְ אַתָּה יְיָ, אֱלֹהֵינוּ מֶלֶךְ הָעוֹלָם, שֶׁהֶחֱיָנוּ וְקִיְּמָנוּ וְהִגִּיעָנוּ לַזְּמַן הַזֶּה.

Baruch ata Adonai Elohainu melech ha'olam sheh'heh'cheyanu vekiyemanu vehigiyanu lazman hazeh.

Blessed are You, Lord our God, Ruler of the universe, Who has given us life and sustained us and has brought us to this day.

Unlike Shabbat candlelighting, the blessings are recited before and not after lighting the wicks.

EATING IN THE SUKKAH

The first thing we do as we enter the sukkah for our meal is to recite the Kiddush for festivals.

On Friday evenings, Kiddush begins here:

(וַיְהִי עֶרֶב, וַיְהִי־בֹקֶר,

יוֹם הַשִּׁשִּׁי. וַיְכֻלּוּ הַשָּׁמַיִם וְהָאָרֶץ וְכָל־צְבָאָם. וַיְכַל
אֱלֹהִים בַּיּוֹם הַשְּׁבִיעִי, מְלַאכְתּוֹ אֲשֶׁר עָשָׂה, וַיִּשְׁבֹּת
בַּיּוֹם הַשְּׁבִיעִי, מִכָּל מְלַאכְתּוֹ אֲשֶׁר עָשָׂה. וַיְבָרֶךְ אֱלֹהִים
אֶת יוֹם הַשְּׁבִיעִי, וַיְקַדֵּשׁ אֹתוֹ, כִּי בוֹ שָׁבַת מִכָּל
מְלַאכְתּוֹ, אֲשֶׁר בָּרָא אֱלֹהִים לַעֲשׂוֹת.)

Otherwise, it begins here:

סַבְרִי מָרָנָן וְרַבּוֹתַי.

בָּרוּךְ אַתָּה יְיָ, אֱלֹהֵינוּ מֶלֶךְ הָעוֹלָם, בּוֹרֵא פְּרִי הַגָּפֶן.

בָּרוּךְ אַתָּה יְיָ, אֱלֹהֵינוּ מֶלֶךְ הָעוֹלָם, אֲשֶׁר בָּחַר בָּנוּ
מִכָּל־עָם, וְרוֹמְמָנוּ מִכָּל־לָשׁוֹן, וְקִדְּשָׁנוּ בְּמִצְוֹתָיו. וַתִּתֶּן־
לָנוּ, יְיָ אֱלֹהֵינוּ, בְּאַהֲבָה, (שַׁבָּתוֹת לִמְנוּחָה וּ)מוֹעֲדִים
לְשִׂמְחָה, חַגִּים וּזְמַנִּים לְשָׂשׂוֹן, אֶת יוֹם (הַשַּׁבָּת הַזֶּה,
וְאֶת יוֹם)

Shemini Atzeret and Torah		Sukkot	Shavuot	Pesach
הַשְּׁמִינִי, חַג הָעֲצֶרֶת		חַג הַסֻּכּוֹת הַזֶּה,	חַג הַשָּׁבוּעוֹת הַזֶּה,	זְמַן חֵרוּתֵנוּ,
הַזֶּה, זְמַן שִׂמְחָתֵנוּ,		זְמַן שִׂמְחָתֵנוּ,	זְמַן מַתַּן תּוֹרָתֵנוּ,	חַג הַמַּצּוֹת הַזֶּה,

(בְּאַהֲבָה) מִקְרָא קֹדֶשׁ, זֵכֶר לִיצִיאַת מִצְרָיִם. כִּי בָנוּ
בָחַרְתָּ, וְאוֹתָנוּ קִדַּשְׁתָּ, מִכָּל הָעַמִּים, (וְשַׁבָּת) וּמוֹעֲדֵי
קָדְשֶׁךָ, (בְּאַהֲבָה וּבְרָצוֹן) בְּשִׂמְחָה וּבְשָׂשׂוֹן הִנְחַלְתָּנוּ.
בָּרוּךְ אַתָּה יְיָ, מְקַדֵּשׁ (הַשַּׁבָּת וְ)יִשְׂרָאֵל וְהַזְּמַנִּים.

It was evening and it was morning.

On the sixth day the heavens and the earth and all their hosts were completed. For by the seventh day God had completed His work which He had made, and He rested on the seventh day from all His work which He had made. Then God blessed the seventh day and hallowed it, because on it He rested from all His work which God had created to function thenceforth.

Blessed are You, Lord our God, Ruler of the universe, Who creates the fruit of the vine.

On Sabbath add the words in parentheses.

Blessed are You, Lord our God, Ruler of the universe, Who has chosen us from all peoples, and exalted us above all nations, and hallowed us by Your commandments. You have given us in love, O Lord our God (Sabbaths for rest), holy festivals for gladness, and sacred seasons for joy: (this Sabbath day and) this day of _____.

On Pesach: the Feast of Unleavened Bread, the season of our freedom.

On Shavuot: the Feast of Weeks, the season of the giving of our Torah.

On Sukkot: the Feast of Tabernacles, the season of our gladness.

On Shemini Atzeret and Simchat Torah: the Eighth-day Feast of Solemn Assembly, the season of our gladness (in love); a holy convocation, as a memorial of the departure from Egypt; for You have chosen us, and hallowed us above all peoples, and Your holy (Sabbath and) festivals You have caused us to inherit (in love and favor) in joy and gladness. Blessed are You, O Lord, Who hallows (the Sabbath), Israel, and the festive seasons.

On Saturday night, we add this as part of the Havdalah service:

בָּרוּךְ אַתָּה יְיָ, אֱלֹהֵינוּ מֶלֶךְ הָעוֹלָם, בּוֹרֵא מְאוֹרֵי הָאֵשׁ.

בָּרוּךְ אַתָּה יְיָ, אֱלֹהֵינוּ מֶלֶךְ הָעוֹלָם, הַמַּבְדִּיל בֵּין קֹדֶשׁ

לְחוֹל, בֵּין אוֹר לְחשֶׁךְ, בֵּין יִשְׂרָאֵל לָעַמִּים, בֵּין יוֹם

הַשְּׁבִיעִי לְשֵׁשֶׁת יְמֵי הַמַּעֲשֶׂה. בֵּין קְדֻשַּׁת שַׁבָּת לִקְדֻשַּׁת

יוֹם טוֹב הִבְדַּלְתָּ, וְאֶת יוֹם הַשְּׁבִיעִי מִשֵּׁשֶׁת יְמֵי הַמַּעֲשֶׂה

קִדַּשְׁתָּ; הִבְדַּלְתָּ וְקִדַּשְׁתָּ אֶת עַמְּךָ יִשְׂרָאֵל בִּקְדֻשָּׁתֶךָ.

בָּרוּךְ אַתָּה יְיָ, הַמַּבְדִּיל בֵּין קֹדֶשׁ לְקֹדֶשׁ.

Blessed are You, Lord our God, Ruler of the universe, Who creates the light of fire.

Blessed are You, Lord our God, Ruler of the universe, Who makes a distinction between sacred and secular, light and darkness, Israel and other peoples, the seventh day and the six days of labor. As You have made a distinction between Sabbath sanctity and festival sanctity, and have hallowed the seventh day above the six days of work, so have You set apart and sanctified Your people Israel through Your holiness. Blessed are You, Lord, Who makes a distinction between degrees of holiness.

Before we actually drink the wine, we immediately add another blessing, our reason for being here this night:

בָּרוּךְ אַתָּה יְיָ, אֱלֹהֵינוּ מֶלֶךְ הָעוֹלָם, אֲשֶׁר קִדְּשָׁנוּ

בְּמִצְוֹתָיו, וְצִוָּנוּ לֵשֵׁב בַּסֻּכָּה.

Baruch ata Adonai Elohainu melech haolam asher kidshanu b'mitzvotav v'tzivanu leyshev ba'sukkah.

Blessed are You, Lord our God, Ruler of the universe, Who has sanctified us with His commandments and has commanded us to dwell in the sukkah.

On the first night this is followed by the Shehecheyanu:

בָּרוּךְ אַתָּה יְיָ, אֱלֹהֵינוּ מֶלֶךְ הָעוֹלָם, שֶׁהֶחֱיָנוּ וְקִיְּמָנוּ וְהִגִּיעָנוּ לַזְּמַן הַזֶּה.

Blessed are You, Lord our God, Ruler of the universe, Who has given us life and sustained us and has brought us to this day.

On the second night, and on the last two nights of the festival, the order is reversed: Kiddush followed by Shehecheyanu followed by leyshev ba'sukkah.

The leyshev ba'sukkah blessing is recited at every meal eaten in the sukkah for the next seven days. If no Kiddush is required, as is the case during the intermediate days, the leyshev ba'sukkah is recited after the hamotzi blessing. If no bread is eaten and, therefore, no hamotzi, the leyshev ba'sukkah is recited after the specific blessing for the particular foods eaten.

There are all different kinds of customs regarding physical stance when reciting Kiddush on Shabbat and on Yom Tov all the year through: standing, sitting, standing for first half, sitting for second half, standing one night, sitting the next day, and so forth. There is also a variation in custom regarding the ritual of washing the hands: some Ashkenazim of German origin ritually wash the hands first, then say the Kiddush, and follow immediately with the hamotzi, without talking in between. Most other Ashkenazim, including ourselves, do it in order of Kiddush, washing, and hamotzi. But once a year—on Sukkot—we switch. Since our sukkah is not large but our crowd often is, the traffic controller decided a few years ago to adopt the German-Jewish custom so as to seat the crowd only once. Thus, everyone washes ritually, goes out for Kiddush, leyshev ba'sukkah, and immediately after—the hamotzi.

Doing it this way has solved not only the traffic-flow problem, but the raccoon problem as well. To wit, this incident of ten years ago: As is always done in the advance setting of a holiday table, the two challot were placed on the silver challah plate, were then covered and were placed on the table. Coming out to the sukkah awhile later, I noticed the challot were gone. Immediately, I lit into whoever had set the table with, "Why didn't you . . ." "But I did," said the innocent child. "No, you couldn't have. They're not here now." "But I did," cried the innocent thing. And then I noticed that the challah cover was on the ground outside the sukkah, and off in the distance I suddenly caught sight of the bushy body with two handlike paws, finishing off the last bit of challah. In the middle of the yard, midway between us, was the second challah he had foraged and dropped en route. He watched me for a moment, and then, somehow knowing I would not race him for his rabid challah, he plodded over to the center of the lawn, picked up his second loaf, turned and gave me another good long look, and then plodded back to his ledge. For that amount of challah, he could have made a leyshev ba'sukkah.

The year after, we made sure not to set the challot out until we were ready to go into the sukkah for Kiddush. But during the year, the raccoon had also gotten smarter and more brazen. He, or his brother, waited until we filed back into the house after Kiddush to wash our hands; he then scurried in and grabbed off our challot—both loaves again. This time, however, he worked fast, and not deftly, messing up our table and spilling the wine. It was on that day that we decided to adopt the wash-Kiddush-hamotzi routine. Thus, although some would be loath to admit the impact of sociology on Sinai, we see that even raccoons can affect halachic procedures.

In instances where the sukkah is a distance from the house, or where the hosts do not want guests in their kitchen, it is a simple matter to set up beforehand pitcher, glass, basin, paper towels, wastebasket so that people can wash their hands right outside the sukkah entrance.

For zemirot at a festival meal, there is a wide range of songs from which to choose. There are many beautiful parts to the Sukkot liturgy and one of the most special is the Hallel, the hymns of praise that we recite each day of the festivals. Another source of zemirot are those Biblical verses related to the festivals themselves, such as "Ve'samachta be'chagecha" (DEUT. 16:14–15)—"And you shall rejoice in your festivals . . . and you shall be *only* happy."

It is a mitzvah to eat in the sukkah all during the holiday, but the mitzvah carries most weight the first night. Apartment dwellers, or people who don't have their own sukkah, make sure to secure an invitation somewhere, or they eat in the shul sukkah, or at least make Kiddush there so as to be able to recite the blessing leyshev ba'sukkah. Homeowners with sukkot go out of their way to invite people who have no sukkah.

The laws of dwelling in the sukkah are fairly lenient. In case of inclement weather or poor health, or rain, one is excused from eating in the sukkah. (We are told to rejoice in the sukkah and not to suffer.) On the first night, however, we make a maximum effort to eat in the sukkah if it is at all possible.

If it rains on the first night, the Rabbis said one should wait until midnight to see if the rain passes. However, later generations of authorities realized this would be a disruption of the joy of the holiday, for oneself and one's family, so the custom arose to wait an hour in case of rain. The Rabbis took it one step further: if one's guests are poor people, the waiting period is waived altogether.

In event the rain does not stop, we go out to the sukkah to recite Kiddush, leyshev ba'sukkah, Shehecheyanu, and hamotzi. We then continue our meal indoors.

Blessing the Lulav

Each morning of the holiday, except Shabbat, we take up the lulav and etrog to recite the blessing. Orienting ourselves toward the east—and Jerusalem—we hold the lulav in our right hand, spine facing us, hadas to the right and aravah to the left. In our left hand, we hold the etrog, pitom facing down. Holding our hands together, with lulav and etrog touching each other, we recite the blessing:

בָּרוּךְ אַתָּה יְיָ, אֱלֹהֵינוּ מֶלֶךְ הָעוֹלָם, אֲשֶׁר קִדְּשָׁנוּ בְּמִצְוֹתָיו, וְצִוָּנוּ עַל נְטִילַת לוּלָב.

Baruch ata Adonai Elohainu melech ha'olam asher kidshanu b'mitzvotav v'tzivanu al netilat lulav.

Blessed are You, Lord our God, Ruler of the universe, Who has commanded us on the taking up of the lulav.

On the first day of Sukkot, we add the Shehecheyanu. Then we turn the etrog so that the pitom is up. Still holding lulav and etrog together, we point the lulav in six directions: front (east), right, back (over our shoulder), left, up and down, symbolizing God's reign over the four corners of the universe and the dominions of heaven and earth. Each time we point to another direction, we give the lulav a little shake.

The blessing over lulav is recited each morning immediately before Hallel. Those who will not have a lulav and etrog with them in shul, as is the case for most women and children, will recite the blessing at home in the morning.

The lulav and etrog are used ritually during other parts of the Shacharit service. They are held in hand all through the chanting of Hallel. At certain key parts of Hallel, we wave the lulav and etrog in different directions. It's a bit difficult to hold the lulav in the right hand and etrog in the left and hold a siddur simultaneously. Thus, the custom is to hold the lulav and etrog in separate hands only for the waving parts, but to hold them together in one hand and a siddur in the other for all the rest of Hallel.

HOSHANOT

Awhile later, we take up the lulav and etrog again as part of another ceremony, this time a processional. After Mussaf, the chazzan carries a Torah scroll in his arms and walks slowly along the outer aisles of the shul, singing responsively the Hoshanah prayer (Help Us). As he passes each row, those who have a lulav and etrog step out into the aisle and follow the procession. In a traditional synagogue, only males join the processional. Many men hold the lulav and etrog in their hands and a young child on their arms. Hoshanot (as the prayer and processional are called) must surely be mysterious, strange, exciting to these little ones who peek out from under their father's tallit. And for those who watch them. I remember some fifteen years ago, in our shul, when there were perhaps fifty men who possessed lulav and etrog. Now there are three hundred or so, slow-moving, chanting, lulav-toting, tallit-covered figures, all friends and neighbors. These Hoshanot are among the most memorable parts of the Sukkot liturgy.

THE SECOND DAY

On the second day of Sukkot, all these procedures are repeated with but two slight variations: at the evening Kiddush, the Shehecheyanu is recited before the leyshev ba'sukkah and not after as on the first night; and the haftorah reading differs from that of the first day.

However, there is another ritual associated with this day that is worth mentioning. In ancient times, there was a joyous water-drawing ceremony, the Simchat Bet Hashoeva. It was performed on the second day of Sukkot which was—and is—the first day of Chol Hamoed in the land of Israel. Water was drawn from a major well in the environs of Jerusalem, carried to the Temple, and splashed over the altar as an offering. Afterward, all the menorot (candelabra) of Jerusalem were lit, and the entire city was bathed in light. A torchlight parade was accompanied by the rich sounds of cymbals and horns. The Rabbis entertained, did acrobatic feats, and performed balancing acts, the most daring of which was the juggling of flaming torches.*

At night, after the second day is over, Havdalah is recited. But since only the first two sacred days are concluded, and not the holiday itself, we omit the blessing over spices, and we end the final blessing with, "Hamavdil beyn kodesh le kodesh," "He Who distinguishes between holy and holy," that is, between different levels of holiness.

WOMEN AND THE SUKKAH

Historically, women were not obligated to eat in the sukkah. Increasingly, however, Orthodox women take every meal in the

---

* After the destruction of the Temple, the celebration ceased to exist, but the Rabbis recorded it in the most glowing terms, claiming, "He who hasn't seen the rejoicing of the water-drawing ceremony has not truly seen joy in his lifetime." In recent years, a few congregations have tried to revive some sort of commemorative celebration, but no formal ceremony has been institutionalized—as yet.

sukkah as do their male counterparts—and not just on the sacred days. A few years ago, during the intermediate days of Sukkot, Goody and I happened to be shopping in Manhattan's Lower East Side. It was lunchtime, and we were very hungry. So we asked a storekeeper, a young man wearing a yarmulke, if he knew where there was a shul sukkah nearby, to eat our sandwiches. He thought it was quite amusing, laughed, and said, "You're ladies. What do you need it for?" He wasn't sure how to get to the shul, so he called out to his partner, "Hymie, these women want to eat in a sukkah. How do they get there?" His partner, of the same persuasion but not of the same mind, came forward and said, "For you two? How wonderful!" and proceeded to give us directions.

THE INTERMEDIATE DAYS

Days three, four, five, and six are called Chol Hamoed, literally, "the weekdays of the festival." These intermediate days have a measure of sacredness to them. In Talmudic times, it would appear that most people refrained from most kinds of work, and the days were celebrated much like the holy days of the festival. Strictly speaking, the Rabbis ruled that work may be done, but only work that cannot be postponed, such as work that will be irretrievably lost or spoiled if not done at this time. Over the centuries, however, and especially in modern times, it was too difficult to take the whole week off, so the definition of work that could not be postponed was increasingly broadened. Most people go to work and restrict it only in a token way.

The rules for work apply equally to tasks done in the home. Here, too, the general rule is: if it can wait, it waits. Laundry, cleaning, and sewing that are not urgently needed are set aside, as are tasks of construction and repair.

Children of yeshiva day schools have been known to resort to a plea of "It's Chol Hamoed!" in resisting any and all homework assignments. But Jewish teachers are not fools either. One of the fine points of Jewish law is that if you must do certain kinds of weekaday work, such as writing, do it in a slightly different manner. For example, start the first line (of, say, a homework assignment) at a slant.

The daily liturgy of the intermediate days is a hybrid. Shacharit consists of the regular weekday liturgy with some relevant insertions, plus Hallel, a brief Torah reading, and the special Mussaf for the festivals. Since most people do work on Chol Hamoed, the services start a half hour earlier than usual for a working day, in order to end the same hour so that people can get to work on time.

There is a halachic debate regarding tefillin on Chol Hamoed. Tefillin are not worn on Shabbat or Yom Tov. If Chol Hamoed is observed as Yom Tov, then one should not wear tefillin. On the other hand, if people go to work, they should don tefillin. Some Jews do wear tefillin on Chol Hamoed, but many Chasidim don't even though they might go to work. And those who put on tefillin for Shacharit remove them before Hallel, so as to signify that it is, after all, one of the festival days.

The blessing over lulav and etrog is recited daily, including the waving ritual. All the meals are taken in the sukkah, to remind us that these days are still part of the joyful holiday.

Whatever day of Sukkot falls on Shabbat, whether sacred day or Chol Hamoed, there is no taking up of the lulav and etrog. There is a special reading on Shabbat of Sukkot—the Book of Ecclesiastes, the most enigmatic, ambiguous, self-contradictory book of the Bible, but every sentence has a ring of truth. It is like life itself: enigmatic, ambiguous, self-contradictory . . .

HOSHANAH RABBAH

Hoshanah Rabbah, the great day of hosannah, starts the eve of the seventh day. Still part of Chol Hamoed, it has special features as we move toward the last of the sacred days of Sukkot. Many traditional Jews—mostly men but some women, too—stay up past midnight or all night, reciting Psalms, or learning Torah. Tradition tells us that on Hoshanah Rabbah the heavenly court places the final seal on the judgment that was handed down on Yom Kippur. There are hardy, devout souls who want to be on duty to mark the final judgment.

Generally speaking, because Hoshanah Rabbah is a regular workday, a day of heavy cooking and preparation for the last two festival days, because services begin very early, and because women are not obligated to be there . . . women seldom go to Hoshanah Rabbah morning services. But they miss something. . . .

In light of the tradition that judgment is sealed this day, the Hoshanah Rabbah morning liturgy symbolically reenacts some Yom Kippur themes. That morning, the ark and bimah table are covered with white as on Yom Kippur. The rabbi and chazzan wear white kittels as on Yom Kippur. After the Mussaf, the Hoshanot processional starts. Instead of one Torah being carried around the congregation, seven scrolls are taken around together. Each one is used to head a different procession. The marchers encircle the shul seven times. Every man in the shul is out in the aisles with his lulav and etrog. In unison, they sing the various chants whose central theme is Hosannah, Help Us.

The judgment of God is not only on human beings: it is also a judgment on nature. Who will live and who will die in nature depends to a great extent on how much water will be granted. On Hoshanah Rabbah, Jews pray for water. To make the message more urgently felt, they reenact an ancient Temple ceremony. With a few dried willow branches in their hands (supplied by the shamash of the synagogue), each man beats the willows against the ground three times until the leaves fall off. It is a reminder, as it were, to God, of what happens to us without sufficient water. We need water to live. Because of the association with Yom Kippur and forgiveness, folklore has it that in beating off the leaves, one is shedding the sins of the past year that were forgiven on Yom Kippur. Would that it were that easy to shake off sins. . . .

Hoshanah Rabbah morning is the last time we will take up our lulav for the year. Although we have finished with it, out of respect for its sacred use we will not throw it away in the garbage. We set it aside, until after Simchat Torah, to dispose of properly. We leave it on the ground outside, to let it decompose naturally; some people weave it into strawlike sukkah decorations for next year; others save a few palm ribs to burn with the chametz (leavened products) before next Passover. This is a way of linking one Biblical festival to another.

On Hoshanah Rabbah afternoon, our family collects etrogim from our friends. We keep one or two, to pomander for besamim (see p. 88), and all the rest we give to my mother. She doesn't quite have a bathtub still, but somehow she manages to produce enough of Sylvia's Three Hundred Proof Etrog Liquor to last the family all the year through.

Lunch on Hoshanah Rabbah is the last time we recite the leyshev ba'sukkah when eating in the sukkah. When evening falls, a new holiday has begun, with its own candlelighting and Kiddush, the holiday of Shemini Atzeret, the Eighth Day of Solemn Assembly.

Shemini Atzeret

Its most unique feature is the prayer for rain—Tefilat Geshem.

It's odd, the places one can have a religious "experience." I would define a religious experience as a heightened awareness of, and sensitivity to, people, nature, time, community, past, future, and God—singly or in any combination. For most of us, these come few and far between, but they carry us far beyond the immediate moment.

In 1974, the year after the Yom Kippur War, our family spent a year in Israel. The children adjusted quite well. Deborah, who was very shy, marched off to school the first day without a backward glance. But J.J., then nine, wanted me to stay in school with him. Just for today, then just for tomorrow, and then just for the day after. After two weeks, I was so much a permanent fixture that the students thought I was the school secretary and the teachers thought I was the new school guard. But the fourth-grade teacher and principal were most understanding. One day, my twelfth day there—it turned out to be my last, since J.J. released me that evening—I was sitting at the back of the room reading my book when suddenly something caught my attention and riveted me for a moment: a few patter drops of rain against the window, and in an instant all the children spontaneously clapped their hands. It was as if they were applauding the heavens, applauding the wondrous ways of God and of nature, feeling joy at the first rain of the season.

Now I have seen children clap over snow. Snow is fun. Snow is snowballs, sleds, and maybe even the closing of school. But rain? Rain is for the earth and the community, things that don't generally engage nine-year-olds. How did they know, these little Israeli children? Did their mothers and fathers tell them? Their teachers? Does it come instinctively of being born in the land of our ancestors? Does it come from two thousand years of Jews saying Tefilat Geshem each year in every corner of the world? Do the children of soybean farmers in Iowa clap when it rains on their school windows? I wanted to know all of these things.

Sixty seconds later I went back to my book, but in those sixty seconds my perception of God and rain and nature and the ancient Israelites had been transformed. I now had insight into something I didn't quite grasp before. Every year since then as I stand for the Geshem prayer, my thoughts inevitably wander back to that classroom, those young children, my teachers. . . . And I know now why it was that J.J. needed me in school for twelve days.

Why do Jews ask for rain on Shemini Atzeret and not a few days earlier, when we give thanks for the harvest? Or on Rosh Hashanah and Yom Kippur when we pray for life? Two reasons: one, the Jews are realists. By observing nature, they noticed the rains simply didn't start two weeks earlier. Why pray for something that just won't happen? Two, the Jews are dreamers; or perhaps in this, too, they are realists? The Rabbis in the Talmud debate whether the prayer for rain should be recited on the first day of Sukkot or the last. It was decided the last day. If the rains would come too soon, they would spoil the holiday of Sukkot by driving us out of the sukkah. Thus, people could not pray for rain with a full heart early in the holiday.

What actually is the Tefilat Geshem? It is an ancient prayer asking for the blessings of rain. This brief prayer is inserted into the repetition of the Mussaf. To it have been added a series of piyutim, medieval religious poems which review all the events in our history that are connected to the blessings of rain.

From this day on, until the first day of Pesach, after which we want no more rain, we will add to our daily Shmoneh Esreh the phrase: "[God] Who brings the winds and causes the rain to fall." Interestingly, the rain phrase is inserted as a preface to the resurrection blessing: "Blessed are You, God, Who restores life to the dead." Rain is compared to resurrection because it, too, brings forth from the ground life which has been barren or "dead" since the last harvest. The Rabbis suggest that rain is as miraculous as resurrection.

On Shemini Atzeret, as on the last day of all festivals (separate but not separate!!), the Yizkor remembrance prayer is recited. In many Orthodox synagogues, an appeal is made for some worthy cause. Inevitably, the rabbi or the appeal speaker will summon the theme of the Torah reading that day, a most famous passage used by fund raisers all year long, but especially now: "Ish K'mat-nat Yado" (each in accordance with the gift of his/her hand, that is, each person according to his/her ability). The Torah tells us that no person should come empty-handed to the sanctuary during the pilgrimage festivals; each should give what he/she can. For some people, tithing themselves is appropriate; for others, it can be too little. . . . "Ish K'matnat Yado" has come to serve as a catch phrase to right all sorts of imbalances and excuses that people come up with to avoid their fair share of responsibility.

Lunch is our last meal in the sukkah. Some people recite only Kiddush in the sukkah but take their meals in the house. In many homes, however, the family lingers over lunch in the sukkah a little longer, as we take leave of the sukkah for another year. Even though we've taken all our meals here for eight days, it hasn't been too much. Even for me it hasn't been a burden. In fact, it has been a source of joy, especially on those Indian summer days of late September. . . .

Simchat Torah (Rejoicing of the Torah)

Simchat Torah is a holiday of pure genius—medieval genius, for that is when its unique format was created.

On Simchat Torah we complete the reading of the last few verses of Deuteronomy, and immediately begin again with the first few verses of Genesis. In that act, we tell the whole story of the unending cycle of study of the Torah. But we don't do it in fifteen minutes, as we easily could. We embellish it in a thousand little ways that express and evoke our great love for the Torah. We do it in an outburst of joy and celebration, laughter and gaiety.

Simchat Torah is ushered in by candlelighting. Since this holiday coincides with the second day of Shemini Atzeret, we follow all of the rituals of that sacred day, including the shehecheyanu at candlelighting, the festival Kiddush evening and day, and the festival liturgy. But the holiday celebration is like no other sacred day in the Jewish calendar.

Unlike most other nights of the holidays, the shul is filled to capacity: men, women, and children.

I'm not sure I would bring a potential convert to my synagogue on Simchat Torah, but I personally would not miss it for all the world—the utter lack of awe, the parody, the humor. It is hard to tell if the shul is a place of worship or a vaudeville show. The regular chazzan is retired for the duration. He is replaced with a lay cantor, who chants the Hebrew prayers of Maariv in the most inappropriate tunes: not just melodies from other holidays such as the Yom Kippur liturgy, but old folk classics like "Oh! Susannah" or even popular contemporary tunes, all sung with exaggerated cantorial embellishments. The little boys tie the ad hoc chazzan's tallit fringes in knots, so that he cannot leave the bimah without stumbling over himself. But of course it is all designed to increase laughter and joy.

After the Maariv, we settle down for hakafot, at which each male member of the congregation goes up in turn to the bimah and is given a Torah scroll. He carries it in his arms in circuit around the synagogue. Those who stand in the pews close to the aisle reach over and kiss each Torah as it passes. There are seven such circuits around the synagogue. As each circuit is completed, there is singing and dancing with the Torah before it is handed over for the next circuit. Children come with small Simchat Torah flags, and empty bags, which they quickly fill up with candy that is showered upon them as they walk around in the Torah procession.

The next morning after Shacharit, the whole system seems to break down again. But there is a perfect order to the chaos. Again, there are seven circuits around the synagogue. In most synagogues in America, one of these seven hakafot is dedicated to the Jews of the Soviet Union. Soviet Jews latched onto Simchat Torah as the one holiday to celebrate Judaism and to defy Russian oppression. This hakafot processional for Soviet Jewry takes place outside, in the street. In many places, the local police will rope off the street for the morning. Our shul is across from a large junior high school, many of whose students are Jewish. As we dance around the Torah, singing "Am Yisroel Chai" ("The Jewish People Lives!"), five hundred faces line up at the windows across the street and peer out. What are they thinking? I wonder.

Following the hakafot, a score of individual minyanim (quorums) are convened throughout the shul so that each adult male can be called up to the Torah for an aliyah. The regular aliyah blessings take on special salience on this day: "Blessed are You . . . Who has chosen us from amongst all the nations and has given us the Torah. Blessed are You, God, Who gives the Torah."

It is customary for each man honored with an aliyah to pledge funds to the synagogue or other worthy cause, such as Soviet Jewry.

Once he has had his aliyah, a man will likely amble out into the vestibule where wine and cake are set up on a buffet table; there he makes Kiddush. If his wife remained seated in the shul, he will probably bring in some wine and cake to her. Just as likely, she's already been offered some by a neighbor.

On Simchat Torah, in many modern Orthodox shuls, the lines separating men and women are less rigid than any other day during the year. For hakafot, men carry the Torah scrolls through the women's section for the women to kiss. Men march down the women's aisles, where they would not be found all year long. Essentially, on Simchat Torah, most women are observers while all men are active participants. It can be a lonely holiday for a woman who wants to be in the center of things, doing, not watching. But because there is so little decorum, and so much opportunity to socialize, and so much going on to watch, most Orthodox women are quite satisfied, in fact perfectly happy, with the role of onlooker.

In recent years, however, as feminist consciousness has risen even among Orthodox Jewish women, the desire to participate more actively in this celebration has grown. In a number of Orthodox synagogues, the women are provided with a Torah and they have their own hakafot dancing with the scroll. Many traditionalists (including status quo women) look askance at this new development, but it is spreading.

The very last aliyah in the shul, except for the three "Bridegrooms," is reserved for the children. Kol Ha'ne'arim—all the children. Every child in the shul, infants held by their fathers, twelve-year-olds who know that this is their last year up there, a hundred or so boys and girls, children gathered together on the bimah, the shul bursting with life. Several large taleitim (prayer shawls) are stretched aloft over them as a canopy; adults pull the tallit taut above the shiny faces with bright and wondrous eyes. There are many favorite moments on Simchat Torah, but this is my sentimental favorite. The aliyah blessing is recited by one adult, who recites along with the children. Parents' voices chime in with their young. After the second aliyah blessing is recited, the rabbi and congregation bless the children with the classic blessing of Jacob: "The angel who redeems me from all evil will bless the children and call in them my name and the name of my ancestors Abraham and Isaac; and may they multiply and increase in the midst of the land."

Memories and associations flood my mind: my sweet husband holding three of our babes in his arms at one time under the Kol Ha'ne'arim tallit. I still see Deborah, sky-blue eyes looking up in wonderment. Does she still remember? At what age are these Jewish memories embedded indelibly in the brain? And Rena, my sister. Does she remember when she was a little girl and afraid of the dark? My father told her to say the Jacob blessing each night, and she would no longer be afraid, for God's angel would watch over her. Every night, for as long as we shared a bedroom, I would hear Rena whisper that blessing after the Shema Yisrael. It must have worked, for no one ever gobbled her up in the dark of the night.

In five minutes, Kol Ha'ne'arim is over. Whatever bit of candy an adult still holds is showered on the children. The congregation spontaneously begins to sing "And you shall see children born to your children. Let there be peace in Israel."

That alone would have been enough, but there is more. What

comes now is the essence of Simchat Torah: the three final aliyot recited by the three chattanim, the three grooms. At Minchah of Yom Kippur, the names of these three special honorees were announced. They are men who are known for their good deeds, their service to the community, their generosity, their Torah learning. The first aliyah goes to the chattan Torah, the groom of the Torah. His portion concludes the reading of Deuteronomy. The second aliyah is given to chattan Bereshit, the groom of Genesis, for whom the first chapter of Genesis, the story of creation, is read. As each new day of creation is described, the congregation chants responsively the last few words. "And it was evening and it was morning, the first (second, . . . sixth) day."

The third aliyah is given to chattan maftir, the groom of the reading from the Prophets. On this day, the prophetic reading describes Joshua's succession after Moses. Not only does the chain of Torah and tradition continue on without end, but the human chain is eternal as well.

I take special pride in the third groom ceremony, the chattan maftir. The first chattanim (grooms) are hallowed traditions going back centuries. The chattan maftir is very new, created some fifteen years ago by my husband when he served as rabbi. Seeking to honor a younger person or a less established one or someone who could not afford the philanthropy frequently honored by the first two groom aliyot, he hit upon the idea of making the Maftir reader also a groom. Since the first two-grooms custom goes back a long way, there are traditional verses of praise and greeting sung in honor of those two grooms. But nothing existed for this third groom, so Yitz composed special grammen (rhyming verses) in his honor.

As it turns out, the chattan maftir affected the other two chattan ceremonies in our synagogue. The traditional verses of greeting the chattan are written in ornate Hebrew and are generally not comprehended by the congregation. By contrast, the grammen for the chattan maftir were in English and were warm, witty, and comprehensible; so the other two honorees were cast in the shadow. By popular demand, grammen were added to the greeting of the first two grooms as well. Thus, good spirits and liturgical creativity spilled over to another area of synagogue life. Most people think of Orthodoxy as conserving or maintaining embattled traditions. I prefer the thought that it embraces the entire past and tradition of the Jewish people—including the ceremonies added out of love and joy or sadness—in each generation. I feel like a special participant in the history of the tradition as I watch the chattan maftir go down the aisle each year. And I think to myself that perhaps someday women will be honored with these special and beautiful synagogue honors.

This is what it's like: as each groom is called up to the Torah, he is ushered in with a special "marriage" ceremony. Several of his close friends accompany him down the aisle, holding the poles of a velvet canopy under which he walks. Some of the candy gets recycled; now it is showered upon the groom like rice at a real wedding. A gaggle of children follows the procession, scrambling to the floor as pieces of candy fall. As the chattan (groom) proceeds with his entourage down the aisle toward the bimah and the beloved Torah, the rabbi sings a rhymed verse which he has composed for the day. It is a This Is Your Life in song, full of humor and warm feelings of camaraderie.

I said I wouldn't bring a potential convert, but I've changed my mind. In fact, I would pick this day above all others to introduce someone to Judaism, just as the wise and spiritually hungry Russian Jews have done. Amid the riotousness, a joy and love for Torah, God, and community shine through. Amid the disorder is a pervasive and satisfying sense of order, of knowing what to expect, of where and how to belong. It is the perfect holiday to bring in someone who is searching for a way to fill an emptiness in his or her soul. No matter the apparent sexism of this day. That, too, we will work out.

Mussaf is anticlimactic. In fact, hardly anyone is left in the synagogue. It used to be that the chattanim offered a joint Kiddush after services, and of course everyone stayed till the last bit of chopped liver was gone. Now that that has been discontinued —probably because of cost for a growing congregation—and everyone is impatient to get home to lunch and a nap before Minchah and Maariv roll around again.

Finally, it's time for Havdalah. Sukkot et al. are over.

It's been a wonderful month. Many highs and a few lows. Starting with Elul, working our way through Selihot, Rosh Hashanah, the solemnity of Yom Kippur, the sweetness of Sukkot, the realities of Shemini Atzeret, the ribaldry of Simchat Torah. During the long, cold nights of winter, as we sip Sylvia's Three Hundred Proof, we will long for these days. But meanwhile, we have spent a lot of time in shul. No one is sorry to see the month of Heshvan come. Bland Heshvan, without a single holiday to mar its face. It is just what we need as we begin to get down to the work we have interrupted so often. A homiletics teacher once said to his class of rabbinic students: "When Heshvan comes, you'll feel like you're on vacation." Maybe that's why the last Havdalah after Simchat Torah is the most wonderful Havdalah of all. I feel like tossing my besamim etrog in the air and shouting, "Hooray! Hurrah! We made it! Now back to reality!"

CHAPTER 19

CHANUKAH

No, Chanukah is not the Jewish answer to Christmas. But as far as American Jewish children go—and their parents, too, for that matter—the fact that Chanukah comes out in December, lasts for eight full days, and has trappings such as Chanukah gelt (coins), gifts, latkes, and lots of candles to light doesn't hurt the Diaspora ego one bit.

There are four levels to the story of Chanukah, each addressing the Jews of any given generation with a different sense of urgency and immediacy. At one level, it is the story of religious freedom and national sovereignty. At the second, Chanukah is about Jewish particularism versus assimilation. The third is a tale of the few against the many, the weak against the mighty and powerful. And the fourth is about lights and miracles.

In the year 167 B.C.E., a small band of Jews—today, we would call them guerrillas—took to the hills of Judea. They had had just about all they could take from the Greek oppressors. And besides, they were in mortal danger. But instead of merely hiding safely in the hills they knew so well, they undertook a risky war against their oppressors. It was a war that would bring them, three years later, victorious to the Holy Temple in Jerusalem.

It had all begun two hundred years earlier, when Alexander the Great conquered that part of the hemisphere. Judea, and its capital Jerusalem, became part of the Macedonian empire. After

Alexander died, in 323 B.C.E., his kingdom was divided into three parts, with Judea falling to the Syrian Greeks. Altogether, this did not affect greatly the lives of the nationals of the various countries, for they were generally permitted to offer fealty and taxes to the nominal ruler, yet maintain a discreet self-autonomy in most areas of life.

Yet, while there was no coercion, the process of assimilating Jews to Greek culture was under way, both in the Diaspora cities and in Judea itself. There were many Jews who welcomed the ways of the stranger. By and large, these were the upper class, the landed gentry, the trend setters, those close to the ruling party. They were the Jewish aristocracy, and there were many of the priestly class among them. These were Jews who were informed by Greek values, enamored of Greek culture, and infatuated with Greek mores. Not only the Greek way of thinking, but the Hellenic style of life appealed to them. In many cases, this meant relinquishing the Jewish way of life and Jewish practices. These Jewish Hellenists frequented the gymnasia, and participated naked in the exercises as their upper-class Greek fellows were wont to do. (Interestingly, however, they were careful to use "kosher" oils to anoint themselves, rather than pagan oils.) Some of these Hellenists ceased to circumcise their children; the more extreme among them went so far as to uncircumcise themselves, that is, to undergo painful surgery that would pull down the foreskin, thereby removing signs of the "primitive" rite their parents had forced upon them as eight-day-old infants.

Although they were a sizable and significant group, in varying degrees of assimilation, by no means did they constitute the whole of the Jewish population. There were many Jews who resented and resisted the religious and cultural incursions of the Greeks. However, as long as it was a matter of assimilation by choice, the devout and faithful Jews, as well as the moderate Hellenists, could criticize their errant brothers, but they themselves could go their own way—the Jewish way. But even this state of affairs was soon to deteriorate.

Under the rulership of the Seleucidan king Antiochus IV, the Greeks stepped up the policy of religious aggrandizement against the semiautonomous Jewish state. In the year 169 B.C.E., a Greek city was established opposite the Temple mount. Not willing to content themselves with heavy taxes levied against the Jews, not satisfied alone with influence by voluntarism, the Greeks instituted religious practices, including pig sacrifices and pagan cultic worship, in the Holy Temple. This was by no means a haphazard act. Their scheme was to render impotent the central locus of Jewish spirituality—the Holy Temple—so as to bring down the entire spiritual enterprise more easily. And to round out the picture, they forbade Jewish religious practices, such as the study of Torah, observance of Shabbat, and circumcision.

The more extreme Hellenists went along with all this, even welcomed and supported it. The moderate Hellenists were made uneasy but remained fairly quiet. Trouble, however, was brewing underneath. The resistance of the masses was growing.

The king did not take kindly to resistance. Having all the power on his side, he crushed the resistance with smashing force. The resisters were given a choice, which represented no choice at all to them: paganization or martyrdom. One of the legends of Chanukah is that of Hannah and her seven sons. One by one, the boys were called into the public square and ordered to bow down to the statue of Zeus. Hannah encouraged each child in his refusal. She was tortured by being forced to watch each one die before her very eyes. After her last son was executed, Hannah took her own life.

But despite this or similar incidents, the king did not get the message; he did not take heed of Jewish determination; he did not understand the implications of Jewish martyrdom. Foolish king that he was, he continued with a heavy hand everywhere. The only thing left for the faithful was to escape or to fight. But with what? With a small, scraggly, unarmed band of farmers, country poor, uneducated, the lowest and most vulnerable strata of society? Jewish children of the next twenty centuries would sing of them as the mighty warriors.

Who organized these guerrillas? An outlaw named Mattathias of the Hasmonean family. But wait: Mattathias was no outlaw. He was a priest, a pious man, a family man, well educated, a person of status and respect in the town of Modi'in, a peaceful little town not far from Jerusalem. Some might even describe Mattathias as a moderate Hellenist, who appreciated certain aspects of Greek culture.

In the year 167 B.C.E., however, pig sacrifices were forcibly introduced into Modi'in. There were many Jews who acquiesced, but Mattathias was not among them. On the contrary, he stabbed a Jew who sacrificed in the new cult, killed the king's agent, and pulled down the sacrilegious altar. Brave but not kamikaze, he could no longer remain safely in Modi'in, so he took to the hills. Thus, he became an outlaw, as did his five sons. Little by little they were joined by other Jews who also wanted to remain faithful to the Torah. Some of them were called Chasidim (pious ones), and initially all they wanted was to be able to escape religious and political oppression and live their lives with fidelity to Jewish practices.

But that wasn't meant to be.

The Hasmonean priest, Mattathias, was not a young man, and he died shortly after he fled. His son, Judah, who came to be known as Judah Maccabee (Judah the hammer), took over the planning and execution of guerrilla strategies.

One of the remarkable effects of this small band of mountain soldiers was to polarize the population. Until now, many Jews quietly obeyed the Greek edicts, passively adjusting to the vicissitudes of the times, unwilling to risk their own necks. Many went along with the Greeks, thinking it wasn't all that terrible. However, when either/or choices were forced upon them, a good many of the populace, including some moderate Hellenists, went over to the side of the Maccabees, as Judah's band came to be known.

All of the things that we know are conducive to guerrilla warfare—familiarity with the terrain, a sympathetic local population, and a win-or-lose, fight-to-the-death attitude—helped carry the Maccabees along successfully despite their numerical weakness against the great Greek armies. Finally, after three years of struggle, the Jews recaptured the Temple mount, cleaned and scoured and purified the Temple, demolished the pig-sullied altar, and rebuilt and rededicated a new one. They also rekindled the Great Menorah, the six-foot-high, golden, seven-branch candelabrum that stood in the inner sanctuary. On the twenty-fifth day of Kislev, in the year 165 B.C.E., Judah offered Korban Tamid, the daily sacrifice, the first in many years. The dedication ceremonies lasted for eight days.

There are several reasons to explain the eight days: the dedication of the first Temple, in King Solomon's time, lasted seven days and people left on the eighth day; another tradition from the apocryphal work, Book of Maccabees (II, 10:6–8), tells us that the Jews were belatedly celebrating Sukkot and Shemini Atzeret. Three months earlier, holed up in the mountainous caves around Jerusalem, they had been deprived of that joy. They vowed then that they would celebrate Sukkot in Jerusalem if they ever made it there alive. So even though it was out of season, they celebrated a full Sukkot, complete with etrog, lulav, myrtle, and willow, as well as with torches that were carried to the Temple on Sukkot from Biblical times onward.

Would that not have been enough of a miracle for later generations to celebrate—the victory of the few over the many, the pious and faithful over the alien anti-Judaic master, and, not the least, the return of national sovereignty? But the victory was fragile, Judah was killed in battle five years later, the Hasmonean descendants betrayed one another in internecine strife, and the worst of them reinvited foreign intervention, which had been cast out at such cost by their ancestors.

But the Rabbis of Talmudic times were not willing to forget the miracle that was. They grafted on to it another miracle, the miracle of the lights, to fix its celebration more firmly.

"What is Chanukah?" the Rabbis asked themselves.
"On the twenty-fifth day of Kislev, the days of the Chanukah festival begin. There are eight days, during which eulogies for the dead and fasting are prohibited. When the Greeks entered the Temple, they defiled all the oil stored in it. After the Hasmoneans had established their rule and prevailed, they searched and found one single cruse of oil, still sealed with the seal of the High Priest. But there was only enough oil to last for one day. A miracle occurred, and the supply lasted for eight days. In the following year, they appointed these days as festival days, with the [recitation of] Hallel and with thanksgiving."
—Shabbat 21b

And that is why Chanukah later came to be called Chag Ha-Urim, the holiday of the miracle of the lights. No one asked why this miracle was not mentioned in earlier sources describing the original Chanukah in detail. It did not seem to matter.

PREPARATION

The basic preparation in advance of Chanukah is to set up the menorah or menorot (plural). A Chanukah menorah is an eight-branch candelabrum, plus one—the shamash. Unlike Shabbat candles, Chanukah lights may not be used for any purpose other than to remember the miracle and to publicize it. (Which, in part, explains the tradition that women not do their housework while the candles are burning—to avoid using Chanukah candles as light.) One doesn't read by the light of Chanukah candles, nor use one candle to light another. Therefore, a Chanukah menorah will always have a ninth candleholder, a shamash, which is used as a "service" lighter. Of course, one could use a match to light all the lights, but the custom arose to keep the shamash burning the same length of time as all the candles, so that if someone inadvertently used the Chanukah lights for illumination, it would be the shamash supplying the light and not the holiday candles.

To publicize the miracle, the menorah should be set up in front of a window, so that passersby can see and reflect on it. This often requires pushing a table over to the window. If the table is still too low, a few books at each end with a board across will raise the menorah to viewing height. If oil is used in the menorah, it is wise to cover the board with heavy-duty aluminum foil.

The menorah can be made from most any material. The only specification is that the eight branches be at even height, while the shamash branch be distinguished in some way—higher, lower, projecting forward or sideways.

Many people use oil, preferring pure olive oil from Israel, for it is specified in the Talmud as "preferred"; only pure olive oil was used to light the Great Menorah in the Holy Temple. However, candles may also be used, and many do use the thin, colorful Chanukah candles. Electric menorot are okay for decoration, but are not acceptable for fulfilling the mitzvah.

The menorah—purists call it a chanukiah, for the word menorah should be reserved for the original seven-branched candelabrum of the Temple—has come to take a special place in Jewish art and self-expression. Judaism is not a religion of many artifacts; therefore, the few that we do have take on unusual prominence. More than Shabbat candlesticks, menorot are a distinctive feature of Jewish memorabilia; every Jewish museum has its collection, as do many synagogues and many individual families. Like synagogue architecture, Jews in every country stylized the chanukiah to reflect the unique approach to design of that particular locale. A chanukiah is not something you put away after its eight-day use. It is often displayed on a shelf or hung on a wall all year long. It is a sign that this is a Jewish home, filled with Jewish symbols.

Some years ago, my nephew, then a twenty-year-old student in Jerusalem, was giving up his furnished one-room apartment. He stored his meager belongings with us for a few days. I found it touching to observe that in addition to his duffel bag of clothing, his entire worldly possessions included a few boxes of books, a Simon and Garfunkel poster, some framed photographs, two mezuzot, and a lovely chanukiah he had made a few years earlier out of wood and glass vials. This is what constituted a Jewish home for him.

One can make a menorah very easily. Anything that can hold candles or hot oil (the oil gets very hot as it burns toward the end) and that can keep the wicks separate from one another and on an even line is a kosher menorah. For example, eight miniature ceramic cups, lined up and affixed with a small dab of glue to a wood or chrome bar, with a ninth cup off to the side, is a simple, easy-to-make, yet very beautiful chanukiah.

We have several menorot that are copies of antique ones. They have cavities for oil and flat backs which hang nicely against a wall all year long. But some of them hang there even throughout Chanukah, for I cannot use them. They don't stand by themselves. I have always wondered how they could have been used, for it would be impossible to hang them and light them in a window simultaneously. At best, they would dangle dangerously. And then I learned that originally the lights were lit outside of the house. In Talmudic times, the Chanukah menorah was positioned against the entrance of the house, opposite the mezuzah, which was to the right of the door. This was done to publicly affirm the Chanukah miracle. In times of danger, the Rabbis permitted the lamp to be hung inside the home. Later, this came to be the accepted way, with the chanukiah hung inside at the entrance opposite the mezuzah. Only in recent centuries have the free-standing menorot become so popular.

No special meal is required for Chanukah, nor is work prohibited during the eight days of Chanukah. The only other preparations are those that contribute to the holiday mood: preparing gifts, gelt, and dreydels for the children, laying in a supply of potatoes and oil for latkes, and decorating the house to look like Chanukah. Jewish bookstores sell all kinds of decorations for Chanukah, but one can also put up crepe paper streamers and hang Chanukah signs to make it look festive.

CELEBRATION

Chanukah lights are lit each night just after dark. If this is not possible, they should be lit as soon after dark as most of the family has gathered. In our house, as in many Jewish homes, each member of the family has his/her own menorah, but we all light together: the menorot are all displayed in front of the windows; on the eighth day of Chanukah, it truly does look like a feast of lights.

CANDLELIGHTING

On the first night, only one light is lit, the one at the far right, as you face the menorah. On the second night, when two lights are lit, the second one, the newest one, is lit first. However, inserting the candles or pouring in the oil should be done in reverse direction, from right to left. Thus, on the eighth night, lights are prepared this way, as you face the menorah:

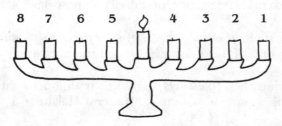

but they are kindled this way:

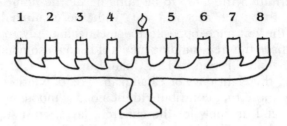

First, the shamash is lit with a match. Taking the lit shamash in hand, but without lighting the other wicks yet, we recite these blessings:

בָּרוּךְ אַתָּה יְיָ, אֱלֹהֵינוּ מֶלֶךְ הָעוֹלָם, אֲשֶׁר קִדְּשָׁנוּ
בְּמִצְוֹתָיו, וְצִוָּנוּ לְהַדְלִיק נֵר שֶׁל חֲנֻכָּה.

Baruch ata Adonai Elohainu melech ha'olam asher kidshanu b'mitzvotav v'tzivanu l'hadlik ner shel Chanukah.

Blessed are You, Lord our God, Ruler of the universe, Who has sanctified us with His commandments and commanded us to kindle the Chanukah light.

בָּרוּךְ אַתָּה יְיָ, אֱלֹהֵינוּ מֶלֶךְ הָעוֹלָם, שֶׁעָשָׂה נִסִּים
לַאֲבוֹתֵינוּ, בַּיָּמִים הָהֵם בַּזְּמַן הַזֶּה.

Baruch ata Adonai Elohainu melech ha'olam sheh'asah nisim la-avotainu ba-yamim ha-hem bazman hazeh.

Blessed are You, Lord our God, Ruler of the universe, Who has performed miracles for our forefathers in those days, at this time.

On the first night, we add the Shehecheyanu. As we come to the last few words of the blessings, we light the candles.

Following these blessings, it is the tradition to sing several Chanukah songs, in particular "Hanerot Halalu" ("These Candles") and "Maoz Tzur" ("Rock of Ages"), the golden oldie of Chanukah. Both of these songs are about miracles and redemption.

At least one day of Chanukah, and sometimes two, falls on Shabbat, which appropriately enough is called Shabbat Chanukah. On Friday night, Chanukah candles must be lit before Shabbat candles, a good half hour before sunset. However, in order that they burn long enough into the night to be seen by passersby (at least thirty minutes after sunset) extra-size Chanukah candles or extra-large vials of oil are used. Some people use the short, stubby Shabbat candles in their menorah. I have found that by using thinner wicks, such as cotton bakery string, on Friday night, the oil lasts a very long time. On Saturday night, the Chanukah candles are lit immediately after Havdalah.

Although Chanukah is a home-oriented holiday, the mitzvah of lighting candles obtains, no matter where you are. If you travel, pack a menorah and candles (oil is messy for travel). And don't forget to repack it the next morning as you leave your hotel.

After candlelighting, we distribute Chanukah gifts and gelt. I'm not sure of the origin of this gift giving, but I'm pretty certain one won't find it in rabbinic literature. Nevertheless, Jews are human, too, and not highly ascetic at that, and since gifts never hurt anyone, especially children ages two to ninety, it is rather sweet that gift giving came to be associated with Chanukah. When our children were younger, we used to give each of them a small gift each night after candlelighting. Contrary to the naysayers, gifts do not distort one's perspective on the holiday nor confuse it with Christmas in the mind of a firmly anchored Jew.

Latkes, grated potatoes fried in oil, are a favorite Chanukah food, linked to Chanukah because of oil. In Israel and in many Jewish homes in America, doughnuts, also fried in oil, are served. Our family, however, remains faithful to latkes. We have a special reason. My father was ready to propose to my mother on their third date. He was quite certain he wanted to marry this wonderful woman, but he had to be absolutely sure, so he asked the key question as they rowed around Central Park lake: "Can you make latkes?" "Sure," said my mother-to-be. Perfect, thought my father to himself. "Well, then, will you marry me?" And they lived happily ever after.

Dreydel is the game of Chanukah. The players spin a four-sided spinner, with each side labeled for relative take. The four Hebrew letters, one per side, are nuhn (n), gimmel (g), hey (h), and shin (sh). These are the initials of the phrase, *Nes gadol hayah sham:* a great miracle occurred there. Depending on what letter the dreydel lands, the spinner takes from or puts into the pot. Nuhn equals nothing, gimmel takes all, hey takes half, shin puts in. Big gamblers we aren't; the game is usually played for pennies and nickels and even then the total stakes are often put into a pushke (charity box) after the game ends.

Why the dreydel? Some conjecture that when the Greeks forbade the study of Torah, the children would keep a top handy. If the Greeks should come upon them in a group studying Torah, they would quickly pull their tops out and pretend they had been playing the game all along.

In addition to candles, there are two other formal observances. One is the Hallel, the special prayer of praise of God that we recite during all festivals. The other is the Al Hanissim prayer, a short passage about miracles that is inserted into silent Amidah and into the Grace After Meals. With such minor liturgical increments for an eight-day holiday, no wonder that candles and gifts took up the slack.

PERSPECTIVES ON CHANUKAH

Next to Rosh Hashanah and Yom Kippur, Chanukah is celebrated by a broader spectrum of Jews than any other holiday. It's not just the lights, the gifts, the hunger for celebration at this particular tinselly time of year. It's the larger message about the relationship of Jews and Judaism to broader cultures, not only to Christianity, but to larger cultural values in general, values which we, as modern Jews, tend to share, embrace, and idealize. Chanukah reminds us that we are a part of it, but also apart from it, and that Jews will always live in the tension between the universal and the particular, between cosmopolitanism and parochialism. It is both easier and harder to be a Jew in America today. Easier, because there is great tolerance, and many Jews feel more comfortable about "returning" and living a more particularist life. Harder, because it is so easy to assimilate and there's no coercion in either direction.

Perhaps in that sense, the contiguity to Christmas is good, for it sharpens the real focus of Chanukah—where and how we locate ourselves in relation to a majority culture.

The Rabbis could have let Chanukah go. Some scholars say that Chanukah had been neglected during the two hundred years following the Maccabean victory, but as Roman oppression grew, the Rabbis revived it: the memory of a successful national revolt couldn't have been sweeter, and the fantasy of independence couldn't have been more passionately re-created. On the other hand, precisely because that nationalist revolt had culminated in absolute failure—in the destruction of the Temple—the Rabbis could really have let it go. Restoration was becoming increasingly a dream of messianic days, and nationalism was removed from the immediate religious agenda.

But the Rabbis didn't let go. Instead, they revived Chanukah and attached to it a more profound meaning, the meaning of the lights. What was the significance of rekindling the menorah in the Temple? It was like turning the lights back on, like saying we are back in business, with our own offerings and our own order of faith. Despite the failure of the Maccabean revolt, it was a resounding religious success. The Hellenists might have overwhelmed the Judeans, but through the Maccabean revolt, the basic rule of Torah for the Jewish people was assured.

The Rabbis understood that that was the real miracle of Chanukah. It was a lesson offered through the efforts not of assimilated Jews in high places, as in the Purim deliverance, but through the medium of the lowly farmer and the poor tanner, the pious mother, the parochial, the unsophisticated, the single-minded, the ones who clung passionately to their ways while their more elitist cohorts marched to the beat of a different drummer. Chanukah was a great victory, not only because the few succeeded militarily against the many, but because if not for their prodding, needling, and forcing of choices, the Hellenists and Hellenizers would have imperceptibly swallowed everyone in their path. I fear to say it, but I, too, a middle-class Jew living in those times, might well have been won over. After all, both

Mattathias and his opponents all started out as moderate Hellenists.

Chanukah is the story of enormous challenge for American Jews, enormous tension. Modern Orthodox live with it more than their right-wing counterparts, but none are immune—right-wingers, modern secularists, universalists, all. And it's a lesson for Christians, too, though they may not know it. The issue is not how to be universalist in this great country, but how to be particularist without rejecting everyone else, how to feel chosen without feeling superior, how to feel covenanted without erasing the covenant of the other, how to integrate positive modern values but not be overwhelmed and swallowed up by them.

It is not easy even for an Orthodox Jew who lives with tradition day in and day out, yet who is often uncertain as to where to draw the lines and which lines to draw. Truly, they were heroes, those sturdy, stalwart, brave Maccabees.

CHAPTER 20

PURIM

The Talmud tells us: When Adar arrives, happiness increases. What the Rabbis really meant was that right in the center of the month of Adar comes the happiest of all Jewish holidays— Purim. The Rabbis ought to know, for they were part of its transformation. Scholars tell us that the Book of Esther, which describes the events of Purim and is read each Purim, was not entered into the Jewish canon until three or four hundred years after the event occurred. What seems to have happened is that Purim was a popular holiday with a soul-warming story that was told over and over again. The people just wouldn't let it die. And although it affected the lives of Jews of a single empire, and was not the only example of deliverance of the Jewish people during those four hundred years, the way it happened is the ultimate and universal fantasy of minority victims everywhere: not only to be saved from extinction, but for the perpetrator to be richly punished. So the Rabbis finally canonized the Book of Esther and established Purim firmly for all time.

THE STORY

In brief, then, the Jews of Persia, a pleasant Diaspora community of the fifth century B.C.E. are suddenly threatened with extinction. The order comes from the unremarkable and flaccid

King Ahasuerus, but it's really Haman, his prime minister, who is behind the whole thing. Haman is an unreconstructed anti-Semite, but what pushes him over the limits of civil tolerance into violence is the fact that Mordecai, a Jew who loiters near the palace a good deal of the time, refuses to bow down to Haman. What is Mordecai doing around the king's court anyhow? He has his reasons which he certainly won't tell Haman.

Mordecai's niece, whom he raised from childhood, is none other than the queen of Persia. But no one knows she's a Jew. And she's not telling either. Even her husband, the king, does not know.

In any event, when the evil decree is circulated, Uncle Mordecai comes quickly again to the palace to inform Esther and to plead with her to help save the Jews. She demurs, but then agrees. She arranges a party for Haman and the king. However, she loses her nerve, so she arranges another party the next day, and then she tells all—her true identity, the threat to her people, and the name of the villain. The king, who obviously still likes and respects Esther, even though he has not been intimate with her for quite some time, is horrified at what's been going on in his kingdom while he's not been paying attention. Mordecai is rewarded, Haman and his ten sons are hanged on the gallows they had newly built for Mordecai, and the Jews are saved.

Mordecai is not only an able and excellent political leader of his people, but a man of religious foresight as well. He writes letters to Jews far and wide, telling them to mark the fourteenth day of Adar on their calendars for celebration, because they have all been saved. He instructs them to send treats to each other and gifts to the poor. The holiday is called Purim, meaning "lottery," and is celebrated the fourteenth day because Haman drew number fourteen from the lottery—the fourteenth day of the month was to have been the beginning of the extermination of the Jews.

Believe it or not, with all of those miracles, the name of God is not once mentioned in the Book of Esther. Very strange. And there are other perplexing questions. What was a nice Jewish girl like Esther doing intermarrying, in the first place? And why was she hiding her identity? She could have done some good for her people all along. And where did a nice Jewish girl learn to play bedroom politics? More about this later.

PREPARATION

Since Purim is a one-day celebration, with none of the Shabbat or holiday prohibitions (for example, cooking, electricity), one would imagine it's a fairly easy holiday for which to prepare. However, if one is a member of a large Orthodox congregation, and in particular if one is a rebbetzin (wife of a rabbi), then not to prepare well in advance for Purim, specifically for the mitzvah of shalach manot, can be an absolute nightmare. Even now that I've gotten it relatively together, I still get a tension headache when someone mentions the words shalach manot.

MISHLOACH MANOT

Let us start at the beginning. Shalach manot, or mishloach manot as it is also called, simply means sending portions of food to friends. Mordecai said in his letter, "Each person should send portions" to his friend to commemorate the day. The Rabbis interpreted this to mean a minimum of two items, either of baked goods or cooked foods or sweets or fruit or drink, although some sources interpret it as requiring at least one baked item in the package. The Rabbis also said you must send a gift to a minimum of one person. That was their great mistake. They should have said a *maximum* of one person. Had they done so, they would have made this rebbetzin and many of her "colleagues" truly happy in the month of Adar. Meanwhile, what happens is that most of the congregation sends packages of shalach manot to the rabbi's family, and if one is a conscientious rebbetzin, she will return a shalach manot package to each one. And if she is naive, she will try to send in kind: to someone who sends two bottles of Scotch and a basketful of Barton's candy, she will not be comfortable sending in return a paper plate with two hamantashen, three walnuts, two red sour balls, and a tangerine. Despite my husband's urgings to the contrary, I used to stay up until 3:00 or 4:00 A.M. after the evening Megillah-reading in order to bake and prepare appropriate packages for my numerous friends in the congregation. And then the next day I would wait near the windows to see who was coming up the walk and then would scurry to get his/her package so that I could appear at the door well organized, calm, and in control. And if someone came for whom

I hadn't prepared a proper package, and couldn't give him/her my plate with three walnuts, I would later assemble a nice package and send my husband and children around the neighborhood delivering it. One year, I made eighty-eight individualized packages. Insanity.

Here are four bits of advice, on how to enjoy this mitzvah:

1. Begin early to prepare the packages for shalach manot. Get sturdy paper plates or small Purim boxes specially sold at Hebrew bookstores, or small colorful shopping bags, or ask the fruit man in the supermarket for the plastic or foam containers. Buy aluminum foil or plastic wrap, or, what makes the prettiest packages, colored cellophane wrap purchased in a large roll (the small rolls cost ten times more per foot. The larger ones can usually be ordered at the local stationery store but need two weeks' delivery time). If you are going to send baked goods, bake in advance, and shop for fruit and candy early.

2. In many communities, the women have organized a system whereby the mitzvah of mishloach manot and tzedakah (charity) are combined, and there's not a lot of work and not a lot of waste. In Merion, Pennsylvania, for example, the women of the Orthodox shul gather together to prepare beautiful packages, which are sent to each member of the congregation. A card is enclosed, with the names of all the people who want to send to this particular family. Since the number of people who contribute to the package is greater than the cost of the package, the Sisterhood brings in several hundred dollars from this project. The funds then go to a charitable cause (oftentimes the shul).

3. For rebbetzins, synagogue klai kodesh, principals, and other community VIPs: Do not try to keep up with the Cohenses. Make all the packages the same; make them all fairly simple and not costly. Being on the other end now, I know that congregants want to send something extraspecial to their communal servants. They understand how many shalach manot a popular leader must send out. No one expects anything fancy in return. The gesture alone is appreciated.

4. Turn the whole thing over to your eighteen-year-old daughter, and hole up in your bedroom for the duration.

If it doesn't get out of hand, mishloach manot can be an absolutely charming and beautiful mitzvah, one which parents and children do together and which gives great pleasure to both giver and receiver.

MATANOT LA'EVYONIM

A second important mitzvah of Purim is matanot la'evyonim: each person is required to give gifts (charity) to at least two needy persons or worthy causes. The money should be distributed on Purim day. If that is not possible, the funds should be set aside and earmarked for later distribution. The origin of this custom is again Mordecai. In gratitude for the miraculous saving, he instructed all the Jews of Persia to send matanot la'evyonim. Mordecai teaches an important lesson: How does one show gratitude and happiness? By helping to improve the lot of those less fortunate.

On the day of Purim, we eat a special seudah, feast, which it is wise to prepare in advance so that the rest of the day is free for other things. No special foods are associated with this holiday, except for hamantashen, the tricornered pastry filled with prune or poppy seed (see p. 484). These are not only sent for shalach manot, they are also served as dessert at the Purim seudah, and served at whatever Purim gatherings one has. It is a gross injustice that Haman, whom we hate so much, should have gained immortality through such a delicious pastry (the prune kind, especially), but Haman had the good fortune to have worn a tricornered hat and Mordecai had the bad fortune to have been given such an unwieldy name. So Haman got the cookie.

One part of the spiritual preparation for Purim is Ta'anit Esther, the fast of Esther, which is one of the minor fasts. From dawn until dusk, the day before Purim (that is, if Purim starts on Tuesday night, Ta'anit Esther is all day Tuesday), Jews fast in commemoration of the fact that Esther fasted before she imposed herself, unsummoned, on the king. Esther also told Mordecai to instruct all the Jews to fast and pray for her efforts to succeed. Ta'anit Esther is not a very difficult fast, nor a sad one, since we all know the happy ending. In fact, I would call it a most perfunctory fast, but fast we do. It forces us to remember the great fear and anxiety the Jews of Persia must have felt in those days.

Some people break the fast immediately after that day has ended and Maariv is recited. Others wait another hour or so until after the Megillah has been read.

CELEBRATION

Purim is a superb holiday. What a funny, wonderful religion that literally commands you to Be Happy on this day. Soon after dark, the regular Maariv is recited. But it's not so regular. In fact, it's quite irregular. The Maariv is done as a parody; the prayers are sung to traditional melodies from other holidays that are completely out of place here and that would upset any straitlaced Jew who is not prepared for some hilarity.

Following Maariv, the entire Megillah, the scroll of Esther, is read. Megillah simply means scroll (although in contemporary parlance it has come to mean a tale). Unlike the Torah scrolls, the Megillah of Esther is rolled around only one winder, which is all you really need if you read the entire work straight through to the end. In accordance with the statement in the Megillah that Mordecai and Esther sent letters to their coreligionists to observe the holiday of Purim, the Megillah is opened out and folded like a letter, several panels at a time. It is as if the original letter of Mordecai is being read again.

The Megillah reading must be heard by everyone, every man, woman, and child. Twice, in fact. If one is bedridden, a reader will go to a person's home so that he/she can hear it being read, with proper cantillations, from the scroll.

Some readers will insert all sorts of voice theatrics, such as a stentorian voice for Ahasuerus' lines or a gentle voice for Esther. In some shuls, the reader dresses up in costume and changes hats with each voice. Can you picture a short, stocky, bearded Megillah reader wearing an organza queen's bonnet, and singing Esther's parts in a high-pitched voice?

Each and every time the name Haman is pronounced, there is a loud booing, stamping, and use of groggers, the traditional noisemakers. Children sound their noisemakers and laugh, parents stamp their feet and boo, babies cry, and Haman's name gets a good "blotting out," as the archvillain deserves. At J.J.'s yeshiva one year, some of the boys used cap guns, horns, laughing boxes, whistles. It's not exactly the way to blot out Haman's name, but it sure fulfills the mitzvah of being happy.

In our synagogue, with eight hundred people assembled, including one thousand children (or so it seems), the shul has rigged up a system of red and green (stop and go) lights that flash green for ten seconds when Haman's name is read, and then red as a signal to the kids to stop their noisemakers so that the reading can continue. It works quite well and is a lot more pleasant than some adult screaming his lungs out to get silence before the reading can continue. Jewish law prescribes that every word of the Megillah be heard; this is quite a challenge with so many children, but the light gimmick helps.

Following the Megillah reading, we go home to break the fast. In some communities, people reassemble for Purim pageants, masquerades, and parties. In recent years Jewish college students in particular have big things going on this evening. They gather in large numbers on different campuses and put on Purim programs. Yeshiva high schools, too, have their own Purim chagigas (parties). And many of the elementary-level yeshivot have Purim carnivals after the morning Megillah reading. At the college-level yeshivot, where the faculty also participates in the Purim chagiga, the students take full advantage to satirize the world around them. Through the use of clever grammen (humorous spoofs in rhyme) and plays, they caricature their rabbis, teachers, and administrators—anyone who holds the balance of power all year long. Whatever ribaldry people carry quietly within them all year spills out at Purim time. Some yeshiva students take seriously the traditional dictum that one must get sufficiently drunk on Purim so as not to be able to tell the difference between blessed Mordecai and cursed Haman. Unaccustomed as they generally are to drinking, there are not a few Purim hangovers at Megillah reading the next morning.

In many synagogues, a masquerade contest for children is held in the social hall, immediately following the Megillah reading. In some shuls, adults come in costume too. Purim is a great holiday for psychiatrists. What they couldn't get on the couch in twenty-five sessions comes right to the surface on Purim. One mild-mannered rabbi I know came dressed one year as Charles de Gaulle, and the following year as Mao Tse-tung. An associate principal, also a rabbi, came to the school's morning Megillah reading and Purim carnival dressed as Mickey Mouse; he got sufficiently plastered to pour some ginger ale down the back of his coassociate principal's back, to the delight of four hundred incredulous children. And what would you say to a pious middle-aged woman who came to the shul masquerade several years ago as the Happy Hooker?

If my memory serves me well, Purim celebration has increased during the last decade as has Jewish consciousness in general since the Six Day War. Purim has come out into the open. Nowadays, many established Jewish newspapers and periodicals publish a humorous issue at Purim time. Ten years ago, this was altogether new. I recall the great wave of shock that swept through the right-wing Orthodox community over a satiric issue that newly appeared, unanticipated, at Purim time, and was taken with great seriousness.

The law is that each person hear the Megillah reading twice: once at night and once after Shacharit. Since most Jews go to their regular jobs on Purim, at least for half a day, two morning readings are scheduled: one at the ungodly hour of seven (preceded by Shacharit at six-fifteen) for those who have to be in a mid-Manhattan office by nine, and one at nine-thirty or so, for students, housewives, and slothful others who can afford to take a day off to deliver shalach manot and prepare for the seudah. By midafternoon, however, the workers, the shirkers, the revelers, the cooks, the kids—each family gathers together for the seudah, the Purim feast. No Kiddush, no double challot, the seudah is simply a good meal, and one of the few festive meals at which liquor or liqueur is served. Families sing songs, especially the old classic "Shoshannat Yaakov," a song expressing the joy of Purim.

For all its joy, Purim is now and always will be tinged with sadness for our family and for several hundred other Orthodox families across the country. Several years ago, on Purim night, while singing and dancing with all his heart in a circle of his beloved students, the beautiful and precious teacher-rebbe-principal of our boys' yeshiva high school collapsed and died of an aneurism of the heart. Only thirty-two at the time, Rav Bak, "Pinky" to his family and friends, had already influenced a large cadre of young people, some in search of their roots and others wanting to understand theirs more fully. In his memory each year, those young men who came under his wide influence and those who were too young to feel it directly, but who go through the system he helped to create, set aside a night before Purim— for one cannot mourn on a holiday of deliverance—and study Talmud the night through, in groups, in pairs, or singly.

It is not that these teenagers grow up before their time; it is that they grow up learning to respond authentically to real sorrow and loss as well as to intense joy; they learn to channel these feelings in a socially constructive manner; perhaps most important of all they learn to feel things deeply. And they learn to remember.

Earlier, I raised three questions: about Esther's morals, Jewish connections, and the whereabouts of God in the Purim story. Mordecai answers them all, in what I believe is the most poignant passage in the entire story of Esther. When Esther demurs, Mordecai bears down very hard. He says, "Do not think in your heart that you will escape in the house of the King from all the other Jews. For if you keep your silence at this time, then relief and deliverance will arise to the Jews from another source but you, and the house of your father, will be destroyed. And who knows but that you were brought to royal estate for such a time as this?" (ESTHER 4:13–14).

That passage is the essence of Purim. Purim is a Diaspora holiday. It is about friends, and enemies; about Jews in high places; about the bonds of kinship and community that are stronger than one's own life.

Purim reminds us of that which Orthodox Jews sometimes tend to forget: that no Jew can ever be written off, that a spark exists that may at some point be ignited, that a commitment to the Jewish people can be as deeply felt by one who is at the very periphery of the community as by one who is at its center.

Jews have made it in America, no doubt about it. For some, the higher they go in status and wealth, the looser their ties. Many Jews assimilate beyond recognition. There are many committed Jews who think the assimilated ones are lost altogether. And forever.

And yet. Esther surely was what we would today call an assimilated Jew, and look what she did. In the final peril, she risked her life to save a people with whom she had all but lost contact.

In doing so, she gave us a second gift—the Esther fantasy. When I contemplate the fact that there are so many Jews in this era who have seemingly lost all connection with community, rather than despair I say to myself, Who knows but that this is all part of the ultimate plan. This, too, is God's design. So when things look their very darkest for the Jewish people, I pull out the old Queen Esther fantasy, and search my mind for who in high places . . . Some feel Henry Kissinger did not understand the Queen Esther message. Tragically Hitler understood it very well. Before he wreaked such terrible havoc, he first eliminated every single assimilated Jew from high places.

There was once a Jewish woman whom I had been trying to involve in some communal activities, a woman on her way up. I asked her to help a particular Jewish cause. I asked her several times, feeling inside of myself a growing and righteous indignation that I was putting myself out and she was doing nothing. But she was not to be persuaded. At one point she said to me something which made me think twice. "Just let me be now," she said. "I can be of more help to you when I've made it. I can help your cause on a larger scale. . . ." Instantly, my mind flew to the Purim story, and I understood her words. (I must admit, however, I'm still waiting. . . .)

Perhaps all of this has something to do with the absence of God's name throughout the entire Book of Esther. It tells us something about the way God works miracles—not only through extraordinary or supernatural acts but through the human initiative of ordinary mortals. And not only through the committed, visible, faithful followers, but through the assimilated and through those who are marginal to the faith community.

That goes for political institutions as well. There are people, Jews and Christians alike, who are troubled by the fact that the reborn Israel has all the flaws of a human state. But the Purim story teaches that it is precisely in such admittedly flawed human realities that divine redemption is brought into being.

Finally, Purim is about remembering. We are told, with one half of our brain, to remember; with the other, to blot out the name of the villain forever and ever. Remember the Amalekites (DEUT. 25:17), remember that evil Haman, remember Hitler. In the midst of my laughter at this funny costume, or that Purim joke, I remember our enemies, past and present. The names change, but not the character or intent. Haman, Antiochus, Hitler, Arafat—all bent on destroying my people. I must remember my enemies with a passion as fierce as my love for the little children masquerading this night in synagogues all over the world. Somehow, we must find a way to be strong enough to protect them.

Purim, then, is the reality we retell, the fantasy it spawns, the antennae we must sharpen, the feelings of kinship it intensifies. A little fancier shalach manot, a little plainer—what does it really matter? I must learn to keep my eye on the ball.

CHAPTER 21

PESACH (PASSOVER)

The Rabbis of ancient times structured the celebration of Passover as a pedagogical device. And it works. Every year there comes my way a small signal or two that reminds me again that the whole thing really does work.

My signal of a recent year: Early one morning, eighteen days before Pesach, I drove to Kennedy Airport to await Deborah, returning from seven months study in Israel. A little blond boy no more than three, wearing denim overalls and red sneakers, was running around nearby. As he ran about, flying a toy plane up and down in a wide arc, he repeatedly sang one tune to himself as little boys often do in accompaniment of their own play. It was the refrain of Dayenu, the ancient seder hymn Jews have sung for centuries on Pesach, proclaiming that this act of God's goodness or that one would have been sufficient. . . . If the little boy managed to nap well on the eve of Pesach, he will have brought joy to the hearts of all the adults as he sang Dayenu with them at their seder. But if not this year, then next year, or the next.

Another year: It was the eighth day of Pesach. Jonathan S.'s Bar Mitzvah took place that morning in shul. Afterward, we all walked to the S.'s for Kiddush. As my husband and I went into the playroom to leave our coats, we overheard a moment of child's play that intrigued us. Seated on the rug were two children, approximately four or five, playing house. The little girl, who was masterminding their play, took "Baby" for herself, and assigned "Mommy" to her little male friend. After eight days of matzah, they must have longed for their peanut butter and jelly sandwiches, for the objects that garnered their attention were a toy toaster and a plastic slice of white bread. Baby said, "Mommy, I want this piece of bread. Is Pesach over yet?" "No, baby," said the little boy. "Wait until . . . five o'clock," and he looked at an imaginary watch. "But I want it, Mommy," said the little girl, feigning a baby's cry with a nasal wah, wah, wah. "It's chametz," said the boy mommy, "and you can't have it." Instantly the baby transformed herself into a normal five-year-old, straightened her spine, and said to her friend reasonably, "But it's not real bread. I can have it. Now say yes." The boy was stymied for a moment and then reached a bit further into his imagination for the answer. "Pretend it's matzah and say, 'I want this matzah,' and I'll say yes."

There they were, two babes, products of Free to Be and a three-thousand-year-old Sinaitic injunction!

Part 1—History

When Joseph, the regent of Egypt, invited his eleven brothers to leave famine-blighted Canaan and bring their father to settle in Egypt, he made them an offer they could not refuse: the best land, good connections, plenty of food, and a respected and protected position even though they were—and would continue to be—outsiders. So they came, settled, multiplied, prospered, and undoubtedly felt quite secure.

Within a few centuries after Joseph's death, however, there arose new rulers who did not remember Joseph. They made the lives of the Hebrews unbearable, tightening the noose inch by inch, setting them up by accusing them of being a fifth column, and, ultimately, reducing them to abject slavery.

One of the universal characteristics of slaves is to surrender hope. The Hebrews, under those latter-day Pharaohs, were no exception. How much hope can you possibly have if you are forbidden to have children? How can you dream of redemption if the monumental struggle to survive occupies your every thought? How much human dignity can you maintain if the master demands a daily quota of stones for his pyramids, but doesn't supply you with the raw materials? How can you think that God loves *you*, descendant of Abraham, if the Egyptians drown your infant sons?

But then, just when things looked bleakest, God calls on Moses to resist the mighty Pharaoh on behalf of this band of miserable slaves. Nor is that all he was called to do. Moses' mission was to shape up the band of slaves, to lead them out of Egypt to freedom, to bring them to the land promised to Abraham.

Pesach, then, is the universal story of redemption, of human dignity, of hope, of freedom. But Pesach is also the particular story of God's special love and special choosing of His people Israel. God and not Moses is the redeemer; Moses is but the heroic messenger. Any other way and the Exodus would have been merely a soothing political memory, a kind but fleeting moment in the history of a particular people.

It is this multifaceted message of Pesach that has made it the central holiday of the Jewish people, and the ultimate paradigm for people of all faiths.

Ordinary people busy with their present lives cannot keep these themes in mind all of the time. To compensate, tradition has served up a hundred and one reminders:

Every single day in the Shacharit service, the whole story is told, including Moses' song at the Red Sea.

The first of the Ten Commandments links monotheism to that act of saving: "I am the Lord your God Who took you out of the land of Egypt from the house of bondage" (EXOD. 20:2).

Shabbat, a day of freedom, is the perpetual counterbalance to the ancient enslavement in Egypt. The Friday-night Kiddush sounds this theme.

Scores of laws that require an ethical sensitivity and benevolence are placed in their proper frame: ". . . because you were a stranger in the land of Egypt, and I took you out" . . . therefore, be kind to strangers, orphans, the disenfranchised, the misfits, the downtrodden.

In tzitzit, mezuzah, in certain laws of kashrut, and also in laws pertaining to the harvest, we are reminded of our great good fortune in the Exodus.

So uppermost must the memory of the Exodus be in our minds that the Talmud tells us that every Jew in every generation should feel as if he or she went out of Egypt with Moses. And in order that the matter not become a dull reflex, once each year the event is compressed, intensified, and reexperienced, so as to reenergize our Exodus batteries for the entire year. On Pesach it is possible to achieve that sensation of the pain of slavery, the hasty departure of refugees who couldn't wait for the dough to rise, the exhilaration at the defeat of the enemy, the exultation of newfound freedom, and the abiding knowledge that God does love us and singled us out—ourselves, our ancestors, and our children's children.

How do you experience an event such as this? How do you get into a slave-to-freeman's skin? Through the use of concrete symbols, through a detailed, graphic, blow-by-blow telling of the story. Why, I always wonder, did the ancient Rabbis go to such extremes in setting forth the mode of preparation and celebration? Merely to put us in the right frame of mind? Yes, but strike "merely," for it is no small achievement to internalize so completely an event that happened three thousand years ago.

Part 2—Setting the Stage

The Torah refers to the festival of Pesach by the name of Chag Hamatzot, the Festival of Unleavened Bread. Matzah is considered lechem oni, the bread of affliction. It is the hard, dry, rough bread that slaves eat, instead of the soft, rich bread of the freeman. But matzah is also lechem cherut, the bread of freedom, for it is the bread the Jews baked as they prepared for a hasty exit, with no time to allow for the dough to ferment and rise. (It also happens to be a more sensible fare with which to travel; a pound of matzah takes up half the space of a pound of bread, is twice as filling, and never spoils.) Thus, in typical Jewish dialectical fashion, the bread of slavery and the bread of freedom are one and the same. And in that there is a most important lesson: the difference between slavery and freedom is not necessarily creature comforts, but rather a relative mastery over one's fate. In slavery, they ate the hard, broken crusts which the master allowed them. In the Exodus, the Jews voluntarily accepted a most Spartan regimen as they set out on their tenuous journey—because they had before them a vision of liberation.*

The basic principle of Pesach observance is this: Seven days shall you eat unleavened bread . . . (Exod. 12:15). Seven days shall there be no leavened products found in your homes for whoever eats chametz, that person shall be cut off from the congregation (Exod. 12:19).

Thus, chametz is not to be seen, eaten, enjoyed, or profited from on Pesach. Banish all chametz, including anything that contains even the slightest measure of chametz. Unlike the regular laws of kashrut, when one measure of forbidden foods in sixty is considered so negligible as to have no effect on the rest of the substance, on Pesach even the slightest measure of chametz in an item renders the total item unfit.

There are two approaches with regard to the elimination of chametz on Pesach: (1) To clean out, destroy, remove, and renounce all chametz. This is known as *biur* (burning) and *bitul* (renouncing) chametz. (2) Since total elimination would constitute an economic hardship for most people, the Rabbis instituted a procedure of *mechirat chametz*: sale of title to the chametz in one's possession.

What is chametz? Contrary to popular belief, chametz is *not* the five grains of wheat, rye, barley, oats, and spelt. Rather, chametz is the leavened product that results when any of these five grains come into contact with water for more than a minimum of eighteen minutes. Thus, all breads, pastas, cakes, cookies, and dry cereals are considered pure chametz.

One could reasonably ask why matzah is permitted. After all, it is baked with flour and water. But matzah baked for Pesach is carefully watched to make sure that no water touches the flour beforehand. When water is added to the flour it is quickly

---

* Credit goes to Irving Greenberg for this original insight on the dialectical meaning of matzah.

kneaded into dough and baked within eighteen minutes, so that no leavening process can take place. That is why only the matzah sold at Pesach time is marked KOSHER FOR PASSOVER. Year-round matzah is not supervised the same way, and could possibly be chametz.

In addition to the five major grains, Ashkenazic Jews (of European origin) do not eat rice, corn, beans, peas, and peanuts, or any derivatives thereof. Flour could be ground of these vegetables and the breads baked from them would look like breads of pure chametz, which might confuse the populace. So the Ashkenazic rabbis barred their use altogether on Pesach. Sephardim, on the other hand, never instituted such a ban and therefore, have always served at the seder wonderful exotic side dishes made of these products.

Preparation: For Men Only

CLEANING

Cleaning for Pesach is the most thorough spring cleaning imaginable. Every corner is vacuumed, every shelf is scrubbed, every drawer cleaned out. Furniture is moved, mattresses are overturned, pockets of garments are turned inside out and shaken clean. What we are looking for are any possible hiding places of chametz. While it seems a bit excessive to some, I am always surprised at how much chametz a good cleaning uncovers. My husband empties out his travel bag—full of tiny pretzel crumbs. J.J. finds his old book bag in a bottom drawer and in it, horror of horrors, is a peanut butter sandwich, hardened like a piece of petrified rock. And once we have started to clean for Pesach, some of us go overboard. Every curtain gets washed and ironed, the rugs are shampooed. At Pesach time, I recall the scene of my father, who like most men of his generation was not big on housecleaning, taking each and every book off the shelves of his extensive library, dusting each book individually, shaking out its leaves, washing the bookshelves . . . Pesach cleaning becomes a combination of classical New England spring cleaning and the relentless ritual search for chametz. This is why, in many well-organized households, Pesach cleaning begins right after Purim. As Lucy L., who works full time, says each year on her way out of shul after the Megillah reading, "Well, tomorrow I've got to get started on Pesach."

The office and the car also must be cleaned thoroughly. In removing the car seats and vacuuming beneath them, one will often find enough change to have made the intensive search for chametz worthwhile.

Only in America. One year, on the night before Pesach, Yitz and I went to make a shiva call. The oldest son of the deceased, a newly barristered twenty-three-year-old, was seated on his hard wooden mourner's stool and was surrounded by a half-dozen young lawyers and secretaries—friends from the law firm Nathan had just joined. At one point I overheard Nathan instruct his office mate, Tom, how to clean out his desk, getting rid of any food, wiping the desk top and drawers with a damp cloth, cleaning out the corners well. I realized that Nathan would not be getting up from shiva until just before Pesach, so Tom, his WASP colleague, would have to do his Pesach cleaning. As I sat there, feeling great love for this country, I thought of my grandparents at age twenty-three, in Poland and Russia, afraid to walk near a church at Eastertime, remaining indoors with shades drawn on Good Friday—to avoid a beating at the hands of some hateful Tomas.

In our house, we do the bedrooms first, beginning three weeks before Pesach. After a room is thoroughly cleaned, no more snacks may be eaten there. When the children were very young, I used to start Pesach cleaning only a week in advance, bringing in two cleaning people a day for the final two days. Anything else was a hopeless waste. I would allow no food upstairs (except baby bottles). After dinner, I would shake out the cuffs of their pants for crumbs. But the final inspection would always turn up something.

Even though food is never taken into the bathroom, one must clean thoroughly there as well, for certain pharmaceutical products, such as vitamins in a grain base, are considered chametz and have to be stored away. Each year, a responsible organization such as the Ⓤ or a local synagogue will publish a list of what is or is not permissible. Many toiletries and druggist items, even those that may contain chametz products, such as grain alcohol, are not necessarily disqualified from possession or benefit. These items fall into the category of nifsal me'achilat kelev —unfit even for animal consumption and, therefore, the special laws of chametz prohibiting any benefit or use do not apply.

Toothbrush holders should be washed well and not used with the old toothbrushes. Every year at Pesach time, the old toothbrushes get thrown out, and every member of the family gets a new one. Some people pour boiling water over their toothbrush holders.

Parakeets, gerbils, and the like, or rather their food and cages, present a problem at Pesach time. These pets live on a grain diet, which is chametz. While the law against eating chametz does not apply to gerbils, the law against deriving any pleasure or benefit from chametz does apply to Jews of all ages. Therefore, cages of pets must be thoroughly cleaned out. The pet can be "sold" to a non-Jewish friend, who will care for it during the holiday. The other alternative, which is an easier and more popular solution, is to alter the diet. Most large pet-food companies, such as Hartz Mountain, will send, on request, a pet Passover diet. Some pet lovers wisely begin by feeding their pets a mixture of the regular diet and the new Passover diet, so that by the time Pesach arrives, the change won't be too abrupt. This business of Passover parakeet food always seemed a bit exaggerated, but that is the law. Moreover, it certainly does firmly implant in a child's mind the concept of ridding the house of chametz.

One important task in cleaning the closets is to check out the pockets of clothing. All members of the family should do this. To observe life on another planet, try to be nonchalantly standing about when a ten-year-old boy empties the pockets of his down jacket. Besides the usual cracker crumbs and gum wrappers, you will be treated to an array of objects and folded papers to which adults are not often privy. Those pocket gleanings hold the keys to the mysteries of the universe; they also provide a clue to the incredible fantasies that ten-year-olds carry around with them.

A liquor cabinet must be locked, its key removed and set aside in a safe place; or bottles of liquor should be stored in a carton which is sealed and put out of sight. Most whiskeys are made of grain alcohol and are therefore not kosher for Pesach. Technically this is pure chametz, but because of the economic loss that would otherwise be involved, most people get rid of it through mechirah (selling it to a non-Jew) rather than biur (permanently ridding oneself of it).

There are different customs regarding what to destroy (biur) and what to sell (mechirah). We store, seal away, and then sell all products that are ta'arovet chametz, admixtures of chametz such as cream of mushroom soup (contains flour) or sauces thickened with grain substance. We also store all dry grains that have not been mixed with water: for example, flour, rice, barley, and so forth. As long as there is no chance that these items have been mixed with water, they could not possibly be considered leavened. These items remain in our house but not in our possession. They stay sealed in our cupboard and we don't set eyes on them for the duration of the holiday.

However, with the exception of liquor, we do get rid of whatever pure chametz—chametz gamur—might be left as we near countdown: breads, spaghettis, dry cereals, pastries. We give away our pure chametz as a gift to a non-Jewish friend rather than sell it as we do with foods of ta'arovet chametz. What little is left of pure chametz on the last evening before Pesach we set aside for the next morning's biur, burning it so as to destroy it completely.

Some Orthodox Jews, however, have the custom of including items of pure chametz in the mechirah—sealing it away and selling possession. They leave out only a minute amount of pure chametz in order to fulfill the mitzvah of biur chametz.

"Some Orthodox Jews do this, some Orthodox Jews do that." Probably nowhere else in the tradition is there a range of custom and interpretation of law as there is regarding the laws of Pesach. Nor is it a matter of one-upmanship in piety. The myriad of details, many of which are themselves a refinement of the basic laws, simply allow for different weightings and interpretations. The thought of having a loaf of bread wrapped and then sealed in a brown bag in the freezer for the duration of Pesach is most strange to me, in fact, a bit revolting, I know not why. And yet, people more careful and more knowledgeable in halacha than I, do permit the practice.*

Our family eats g'bruck the first night of Pesach, but my sister's family does not. G'bruck is matzah products cooked with water, such as matzah balls. (Some fear that unintentionally it may become chametz.) Some people kasher their dishwashers; others follow rabbinic opinion that forbids it. In our community, two of the learned Orthodox rabbis, good friends, both ordained in the same yeshiva, have come out each with different p'sak—religious decision—in several areas. Rabbi A. says Formica must be covered for Pesach, and Rabbi M. says it need not be; Rabbi A. says Pyrex can be kashered; Rabbi M. says no. And each has perfectly legitimate halachic explanations for his decisions.

Thus, I shall proceed to explain the procedures according to the majority ruling, but on each matter one should consult his/her local rabbi. One should not hesitate to call a rabbi with any question, no matter how ridiculous it may seem. The rabbi will never laugh or think it foolish. He has probably answered it before.

THE KITCHEN

The kitchen is where most of the work lies, for the entire kitchen must be made Pesachdik (fit for Passover). In addition to biur and bitul of chametz, there is also an issue of utensils that have been used for chametz all year. These cannot be used as is for Pesach. They must either be sealed away or, where possible, transformed from chametz to nonchametz status. This process of transformation is called kashering for Pesach.

The whole project is no small matter. All dishes, cutlery, utensils, pots and pans, serving pieces, trays, sink racks, drainboards, kitchen gadgets, storage areas, freezer, refrigerator, stove top,

---

* This is permitted on the grounds that it prevents a more serious problem of chametz she'avar alav ha'Pesach . . . leavened products that were in a Jew's *possession* during Pesach may not be eaten after Pesach. Since this one is sure and that one is doubtful, that is, the bread in one's freezer we definitely know was renounced (sold to a non-Jew), while the bread in the supermarket might have been owned by a Jewish storekeeper during the eight days, some say it is better to sell one's own bread and buy it back eight days later than to buy a "questionable" loaf from the grocery after the holidays.

oven, dishwasher, blender, food processor, toaster, electric mixer, spice rack, in sum, everything we use all year long, may not be used as is for Pesach, because they have been used with chametz all year and, as a result, have absorbed chametz.

STORAGE AREAS

All cabinets, cupboards, and drawers should be thoroughly cleaned out and wiped with a damp cloth to pick up any bits of chametz lurking there. If these spaces are now to be used for Pesach utensils and foods, as they are in most contemporary kitchens of limited cabinet space, they should be first lined with fresh lining paper. For those who line their cupboards only for Pesach, a perfect, cost-free, flexible size, temporary shelving is discarded IBM printout, reverse side.

Most of the year-round utensils cannot be kashered for Pesach, and if they are to be stored in their regular cabinets or drawers, these storing places should be locked or tied so that one would not inadvertently open them during the holiday. We tape our non-Pesach cupboards closed with a colorful strip of Mystik tape as a reminder that these cabinets are off limits. Labeling the cupboards PESACHDIK or CHAMETZDIK is also helpful during the preliminary transition—especially when there are a number of people in the household who have not participated directly in transforming the kitchen.

REFRIGERATORS

Refrigerators or freezers, like other storage areas, should be emptied, washed thoroughly, with special attention given to the racks and the rubber gasket linings, whose folds can collect food. The shelves should be lined with paper or aluminum foil. To ensure circulation of cool air, slits or holes should be made in the paper or foil.

KASHERING

Some of the appliances we use year round with chametz can be kashered for Pesach. Here, too, however, there is some variation in rabbinic opinion, which is why, in all instances, one should consult a rabbi. The broadest principle is this: any item that can be thoroughly cleaned of chametz can be kashered. This basic principle, however, like all basic principles, has more exceptions than inclusions. A utensil that is made of one solid piece, such as a seamless pot with no folded lip, or a stainless-steel serving dish, or a set of flatware with no joints can be kashered, while a set of fine bone china cannot be. Under the broadest principle of perfect cleaning, it would seem that a set of fine china would qualify, but regrettably this is not so. China, earthenware, and porcelain are all considered porous materials. Having absorbed through heat the taste of chametz all year long, they would require hagalah, immersion in boiling water, to be kashered. But they could not withstand such high heat without breaking. Therefore, no kashering is permitted of these items. So, into brief storage goes our china, and out come the Pesach dishes that, for all the bother, still feel like an old friend returning once a year.

Some rabbis permit hard but not soft plastic to be kashered through hagalah—boiling water—which would misshape soft plastics. Pyrex and Corelle are considered as glass, and indeed, they simply are hardened glass. Thus, in a similar rabbinic view, they need only be kashered in the manner of any utensil that has been used with heat. Enamel is considered a porous substance, yet it can withstand the heat required to kasher it. Nevertheless, for other reasons (largely because it cracks and chips easily), it is put into the same category as china, and cannot be kashered. On the other hand, a refrigerator whose insides are enamel can be kashered simply by washing it clean. The reason: it hasn't absorbed chametz through heat.

And so it goes. Intricate, seemingly arbitrary, and yet quite logical when one relates each item to the general principles of law.

There are four alternate methods of kashering for Pesach: (1) hagalah—immersion in boiling water; (2) libun—purification by flame; (3) irui—pouring boiling water over the surface; (4) milui v'irui—soaking in cold water.

The general principle of which method to choose is known as k'vol'o kach polto, as it absorbs, so it sheds. The same means by which chametz was absorbed into the utensil, so it should be expelled. For example, an oven can be kashered by the heat from a fire (its own or a blowtorch); a pot that absorbed chametz in the cooking process, that is, with water, can be kashered by immersion in boiling water.

It goes without saying that all items to be kashered should first be thoroughly cleaned. If hagalah is to be the method of kashering, the utensil must be set aside after cleaning for twenty-four hours without use and then kashered. As a result of this twenty-four-hour hiatus, one must plan ahead very carefully. Finally, all kashering must be completed before ten in the morning on erev Pesach.

Hagalah. Hagalah requires total immersion in boiling water.* STEP ONE: To kasher the pot in which other items will be immersed, fill a very large pot with water to within one inch of the top rim. Heat until the water comes to a rolling boil. Then, to make sure that this entire pot is "immersed" in water, add to it a stone, or a solid piece of nonrusting metal, that has been superheated directly over an open flame. When it is very hot, lift it with a large pliers and drop it into the boiling water. This hot rock or metal will cause the boiling water to overflow the sides. It is considered as if the entire pot was immersed in water.

This whole process can be quite messy, although it does have some novelty to it. If you have a large enough pot that is already Pesachdik and can be used for kashering smaller utensils, you need not do this. Skip to step two. Meanwhile, here are some suggestions to minimize the mess in your own kitchen:

Put plenty of newspapers on the floor near the stove, and underneath it, to absorb the overflow. Also place a nice thick towel between you and the stove. Place a lit candle nearby, so that when your light and pilot go out as a result of the water overflowing, you can relight safely without gas smelling up the house. Instead of a rock, I use a very large hammer. I heat up its metal head superhot. The wooden handle gives me a cool, long-arm's reach so that I can insert and retrieve the metal head with ease. Some people use a knife sharpener; it has the same advantages.

* Many shuls do kashering through hagalah a few days before Pesach. Ask the synagogue sexton which hours.

STEP TWO: Into this large pot of boiling water we can now immerse other smaller utensils for kashering. The ratio of item to water must be one to sixty. A utensil need not be kept in water for any length of time. Immerse it completely in the boiling water —even for an instant—and then you can take it out. Add a hot rock or metal head if the water has stopped boiling. Rinse the utensil under cold water, and it can now be used for Pesach. If the entire utensil cannot be submerged all at once, then do half first and then rotate it so that every part is submerged consecutively. A large net or a perforated basket is useful for putting smaller items into a large pot for kashering. I have neither of these, so I find a nylon net lingerie bag to serve my purposes quite well.

STEP THREE: After the smaller items have been kashered, the large pot should be rekashered, that is, water boiled, hot stone, boil over the sides, rinse in cold water.

Libun.   Libun is a flame kashering process. Teenage children and other pyros will happily do this job. It requires the use of a blowtorch, a medium-sized tool that can be purchased in any hardware store quite inexpensively.

In contrast to hagalah, where boiling water forces out the chametz, libun destroys it by burning it up. Libun is generally used to kasher items that acquire chametz through direct contact with the source of heat. Baking utensils, oven interiors, and stove burners fall into this category. Interestingly, libun can be used in place of hagalah, but not vice versa. A roasting pan cannot be kashered through hagalah, but a stainless-steel sink can be kashered either by libun or hagalah.

One of the advantages of libun is that it can be applied immediately after washing the item clean. One need not set the item aside for twenty-four hours before kashering it. The process is very simple: pass the blowtorch over every inch of the surface until the surface is heated to a glow. You can tell when you've hit upon a crusted food particle; you actually hear it sizzle.

Irui.   Irui is a boiling-water process, but in this case it involves pouring water rather than immersion. Irui is useful for vessels and utensils that are too large to submerge or too stationary. A stainless-steel sink, for example, is kashered through irui. Boil a large kettle of water, or kettles, if the item's surface is very large.

Pour the boiling water over the entire surface; rinse with cold water. In irui, as in hagalah, the item to be kashered has to be set aside for twenty-four hours prior to the boiled-water treatment.

Milui v'irui. Milui v'irui is the easiest, but also the lengthiest form of kashering. It is used to kasher glassware that has been used primarily for cold food or drink. It is a soaking process, and it requires three days minimum, in advance of Pesach.

Take a large vessel that was cleaned and not used for twenty-four hours. Fill it with water and put the glassware in completely submerged. After twenty-four hours, drain the water and refill. Again, after the next twenty-four hours, drain and refill. When this third twenty-four-hour soak has been completed, the glassware is usable for Pesach. Before we had a second bathtub, which is what I now use to kasher glassware, I used a large plastic laundry basin.

A friend of mine came up with an ingenious device for milui v'irui. On her apartment terrace she placed a large, clean, plastic trash barrel. Approximately one inch from the bottom of the barrel, she cut a small hole, which she then plugged up with a cork. After each twenty-four-hour period, she pulled the plug, let the water drain, and then refilled it by running a line of plastic tubing from her kitchen faucet. The whole thing looked pretty primitive, with rubber bands and corks, but none of her glassware ever broke. I always have at least one glass casualty.

Here is how the following items may be kashered:

Gas stoves. The stove top should be thoroughly scoured, including the jets and the area below the jets where food spills over. This bottom area should be lined with aluminum foil. The grates can be kashered through libun, either using a blowtorch or using the gas jet itself as a flame source. The grates should be red-hot. I always kasher the grates after nightfall. I turn the grates upside down on the burners, so that they will be closer to the flame, and I turn the jets on full blast. After fifteen minutes, we are ready to test for libun. We turn out the kitchen lights, and then each child quickly turns off a jet and announces whether or not the grate is glowing red-hot. After fifteen minutes, it never fails to glow, even if only for two or three seconds.

The enamel or stainless steel top frame should be covered with a Pesach blech, a tin or copper sheet that has cutouts for the burners. Or, the entire top of the stove can be covered with aluminum foil; openings for the burners are easily cut out with a knife.

Electric stoves. An electric stove top is cleaned thoroughly. The electric burners must be kept on at maximum heat for only five minutes, which is safely longer than it takes to get them glowing.

Ovens and broilers. The oven and broiler should be cleaned with a chemical oven cleaner and steel wool. After the oven has been inspected and pronounced perfectly clean—some examine the insides with a flashlight—it can be kashered in two ways. One is to kasher it with a blowtorch, including the walls and floor and racks of the oven. The second way requires that the cleaned oven not be used for twenty-four hours. After this hiatus, the heating unit is set at its maximum heat for the time period of its normal longest use. The broiler is treated exactly the same way. Immediately after this kashering process, the oven can be used for Pesach.

A self-cleaning oven is a wonderful thing to own, for the self-cleaning cycle kashers it perfectly. It should be cleaned thoroughly on the self-clean cycle, residue ash wiped out, not used for twenty-four hours, and then self-cleaned again, this time for kashering.

A continuous-cleaning oven is treated like a regular oven, kashered with blowtorch or its own heat.

A microwave oven is kashered through autoclave. It is cleaned, not used for twenty-four hours, and then a pot of boiling water is set inside and heated further until a dense steam fills the entire oven.

Dishwashers. There are different opinions concerning dishwashers. A number of authorities agree that dishwashers with stainless-steel interiors can be kashered through their own autoclaving. The plastic or rubber racks, however, cannot be kashered and must be replaced with special Pesach racks. (Many people will order an extra set of racks when purchasing the dishwasher.)

Process: Remove the regular racks and store them away until after Pesach. Wash out the dishwasher very well and then do not use it for twenty-four hours. Run the dishwasher through a complete cycle at its hottest temperature. Insert the special Pesach racks. Remember to switch racks again after the eighth day.

When it comes to porcelain interiors, there is less accord. Interestingly, the Israeli chief rabbinate ruled more than a dozen years ago that porcelain dishwashers could be kashered in the same manner as metal ones. The American Orthodox rabbinate, however, is very divided on the issue.

Smaller appliances.   Electric coffee makers can be kashered by hagalah if no chametz-based coffee was used in them during the year.

Food processors.   The word is getting better every year. Five years ago, when food processors first came out for home use, several rabbis pronounced they could not be kashered. Now that processors are more common items in the Jewish kitchen, there has been closer rabbinic scrutiny of the matter. Today, most rabbis agree that processors may be kashered if they are dismantled and attended to properly. Dismantling is a simple process. The Pyrex or plastic bowls can be kashered through hagalah; the metal parts through libun; the blade, libun or hagalah; the motor, washed perfectly clean. The dough-mixing attachments, however, are not kashered and not used.

The same procedure applies to a blender.

People often keep separate blender jars and food-processing bowl and blades for Pesach. All they have to do is lock away their year-round parts and wipe the motor base clean before setting up the Pesach attachments.

Kitchen surfaces.   Table and counter tops made of Formica or wood are washed clean and then covered with a plastic or oilcloth.

A baby high chair should be washed thoroughly and its tray covered with contact paper.

Sinks are scoured well, including the sink drains. They are then not to be used with hot water for twenty-four hours. After that period has elapsed, the sink is cleaned again, hot water run over its surface, and then kashered by means of irui—boiling water poured over every inch of sink surface, spigots, and faucet. Porcelain enamel sinks cannot be kashered through irui. In those instances, only the spigots, faucet, and drain are kashered by pouring boiling water over them, and the sink itself is lined with plastic or wooden sink liners.

SHOPPING FOR PESACH

When I was a young child, growing up in Seattle, Washington, there was an aura of mystery about acquiring foods for Pesach. I remember that my grandfather made his own wine in a little porch at the back of his small frame house. Before Pesach my father and four of his brothers would take us children out to a farm for Pesach. There, they would milk the cows and bring home enough milk for each of their families. My grandmother made her own sweet cream and sour cream. When the children would visit, she would always serve us thick sour cream and silky raspberry jam, all homemade. There was no such thing as Passover cakes and rolls, as they have nowadays, nor was there butter. On Pesach, my mother made a delicious avocado spread, which we ate on matzah. It was the only time during the year that we ate avocado. To this day, I think Pesach when I eat avocados in December.

Today, there is no mystique in shopping for Pesach. Everything that one can buy kosher all year long is available for Pesach —and then some. Supermarkets have whole aisles set up with kosher for Passover foods. All manner of cheeses, sauces, canned and frozen prepared foods, spices, desserts, baby foods, and even something to fool the gods—Pesach noodles!

Still, one cannot throw all caution to the winds when shopping for this holiday. First, not every label of rabbinic supervision can be unconditionally relied upon. Simply a stamp marked KOSHER FOR PASSOVER or **K P** or even an individual rabbi's name or the ordinary **K** are not secure enough. One has to check further.

Second, a lot more things require supervision than one would imagine. Would you think that plain ground pepper would not require a hechsher (rabbinic certification)? Well, it does. In general, canned goods, processed foods, condiments, spices, and beverages require rabbinic supervision.

And so do all baked goods. During the last few years, as the celebration of Passover has grown, there have been unscrupulous bakeries that sell special cakes for Passover, advertising them to the hilt, when in reality these cakes are no different from their yearlong confections and are the antithesis of what Pesach observance is all about. Perhaps the bakers justify themselves by claiming that all they intend to do is to cash in on the holiday spirit in true American entrepreneurial fashion. But still, the unaware buyer must be protected. Unless a bakery thoroughly cleaned out every bit of its year-round chametz, and unless it is under rabbinic supervision, and changes its ingredients, its Passover cakes are not kosher.

Third, and to make matters more confusing, not everything that is marketed as such and that has a reliable stamp of supervision actually requires it; for example: pure tea, pure coffee (100 percent with no additives), eggs, sugar, and salt; also pure fruit juices other than grape juice; and dairy products that are year-round kosher, such as milk, butter, sour cream, cottage cheese, and farmer cheese need no special Pesach label if purchased before the holiday. Similarly, products such as soaps, paper goods, and aluminum foil that we use all year long require no additional certification. Kosher meat, poultry, and fish need no special hechsher either. These can be bought well in advance of the holiday, when prices are lower, rinsed under cold water, and stored in a plastic bag in the freezer. And of course all fresh fruits and vegetables need no special supervision.

COSTS

The food bills at Pesach time are gruesome. This is so for several reasons: we have to stock our pantries from scratch; there is a minimum of ten festival meals, often with company (two meals each on the first two and last two days, plus two on Shabbat); much wine is used for each seder. And then there is the pricing of foods. Not only do fish and meat prices jump, as a result of supply and demand—or what the kosher market will bear—but also foods with a seal of rabbinic supervision are higher priced. Over the years, I have kept general track of food inflation by mentally noting the approximate cost per grocery bag. In my supermarket, I figure it now costs an average of ten dollars per bag. At Pesach time, however, the cost jumps to almost fifteen dollars per bag.

Some of the expenses of Pesach will be neutralized the week following the holiday, when we mingle our "repurchased" chametz supplies with our Pesach pantry leftovers, and when we all go on diets after so many matzah balls. Besides that, however, there are several things one can do to bring the cost down a bit: (1) if freezer space allows, buy meat and fish two weeks before the prices go up. (2) Don't overbuy. It helps to do your advance Pesach shopping starting out with a detailed list in hand and two pizzas and a large Coke in your stomach. (3) Instead of buying canned fruits and vegetables, which are exceedingly high with the Passover label, buy fresh produce. (4) Cut down on the size of meals; make a menu and stick to it. (5) On foods that are permissible to buy without the Passover label—such as pure fruit juices, tea, sugar, club soda, honey, frozen vegetables—judge your purchases in terms of the price differential.

And finally, on processed foods that require a Passover label: certainly it costs more to produce a small quantity of rabbinically supervised food just for Pesach. For those who can afford it in a particular year, it is fine that everything is available. For those who can't afford it, that's okay too. Our grandparents managed quite well on Pesach without such items as anchovies, dried apricots, mushroom soup mix, pickles, potato chips, cranberry sauce, ice cream, and sherbet. One year I thought I must have every one of those items, or my poor family and guests would feel deprived! The next year, I was determined to keep my costs down so I bought none of those items. And still we ate like royalty!

Nor did I feel resentful the week before Pesach as I passed these items by on the supermarket shelves. On the contrary, I was pleased to see such a variety of prepared Passover foods available. I only hope they'll be there next year, when I'll feel the pinch of inflation less. The fact that I, and others like me, exercised an individual power of check and balance in a free-market system allows me to believe the prices won't move too far beyond my reach by next Pesach. There's really no price gouging if no one is forcing me to buy the luxury extras.

WOMEN AND PESACH

Several years ago, after I had tried without success to get on a quiz show that gave away fantastic prizes, I had a most vivid dream. I had won the jackpot, and the quizmaster rotated before my eyes a house that was the exact twin of mine. Every corner was spotless, the closets filled with holiday clothing—everything hemmed—color-coordinated ribbons, lacy knee socks and shiny black patent Mary Janes for the girls, white shirts and perfectly pressed pants for the boys. The kitchen cupboards were stuffed with kosher for Passover foods. All of my ancient Pesach pots and pans were in their proper places. The refrigerator had plastic containers labeled MATZAH BALLS, CHICKEN SOUP, GEFILTE FISH. The seder table was beautifully set with my own Pesach dishes. There were pillows at everyone's chair for reclining. The quizmaster then presented the key to me and, like any good winner, I screamed and hugged him and cried tears of joy. The tears awoke me instantly, to my great dismay, for I wanted to stay longer with that dream.

My husband chuckled when I reported the dream to him, but my "housewife colleagues" were stunned into silence by the sheer gloriousness of it all. It was, I realized, the absolute and ultimate fantasy of every Jewish housewife.

I have spent an inordinate amount of time in a discussion of preparation, because that's what it takes to get ready. By now, the reader has guessed why the section above was entitled, "For Men Only." Traditional Jewish women know exactly the procedures outlined above. And while many men know the law in theory, they are not familiar with it in practice. Nor do they have any idea of the time, energy, and planning it takes to clean closets, move furniture, store utensils, boil, kasher, shop, inspect labels, cook, bake . . . I recall when the wife of an illustrious and brilliant rabbi was taken ill, two weeks before Pesach, and had to be confined to a hospital bed. The rabbi had to move out of their house with their three children for the duration because he could not possibly "make Pesach"; this, despite the fact that it was he to whom a hundred women had turned with questions on kashering for Pesach.

My mother used to say that the Jewish housewife was the only one who didn't go out of bondage on Pesach. Happily, today, more men are sharing in household tasks, including preparation for Pesach. Others, men and women more resistant to changing their ways and inherited roles, have presumably worked things out to their mutual satisfaction. At the very least, those who do not participate equally should appreciate a bit more those who labor in the home. They ought to give life-experience credit to a woman who has made Pesach. Even though no one will understand it, I think I shall add "made Pesach twenty-two times" to my résumé.

Having said all that, I would like to offer these suggestions, particularly for women who have traditionally masterminded the entire operation, and who now work outside the home as well:

1. Make a master list of everything that must be done, then divide or negotiate up front exactly who does what.
2. Announce to other members of the family that when it's work time for Pesach no one sits until you sit. If they've finished one task, they should come and ask, "What can I do now?"
3. Say to yourself, and to your family: "I shall not work on Pesach preparation unless at least one member of the family works alongside me."

Even if you stick to these rules only 50 percent of the time, it will make a difference between coming into Pesach exhausted like a slave or exhilarated like a free person.

Part III—Spiritual Preparation

While the spiritual preparation is nowhere near as demanding as the physical (although what is ridding our lives of chametz if not a spiritual preparation????), it, too, begins well in advance. In the six-week period preceding Pesach, there are five special Sabbaths. Four are entitled after the special Torah reading of that Shabbat; the fifth takes on luster because of its proximity to the holiday itself. All together, the five Sabbaths serve as a kind of countdown toward Pesach.

First comes Shabbat Shekalim. Its special Torah portion recalls the donation of a shekel to the Temple economy, a form of communal membership dues. The second Shabbat, which precedes Purim, is called Shabbat Zachor, the Sabbath of Remembrance: "Remember what the Amalekites [from whom Haman descended] did unto you . . ." as your ancestors tried to cross the desert. The third is Shabbat Parah, when we read about the ritual of the Red Heifer, the ceremony of symbolic purification of the people. We are reminded to purify ourselves morally and also to begin the purification rites for Pesach. Finally, there is Shabbat Hachodesh (the month). It is the Shabbat prior to the first of the month of Nissan. The Torah readings describe the fixing of Nissan as well as the regulations and preparations for Pesach.

As if that countdown weren't enough, there is one more Shabbat. It is called Shabbat Hagadol, the Great Sabbath, the one immediately preceding Pesach. A number of traditions have sprung up concerning Shabbat Hagadol: that it was on this Sabbath that the Jews of Egypt sprinkled a few drops of lamb's blood on their doorposts signaling the Angel of Death to pass over the Jewish households without afflicting the firstborn; on this Shabbat, the rabbi would hold a long and learned discourse and also answer questions about Pesach.

Today, on Shabbat Hagadol, most Orthodox synagogues conclude Shacharit services quite early; people go home for lunch, a nap, and then return in the late afternoon for the rabbi's Shabbat Hagadol presentation, a learned discourse that is related to Pesach. Many rabbis will give their congregations an advance list of textual references so they can come to the session prepared.

MAOT CHITTIN

This literally means "money for wheat." It is a requisite charitable contribution over and above one's normal gifts of tzedakah. Every synagogue and every Jewish organization has a Maot Chittin drive before Pesach. The funds enable poorer Jews to have everything they require to make a proper and festive seder—wine, matzah, fish, and fowl. Some Jewish organizations have also taken care to see that in countries of the world where Jews cannot get matzah, these supplies are shipped directly rather than money contributions. It's something of a minor miracle that matzot baked in Brooklyn can reach Asmat, New Guinea, in time for the seder.

KOL DICHFIN

At the seder, we recite the words "all who are in need (Kol Dichfin), let them come and eat." In order that these not be empty words, we are supposed to plan ahead and invite guests who, because of lack of funds or of knowledge, would otherwise not enjoy a seder of their own. In some congregations, a communal seder is held just for this purpose. Our shul tried a communal seder for several years, but it never really caught on. Now, the rabbi places a Kol Dichfin ad in the local newspaper, inviting strangers who would have no seder to call the synagogue. Shul members are requested to host in their homes. Admittedly, not too many respond on either side, but the solicitation for shul families to host strangers has an amazing way of swelling the Maot Chittin fund. . . .

EREV PESACH

As we approach the holiday itself, the activity regarding chametz intensifies. On the eve of Pesach, there are four stages: bedikah, bitul, biur, and mechira.

BEDIKAT CHAMETZ

The night before Pesach, immediately after sundown, we undertake a thorough search for chametz throughout the entire house. The custom is to darken the house for the search, so that we focus on the places illuminated by the candle. With all the family gathered around, a single candle is lit, and the following blessing is recited by a head of the household:

בָּרוּךְ אַתָּה יְיָ, אֱלֹהֵינוּ מֶלֶךְ הָעוֹלָם, אֲשֶׁר קִדְּשָׁנוּ בְּמִצְוֹתָיו, וְצִוָּנוּ עַל בְּעוּר חָמֵץ.

Baruch ata Adonai Elohainu melech ha'olam asher kidshanu b'mitzvotav v'tzivanu al biur chametz.

Blessed are You, Lord our God, Ruler of the universe, Who has commanded us concerning the destruction of the chametz.

Then with candle, feather, and wooden spoon in hand the search is on. The candle is used to light dark corners; the feather serves as a whisk broom to brush up crumbs into the makeshift dustpan—the wooden spoon.

But wait! Had we not described a moment ago the most rigorous cleaning imaginable? There's no chametz in the bedrooms or the living room. Why bother searching? Why say a blessing on removing the chametz? Chances are the search will prove fruitless, and all we'll have for our efforts is a b'racha levatala—the forbidden use of God's name in vain (see p. 154).

But Jews have thought of everything! To put a little excitement into the search, and to assure that we don't recite an inauthentic blessing, one member of a household—usually the mother—hides ten bits of bread throughout the house. Some people wrap each piece in plastic to avoid tiny crumbs on the rug, but most of us search for our chametz in the raw.

Why ten? No, it has nothing to do with the ten plagues, or with the Ten Commandments. It is simply an easy number to remember, and it avoids altogether the family's exasperated second search, as you sheepishly try to recall, twenty minutes later, whether you hid six or seven pieces about the house. But there's no law about ten; even one or two pieces will do.

BITUL CHAMETZ

As soon as all the pieces are collected and deposited, along with spoon and feather into a paper bag, everyone gathers for the second part of this ritual: the recitation of the formula for bitul chametz, renouncing all ownership. This formula is known as the Kol Chamira, after its first two words:

כָּל חֲמִירָא וַחֲמִיעָא, דְּאִכָּא בִרְשׁוּתִי דְּלָא חֲמִתֵּה, וּדְלָא בְעַרְתֵּה וּדְלָא יָדַעְנָא לֵהּ לִבְטֵל וְלֶהֱוֵי הֶפְקֵר כְּעַפְרָא דְאַרְעָא.

The language is Aramaic, so the custom grew to repeat the formula again in one's native language: "All leaven and all chametz which is in my possession, which I have not seen or destroyed, nor have knowledge of shall be null, void, ownerless, and as dust of the earth."

We then put the bag in a safe spot until the next morning, when we will burn the chametz.

The whole ceremony strikes my fancy. It is a fascinating insight into the conglomerate nature of Jewish ritual. It's hardly likely we will find anything at all, but we just might, so the law is, unequivocally—search! Even if you are going away for Pesach, even if you lock your door and sell the whole house, still you must do bedikah before you depart—up to thirty days before Pesach. A flashlight would be more sensible to use—brighter, safer, and halachically permissible —but candle it was, so candle it is! A wooden spoon seems odd, but really it makes perfect sense if you plan ahead for tomorrow's burning.

We carefully hide bits of chametz, such a clever and playful act, for the children who would otherwise be frustrated and lose interest if nothing ever turned up. And that formula! As if waving a verbal wand can wave away all responsibility for chametz. But what else can we do? We are bidden to eliminate *all* chametz. Yet we are realistic enough to know that it's not all totally within our control. So we trot out our handy ancient formula.

And it all works! I'm not sure why, but it does. The fact is that it matters greatly to me that there be no chametz about the house. Perhaps it's the sheer force of Biblical and rabbinic law; perhaps it's the way Jews for three millennia have said good riddance to chametz; whatever, it certainly has altered my psyche regarding leavened products these eight days. When I come upon two little boys playing "pretzel keys" before Pesach, my anxiety level mounts. But just as instinctively, the Kol Chamira comes into mind—and calms me.

That's Judaism!—a little pedagogy, a little pageantry, a little fantasy, a little realism; a game of hide-and-seek, a mnemonic device, some superstitious behavior, a little pedantry and regimentation, a magical formula, a measure of faithfulness—in short, something to appeal to everyone.

BIUR CHAMETZ

On the morning before the seder, we stop eating all chametz. The exact moment of end time is calculated by the experts, according to the length of day. "Day" in this case means daylight, from dawn to dusk. At this time of the year, one third of the daylight is over by approximately 9:30 A.M., so there's enough time to eat a last breakfast of chametz. After "eating down" our chametz supplies for two weeks, we end up with very little to give away or burn. As most parents of teenagers will know, this frugality is not without its emotional costs, for we subject ourselves to that constant refrain of, "There's nothing in the house to eat" from that peculiar breed aptly referred to as the "bottomless pit." J.J., to whom some General Mills executive directly owes his swimming pool, cannot "live" without dry cereal. I am sure that we must be the only Orthodox family in the world found wandering down the cereal aisles two days before Pesach. We buy for J.J. the junkiest junk cereals we can find, the kind he isn't permitted all year long. He has five bowls of cereal for dinner the night before Pesach and five more bowls for breakfast before the end time for chametz. In this manner, we manage to avoid withdrawal symptoms up until halfway through the week.

Within one hour after that end time, we must do biur chametz, the final act of purging leaven from our lives. All chametz gathered in the search last night, plus whatever is left after breakfast, is thrown into the fire. Apartment dwellers do this in their incinerators; house folk light a small fire outdoors. Because the fire is small and self-contained, it is possible for those whose apartment buildings have no incinerators (new ones may have compacters instead) to burn their chametz on the terrace or in a nearby park; or one can take it to the synagogue for disposal. We use a coffee can or a large juice can. We insert the bag with chametz, spoon, and feather, douse it with kerosene, and set it aflame. As it burns, a head of household recites again the Kol Chamira—the nullification formula—this time in a slightly broader form: "All leaven and all chametz that is in my possession that I have seen or not seen, destroyed or not destroyed, let it be null and void and as dust of the earth."

MECHIRAT CHAMETZ

So much for the chametz we shall burn or of which we shall disclaim ownership. What about all that stuff sealed away in our cupboards—goods that would constitute an economic hardship were we to lose them altogether? For that, the Rabbis of Talmudic times devised the legal sale of chametz.

We cannot sell our remaining chametz to another Jew, even one who doesn't observe Pesach because, in democratic fashion, halacha clearly states that what is forbidden to one Jew is forbidden to another. Thus, each of us must sell it to a non-Jew; however, we should like to do so in a manner that would not cause us irreversible loss. This would be a pretty difficult thing for each Jewish householder to achieve were it not for the laws of agency concerning the sale of chametz. The rabbi of the community becomes a wholesaler, so to speak. During the week before Pesach, the head of each household appoints the rabbi as his/her agent to negotiate the sale. A bill of sale contract that would be legal in any court is drawn between the rabbi and a non-Jewish buyer. The contract gives the purchaser full and unconditional title to all the goods and free access to them. The sale goes into effect at approximately 10:00 A.M. on erev Pesach.

How can we resume ownership after the holiday? It works this way. At the drawing of the contract, the non-Jew, a person of goodwill and one whom we can trust not to exercise his rights of full access, will put down a nominal deposit of, say, ten dollars on a half-million-dollar contract. He has eight days to come up with the balance. At the end of eight days (right after Pesach is over) the rabbi contacts him. If he can't produce the money, he forfeits the sale. Which is what always happens. In this manner, we are able to abide by the Sinaitic injunction of ridding ourselves of all chametz, yet we manage to avoid permanent loss of our goods. An easy solution all around, and one that maintains our links to tradition. (Now why couldn't the Sages have found a solution for china and earthenware?!)

FAST OF THE FIRSTBORN

Most of the ancient primogeniture rules no longer apply, but here and there are rituals to remind us that distinctions once were made. In Egypt, the plague of the firstborn son, the most favored child, was the bitterest of all. It was the final act that made Pharaoh succumb to Moses' request. The Jews were spared this terrible ordeal, and in gratitude for that miracle, tradition requires that the firstborn son fast on erev Pesach.

But fasting is a hardship, especially when one needs energy to get through the seder that night. Consequently, the rabbinic practice of a seudat mitzvah, a meal that takes on religious significance in celebration of a Brit, wedding, Bar Mitzvah, or siyyum (the completion of a Talmudic tractate) is widely observed.

Now one cannot always count on a Brit for that day, and no one in his/her right minds would schedule a wedding or a Bar Mitzvah celebration on erev Pesach. So the custom arose for the congregation to target for that day the completion of a tractate of the Talmud and thereby celebrate a siyyum. This takes place in the synagogue immediately after Shacharit services. The worshipers study the last few lines with a scholar who has completed the tractate. A beautiful prayer known as the hadran is read; it is a paean of praise to God for the privilege of studying Torah. Following the siyyum, all present partake of a light seudat mitzvah. Once the fast is broken by a seudat mitzvah, there is no requirement to fast for the rest of the day. As one would imagine, the shul is full of firstborn sons of all ages on that morning.

THE SEDER TABLE

Over and above the normal preparation for a festive holiday meal, there is much to be done in advance for the seder. The following items should be set on the table:

Wine. Enough to fill four or five cups per person. How much wine fulfills the mitzvah of the four cups? The two most commonly held opinions are 3.3 ounces and 5.2 ounces. Some people, mostly children and others who cannot drink all that wine with impunity, substitute grape juice after the first or second cup. Certain authorities frown on the use of grape juice, but no one disputes the fact that it is halachically permissible to recite the same Kiddush over it. A wine cup is set at each place with a saucer underneath to keep things tidy. Also placed on the table is a large goblet, which will be filled later with wine for the ceremonial cup of Elijah.

Matzah. Shmurah or regular. Three are placed at the head of the table to be used ceremonially, but there should also be enough on the table for each participant to have at least half a matzah. All the matzot (plural) should be covered. There are special matzah covers available that have pockets for the three matzot, but any cloth napkin will do.

What is shmurah matzah (or matzah shmurah to be more grammatically correct)? *Shmurah* simply means "watched" or "guarded." The Torah says, "U shmartem," "and you shall observe [the festival of] matzot." Literally, that verse also means, "And you shall watch the matzot" so that they don't become leavened. Some of the Rabbis interpreted the verse to mean that the wheat must be watched from the time it is cut; most rabbinic authorities, however, interpret the watch as beginning from the time that it is ground into flour as is the case for all kosher for Passover matzot (see page 402). Of late, a compromise custom has grown among traditional Jews. Since the obligation to eat matzah is only for the first night (that is, chametz is forbidden all the days of Pesach, but matzah is required only for the first night), many people use shmurah matzah for the first seder, or for both sedarim (plural), and then use regular matzoh all the rest of the week.

There are two different types of shmurah matzah: hand-baked and machine-baked. Hand-baked shmurah matzah is round, hard, and brittle and, in this family's opinion, infinitely more delicious. It also costs more: seven dollars per pound for hand shmurah, four dollars for machine shmurah, and one dollar for regular matzah. One must remember to order shmurah matzah in advance, through the synagogue sexton, local yeshiva or Jewish grocery store. If one has the time, it is a most interesting and worthwhile experience to take the whole family to a factory where they bake shmurah matzah.

In setting out the matzot before the holiday, one must remember not to eat any. So as to heighten our taste for matzah and for the mitzvah of eating it, we are not permitted to eat matzah on erev Pesach. Most Orthodox Jews observe the custom of not eating matzah from the first day of Nissan; if you're a matzah lover, this hiatus certainly does increase your appetite for it at the seder.

Hard-boiled eggs. One per person, for dipping in salt water at the beginning of the meal.

Bowls of salt water. For the dipping of karpas (a vegetable) and eggs.

Pillows. These are placed at everyone's chair for reclining.

Haggadot. One per person so that each can follow the seder service.

All the items for a seder plate:

One egg. This should be slightly roasted on the open flame (remember to boil it first).

One zeroah. A shank bone, also roasted (a kosher butcher will supply the bone).

Maror. Bitter herbs: the root of a horseradish, peeled and then grated or cut into chunks. Some use romaine lettuce; we put both on our seder plate.

Karpas. A vegetable, either boiled potato or fresh celery or parsley.

Charoset. A mixture of fine-chopped apples and walnuts and wine, made to resemble mortar.

The seder plate items are arranged as follows:

egg	zeroah
maror	
vegetable	charoset

This arrangement is of both practical and theological significance. They are arranged in order of use. The vegetable is used first, maror and charoset next; the roasted egg and zeroah are not eaten at all at the seder. The religious principle is that one does not bypass (reach over) one mitzvah in order to perform another.

If there are many diners at the table, and it is not possible to get enough of everything onto the seder plate, additional bowls of charoset, maror, and vegetables should be prepared.

The seder plate, like the three matzot, is set near the leader. If there are several heads of household present at a seder, it is a nice gesture to set out a seder plate for each one. In most Orthodox homes, the male head of household or the most learned guest orchestrates the seder, but the fact is that anyone who is capable can lead.

Any plate can be used as a seder plate, but it is fitting to use a special ceremonial plate. There are many of these on the market; or, a moderately talented person can transform an ordinary piece of chinaware into a seder plate quite simply, using lead-free hobby shop enamel and painting in the proper symbols in their correct positions.

Everything has its meaning.

As always, wine is used to sanctify the occasion. Wine is a symbol of joy. Four cups—four different expressions of joy—are related to the four different verbs used in the Bible to describe God's saving acts; each different nuance, like each additional cup of wine, has a cumulative effect, heightening the glow, increasing the joy:

Ve'hotzaiti—and I will bring you out.

Ve'hitzalti—and I will save you.

Ve'ga'alti—and I will redeem you.

Ve'lakachti—and I will take you to me as my nation.

There is also a fifth verse:

Ve'haivatee—and I will bring you into the land I promised Abraham, Isaac, and Jacob.

Because of the long, long exile from that land, Jews did not drink the fifth cup. Instead, they set it aside as a cup for Elijah the prophet, who will herald the Messiah, who will bring us back to the land. Now that we have been restored to the land of Israel, some Jews follow the custom of drinking a fifth cup, which is inserted into the second half of the seder, between the original third and fourth cups. The former fourth cup now becomes the fifth. But even those who drink five cups still fill one more for Elijah.

The eggs dipped in salt water are a custom primarily in Ashkenazic homes. There are several explanations: eggs are a sign of spring; eggs are a symbol of rebirth and the renewal of life; eggs dipped in salt water (tears) are a sign of mourning for the Churban—or for the Egyptians who drowned in the Red Sea; and finally, starting off with an egg is simply the way meals were begun in ancient times.

The matzah—as we said earlier—is the bread of affliction and the bread of freedom and hope. In contrast to the usual two whole loaves of challah on Shabbat and holidays, three whole "loaves" of matzah are used at the seder. At the beginning of the seder we break the middle matzah in two and hide the larger half for afikoman. Thus, by starting off with three, when we get to the motzi matzah ritual awhile later, we will still have the requisite two whole "loaves" (plus a half).

The *roasted egg* is a symbol of the Korban Chagigah, the festival sacrifice we no longer bring.

The *zeroah* is a reminder of the Paschal sacrifice, thus also Zecher Le'churban, in memory of the Churban. Why was the shank bone picked over every other part? Because its Hebrew word is zeroah (arm), which is the same word used to describe God's outstretched arm as He delivered us from bondage.

Maror, so we should taste the bitterness the Israelite slaves had to endure.

Charoset, the mortar the slaves had to prepare in building cities and pyramids for the Pharaohs. I once read a tale by a woman who found herself somewhere in Africa at seder time. Determined to have a seder, she acquired matzah, bitter greens, an egg, and a substitute for wine. But apples and nuts were nowhere to be found. Ingeniously, she located a brick and placed it at her seder table. I daresay her charoset was more authentic than the delicious mixture we eat.

Karpas, the vegetable, is a sign of spring, vegetation, new growth, and new hope. In typical Jewish dialectic, we dip it in salt water, which represents tears of life.

The pillow for reclining symbolizes the way free people eat. It's the best we can do, given the fact that there are no Roman

couches around these days. In some homes, only the leader of
the seder services reclines; in others, only the adult males; in our
house, as in many Orthodox homes, everyone gets a pillow.

The Talmud discussed whether women should recline: "After
all, reclining," says one rabbi, "is only for important people."
Fortunately, he is answered, "All of our women are important
people. . . ."

Haggadah means "telling": it is the book that contains the
order of the seder service. There are hundreds of unusual haggadot available, and one can spend many delightful hours in
selecting. Each person should use a haggadah tailored to his/her
own level and interest. There are now on the market several
beautiful haggadot designed especially for children.

Although using a uniform one at the table for every family
member and guest has certain advantages—such as finding the
place—this is outweighed by each person's sharing with the
whole group the unique commentaries from his/her haggadah.
One of my favorites happens to be a richly illustrated archaeology haggadah, with commentary on the traditional text based on
contemporary archaeological discoveries. When we reach certain historical descriptions, I proudly display my pictures and
instant archaeological knowledge. The next night I switch and
use a hagaddah with no illustrations whatsoever, but with a clear
explanation of text and a rich collection of rabbinic interpretations, in good-size print so I don't have to wear reading glasses.
Last year, I tried a feminist haggadah, but that particular one
wasn't quite satisfying. I still can't seem to compare woman's lot
to slavery and oppression. Moshe uses the updated halachic
compendium commentary, while Yitz reads from two or three
haggadot at one time.

CANDLELIGHTING

The candlelighting for Pesach is the regular festival candlelighting (see p. 323); on the first two nights the blessing is followed by
the Shehecheyanu.

THE SEDER

Immediately after Maariv, the seder should begin. In some families, the male head of household puts on a white kittel, to give

the seder an added sense of sacredness. The order of the seder, which is given at the beginning of the haggadah, is:

KADESH	blessing over the wine
U'RECHATZ	washing the hands
KARPAS	eating the karpas
YACHATZ	dividing the matzoh
MAGGID	telling the Passover story
RACHTZAH	washing the hands
MOTZI MATZAH	blessings over the matzah
MAROR	eating the bitter herb
KORECH	the sandwich
SHULCHAN ORECH	the festival meal
TZAFUN	eating the afikoman
BARECH	Grace After Meals
HALLEL	Hallel
NIRTZAH	conclusion

We "introduce" the seder by singing out the order in Hebrew, in rhymed verse—a mnemonic device.

1. Kadesh: Cups of wine are filled, and then the Kiddush is sung. In some homes, only the leader of the seder recites the Kiddush, while the others answer Amen. In other homes, all sing the Kiddush together. The most common custom is to stand for Kiddush and to sit for drinking. A sip will not do: one must drink at least a rov-kos, at least half the cup. This is so for each of the four/five cups of wine. Although pillows are at our seats, it is difficult to actually recline throughout the entire service, when one is sitting erect at a table. While drinking the four cups, however, we do recline leftwise against a pillow. Why to the left? Ritual often has practical meaning: (a) Because the esophagus is to the left. Were we to lean to the right, there would be danger of food going down the windpipe. (b) To the left, so that we can hold a cup steady with our right hand.

2. U'rechatz: Next, the ritual washing of the hands. Since no bread will be eaten, no blessing over handwashing is recited. The Talmud tells us that the eating of any food dipped in liquid requires a prior washing of the hands. This is done by filling a cup with water and pouring it over each hand, two or three times, alternating hands.

3. Karpas: Thus, we are ready to dip the vegetable in salt water. This is the first dipping ritual. Why dipping? So the children should ask, as they will a moment later, in the Ma Nishtana. One answer: salt water is like the sweat and tears of a people in bondage.

Some people say only a small amount of vegetable should be eaten; others say half or a whole potato per person. We follow the latter custom, which makes much more sense. I'm sure this was thoughtfully introduced by the Rabbis to stave off light-headedness from half a cup of wine on an empty stomach; also, to enable us to concentrate on the epic-telling part of the seder and not on what otherwise would be a growling stomach.

4. Yachatz: Taking out the middle of the three matzot, the seder leader breaks it into uneven halves. He wraps the larger part in a napkin and squirrels it away for afikoman. This ingenious device, probably more than any other part of the seder, has been single-handedly responsible for keeping children alert throughout. From the moment the seder leader wraps the half matzah in a napkin, the children keep their eye on it. At the first opportunity, they "steal" this afikoman and then hide it. Ransomed, it might be worth a king's fortune. Experienced parents of young children offer this advice: To prevent youthful tears, intrigue, power plays, and manipulation, simply announce at the outset that the afikoman is a collective enterprise. It belongs to the whole pack and not to any one child.

5. Maggid: The seder plate is lifted for an instant, and the matzot are uncovered. This signifies the beginning of the haggadah, the telling of the story. After the opening passage of ha lachma anya, the matzot are again covered, the wine cups refilled, and the youngest child proceeds to recite the Ma Nishtanah, the four questions:

מַה נִּשְׁתַּנָּה הַלַּיְלָה הַזֶּה מִכָּל הַלֵּילוֹת:

שֶׁבְּכָל הַלֵּילוֹת אָנוּ אוֹכְלִין חָמֵץ וּמַצָּה, הַלַּיְלָה הַזֶּה כֻּלּוֹ מַצָּה.

שֶׁבְּכָל הַלֵּילוֹת אָנוּ אוֹכְלִין שְׁאָר יְרָקוֹת, הַלַּיְלָה הַזֶּה

(כֻּלּוֹ) מָרוֹר.

שֶׁבְּכָל הַלֵּילוֹת אֵין אָנוּ מַטְבִּילִין אֲפִילוּ פַּעַם אֶחָת,

הַלַּיְלָה הַזֶּה שְׁתֵּי פְעָמִים.

שֶׁבְּכָל הַלֵּילוֹת אָנוּ אוֹכְלִין בֵּין יוֹשְׁבִין וּבֵין מְסֻבִּין,

הַלַּיְלָה הַזֶּה כֻּלָּנוּ מְסֻבִּין.

How different is this night from all other nights? On all other nights we may eat either chametz or matzah; why on this night only matzah? On all other nights we eat other kinds of herbs; why on this night bitter herbs? On all other nights we do not even dip the herbs once; why on this night do we dip twice? On all other nights we eat either sitting or reclining; why on this night do we all recline?

The matzot are again uncovered and remain in view as we begin to answer these questions by reciting the haggadah. These are verses from the Torah and Talmud, tales, allegories, commentaries, psalms of praise, plagues, miracles, songs, and rituals. Cut and dried, the whole section can be read in half an hour, but no one ever does it cut and dried. It is designed to invite questions, reflections, comments, interpretations—old ones, as well as those inspired on the spot. Unlike other forms of prayer, which should not be interrupted, seder participants are encouraged to explain, interpret, and otherwise comment on the events of the Exodus, interrupting at any point to do so. In some families, all read the haggadah aloud together; in others, individual members take turns reading solo while the others follow. Any combination is fine, as long as the story gets told. A good Maggid can take upwards of two hours. Maggid concludes with the second cup of wine.

6. Rachtzah: The ritual washing of the hands, with its blessing.

7. Motzi matzah: The two whole squares and one-half square of matzah are now held up by the leader of the seder, and the hamotzi blessing is recited. Then, the bottom matzah is put down. While still holding the top and half of the middle matzah, the seder leader recites the special matzah blessing ". . . Who has commanded us to eat matzah." Each person receives a piece of the top whole matzah (a symbol of freedom) and a piece of the broken middle matzah (a symbol of slavery). These are to be eaten together while reclining to the left.

8. Maror: The bitter herb is taken and dipped into the charoset; the blessing over eating maror is recited. This is the second act of dipping.

9. Korech: A sandwich is made out of pieces from the bottom matzah, with maror in between. We are instructed: "Matzot and bitter herbs shall you eat." In rabbinic times, there was a difference of opinion as to whether this meant matzah and maror should be eaten separately, or eaten together. The latter interpretation was offered by Hillel, the first century rabbi who lived while the Temple still stood. Although the majority rabbinic opinion concluded that the mitzvah—or, rather, mitzvot—is to eat matzah and maror separately (as we did a moment ago), we nevertheless also acknowledge Hillel's custom by reciting a description of it and then eating the "Hillel sandwich."

10. Shulchan Orech: The meal. A regular festive meal is served. Some begin with the eggs dipped in salt water. Chicken soup and matzah balls are a standard treat at the seder meal. It is a custom not to serve roast meat at the seder because of its similarity to the roasted lamb that was used for the Paschal sacrifice which is forbidden to us since the Churban. While it is hardly likely that anyone would misconstrue or mistake a slice of roast beef for the Paschal sacrifice, nevertheless, cooking in a different way for this night does remind us of the life of Jews in Temple times. In our house, we serve a pan-braised brisket, simmered in water and spices; also, boiled chicken, which is delicious once a year.

11. Tzafun: Means hidden. After a search that is more show than search, parents negotiate to ransom the afikoman, which the children have hidden. The afikoman is the final part of the meal, the halachic dessert which follows the culinary dessert. It

commemorates the Paschal lamb which was the last item to be eaten at the seder meal in Temple times. The children know we cannot conclude the seder without the afikoman, so they bargain for a game, a toy, a bicycle, a sweater—whatever the market will bear. A piece of afikoman is distributed to everyone, and the meal has concluded. There is no more eating that night after the afikoman.

12. Barech: The Grace. A third cup of wine is filled and the Birkat Hamazon is recited. Grace concludes with the blessing and drinking of the third cup of wine.

Immediately, the cups are again filled, as is the large goblet set aside for Elijah. Someone goes to open the door for Elijah. A brief prayer is recited. It is a hymn that was entered late into the haggadah during the Middle Ages. It was at the time of the blood libels when Jews were accused of mixing Gentile blood into their matzah. Jews were sorely victimized as a result of the blood libels, and this prayer, in essence, asks God for revenge against our enemies.

The overall tone of the haggadah service is one of compassion, even for the Egyptians. For example, in the Maggid section, when we tell the story of the ten plagues, we remove a drop of wine from our cups at the mention of each plague, to symbolize that our joy is not complete, our cup runneth not over; for even though the Egyptians deserved that punishment, we feel some remorse that our redemption was brought about through the suffering of others.

But here, at the cup of Elijah, who will ultimately herald the messenger of redemption, we ask forthrightly for revenge against our enemies. In some homes, it has been a custom to insert a memorialization to the victims of the Holocaust who collectively suffered more than slaves and more than blood libel victims.

Opening the door represents not only a welcome to Elijah through the front door, it also makes the statement that we are not afraid, despite the dangers we face as Jews—because we have faith in the Ultimate Redeemer and in a final redemption.

In some haggadot, this ceremony of Elijah's cup is bracketed as part of the Hallel section; in others, it is the concluding part of barech. Whichever, the front door is closed, the fourth cup of wine is poured, and the mood shifts, as we now turn to Hallel.

13. Hallel: Songs of praise. Actually, half of the Hallel was recited earlier, as part of the Maggid recitation, so only the remaining half is recited now, plus several additional psalms of praise and thanksgiving. There are many melodies that developed around the particular verses of Hallel, and the family sings these together.

14. Nirtzah: This is the concluding part of the seder. As we call out the word, our minds fly momentarily to Yom Kippur, at the end of Ne'ilah—the only other time of year when we call out the same word. The words mean acceptance, which we now request. Technically, as after Ne'ilah, our formal prayer requirements for the seder service have been completed, and we ask that our prayers and praises be acceptable; we also ask that we be privileged to celebrate the seder service again next year and the years thereafter. Like all of Jewish prayer, we never end at the ending. We add a few more songs, a few more hymns, a few more memories. Some of the favorite seder songs, such as "Ehad Mi Yo'deah" ("Who Knows One?") and "Chad Gadya" ("One Kid"), are part of the concluding Nirtzah section. These songs motivate the children to stay awake until the very end. The final song is the song that has symbolized the ultimate redemption for Jews for two thousand years—"L'Shana Ha'ba'ah Be'Yerushalayim," "Next Year in Jerusalem."

For one who is not familiar with the melodies and words of the seder, there are now tapes and records of the seder service that can be played any number of times before the holiday. The seder, in great measure, is designed to hold the interest of children throughout, and it helps if they have familiarity with its song and verse.

THE SECOND SEDER

In the Diaspora, a second seder is celebrated on the eve of the second day. With some very minor exceptions, the two sedarim are exactly the same. Or, as a friend says to his father each year before the second seder begins, "Do it again, Dad, until you get it right!" To some extent, the second seder is anticlimactic. Certain distaff members of my extended family claim that one of the bonuses of settling in Israel is having only one seder.

LITURGY

The regular festival liturgy is followed, including Hallel recited every day, and the Yizkor memorial service recited on the eighth day. There are some special additions to the holiday liturgy, most notably: Tefilat Tal, the prayer for dew, recited during Mussaf of the first day; and the counting of the Omer, beginning with the second night. There are also special Torah readings, such as the entire eight chapters of Song of Songs, read on the intermediate Shabbat; the Vision of the Dry Bones in the Book of Ezekiel; and the story of the crossing of the Red Sea, which took place on the seventh day of the Exodus and is read on the seventh day of Pesach, as is the song of thanksgiving that Moses sang.

Moreover, during Pesach, we switch over to our "summer wardrobe" of prayers. At Minchah, on the first day, we drop the verse, "Who brings the winds and brings down the rains." We substitute for it, "Who brings the dew." And beginning with the first Maariv of Chol Hamoed—which starts the third day of Pe-sach—and until winter rolls around again, the ninth of the eighteen benedictions is slightly reworded to adapt to our needs in nature. We ask God to give us blessings on the earth rather than to give us rain.

THE COUNTING OF THE OMER

The Omer count is a prime example of the layering that can take place when a religion is both ancient and modern. Through successive generations and events in history, new layers of meaning have been attached to this particular ritual. In thinking about the Omer and its sweep through history, I feel a sensation that must be similar to that experienced by an archaeologist as he/she examines a cross section of a geological formation and breathtakingly considers its strata.

But first, what is the Omer? It is a simple counting ritual. We count one day and then two, all the way up to forty-nine. Starting with the second night of Pesach, which is one on the Omer count, we count each day until we reach Shavuot, seven weeks later. That's all it is: a benediction on the mitzvah of counting, and a one-line count. Often it is concluded with a very brief (nine-word) recitation, and some people add a short introductory verse. With everything, it still takes no more than sixty seconds, and yet it summons up several of the most crucial periods of Jewish history.

It all starts with a commandment from the Torah: "And from the day after the Sabbath [Pesach], the day on which you bring the omer [a measure of barley] of wave offering, you shall count seven full weeks."

Thus, on the sixteenth of Nissan, the day after Pesach began, a measure of barley was brought to the Temple. It was offered as a symbol of thanksgiving and as a plea to God to protect the harvest from injurious winds, a matter of great consequence in an agricultural society. The forty-nine days of consecutive counting came to be known as Sefirat Ha'Omer or simply "Sefirah," the counting.

But why count for forty-nine days? They could have marked Shavuot on their ancient calendars, as they did other holidays, and celebrated it in its proper time. The Rabbis explained that this was in order that the people not lose sight of the connection between the physical redemption and revelation. The counting of days links one to the other, with Shavuot providing closure to Pesach.

After the destruction of the Temple, when there was no more barley offering, the Omer count served as a reminder of yearning for redemption and return to the land. It is then that the concluding Harachaman verse was added, a plea that the Temple worship be restored. . . . It is by means of that continuous longing that the Jewish people managed to keep the dream of redemption alive.

During the post-Churban era, symbols and expressions of mourning were attached to the Sefirah period: marriages were prohibited, musical instruments were not used, the cutting of hair was not permitted. There are a number of medieval sources that associate this particular period of mourning with the plague which, the Talmud describes, decimated the school of Rabbi Akiva, killing many thousands of his disciples. Some sources explain that on the thirty-third day of the Omer, the plague was miraculously interrupted, and no more of Akiva's students died. Another tradition connects the days of the Omer to Bar Kochba, the Jewish general thought by Akiva to be the political messiah. Bar Kochba led the revolt against Roman Emperor Hadrian who persecuted the Jews, in particular scholars such as Akiva. On the thirty-third day of the Omer (Lag B'Omer), the persecutions momentarily stopped; the revolt had a change of fortune. Although it was ultimately defeated, the glorious moment was not forgotten. Thus, today, on the thirty-third day of Omer, there is a pause in the mourning restrictions: weddings are performed, music, haircuts—all are permitted. Yeshiva day schools and Jewish youth organizations often schedule outings or picnics on Lag B'Omer.

In modern times, the Sefirah period coincides with the season of the Warsaw Ghetto Revolt and the days set aside for Holocaust Commemoration—when the mood of mourning is altogether appropriate. However, also during this Sefirah period, we celebrate the rebirth of Israel and the reunification of Jerusalem. Thus, after so many years of the Omer count, there are two additional days that interrupt the mourning: Yom Ha'Atzmaut and Yom Yerushalayim. Hallel is recited; some rabbis perform weddings on both days; some only on Yom Yerushalayim.

Procedure. The counting ritual is performed at night, preferably right after nightfall following Maariv.

The blessing:

בָּרוּךְ אַתָּה יְיָ, אֱלֹהֵינוּ מֶלֶךְ הָעוֹלָם אֲשֶׁר קִדְּשָׁנוּ בְּמִצְוֹתָיו, וְצִוָּנוּ, עַל סְפִירַת הָעֹמֶר.

Baruch ata Adonai Elohainu melech ha'olam asher kidshanu b'mitzvotav v'tzivanu al sefirat ha-omer.

Blessed are You, Lord our God, Ruler of the universe, Who has sanctified us with His commandments, and commanded us regarding the counting of the Omer.

Then immediately we state what day of the count it is. For example:

Hayom yom revi'i laomer.

Today is the fourth day of the Omer.

After seven days, we state both the number of days and its equivalent in weeks. For example:

Today is the thirtieth day of the Omer, which is four weeks and two days of Omer.

Or

Today is the forty-sixth day of the Omer, which is six weeks and four days of Omer.

The reason for this double count is that the Torah states in one place:

And you shall count fifty days.

And in another:

And you shall count seven full weeks.

So to be properly correct, we do both.

After the declaration of day, many Jews recite the prayer:

הָרַחֲמָן הוּא יַחֲזִיר לָנוּ אֶת עֲבוֹדַת בֵּית הַמִּקְדָּשׁ
לִמְקוֹמָה.

Harachaman hu yachazir lanu et avodat bet hamikdosh limko-mah.

May the Merciful One restore to us the service of the Temple in its place.

The Omer should be recited standing and at night after dark. If you should forget at night, there is still the next day in which to count—but without the blessing: only the declaration of days is made. The next night, you may resume the count with the blessing again. If, however, you've missed an entire day, it is as if you've broken the continuous thread of counting and, therefore, while you may—and should—resume declaring the days until Shavuot, you do so without the b'racha.

That is why we try to do whatever we can to help us remember. For those who pray regularly or with a minyan, it's no problem to remember. But for others, it is well to prepare something to remind you. Religious bookstores sell Sefirah counters, like calendars with movable parts to change the day. J.J. tacked up on the refrigerator door a replica of a Sefirah calendar that he received from one of his youth organizations. With a wide-tipped purple marker, he wrote all around it, "Count Count Count." You can't miss it. Otherwise, I probably would have.

CHAPTER 22

YOM HASHOAH— HOLOCAUST REMEMBRANCE DAY

The destruction of European Jewry, like the enslavement in Egypt or the destruction of the Holy Temple, did not occur in a single day. Its unremitting horror ran the full course of a dozen years. Moreover, its effects were so total, so shattering, that in measures of cosmic time, the event goes on interminably. European Jewry, once the vital nerve center of world Jewry, will never spring to life again. What could have been will simply never be.

Nevertheless, though its magnitude may warrant it, we cannot mourn the event every day of our lives until eternity. We are a life-affirming people—and one of the ways that Jews of this generation have responded to the Holocaust is to build and protect Jewish life with special zeal. Israel, Soviet Jewry, Jewish learning, the increased Jewishness of Jews—a Holocaust consciousness that is deeply embedded in our psyche is what continually prods us, whether we speak of it or not.

On the other hand, not to actively mourn would not be true to our deep feelings of grief at the great loss and suffering of our people. So Jews of this generation have set aside a special day each year—to focus our memory and our mourning. That day is the twenty-seventh day of Nissan, which falls between Pesach and Shavuot, in the springtime of a Jew's heart.

How is a date picked for immortality on the calendar? All of our ancient religious commemorative days are either Biblically ordained or enacted by rabbinic legislation. The date for Yom HaShoah is the product of a coalition: ghetto fighters, secular members of the Israeli Parliament, the traditionalist bloc in government, rabbinic sages, survivors. All had different ideas. Some preferred the anniversary of the Warsaw Ghetto uprising; others wanted to attach Yom HaShoah to a waning fast day, the tenth of Tevet, to give that event new meaning, and to revive its observance; still others wanted to graft Holocaust commemoration onto Tisha B'Av, destruction upon destruction; and there were those who felt the Holocaust and Israel are organically related and therefore wanted Yom HaShoah to be adjacent to Yom Ha'Atzmaut. In the end, a compromise was achieved. A thousand years from now it will not matter that human beings argued over the merits of this day over that one. It will be, even as it is beginning to be in our own time, a yom kadosh, a holy day set apart from every other day of the Jewish calendar.

THE EVENT

Unlike historical events of our ancient past, we know almost every detail. The Nazis kept records, the postwar trials produced evidence, Allied governments classified documents, and the survivors gave corroborative testimony. We know more horror than we can possibly assimilate.

The basic facts are these: Hitler came to power in 1933. From that moment on, until World War II was over in 1945, every single Jew in Europe was vulnerable. With intensified zeal and step-by-step methodical madness, Hitler put into effect his plan to make the world *Judenrein*, altogether clean of Jews.

At first there were restrictions to remove Jews from the mainstream of society, from politics, art, academic and economic life; to isolate them so that they became "the other"; to cause them economic hardship and physical and social degradation. The next step was to set them apart physically, in ghettos and with a Jew badge, thus further removing them from protective society. Now, they could be more easily targeted, more highly vulnerable. The third step was to incarcerate them in concentration camps, and to torture. Finally, when it seemed as if most of the world's great powers didn't really care, Hitler put into effect his Final Solution: the extermination of every Jewish man, woman, and child.

Age, wealth, talent, health, connections—nothing mattered but race. Gas chambers, crematoria, medical "experiments," mass shootings, open graves—these were his tools of power. By the end of the war, six million Jews—over one third of world Jewry—had been wiped out.

To give expression to an event of such magnitude seems almost an inhuman task. How can we possibly encapsulate a madness of such awesome proportions? And how can we experience it as part of our religious calendar?

The answer is: we really do not yet know. We are still too close to the event, still too numb to do the right thing, say the right words, feel secure in including this and leaving out that. From the moment in history at which we are now poised, we understand this is exactly how it happened at the time of the Churban: to those who did not actually live through the event fell the task of sacralizing it.

Nevertheless, it is a process that has begun to unfold before our very eyes. I remember how the day was marked five years ago, ten years ago, and fifteen years ago, and the signs are unmistakable. In 1965, the rabbi of our shul organized a Yom HaShoah program. It was the only such event of its kind in the area, which encompassed several synagogues, Hebrew schools, and yeshivot. The entire program consisted of one speaker—Elie Wiesel. Wiesel had kept the memory at center front for two decades when all other survivors were too paralyzed to speak, but in 1965, he was hardly well known. Forty people showed up. There were no prayers, no hymns, no Kaddish. And no children were present.

In 1982, Elie Wiesel commemorated Yom HaShoah in the White House, along with the president and other American leaders. Millions of American citizens remembered the victims along with Wiesel, American citizens who did not even know the word "Holocaust" five years ago. And this year in our community, every synagogue, every school, had its own commemorative program.

In our synagogue, hundreds of people came; the event was called a Yom HaShoah Family Service, and the synagogue bulletin and announcement made sure to add, BRING THE CHILDREN: DO NOT FORGET, with its double meanings perfectly clear. The service was held in the sanctuary, not in the social hall as of eighteen years ago. Interspersed throughout the program were several of the formal prayers taken from the traditional liturgy, the classic locus of Jewish sacredness. Survivors gave testimony, children participated formally in the program, remembering, asking questions, singing songs that evoked poignant feelings in the listeners. Fifteen years ago, there was one commonly used film on the Holocaust. Today, every synagogue and school showed a different film. Six candles were lit, each frail flame representing a million victims.

COMMEMORATION

There is no standard format as yet. But we live in modern times, with modern means of communication. Every aspect of life moves at a faster clip, including memorialization of events that are both history and of the immediate moment. And so we begin to see the basic outlines, simply by observing the similarities in unrelated and spontaneous commemorative programs throughout the country.

A Maariv (evening) service

The lighting of candles

Prayers from the standard prayer book, including the El Maleh Rachamim, and the Kaddish

Recitation of Holocaust poems and witness literature

Testimony of survivors

Films of the Holocaust

Songs of the Partisans (in Yiddish, the language whose heartland was destroyed in the Holocaust)

The Ani Ma'amin, the declaration of faith and hope that the victims sang on their way to the gas chambers, their final act of human dignity

Home celebration is less formalized and standardized, and, in fact, less ritualized. Some people light a yahrzeit candle; some people light six such candles. We light a candle and sit in the semidarkened living room for a few moments, either talking or just quietly reflecting. We don't play the piano, nor music on the radio during Yom HaShoah; at dinner, each child talks about the Holocaust programs they experienced in school or in their youth groups. While we have very little formal ritual at home, our lives in general become more subdued on that day.

Some schools have a full week of Holocaust commemoration. Films are shown, outside speakers are brought in, a special assembly is convened, and special prayers are said. Various organizations, such as Zachor, Holocaust Resource Center; the Anti-Defamation League; the various boards of Jewish education in different cities; and the United States Holocaust Memorial Council, have published Holocaust curricula that are available upon request. Ten years ago, the debate over whether to teach children about the Holocaust could still be heard. Today, it is part of the natural instruction of a Jewish child, beginning at a very young age.

It will take a generation or two—or perhaps even longer— until the liturgy becomes standardized and the features of the day structured, formalized, and uniformly observed.*

One can only project what the day might be like: a month before the memorial day, the yeshiva day schools will begin to prepare the children through intensive review of the historical facts. Perhaps Yom HaShoah will be declared a fast day, preceded by a meal of potato peels, watery soup, ashes, and something more bitter than maror. Perhaps our great-grandchildren will all wear yellow-starred armbands on that day, or a striped garment, or hard shoes made of mud and twigs. There will no longer be any survivors, but the grandchildren of survivors, who will surely have a special role in witnessing, will retell the story. Perhaps they will read from a parchment scroll, singed at the corners, to remind us of the thousands of Torah scrolls the Nazis burned, together with Jews sealed in flaming synagogues. Per-

---

* Zachor, Holocaust Resource Center, has sponsored an extensive Holocaust liturgy project.

haps the Book of Job will be read in the synagogues, with or without its last chapter.

There are no neat theological categories into which future generations can fit the events of the Holocaust. True, there are meanings that Jews of this generation have begun to assimilate; and whatever form Yom HaShoah takes, it will incorporate some of those meanings: that to forget the victims is to fail them once more; that the fate of the Jews is unique; that the Jews stand alone; that modern universalist values are no guarantee of moral progress; that the response to unspeakable evil is to give love and new life—conflicting messages, each with its own truth.

One cannnot precisely call these theological categories. Yet, Jews of the future will somehow find a way to be faithful to the memory of the victims, to link themselves authentically to community and tradition, and perhaps even find a way to speak of God after the Holocaust.

CHAPTER 23

YOM HA'ATZMAUT— ISRAEL INDEPENDENCE DAY

For the last two thousand years, Jews have experienced very few miracles. To be sure, individual acts of miraculous saving have been many. They have been told and retold, and they warm the heart. But national miracles, great acts of deliverance equal to the Exodus, or the Maccabean conquest and return? None such have entered our Diaspora history books for the last two thousand years.

Until now. Until this very generation. Until the creation of the Third Commonwealth, the rebirth of the State of Israel, the return of Jews to sovereignty in the land of their ancestors.

The story of Yom Ha'Atzmaut is essentially three tales in one. It is the story of a love affair of the Jewish people for this land; it is also a messianic dream; it is also a desire for national and political status and security. All three themes are interwoven.

Some say the love affair begins with the last Churban, in the destruction of Jerusalem and the exile of Judeans by the Romans in 70 c.e. Some say it begins with the Churban before that, in 586 b.c.e. Some say it begins with the naming of the people and the land by the same name. Most contemporary Jews would probably begin the story with the covenant between God and Abraham, with God promising this land to Abraham and his descendants.

Wherever one begins, this much is true:

Israel has become the center of the universe for Jews of countless generations, and Jerusalem, the epicenter. There are a hundred ways we have kept this love affair fresh in our minds, and in our hearts. When a Jew died in the Diaspora, a bit of soil from the Holy Land was thrown into the grave. When Jews pray, they face Jerusalem. At every Jewish wedding, amidst our joy, we shatter a glass, a form of Zionist protest and messianic longing. When we build a home, we leave a small part unfinished, in memory of the destruction and our exile from our beloved land. Rabbinic and medieval Jewish literature is replete with statements of intense love. In the Talmud, we read, "Rav Abba used to kiss the stones of Acco; Rabbi Chanina would mend its roads; . . . and Rav Chiyya bar Gamda would roll himself in the dust of the Holy Land; all this, in order to fulfill the verse, 'For your servants delight in her stones and love her dust' " (KETUBOT 112A–B). The Rabbis even ruled that if a man or woman wants to settle in the Holy Land, and the spouse refuses, that is sufficient grounds for divorce.

Countless Jews throughout the Diaspora period were swept up into the messianic movements that promised a return to the Holy Land. Many great rabbis, such as Nachmanides and Judah Halevi, themselves went to settle in the Holy Land. The mourning fast of Tisha B'Av and the other fasts related to the Churban are a confirmation of the love for Israel, and in our prayers every day, three times a day, the theme of return is a most prominent one. Even in our Birkat Hamazon we make a simple, outright plea: "And rebuild Jerusalem, the holy city, speedily, and in our day. Blessed are You, God, Who rebuilds Jerusalem."

When you love someone, you not only talk and think about him (or her), but you identify with him, and with what he or she is doing at a given moment. That is how we can understand the holiday of Tu B'Shvat that has been celebrated by Jews of the Diaspora for two thousand years. Tu B'Shvat is the New Year of the Trees, but if you live in New York, and the fifteenth day of the month Shvat comes out in January, as it usually does, the rebirth of trees is the furthest thing from your mind. And yet, if you are a Jew, in love with the Holy Land, you have no trouble at all spanning time and oceans and seasons. Tu B'Shvat is when the sap begins to rise in Israel's fruit trees. Diaspora Jews have celebrated this day by eating fruits that grow in the land of Israel, such as bokser, the fruit of the carob tree, and almonds, which will soon begin to flower and bear fruit in the hills of Judea and of Galilee. And if you can't be there physically to plant a tree in the Holy Land, then you send money to purchase the sapling which a child in Israel will plant on this day.

All that, in very small measure, is part of the dream and the love and the longing.

The immediate history of Yom Ha'Atzmaut begins with nineteenth-century nationalism, which stimulated Jews as it did all other peoples. In addition, the political Zionists, such as Moses Hess, Tzvi Hirsch Kalisher, Leon Pinsker, and Theodor Herzl, built upon the hopes for messianic return and redemption in their strivings to create a Jewish national state. Since they were evoking latent feelings that were continuous with Jewish tradition, the impetus for their followers came as much from Jewish memories as it did from European nationalism. Also, the pogroms of Eastern Europe played no small part in pushing the process forward.

In 1897, Theodor Herzl convened the first Zionist Congress in Basel, Switzerland. Herzl is rightly called the father of modern political Zionism. Though he died an early death not too many years later, his enormous and single-minded efforts on behalf of the Jewish state bore fruit half a century later.

In the early 1900s, the Turks ruled Palestine. After World War I, a British mandate over Palestine superseded Turkish rule. All the while, there was a yishuv population that had settled in the Holy Land and that was slowly organizing itself into what would someday be its independent government. In the early 1920s, for example, the Jewish labor organization and the Jewish self-defense forces were formed.

During the 1930s, largely as a result of Arab pressure on the mandate government, the British Foreign Office issued several White Papers limiting Jewish immigration. Nevertheless, from '33 to '39, with the specter of Nazism over Europe, additional Jews were smuggled into Palestine. This was known as Aliyah Bet. An illegal immigration. There was no other choice.

Relations between Jews and Arabs continued to deteriorate. In

1937, the British commission, under Lord Peel, recommended a partition of Palestine into two states. The Jews accepted the partition; the Arabs were against it, and revolted. Arab riots, which were not uncommon in the twenties and thirties, again broke out. In the 1940s, World War II conditions sealed off all immigration. A very small number of Jews managed to escape the nightmare of Hitler's Europe. Of those, only a handful were able to get past the British.

In 1947, the world had a change of heart. Partly in response to the devastating blows of the Holocaust, the nations of the world voted in favor of partition. It was to go into effect on May 14, 1948, when the British would withdraw their forces from the Middle East. On that day, Israel declared itself an independent state. On that day, the fifth day of the month of Iyar, the seven Arab nations that surrounded Israel declared war. The War of Independence lasted until 1949 when cease-fire agreements were struck with Egypt, Jordan, Syria, and Lebanon. In 1949, Israel became a member of the United Nations. Some people cite as proof of the miraculous nature of Israel's resurrection as a state the fact that the Soviet Union voted in favor of partition and in favor of membership for Israel in the United Nations.

In 1950, the Israeli Parliament passed the Law of Return, that every Jew could come home and be granted citizenship, no matter what state of health, no matter what degree of financial need. More than a law, it was a fulfillment of the yearnings of Jews for two thousand years.

CELEBRATION

The celebration of Yom Ha'Atzmaut has not yet fully incorporated the broad range of emotions that Israel evokes in a Jewish heart. However, the character of the day is still in flux and, year by year, the gap between feelings and ritual expression is shrinking. As one would expect, we can see the metamorphosis of Yom Ha'Atzmaut most clearly in Israel. In the early years of the state, Independence Day was marked by military parades. The Israelis were flexing their muscles, showing the world "we can be a state like all other states; we have an army to protect ourselves." I remember going to the center of town in Jerusalem in 1969, on

Yom Ha'Atzmaut, and watching people with noisemakers, streamers, and funny hats, and thinking to myself, This is all perfectly legitimate but somehow not to my liking. Unfairly, perhaps, I felt disappointed.

Today, Yom Ha'Atzmaut, or the celebration thereof, has matured, just as Israel has matured as a state. First of all, it is linked to Yom Hazikaron, the day of remembrance of the fallen soldiers. This has a sobering effect; Israelis come into Independence Day from the depths of pain and loneliness, which explains in part why Yom Ha'Atzmaut is beginning to evolve as a religious holiday. Jews, even secular ones, are grappling with the religious values of the state. In 1982, there was no military parade, though no one would for a moment doubt the importance of the military in the survival of the state. There has also been a subtle shift to celebration as a family holiday, including seudah, a feast. The rabbinate has published a ritual guide, and communal prayer is a prominent feature of this day. There is talk of an Israel haggadah, a Yom Ha'Atzmaut seder, at which the entire story will be told, comparing it, of course, to other holidays of miracle, victory, and redemption.

In the United States, we are beginning to see the outlines of religious commemoration and celebration. An evening service is held in the synagogue, attended by all members of the family. Often, these services are followed by a lecture and a film on Israel. Afterward, usually in the synagogue social hall, there is a kumsitz, the word Israelis often use for a social gathering. Israeli foods such as falafel are served, the band plays Israeli music, and there is Israeli singing and dancing. In cities with large Jewish populations, there are Israeli Day parades with floats whose theme has some connection to the modern State of Israel or to the history of Zionism. Israeli dance groups often schedule a joint dance festival around the time of Yom Ha'Atzmaut.

At the morning service on Yom Ha'Atzmaut, Hallel is recited, just as it is on other holidays of deliverance such as Chanukah, Pesach, and Purim. There is a debate among traditional Jews in America as to whether to recite these prayers of thanksgiving with or without the introductory b'racha, which elevates the prayers to the status of performance of a mitzvah. Some Jews are afraid to change anything that was not established by the

Rabbis of yesteryear. However, most Orthodox rabbis do acknowledge the monumental act of deliverance in the creation of the State of Israel and therefore instruct their congregations to recite the Hallel with its opening b'racha.

We are only at the beginning, just as Israel the state is only at the beginning. In fact, the words we use to describe Israel in our prayers are raishit tzmichat ge'ulatenu, "the beginning of the flowering of our redemption."

Israel, the modern nation-state, is not without its problems. Integrating two cultures, Oriental and Western, is extremely difficult. It faces an enormous task of resettling Russian Jews, the problems of peace at its borders are never ending, and most difficult and troubling of all is the problem of Palestinians, both on the West Bank and elsewhere. The Palestinians fled in 1948, and have since raised their children in refugee camps because they were not integrated into any other Arab societies. It is a problem because they, too, have their memories and their dreams which they pass on from generation to generation. And so the dilemma escalates rather than quiets.

Still, I am a Jew more than I am a universalist. So to me, the right of Jews to legally resettle in their homeland, with the sanction of the nations of the world, is not something I will yield easily. For me, all things are not equal. My roots in that land go very far back; therefore, my compassion for humanity-at-large must be reconciled with my self-interest, my very identity.

When I arrived at the Jerusalem shoemaker's shop, just as he had closed up to go home and get ready for Sukkot, and I said to him, "Please, my daughter's shoes, for the holiday . . ." he pulled back his tin overhead door, took her shoes in hand, and quoted a verse from the Torah: "And when your brother is in need, do not stand idly by." I had a sense that there was something else going on here besides the shoemaker, me, and a pair of shoes. No shoemaker from the Bronx can make the Bible come alive for me in quite the same way. Or to meet a woman whose family has lived in Jerusalem for eight generations; to see children playing in the sunshine near the sprinklers, oblivious to the rifled guard who protects these most valuable of our treasures; to come upon a mountain that is half brown and half green, and know that somewhere in the green half is a tree planted forty years ago by a Jewish child in a Hebrew school in Kansas City, Missouri, or New Orleans, Louisiana; to mourn with friends, one who lost a son and one who lost a son-in-law in the Lebanese war; to worry about my David whose bus is pelted with rocks as he travels from Jerusalem to his yeshiva in the Etzion bloc—these are my roots and my connections. The sum of all these experiences is greater than its parts. That's what Zionism is all about, and what Yom Ha'Atzmaut celebrates—an abiding love for Jewish settlement in a Jewish homeland.

The story is told of the disgruntled traveler to Israel. He complains about the heat, the dust, the narrow streets in Jerusalem, the noise and crowds in Tel Aviv, the non-English-speaking chambermaid, the cabdriver who drives too fast, the lack of buying power of his dollar. The whole trip, he complains. Finally, at the airport for the return flight home, he starts again—this time, about the long lines and the thorough security check. Exasperated, his cotraveler turns to him. "This is the first Jewish state in two thousand years and all you do is complain, complain, complain." The disgruntled traveler replies: "First Jewish state in two thousand years, and it had to happen to me!"

Most Jews, however, are like the big United Jewish Appeal donor who makes his first trip to Israel after years and years of committed work and generous giving. Upon his return, his friends ask him for a report. "Friends," he says, "you know all those lies they've been telling us about Israel all these years? Well, they're all true."

Like every normal person, I should like to enjoy a long life. Like everyone else my age, I would like someday to enjoy the blessings of grandchildren, and even great-grandchildren. Besides the pleasure they will give, I have something special to tell them: that I lived in the eye of a miracle. I remember my parents and sisters and neighbors gathered in front of our console radio, listening to the UN count on partition. When the chairman called out the deciding vote, everyone hugged and cried, and my father opened a bottle of Scotch for a le'chayim. I remember David Ben-Gurion's immortal words on the fifth of Iyar, May 14, 1948, as he declared Israel an independent state, with its provisional government. Moments later, one could hear the singing and dancing in the streets of Tel Aviv, and the sounds of guns and warfare in the distant background. I will tell my grandchildren that my second cousins fought in the War of Independence, that I know people who came on Aliyah Bet, and that I once met and conversed with David Ben-Gurion in person, that I was on a kibbutz in the Negev when the Sinai campaign broke out in 1956, and that the Monday morning of the Six Day War is as vivid to me as yesterday.

"Two thousand years, and it happened to me! Come here and touch me." That's what I'll say to them.

And that is what they will tell their grandchildren, at a Yom Ha'Atzmaut seder.

CHAPTER 24

SHAVUOT

Sung to the tune of Mah Nishtana:

Why is this festival different from all other festivals?

Because on all other festivals we celebrate eight days,

On this festival, only two days.

Because on all other festivals we eat chicken soup,

chopped liver, and roasts;

On this festival—blintzes and cheesecake.

Because on all other festivals we catch a good night's sleep.

On this festival, it's *tikkun* study all night long.

Because on all other festivals we celebrate our physical
    redemption;

On this festival—the Revelation.

Moscow, June 1976: My husband and I are in the synagogue
on Archipova Street. At the moment it is filled with six hundred
aging Jews. Halfway through the service, a group of thirty foreign college students enter, handsome Nordic types—which is
as it should be if you come from the University of Copenhagen.

A small dark girl is seated behind me. Lisa, it turns out, is Jewish, one of three Jews in the group. She is an exchange student from Rutgers University, spending the year with a Danish family. Five minutes of whispered landsmanschaft and we rapidly locate our mutual acquaintances. Her uncle is a well-known professor of Jewish studies. She spent eight years in Hebrew school.

After a few moments I learn why some of the girls are wearing jeans under the Bessarabian babushkas they have so cleverly wrapped around their middles. They are not shul hopping; simply, they are on an architecture tour of religious institutions in Moscow. Had they known they would be walking into the midst of a service this Thursday morning, they would have dressed more conservatively. Never mind: the Russian Jews are happy to see foreigners in any size, shape, form, or relative state of undress. Just before they leave, Lisa leans over and asks, "Why is the synagogue so crowded today; is it like this every day?" "It's Shavuot, a holiday . . ." I couldn't finish my sentence. Her eyes lit up. "Oops! you're right, I completely forgot; my mother forgot to write me. It's like my anniversary. I was confirmed on Shavuot. . . ." And with a warm hug to some elderly Russian women, Lisa is off to celebrate Shavuot—and Greek Orthodox architecture.

Of the three Biblical festivals, Shavuot is currently the least known outside of its celebrating community. That, however, does not diminish its stature within. Of the three, it might be the shortest in duration, but it lacks nothing in the way of intensity of feeling and depth of meaning. For those who really get into it, there is a sensation of reenacting an event that occurred some three thousand years ago, a cataclysmic event that took place, tradition tells us, fifty days after the Exodus from Egypt. The event: Revelation at Sinai and the giving of the Ten Commandments.

But the holiday Shavuot didn't start out that way. Originally, the Bible describes Shavuot as an agricultural festival, a feast of the summer wheat harvest in the land of Israel. The first wheat ripens approximately fifty days after the first barley. The first barley offering was brought to the Temple one day after Passover began. From that day on, the Jews were told to count up seven full weeks from one harvest to the other, and at the end of the count they were commanded to celebrate Shavuot which literally means "Weeks."

The Torah refers to this day also as Chag Habikkurim, the Festival of the First Fruits. The Jews would make pilgrimage to Jerusalem, bearing as gift offerings the first fruits of their land, in particular, the Biblical "seven kinds" with which the holy land was abundantly blessed. Inasmuch as the national economy could not make a go of it on grain and fruit offerings, the wealthy landowners would bring their gifts in baskets of silver and gold. In an agricultural economy, Shavuot was a time of great bounty, of joy, an occasion for the nation to come together to give thanks.

In time, however, the emphasis of the day shifted from agriculture to history, so that today Jews in every part of the world, including those in agrarian economies, celebrate the Revelation foremost and the harvest secondarily. Shavuot is an example of the Jewish people's ability to transform the meaning of a moment, to move from nature to history, from biology to spirit.

Some say the shift in emphasis occurred during the conflict between the Sadducees and the Pharisees, the two major Judean parties of the first century C.E. The Sadducean leadership was comprised of wealthy landowners and members of the priestly class, people who had a vested interest in the Temple cult and harvest celebration of this holiday. On the other hand, the Pharisees, who were mostly scholars and folk people, derived authority from their knowledge of the oral tradition. Quite naturally, then, they wanted the historical event of theophany at Sinai—which was the source of all of tradition—to be the preeminent focus of the day. Moreover, they wanted to maintain the theological link between Shavuot and Pesach, as if to say that Revelation and Exodus were but two parts of the same experience. Freedom without Revelation, said the Rabbis, would have been of little significance. It was the completion of that redemptive act with the giving of the Torah that created the Jewish people.

With the destruction of the Temple in 70 C.E. and the ensuing exile from the land, it was only natural for the people to gravitate toward the spiritual cathexis of the holy day—the Torah and the covenant. The Pharisees didn't eliminate the agrarian characteristics of the day, or the prayers that refer to celebration as it was in Biblical and Temple times. What they did was to add and reinforce other customs and prayers that supported the ancient tradition that the Revelation occurred on Shavuot. Those customs and prayers are all part of the celebration today.

PREPARATION

In contrast to Pesach and Sukkot, which celebrate a physical redemption, most of the preparations for Shavuot concern the spirit rather than the physical props such as are required for Pesach and Sukkot.

In the Bible, the three days preceding the Revelation are described as very special days. They are called Sheloshet Yemai Hagbalah, three days set aside to get ready to receive the Torah, three days during which the Jews were told to purify themselves and abstain from having sex. Today, there is no formal observance of Sheloshet Yemai Hagbalah. The only vestige of those three days is that the Sefirah (the mourning period for the Hadrianic persecutions, ca. 135 C.E.) ends three days earlier, instead of ending with the onset of Shavuot. Those who missed their chance on Lag B'Omer, and who haven't had haircuts all during Sefirah, may now do so. Those who grew Sefirah beards—and the number in the Orthodox community is growing these days—will now shave them off. Also, marriages are performed during these three days. The injunction against sex on Sheloshet Yemai Hagbalah was in effect only at Sinai.

There are men who take seriously the idea of purifying themselves for reenactment of the Revelation. They go to the mikvah, which is open for men's use on the day preceding Shavuot.

For many, the most important preparation for Shavuot is, oddly enough, a good long afternoon nap on erev Shavuot. In a moment, it will become clear why.

Shavuot is a little jewel, a Jewish housewife's dream. There is no massive housecleaning, no need to cook and plan for umpteen holiday meals, and if there's a lot to be done before the end of the academic calendar, then two days of holiday and not eight are just enough. (Although I sometimes suspect that the lesser preliminary efforts required of a woman have made Shavuot universally the least known of the three festivals. How's that for Jewish mother power?!)

All the festival rules regarding candlelighting, Kiddush, meals, food preparation, work, as well as most of the festival liturgy, apply to Shavuot. But there are some exceptions, which give the holiday its own special character.

On Shavuot, we eat dairy for the festival meals or at least for some of them (which diminishes somewhat the housewife's gain because, as everyone knows, dairy meals are harder to prepare than meat meals). In our house, as in many Jewish homes, we eat no meat during Shavuot, unless it happens to come out on Shabbat. Somehow, Friday night without chicken is just not Shabbat.

Foods, like cheese blintzes, cheese kreplach, and cheesecake are served. The symbol of kreplach, a three-sided pastry filled with cheese, is that God gave the Torah in three parts (the Torah, the Prophets, the Writings) to three categories of people (Kohen, Levite, and Israelite) through a third-born child (Moses, whose older siblings were Aaron and Miriam) in the third month of the year (1. Nissan, 2. Iyar, 3. Sivan).

Jewish lore offers several origins to the dairy tradition: Moses was drawn out of the water on the day which later came to be Shavuot. He was willing to be nursed by only a Hebrew woman. On his merit, that of choosing a Jewish mother's milk, we eat dairy. Another, less fanciful reason is that until the Jews received the Torah they were not bound by the laws of kashrut. Upon receiving the Torah, all their pots and pans and dishes were rendered trefeh (unkosher). So they ate dairy until they could kasher their utensils. . . .

Another explanation grew out of allusion to the verse in Song of Songs (4:11) that "knowledge of the Torah is like milk and honey under the tongue." From this verse also grew the custom of serving at each meal two challot that are sweet and baked with honey.

Another food custom is to prepare or buy challot that are a bit longer than usual. These challot are a symbol of the "wave offering"—the two loaves of bread that the Jews were required on Shavuot to bring from their farms to the Temple (Lev. 23:17). The officiating priest would then wave these loaves before the altar.

In addition to food customs, the tradition arose to decorate the synagogue and the home with plants, flowers, branches of trees. The synagogue never looks more beautiful than it does on Shavuot. It feels like a wedding is taking place, and in a way it is. One explanation of this custom is that the giving of the Torah took place on a mountain encircled with green (either this was an exilic fantasy, or several millennia of erosion have denuded Mount Sinai and environs of greenery; it is now a rather brown mountain—if indeed that is Mount Sinai); another is that the infant Moses was saved from certain death by being placed in a basket of reeds and floated on the river of reeds. We spread greenery all around to remind us of that miracle. Although I've never seen it, I've read that in some synagogues reedlike grasses are spread on the floor of the shul. And of course all the greenery is a sensate reminder that Shavuot started out primarily as a harvest festival.

There is also a hint in the tradition that the Jews adopted this custom of greenery from their Christian neighbors in medieval Europe. Some rabbis even forbade it, since it looked too much like Church practices. Whatever the reason, this appealing custom has been with us for a long time.

CELEBRATION

In the Diaspora, Shavuot is celebrated two days: the sixth and seventh of Sivan. In Israel, only one day.

On the first night of Shavuot, the regular Maariv for festivals is recited. After prayer, the evening meal is taken. Then Shavuot begins to take on a character all its own: tikkun leil Shavuot, the all-night study session.

As traditions go, this is a fairly late one, begun by the Kabbalists in the Middle Ages. In the major mystical work, The Zohar, there is a passage that praises those who stay awake all night in anticipation of receiving the Torah. Since God, the Jews, and the Torah are bound together, as if in marriage, one should stay awake the night before preparing "ornaments" for the bride.

What are these ornaments, these jewels? None other than the words of the Torah. Jews gather in synagogues after the meal (and, for some, after a little catnap) and spend the entire night together studying selections from the Torah, the Prophets, and the Talmud. At the conclusion of the tikkun, as the sun rises, the morning services are recited.

The tikkun book can be purchased in a Jewish bookstore. Or one can put it together following a list; all the necessary books are easily available.

The selections are taken from the written and oral law. It was organized that way to underscore the indivisibility of the two. The readings consist of three to seven verses from the beginning and end of every portion of the Torah. Certain sections, however, are read in full:

Creation (GEN. 1:1–2:3)

The Exodus and the song at the Red Sea (EXOD. 14, 15)

The giving of the Ten Commandments (EXOD. 18–20; 24:1–18; 34:27–35; DEUT. 5:1–6:9)

The grand review of the essence of the Torah (DEUT. 10:12–11:25), contains the Shema prayer.

The same method is used for the Prophets: that is, the first and last few sentences from each book. The special full reading is Ezekiel, the entire chapter 1 (The Vision of the Chariot). The twenty-four minor Prophets are considered as one book, so three readings represent the entire work: (HOSEA 1:1–3; HABAKKUK 2:20–3:19; and MALACHI 3:22–24). The Book of Ruth is read in full; and of the Book of Psalms, chapters 1 and 19 are read. Next, the first and last few passages of each of the 63 treatises of the Mishnah are studied. This is followed by a reading of Maimonides' 613 mitzvot. Chasidim read selections from Kabbalist literature. If it seems like a whole lot of material, remember that it represents eight to ten hours of continuous study—approximately one fourth of a full term's work for a college course.

If you don't have a good long nap beforehand, instead of readiness to receive the Torah, the only thing you will feel the next morning is spaced out. Moreover, you will be out of sync for the rest of the holiday. The Jewish people are dreamers, with a practical bent. Since not everyone can nap, and some are less hardy than others, there are many modified forms of tikkun leil Shavuot. In some communities it is the custom to study three or four hours and then break at midnight so that everyone will be refreshed for the Torah reading the next day. Unlike grown-ups who appreciate a night's sleep, youngsters find it a novelty (to try) to stay awake all night. But here, too, there must be modification—a program of study geared to their level and interests. Otherwise, they will surely be found napping the night through beneath the juice and cake table.

In addition to the regular festival prayers on Shavuot morning, there are three special highlights: First, the Torah reading on the first day is the Revelation of the Ten Commandments (Exod. 19:1–20:26). The description is so graphic that one can fairly see the crowds milling around. There must have been a good deal of preliminary confusion and disorder, despite Moses' firm and orderly hand. After all, who knew what to expect?

The Rabbis tell us that each Jew in each generation should consider him/herself as having received the Torah at Mount Sinai. As we reach the section of the Ten Commandments, the entire congregation stands for its reading. Even the little children are quiet in shul, as they sense an awe in this, their second home.

The second feature is the reading of Akdamot. These are recited immediately before the Torah reading, or, in some congregations, right after the first verse of the Torah had been read. Akdamot are liturgical poems of loyalty of the Jews to the Torah; these were composed in the eleventh century. The language is Aramaic, thus, the haunting melody with which Akdamot are chanted is what many people find most moving.

Third, on the second day of Shavuot, the entire Book of Ruth is read before the Torah reading from Deuteronomy. Ruth was a Moabite woman who refused to abandon her husband's family after he, his father, and his brother die. She leaves Moab to accompany Naomi, her mother-in-law, back to Judea. There, Ruth meets and marries a relative of her deceased husband. Through Ruth the convert, new life is given to the family. Ruth is the ancestor of King David, who died on Shavuot, and from whose line the Messiah shall come. Appropriately, the story of Ruth takes place at harvesttime.

On the second day of the holiday, as on the final day of all festivals, the Yizkor memorial prayer is recited. In many an Orthodox shul there is an appeal during Yizkor for the Hebrew school or a local yeshiva. The speech for this Yizkor appeal is the easiest of all, since it fits so well with the overall theme of love for the Torah.

Throughout the book, I have hardly described customs that used to exist but that no longer exist. But I shall make an exception for one now, for two reasons: one, to tell what it was, for it conveyed the sweetness and love of the Torah, and a parent can easily duplicate these customs today, and two, to tell what we have substituted, given the different ways our lives are programmed these days.

In European Jewish communities of pre-modern times, it was the custom to begin teaching children Torah on Shavuot. At dawn, the children were taken to the synagogue. They were taught to recognize the letters of a Hebrew verse written on a special slate, a verse they had memorized almost from infancy. One such verse was: "Torah tzivah lanu Moshe," "Moses commanded us the Torah." The teacher would recite each letter and the child would repeat the letter after him. As the child mastered each letter, it was checked with a dab of honey, which the child then licked off. Another custom was to bake a special milk and honey cake and ice it with verses from the Torah. It seems we also had our equivalent of the Easter egg. An egg was boiled for each child, and Torah verses were written on it. After reading the verses, the child was given the cake and the egg to eat. Although it seems strange to gobble down verses of the Torah, nevertheless it was legitimated. That was the Jewish version of motivation theory.

These customs are no longer practiced because we now have an orderly, externally imposed educational system and we follow a standard academic calendar. Nevertheless, in many a Jewish day school, we have plucked out of the educational system an event which is linked in theory and practice to Shavuot and to the older customs. Today, the custom is to distribute to the young child his/her very first own book of the Bible, their first Chumash. Sometime around Shavuot, the parents of the first graders are invited to school for an hour; the principal makes a brief speech to the children about the preciousness of the Torah; the Hebrew-studies teacher adds a few words on a related theme;

and then each child is called to come up, one by one, to receive his/her own small Chumash, usually the Book of Genesis, in Hebrew script as in the Torah scroll itself. In our children's day school, the S.A.R. Academy, one or two handy parents in the class are asked to sew colorful felt book covers complete with the child's name stitched onto the front cover. If our Goody grows up to be a Torah scholar, it will be in part thanks to the principal, to her first-grade teacher, to her grandmother who also came to share that event, and to that mother who lovingly sewed up the first Chumash book cover for Goody.

It is a ceremony for which it is unequivocally worth giving up a day's work. While no words such as generations, continuity, inheritance, and chain of tradition, and so forth are used—for six-year-olds don't quite grasp those concepts and it's their day— nevertheless, these are the sentiments that fill to overflowing the minds and hearts of every adult present.

That event is really what Shavuot is all about. It is about the Torah, and about the covenant. A covenant has many dimensions to it. A Jew knows that if he/she breaks it, he/she breaks it for all generations to come; all that effort to keep it going for a hundred generations might possibly go down the drain. Conversely, bringing our children into the covenant, watching them as they move closer toward it, step by step, validates and strengthens our own commitment, our own love for Torah and tradition.

The covenant between God and the Jews suggests many things. A covenant is like a good marriage: open-ended, you never know what the next day will bring, yet deep down you know that you'll remain faithful. There's a steadiness about it, a commitment that is somehow more than just the sense of working at it to make it go. An open-ended relationship means that in times of pain and suffering the partners grow closer together, just as does a strong family. In three thousand years of ups and downs, neither partner has said, "Enough already." That's what a covenant is.

And that's what the Book of Ruth is really all about—that you can love after evil, that you can have passion and compassion after tragedy, and more than that, that to go on being human you must feel those very feelings. Ruth is a simple yet profound tale—a commitment of love that is stronger than logic, of little acts of goodness that are, in the long run, of cosmic significance. And perhaps Jews in this generation can understand this better than all the Jews who went before us.

Sometimes a little ritual can say more than a thousand philosophical treatises. The Sephardim, possibly because they were our best philosophers, developed the perfect ritual for Shavuot. Perhaps in the next thousand years, the Ashkenazim will take it up as well. Immediately after the ark is opened up on Shavuot morning, Sephardic Jews read a ketubah, a marriage contract between God, the groom, and Israel, the bride. In the ketubah, God invites the bride to His palace, and promises to bind Himself to her forever. The bride says, "Na'aseh Ve Nishmah," "We will do and we will listen." We accept. These are the very words that were used by the ancient Jews at Sinai. The groom then gives His gift to the bride—the Torah and the oral law.

This is an incredible season to be a Jew, if you have the emotional stamina for it. Springtime in a Jew's life is like being a manic-depressive. One goes from tears to laughter, joy to despair, and back again in dizzying proportions: Purim, Passover, Holocaust Remembrance Day, the anniversary of the Warsaw Ghetto uprising, Israel Independence Day, Jerusalem Liberation Day . . . Sometimes, it seems almost more than the heart can bear. Yet Shavuot caps it all, with its emphasis on the covenant, its steadiness, its security, its reminder of who we are. Shavuot gives meaning and makes sense out of everything else.

CHAPTER 25

TISHA B'AV
AND OTHER FASTS

It would seem only natural, would it not, that whereas we rejoice and celebrate with feasting, we mourn and memorialize without. Food gladdens the soul, fasting chastens it. Thus, on days we recall tragedies, such as the destruction of the Holy Temple in Jerusalem, the Rabbis ordained a fast.

Tisha B'Av is linked to two of the most incredible eras of Jewish history. Therefore, let us take a moment to place the immediate events within the larger Jewish historical framework:

In approximately the year 1750 B.C.E., Abraham embraced monotheism. He left his father's home and, along with a cadre of believers, set out for Canaan. Canaan was the land God promised to him as a sign of the covenant between them.

Years later, this Promised Land was temporarily blighted by famine, so Abraham's grandson Jacob, plus eleven sons, one daughter, and their families, left Canaan and settled in Egypt. Since Joseph, the long-ago-betrayed-but-now-forgiving brother, was regent of Egypt, their fortunes were pleasant indeed.

Four centuries later, however, the descendants of Jacob and Joseph found themselves in altogether different circumstances. They were now reduced to slavery, and they needed a savior.

Enter Moses. Approximately 1250 B.C.E., Moses led the tribe of Hebrew slaves out of Egypt to freedom, and to the promise of return to the land of their ancestors. En route, however, Moses died. Joshua took over the leadership of this band of slaves turned freemen. Through conquest and resettlement they reestablished themselves in the land of the patriarchs and proceeded to divide up the land according to tribal origins, this portion for the children of Simeon, that for Levi, Judah, and so on. Within the next hundred years, a kingdom was established to unify the twelve separate tribes. Under the third king, Solomon, son of David, a great Temple was built. This took place during the tenth century B.C.E.

This Temple was the center, the heart of the nation; it was the physical symbol of a thriving, wholly independent theocracy. Kings might come and go, the Northern Kingdom might split off from the Southern Kingdom, but the sacrifice, worship, and gathering that took place on the plaza of the Holy Temple—that was what created a sense of Jewish sovereignty, stability, and nationhood. In fact, the Jewish Commonwealth was numbered according to the years the Temple stood.

In the year 722 B.C.E., the Northern Kingdom was invaded and conquered by its neighbors farther north, the Assyrians. The land was resettled by the conquerors and the Ten Northern Tribes were all but gobbled up by foreign invaders, or "lost" as historians came to describe these ten tribes. The Temple, however, was not touched. Fortunately, it had been built in Jerusalem, which was part of the Southern Kingdom of Judea, as the territory of Judah and Benjamin was known.

But, as history reminds us over and over, nothing lasts forever. In 586 B.C.E., almost four hundred years after it was built, the first great Holy Temple was destroyed. The Babylonians to the east and the Assyrians to the north fought over this crossroads territory. The Babylonians won. They crushed the Judeans in their revolt for independence, utterly demolished the Temple, and, as was most common in those days, "resettled" all but the lowest strata of society. They left behind the poor, the marginals, the uneducated, the misfits, so that there would remain no significant human resources to muster in an attempt at rebuilding the vital, sacred, nerve center—the Temple.

A shattering loss. The absolute end of the First Jewish Commonwealth. In response, the religious leaders of the community established four fast days to commemorate the destruction of the first Temple:

The tenth of Tevet, when the siege of Jerusalem began.

The ninth of Tammuz when the walls were breached.

The ninth of Av when the Temple was sacked.

The third of Tishrei when Gedalia, the provisional governor of the remaining Jews in Jerusalem, was slain and the last Jews fled Judea.

Yet history also teaches us that as long as an idea lives, nothing is irreversible. Shortly after the exile, Judea changed hands again; the exiles were not only allowed to return, but were granted permission to rebuild the Holy Temple. Who would have believed that only seventy years after the Churban, the ultimate destruction and degradation, the second Holy Temple would be magnificently erected, the Second Jewish Commonwealth back in business?

And yet. Though History may be fickle, the Memory remains faithful. Even though the Second Commonwealth now flourished, and the Temple occupied as central a place as ever, no one saw fit to rescind the mourning for the Churban, and for those who had fallen.

The Second Commonwealth was even more stable than the first. It was a period rich in religious creativity: canonization of the Bible, the flowering of the oral tradition, the nourishment of sectarian ideas, and, as the end approached, the growth of messianic movements. Moreover, the Second Commonwealth lasted for almost six hundred years.

In 70 C.E., Jewish nationhood came to an end. This time, it was Rome and not Babylon. But the sequence was the same: an unsuccessful revolt by the Judeans, the siege of Jerusalem, the breach in the walls around the city, and finally the destruction of the Holy Temple. By strange coincidence, the dates were almost identical: the breach of the walls—the seventeenth of Tammuz; the sacking of the Temple—the ninth and tenth of Av. To these dates, then, was attached mourning for two destructions. The reason the seventeenth of Tammuz was chosen as a fast to mourn the breached walls, and not the ninth of Tammuz, when the first walls of Jerusalem were breached in 586 B.C.E., is that Churban II was considered a harsher, more permanent, more profound tragedy by generations that followed: more lives were lost, the Temple was never rebuilt, and the exile was to last nineteen hundred years.

How does one mourn for something that happened so long ago, much of whose bitterness has been muted by the return of modern Jews to Zion and Jerusalem? How does a community summon up distant pain? By reliving the event that was, by telling of it with clarity of detail as if it happened last year, by taking on other symbols of grief and mourning.

COMMEMORATION

To begin reliving the events, we start with the siege, on Asarah (tenth) B'Tevet. This day, which usually comes in January, is set aside as a minor fast, a daylight fast. That means that the fast begins as the sun rises and ends as it goes down. Some people rise very early in the dark hours of the morning to eat a good breakfast so as to make the fast easier. Moreover, since January daylight hours are short, Asarah B'Tevet is the shortest of all fasts. Many pre-Bar and -Bat Mitzvah children try their first full-day fast on Asarah B'Tevet.

Besides fasting, the only other deprivation on minor fast days is washing or bathing.

Special prayers are added to the regular liturgy. A special Torah reading known as Va'ye'chal (Exod. 32:11–14; 34:1–10) is recited on all fast days at both Shacharit and Minchah.

To all intents and purposes, the siege is put out of mind for the next few months. Then, as we near the date of destruction itself, the mourning begins again, slowly, steadily increasing in intensity until we reach the peak of anguish on the day of actual destruction.

This cycle begins with the minor fast of Shivah Asar B'Tammuz, the day on which the supposedly impenetrable walls around Jerusalem were penetrated and the enemy entered the city. It was the beginning of the end.

Between the Shivah Asar B'Tammuz and Tisha B'Av is a span of three weeks. During the Three Weeks, Jews do not celebrate weddings, play joyful music, dance, wear brand-new clothing, or get haircuts. Long hair in olden times was a sign of mourning. Some men do not shave during the Three Weeks, although many of those who go to business do shave. In Jewish summer camps, the local barber in the nearest town is usually brought to the campgrounds a day or two before the Three Weeks for wholesale clippings.

The latter part of the Three Weeks, from the first to the ninth of Av, is known as the Nine Days. The laws of deprivation and mourning intensify during the Nine Days:

No laundry, except that which is essential.

No swimming.

No eating meat or poultry, except on Shabbat or at a seudat mitzvah feast in honor of the performance of a mitzvah. Such occasions might be a siyyum (completing a tractate of the Talmud), a Brit, a Pidyon Haben, or a Bar Mitzvah that is celebrated on Monday or Thursday (when the Torah is read).

Likewise, there is no drinking of wine, except for Shabbat. Even the Havdalah wine, which is drunk after Shabbat has ended, is given to a child to drink.

Some people refrain from full showering or tub baths during the Nine Days.

The Nine Days should really be called the nine and a half days, since all of the above restrictions remain in effect until the middle of the tenth day of Av. Although the actual fast of Tisha B'Av (the ninth of Av) completes the mourning period, the other restrictions are observed an additional half day in commemoration of the fact that the Temple continued to burn and smolder through the tenth of Av.

The ban on swimming, coming as it usually does in summertime, can be a real deprivation. Summer-camp administrators and parents have their hands full if a heat wave strikes during the Nine Days. As Gary P., then age twelve, once remarked wistfully during the course of the Nine Days, "Why couldn't Nebuchadnezzar [the Babylonian king] have destroyed the Temple in the middle of January!" But, that is the law, and so the ban is widely observed in the Orthodox community.

Unlike other fasts connected to the Churban, Tisha B'Av is a major fast, not only in importance but in length of time. Tisha B'Av begins at sunset and lasts until sundown the following night. It is the longest, hottest, most difficult fast of the year. The custom is to eat a large meal before Minchah (midafternoon) on erev Tisha B'Av and then, just before sunset, to eat a small meal, the formal prefast meal (seudah mafseket). For this prefast meal, some follow the custom of eating a piece of bread and a hard-boiled egg, with the bread dipped into ashes.

During the fast itself, the same restrictions that apply to Yom Kippur apply here:

No eating or drinking.

No washing or bathing except for necessary washing (upon rising, or soiled hands, or after elimination).

No anointing (no cosmetics).

No wearing leather shoes.

No sexual relations.

There are two additional restrictions on Tisha B'Av that point up the distinction between a fast of mourning and one of atonement.

On Tisha B'Av, the Rabbis prohibited the study of Torah, except for the Book of Job and certain parts of the Prophets and Talmud directly related to the Churban. The reason is perfectly logical. Torah gladdens the soul, and Tisha B'Av is not the day for that.

The second unusual prohibition is that of greeting friends. Instead of a big hello or broad smile, we give a controlled nod of the head; or we start a conversation right off without the preliminary hello or how are you? This custom of restricted greeting is borrowed from shiva, where the mourners and guests do not formally greet each other (see chap. 14). It sounds as if it would be awkward, but generally it isn't terribly so, for everyone in the community understands the law and anticipates the modified behavior. For others with whom we work and live, our greetings are simply more subdued, and the difference is barely noticeable. One does not have to wear Tisha B'Av on one's sleeve unless one is so inclined.

Why should restricted greetings be a sign of mourning? It was only when I finally experienced the discomfort that I understood what the law was about. When Yitz and I were first married, we were closely affiliated with the Orthodox community in Brookline, Massachusetts. Subsequently, we moved to New York, but always returned to Gloucester, Massachusetts, for our summer vacations. The logical thing to do, since there was then no Tisha B'Av minyan in Gloucester, was to drive to Brookline, to our old shul. But it was a source of confusion for me. On the one hand,

I would be seeing friends whom we hadn't seen in a year. If it weren't Tisha B'Av, we would have thrown our arms about each other and hugged.

Even restraining our formal greeting, even talking in quiet tones, it was still like a great party to me, getting together each year with so many old friends. How wise the Rabbis were: law on restricted greeting is really the law against rejoicing. Instead of a global, "You shall not rejoice," which would be incomprehensible, they said, "You shall not do this little thing or make that small gesture." I never knew how much pleasure there is in greeting a friend until the Rabbis forbade it on Tisha B'Av.

The work prohibitions of Shabbat and Yom Tov are not in effect on Tisha B'Av. Yet, in the spirit of mourning, it is the tradition to restrict work activities somewhat. The law permits work in cases where refraining from work would entail a loss. Loss has been rather loosely defined to include salary, time, and momentum. Most Jews do work on Tisha B'Av, but some follow the tradition of not going to work until midday.

THE LITURGY

The synagogue services on the eve of Tisha B'Av are most unusual. To set the tone, the curtain covering the ark is removed or is replaced with a black curtain. Either way, the ark, and by extension the whole shul, looks bare. The lights are dimmed, a few candles are lit. The prayers are recited in a mournful tone.

After Maariv and Kaddish all the congregation move out of their pews and seat themselves on the floor or on the steps of the bimah. Some hold candles as they follow the reading of Eichah, the Book of Lamentations. The reader reads it in a mournful, weeping voice. He starts out very softly. With each chapter (there are five) the reader increases his volume. At the last sentence, the entire congregation joins in. We sing a poignant melody to the words, "Turn us to You, O Lord, and we will return. Renew our days as the days of old." Following Eichah, other lamentational prayers (Kinnot) about other tragedies in Jewish history are recited. The service concludes with another Kaddish, after which people disperse quickly and go home.

The Rabbis of ancient times set this scenario. One is tempted to say they were great stage managers, for even if you entered the shul lighthearted, and even if the burden lightens as soon as you leave, the experience in shul itself is weighty, sorrowful, and memory-laden. But the Rabbis weren't stage-managing anything. It was what they remembered, how they felt, and what they themselves did that became part of our tradition.

The first two chapters of Eichah in particular, describing the ravishing of the young girls of Jerusalem, the enslavement and exile of young innocents, and most gory of all, the starvation that led mothers to eat the flesh of their dead children, make my own flesh crawl, my stomach tighten, and my heart constrict in pain. A decade ago, when our own children began to enter the large world of Jewish memories, I dreaded each Tisha B'Av, when, one by one, they would begin to understand those words and ask about such horrible things.

At the morning service, men do not don tefillin or tallit, just as an onen, a newly bereaved person, refrains from doing so until after the burial of his relative. By midafternoon the sacred Temple has been sacked, the Commonwealth buried, and so, men don their tefillin and tallit for Minchah.

During Shacharit, there are three aliyot from Deuteronomy (4:25–40), after which the third person reads a selection from Jeremiah (8:13–9:23). The Torah and Haftorah are chanted in the same mournful melody as Eichah. There are additional special prayers, such as Anenu, Answer us, answer us, O God, on this day of our sorrow.

Minchah, too, is unusual if only because it is the only time during the year that men wear tefillin in the afternoon. But there are also special prayers of comfort (Nachem), as well as the Va'ye'chal Torah reading that is recited on all fast days. After the Six Day War and the reunification of Jerusalem in 1967, the ancient Nachem prayer was emended by the Israeli rabbinate to reflect this miracle in our times. Some congregations in America have adopted the emended version, which seems most appropriate.

WHY FAST?

Why fast? What does fasting really achieve? It is altogether possible to remember and grieve without it. And perhaps one could even say the reverse. Sometimes fasting on a difficult fast day takes our mind away from the larger thing and brings it to light on thoughts of food. I remember one August afternoon several years ago, J.J.'s first full Tisha B'Av fast. He was then almost thirteen, almost six feet tall, and consuming almost five thousand calories on a normal day—and still you could count every rib from five feet away.

That afternoon, J.J. was stretched out on the living-room couch and was writing something on a pad. As I passed through the room, I asked, "What are you doing, J.?" "Just making a list for myself." I didn't think to ask what the list was about, since J.J. is the world's all-time master list-maker. An hour or two later, I passed through the living room again and J.J. was fast asleep, paper and pen on his chest. The list was entitled, "What to Eat After Tisha B'Av Is Over."

Three slices of rye bread, thick with butter
Two bagels and cream cheese—lots of cream cheese
Two glasses of milk—large-size glass
Bananas . . .

And so the list went. Obviously, the poor kid was famished. Thoughts of the Churban were the furthest thing from his mind that afternoon. I knew that he was probably dreaming of food. It reminded me of my own late-afternoon hours of a fast as I mentally rummage the refrigerator shelves.

Why fast? After all, the Jews have returned to their homeland, Jerusalem is reunited, the Third Commonwealth is strong, despite its problems. Why fast?

Because fasting is a tangible symbol of grief, of mourning, of suffering. Fasting focuses the memory onto the event, it heightens empathy for the martyrs. It sharpens the feelings of identity, not only with the traumatized Jerusalemites of old, but with the loving, memory-rich community of the present.

Fasting, then, and the feelings of grief it crystallizes are a testimony to the power of memory. Through the process of remembering, we can never let ourselves become reconciled to defeat and destruction. What does that really mean? It means that somewhere in the recesses of the mind we understand that we can build atop the ruins. Memory is protest, memory is activism, memory is the incredible power to turn grief and destruction into hope. Not to remember, not to relive, not to retell, not to mourn, not to feel pain, is to be finally and ultimately defeated —and not the other way around.

In the summer of 1979, we were all in Jerusalem on Tisha B'Av. We had gone to the Kotel, the Western Wall, for the evening prayers. The men in our family were on one side of the mechitza (the divider), the women on the other. We—Deborah, Goody, two sisters-in-law, and I—sat on the hard stone floor in a small group encircled around an American rebbetzin who read Eichah for us. She read it beautifully, with a wailing voice, and full of emotion. But for me the mood was continually broken as her PR person and camerawoman kept taking pictures of her. A few times I felt a pang of sadness at her words, but for the most part I could not get into the spirit of things. I felt like a Dr. Jekyll and Mr. Hyde. Someone near us would begin crying, and I would hear the rebbetzin cry, and feel like following suit. And then a moment later the camera would whir or click, an old friend would pass by, some beautiful, young, healthy Jewish child would scramble up the grassy side bank, my eye would catch sight of the broad stones of the wall—and I would feel like throwing my head back and laughing with joy.

Afterward, on the large stone plaza far back of the Kotel, our family regrouped. We walked very leisurely to the exit, seeing old friends whom we hadn't seen in a long while. I loved every minute of it. Where was my anguish? It was nowhere to be found.

The next morning, we went off again to the Kotel. I detached myself for a few moments and went off quietly to do that which an Orthodox Jew is not permitted to do—to go up to the area of the Temple mount where a great mosque now stands. Despite my prayers about Temple sacrifice, I have never been able to get myself to imagine or long passionately for restoration of the Temple service. But standing there a moment in the hot wind, and in a hostile environment, I felt a sadness and void wash over me. How shortsighted and passive our people were, not to have reclaimed that holy spot in the second century or the third century or the fifth century or the eighth century—before it was too late. How sad there was no magnificent edifice of our own there.

Surely there must have been a wedge at some time, in some person, in some benevolent ruler other than Emperor Julian, who gave permission to rebuild the Temple in the fourth century but died before it could be effected. Could there be, rotting in hell, some rich, third-century Italian Jew who was asked to contribute to the rebuilding of the Temple, but who refused the opportunity of a lifetime, of a thousand lifetimes?

Two minutes later, I went back down to the Kotel, to my people, and all thoughts of what could have been were swiftly banished.

Later that afternoon, we had all planned to return to the Kotel a third time, for Minchah and Maariv, but I fell asleep. No one wanted to wake me, so they left without me. I awoke in due time, and sped out to the Kotel in a taxi, to arrive just at the end of Minchah, when the men were peeling off and wrapping up their tefillin.

There were thousands and thousands of people—old people, babies, teenagers in olive green, young singles, large extended families. Some were praying, some were watching, some were waiting. A few curious birds flew overhead, trying to decipher human mating calls. The afternoon sun was beginning to give off its golden glow against the walls. Suddenly, the fatigue, the hunger, were out of my mind. As I made my way through the crowds, searching for my two daughters, I said to myself, How beautiful, how vibrant, how incredibly lucky we are. Why I would fast a hundred days just to be where I am right now! I would fast a thousand fasts of Tisha B'Av so that my husband and sons and daughters could be somewhere in this crowd, on this day, at this ancient wall, in Jerusalem.

And that is exactly what had happened. My ancestors kept the Jerusalem watch for me. It was only through their longing and their fasts that I was privileged to see this in my lifetime. It was only because they felt so much anguish on this day that I could feel so much joy. It was their shattering of a glass that intruded the destroyed Temple into every joyous wedding; their ruling to leave every new home with a spot unfinished—zecher le Churban, in memory of the destruction; their willingness to say, a billion times over, since the day of destruction, "If I forget thee, O Jerusalem, let my right hand wither." . . .

Can I do any less?

AFTERWORD

As the reader has probably noticed, there has not been a great deal of talk about God in this book—a serious defect, which opens me up to the classical criticism about traditional Jews: that they are ritualistic, consumed with picayune details and not with larger matters of spirit and faith.

But I think it misses the whole point of halacha, for halacha is nothing if not a faith principle. In its very essence, it is an expression and a channel of love. The bottom line is this: we observe halacha because God commanded us. To act and to do, it seems to me, is at least as high a form of faith as to say, "I love" and "I believe."

That is how we must understand what the Jewish people have done since Sinai. Take kashrut, for example, a code of law we are told to observe without being given any rational reason except, perhaps, that amorphous quality of holiness. In developing halacha around the Biblical laws of kashrut, with layer upon layer of tradition, the Rabbis went way beyond the original revelation concerning forbidden and permitted categories. They did this because they felt it to be a voluntary expression of love, faith, and trust in God; they were not content merely to obey the explicitly commanded. Thus, in and of itself, ritual is a vehicle of love and faith.

Second, the whole of Jewish practice testifies to our belief that we fill a special role as God's Chosen People. Observance of halacha has always been one of the powerful ties that binds us to each other and strengthens this collective sense of oneness. Unity means nothing more and nothing less than a thousand shared memories, shared experiences, shared actions.

Third, halacha—ritual, a traditional way of life—serves another function. I speak not of the salvific function of law, that is, scurrying around like busy little bees, consumed with ritual, in the hope of getting into God's good graces. Rather, I speak of the very human function of halacha—how to walk through life with some moral anchors and a modicum of dignity, goodness, restraint, and purpose.

Rava, the great Talmudist, taught: At the end of a person's life, he or she is brought to the heavenly throne. God, too, has His questions, very specific ones at that: "Were you honest in your dealings with others? Did you set aside regular times for study of Torah? Did you occupy yourself with building a family? Did you look forward to redemption? . . . (SHABBAT 31A).

This is what one might call the examined life. To be able to answer yes at the end of our days—that is what living a traditional Jewish way of life is all about.

RECIPES *

Challah

2 envelopes dry yeast
½ cup lukewarm water
2 cups boiling water
¼ cup vegetable oil
2 tsp. salt
2 tsp. sugar
2 eggs, beaten
7 to 8 cups flour, depending on atmospheric conditions
    that day

In a small bowl, combine yeast and lukewarm water. Allow to stand about 5 to 10 minutes to work.

In larger bowl, put in boiling water. Add oil, salt, and sugar, and stir until sugar is dissolved. Cool mixture to lukewarm and then add the yeast mixture. Add beaten eggs (reserving 2 tablespoons of egg mixture for brushing loaves before baking). Add approximately 3 to 4 cups of flour and stir, to make a smooth

---

*These recipes were all contributed by my mother, Sylvia Genauer. She calls them her "plain, basic" holiday recipes. I call them "kosher gourmet."

batter. Then add remaining flour to make a dough that is smooth and elastic and manageable. Knead dough for a few minutes. Shape into a ball and grease entire surface of dough lightly with oil and place in a greased mixing bowl. Cover with clean cloth, and set in warm (not hot) place until dough rises to double in bulk (approximately 2 to 3 hours). Knead again, and divide into two even balls to make two challot.

Now "take challah"—remove a small piece of dough, the size of an olive, and throw into the oven, making appropriate prayer:

בָּרוּךְ אַתָּה יְיָ, אֱלֹהֵינוּ מֶלֶךְ הָעוֹלָם, אֲשֶׁר קִדְּשָׁנוּ בְּמִצְוֹתָיו, וְצִוָּנוּ לְהַפְרִישׁ חַלָּה.

Baruch ata Adonai Elohainu melech ha'olam, asher kidshanu b'mitzvotav v'tzivanu lehafrish challah.

Blessed are You, Lord our God, Ruler of the universe, Who has sanctified us with His commandments, and has commanded us to separate challah.

Cut each ball into 3 pieces. Roll each piece into a long strip, slightly tapered at the ends. Press the top 3 ends together and start braiding the challah until the end, and press the bottom ends together. Prepare the second loaf in the same way. Place the 2 challot on a greased baking sheet, or in 2 bread loaf pans, 9 x 5 x 3 inches (greased). Set in warm (not hot) place away from drafts. Cover with clean dish towel and allow to rise to double the bulk. For a crispy crust, add a spoonful of water to the reserved egg and brush onto the loaves. Sprinkle with sesame or poppy seeds—if desired. If you desire a soft crust, brush loaves with melted margarine. Bake in hot oven (400°) about 10 minutes. Then reduce heat to moderate (350°) and continue baking about 30 to 40 minutes, until desired brownness.

If you bake challot in loaf pans, remove them from pans immediately when they come out of the oven, and place them on a rack.

Gefilte Fish

4 lbs. ground fish: pike, whitefish, pickerel, and carp are
  the popular varieties
4 onions
3 carrots
3 stalks celery
About 2 qts. water
3 large eggs
3 tbs. matzah meal (and if too loose, you may add a
  little more)
Salt and pepper to taste
1 tsp. sugar (optional in both broth and fish)

Have fishman fillet and grind your fish. Take home the bones, skin, and head for the broth. Clean bones, skin, and head well, and salt.

Into a large kettle, place cleaned heads, skin, and bones, 2 sliced onions, 2 carrots, 2 stalks of celery, salt and pepper to taste, and sugar if desired. Cover with 2 quarts of water. Cover pot and bring to boil.

Using processor or grinder, grind 2 onions, 1 carrot, and 1 stalk of celery, and mix with ground fish. Season to taste with salt and pepper, and a spoonful of sugar, if desired. Turn into a mixing bowl, add ¼ cup of cold water, and keep blending the entire mixture. Then add the eggs, one at a time, and keep blending. Finally, add the matzah meal to make a nice consistency that you can handle. Check seasonings here. Wet hands with cold water, and shape round balls or elongated ones by rolling from hand to hand. Make size of balls depending on whether fish is to be main course or the appetizer. Drop each ball into the boiling broth *carefully*. The balls should not break when you drop them into the water. If one does, add a little more matzah meal to the remaining batter and blend. And then continue. Bring the pot back to boil, cover, then turn heat to low and simmer for about 1½ hours. Check the water from time to time to see that the pot isn't dry.

When done, allow fish to cool before removing onto a tray. Remove the carrots to use for garnishing. Then pour the rest of the liquid through a sieve, so that you can have a clear broth to serve with the fish, if desired. Serve hot or cold, with horse-radish.

Rena's Favorite Recipe— Hamantashen

Preheat oven to 365°

Dough

3½ cups flour
1 cup sugar
1 tsp. baking powder
Dash salt
1 cup melted Crisco
3 eggs, beaten
¼ cup orange juice
Rind of 1 lemon

Filling

2 lbs. prune lekvar or apricot lekvar

Add to it:

Juice of 1 lemon
½ cup chopped walnuts
Rind of 1 orange
1 or 2 tbs. bread crumbs (to make lekvar drier)

Make dough by blending all the ingredients. Roll out on floured board until nice and thin. Cut out 2-inch rounds with open end of glass. Fill with lekvar recipe. Fold up 3 sides to make a tricorn. You can either leave center open or seal the dough completely. The open ones look prettier.

Bake on greased cookie sheet, at 365°, for 25 to 30 minutes, until done as desired.

(Purim) Hamantashen— Dairy or Parve

Preheat oven to 375°

Dough

4 cups flour
2 tsp. baking powder
½ tsp. salt
1 cup butter or margarine
1½ cups sugar
2 eggs
4 tbs. orange juice or pineapple juice
¼ cup club soda or seltzer water
1 tsp. vanilla

Filling

2 lbs. lekvar

Add to it:

Juice of ½ lemon and rind of 1 lemon
½ cup chopped walnuts
½ peeled, grated apple

Blend flour, baking powder, and salt. Cream shortening and sugar. Add eggs. Add flour mixture to creamed mixture, alternately with liquids. Add vanilla. If dough is too loose, add more flour.

Roll dough to ⅛ inch to ¼ inch thickness. Cut dough with open end of glass to make two-inch circles.

Place mound of filling in each 2-inch round. Pinch dough up on 3 sides to form a triangle. Place on greased cookie sheet and bake until lightly browned, about 40 to 45 minutes.

Tzimmes for Shabbat or Rosh Hashanah

¼ cup margarine
6 to 8 carrots, sliced
3 sweet potatoes, chunked or sliced in 1-inch rounds
3 peeled, sliced apples
¼ cup brown sugar
A minimum of salt
Water to cover all

Cook in covered pot over low flame, for 1 to 1½ hours. You may add honey for Rosh Hashanah, or at any time. You can vary this recipe by adding some dried apricots, or a few prunes or whatever you fancy.

Carrot Cake

(Good any time; also for Rosh Hashanah)

¾ cup oil
½ cup brown sugar
1 beaten egg

Add:

1¼ cups flour
½ tsp. salt
1 tsp. baking soda
1¼ tsp. baking powder
1 tsp. cinnamon

Add:

1 tbs. water
1 tbs. lemon juice
4 medium grated carrots (approx. 1½ cups)
(Mixture should be moist but not drippy)

Bake in small, round mold pan with open center at 350° for 40 to 45 minutes. The mold should be lightly greased.

Potato Kugel for 5 to 6

5 large Russet potatoes, peeled and grated
1 onion, grated
2 eggs (3, if small)
⅓ cup oil
Salt and pepper to taste
2 tbs. matzah meal

Peel and grate potatoes—add grated onion. (All this can be done easily in a processor using the chopping blade rather than the grating one.)

Add eggs and beat well, and then add oil, salt, pepper, and matzah meal.

Pour into well-greased casserole pot and bake at 400° for at least 1 hour (usually, about 1 hour and 15 minutes).

Tsholent for 8 to 10 People as a Side Dish

(If you want to use this as a main course for 6 people, increase the amount of meat)

1¼ cups large lima beans
½ cup red kidney beans
1 cup barley
1½ to 2 lbs. flanken
3 large potatoes, in large chunks
Coarse salt to taste
Pepper to taste
3 tbs. brown sugar
1 tsp. minced garlic
Paprika for color

Check over lima beans, red kidney beans, and barley for any rotten beans. Discard those. Wash all beans and barley very well. Place in a large pot or Dutch oven. Cut up flanken and put into pot. Then fill with water to cover, with about 2 inches above the ingredients. Bring to a boil, and skim off the scum. Cover and cook for 1 hour, at medium heat. Add the potatoes which have been cut into chunks. Now cut heat down to very low and allow to cook for four or five hours on top of stove. When you put your tin on the stove for Shabbat, you place your finished tsholent on a hot spot and leave it for Shabbat. It will stay hot and won't spoil since the tsholent will already be cooked. The trick is to keep it hot but not cooking.

Method #2

Another method is to cook the tsholent on the top of the stove for 1 hour, add the potatoes, and cook for another ¾ hour, and then place in oven at 275° for the rest of Shabbat. Do not stir tsholent, either on top of the stove or in the oven.

Method #3

Place all the ingredients in an electric Crock Pot, cover with water, the same as recipe #1. Turn to Automatic, which will start the Crock Pot; it will adjust itself to simmer even though the arrow will still be pointing to Automatic.

Cheese Blintzes (Crepes) for Shavuot

Leaves

1 cup flour
1 tsp. salt
1½ cups milk or water
3 eggs

Filling

4 to 5 packages farmer cheese 2–2½ lbs.

Add to it:

2 egg yolks beaten
1 tbs. butter
1 tbs. sugar
Pinch salt
¼ tsp. vanilla

Prepare leaves first. Place flour in bowl, add ½ teaspoon salt. Make a well, then gently add liquid into well, a little at a time, and draw flour into liquid. Keep stirring, until all flour is absorbed with liquid, and batter has no lumps. Then add eggs, which have been lightly beaten. Mixture should be light, smooth, and more to the watery side.

Use 7-inch frying pan. I use the Wear-Ever SilverStone frying pan, which is excellent for blintzes and crepes, as the batter never sticks to its bottom. Heat the frying pan over moderate flame, using very little butter. Pour about 2 tablespoons of the batter into pan, and shake it around to cover the entire bottom. Place the pan on the burner. You will see the sides of the leaf getting a little dry. Flip leaf onto a clean dish towel so that the bottom side is on top. Grease pan with paper towel pad each time before pouring in batter for leaves. Continue making each leaf separately, and turn them onto a clean towel. CAUTION: each leaf only takes about a minute, so don't leave the stove.

When all the leaves are made, place the cheese filling on one end of each leaf, and start rolling the dough over the cheese. Then fold over sides, and continue rolling until you have a blintz, neatly sealed. Place them on a buttered dinner plate until you are ready to fry them. Heat oil in pan, turn to moderate heat, and place blintzes in to fry, turning once to brown. Remove and serve hot.

Noodle Pudding with Cheese for Shavuot

This is a good substitute for blintzes on Shavuot, and much easier to make.

½ lb. fine or medium noodles, cooked
1 lb. farmer cheese
½ lb. cream cheese
¼ cup unsalted margarine or butter
¾ cup sugar
1 cup sour cream
3 eggs
1 tsp. salt
1 tsp. vanilla

Combine all ingredients and bake in greased oblong pan. (I use a foil pan.) Cook at 350° for 1 hour.

Salt and Pepper Noodle Ring for Shabbat

½ lb. cooked fine noodles
3 eggs
3 tbs. oil
Salt and pepper to taste

Cook noodles in salted water, for about 8 minutes. Drain in colander. Beat eggs and add to noodles. Add oil, and salt and pepper to taste.

Bake in greased kugel pot or baking dish for 1 hour, in moderate oven, 350°–375°.

Sweet Noodle Pudding

(Also to be used as side dish for Shabbat)

½ lb. cooked noodles, fine or medium
2 tbs. oil
3 eggs, separated
1 cup sugar
3 peeled, sliced apples
¼ cup raisins
1 tsp. cinnamon
½ tsp. vanilla

Add oil to cooked noodles. Add egg yolks, sugar, and other ingredients. Beat egg whites stiff, and fold into mixture. Bake in greased pan or round casserole dish at 375° for 45 minutes, or until done.

Sponge Cake

(This is my special first recipe—and I am still making the same one after forty-nine years of marriage)

Preheat oven to 350°

1½ cups flour
1½ tsp. baking powder
Dash of salt
6 eggs, separated
1½ cups sugar
½ cup very cold orange juice or water
1 tsp. vanilla

Sift the flour, baking powder, and salt several times. In a very dry bowl, beat egg whites with half of the sugar until stiff but not dry. (Beaters, too, should be absolutely dry!) Set bowl aside.

Beat egg yolks with remainder of sugar. Gently add flour alternately with orange juice or water until all are blended. Fold in egg whites by hand, into yolk mixture—gently, until all is blended. Blend in vanilla.

Pour into spring tube pan, 10 x 4 inches, which must be dry: *no grease*. Tap pan lightly on floor to release any air bubbles. Place in moderate oven at 350° for 50 to 55 minutes. Test by pressing index finger gently on top. If it springs back, the cake is ready. Don't let the cake get too brown on top, as that will also dry up the sponginess. Turn cake upside down, immediately, and allow to cool on cake rack. When cool, loosen cake with a knife, going all around; then unspring sides of baking pan. You can then run a knife under the bottom of the sponge cake, and you can remove the cake. If you are using a regular tube pan, which I use, you have to turn the cake upside down immediately and cool the cake. Loosen the cake with a knife, going all around, while keeping the knife close to the side of the pan and going down to the bottom of the pan. If you use a cut of brown paper to fit on the bottom of the tube pan, the cake will also be easier to take out. You can use this recipe for strawberry short-cake or any other cake you want to layer with fruit.

Chicken Soup

3 qts. water
3–4 lbs. chicken
3 ribs celery
2 or 3 carrots
1 parsnip
1 root
1 leek or 1 onion
2 sprigs dill (optional)
Salt and pepper to taste

Clean chicken well. Place all ingredients in a 5-quart pot. Cover with cold water and allow to come to boil over moderate heat. Skim the scum and foam that rises to the top as the soup boils. Then turn down the heat to simmer. Cover pot and simmer for 1½ to 2 hours. Taste for seasoning. Remove chicken from soup. Add sprigs of dill for 3 to 5 minutes—no longer—and remove dill immediately from soup. If you don't like dill, the soup will be as delicious without it.

Knaidlach for Chicken Soup

4 eggs
1 tsp. salt
Dash of pepper
½ cup water
⅓ cup melted shortening
1 cup matzah meal

Stir eggs lightly with fork. Add salt, pepper, water, and melted shortening. Stir in matzah meal. Place in refrigerator for 15 minutes or longer, if desired. Make balls; drop them into 2 quarts of boiling water, to which 1 tablespoon of salt has been added. Cook for about 20 minutes; remove from water when done.

Stuffed Cabbage for Sukkot, Simchat Torah, or Whenever

12 to 15 large leaves of cabbage
1½ lbs. freshly ground beef
1 medium onion, grated, or 2 sautéed onions
⅓ cup uncooked rice, selected and washed
Salt and pepper to taste

There are 3 methods for softening cabbage leaves. *One:* pour boiling water over a cored cabbage; water should cover the top of the cabbage. Cover, and allow to soak for 15 minutes. *Two:* Shortcut. Cut out core of cabbage. Place in freezer for *at least* 24 hours. When cabbage defrosts, (allow several hours), the leaves will be pliable and ready to stuff. *Three:* Core cabbage, remove leaves, steam in a colander over boiling water for several minutes, until leaves are pliable enough to roll.

Now here are two sauces in which to cook the cabbage:

Sauce #1

2 large diced onions, melted in
⅔ cup brown sugar. Add
2 cans tomato sauce (16 oz.)
1 can of water
2 tbs. lemon juice
Handful of raisins, if desired

Bring to a boil. Season if necessary, with additional salt and/or lemon juice.

(This sauce is also good for sweet-and-sour meat balls.)

Sauce #2

1 10-oz. bottle of ketchup
2 large cans whole cranberry sauce

Bring to boil in a wide-bottomed pot.

Combine the chopped meat, onion, and rice. Salt and pepper to taste. Place meat filling in cored end of leaf. Roll up once until meat is covered, then fold over the sides, and continue rolling to end of leaf, tucking in all edges.

Place some leftover leaves on bottom of dutch oven or large pot. Pour sauce into large pot. Place the stuffed cabbage in pot.

Make sure the sauce covers the stuffed cabbage. Turn the heat to moderate, and, when the cabbage begins to cook, turn down to simmer. Allow to cook approximately 1½ to 2 hours. Check to see that sauce doesn't boil out. If necessary, add more sauce and seasonings.

GLOSSARY

ALIYAH 1. the honor of being called up to the Torah to recite a blessing; 2. each one of the seven parts of the weekly Torah portion.

AMIDAH a prayer of benedictions recited silently and in a standing position; the central part of the prayer service.

AVEL a mourner, one who observes Jewish laws of mourning for a deceased family member.

BA'AL TEFILA one who leads the congregational prayer service.

BENTSCHEN (Yiddish) recitation of Grace After Meals.

BET DIN Jewish court of law guided by principles of halacha; three males preside.

BET MEDRASH (or beis medrash) the study hall of the synagogue.

BESAMIM spices, used in the Havdalah service marking the conclusion of the Sabbath.

BIMAH 1. the front platform of the synagogue where the ark containing the Torah stands; 2. the platform which contains the Torah reading table.

BIRKAT HAMAZON the Grace After Meals.

B'RACHOT blessings and benedictions.

CHAG 1. a holiday; 2. the three pilgrimage festivals: Pesach, Shavuot, Sukkot.

CHALLAH 1. the braided ceremonial bread used for the Sabbath and festivals; 2. the law concerning removal of a piece of dough for consecration.

CHASIDIM   1. members of a religious and mystical revival movement;   2. sectarian Jews who follow the leadership of a charismatic rabbi, known as a rebbe.

CHAZZAN   the cantor or prayer leader of the synagogue or services.

CHEVRA KADISHA   the society or fellowship which performs the tasks of burying the dead in accordance with Jewish law.

CHOL HAMOED   the intermediate days of a festival.

CHUKKIM   Jewish ritual laws for which no specific reason is given for their observance.

DAAVEN   the Yiddish term meaning to pray.

ERUV   1. the general term for several types of rabbinic enactment intended to promote the sanctity of the Sabbath;   2. the symbolic boundary around a town which encloses and transforms it into a private domain, thereby permitting one to carry objects within the circumference on the Sabbath.

ERUV TAVSHILIN   a safeguard to the sanctity of the Sabbath which allows cooking preparations for the Sabbath to be done on a festival day which falls the day before the Sabbath.

ETROG   a citron; one of the four species used ritually on Sukkot.

GELILA   rolling the Torah scroll closed and replacing its covering and ornaments.

GEMARA   the larger section of the Talmud consisting of interpretation and discussions of the Mishnah.

GET   a writ of Jewish divorce.

HAGALAH   kashering a utensil by immersion in boiling water.

HAGBAH   raising the Torah scroll aloft in an open position for the congregation to see.

HALACHA   Jewish law; the Jewish way of life (halachic: of halacha).

HALACHOT   laws of Jewish tradition; laws of a ritual or ethical nature.

HAMOTZI   the blessing recited before eating the bread.

HAVDALAH   the ritual service marking the end of the Sabbath or a holy day.

HOSHANOT   the prayers recited on Sukkot during the circuits around the synagogue, carrying the lulav and etrog in hand.

KABBALAT SHABBAT   the opening section of the Friday-evening service, the prayer service which ushers in the Sabbath.

KADDISH   the mourner's prayer.

KASHER   the act of making kosher, as in preparing raw meat or purifying a utensil.

KASHRUT   laws or system of dietary laws of Judaism.

KAVANNAH   awareness and intention of preparing for and performing rituals; also, concentration as in prayer.

KEDUSHA   the holiness passage; part of the repetition of the nineteen benedictions; recited only with a minyan.

KEPAH   a skullcap worn as a covering of the head.

KRIAH   the act of making a tear in the garment of a mourner.

KIDDUSH   the sanctification prayer proclaiming the holiness of Sabbath or holidays; recited over a cup of wine.

KOHEN   a Jew of priestly descent; a descendant of the house of Aaron the High Priest.

KOSHER   1. permissible to be eaten according to Jewish dietary laws.   2. an act performed on an item prepared in accordance with Jewish law.

K'VOD HAMET   the Jewish principle of honoring the dead.

LASHON HARA   speaking evil of someone when he or she is not present.

LEVI   tribe that assisted the priests in the Temple and all descendants thereof.

LIBUN   kashering by application of a direct flame.

MAARIV   the evening prayer service.

MAFTIR   the final section of the weekly Torah portion.

MECHITZA   the divider set up between the men and women in an Orthodox synagogue.

MEGILLAH   a parchment scroll, generally referring to the Book of Esther.

MELAVEH MALKA   a festive meal conducted after the end of the Sabbath.

ME'SHEH'BAY'RACH   a prayer for a sick friend or relative recited during the Torah reading.

MEZUMAN   an invitation to recite the Grace After Meals in the presence of three or more adult Jewish males.

MEZUZAH   a parchment scroll inscribed with the first two paragraphs of the Shema, and placed on the doorposts in one's home.

MIKVAH   the ritual bath used for purification purposes.

MINCHAH   the afternoon prayer.

MINYAN   a quorum of ten or more men constituting a spiritual congregation.

MISHNAH   a part of the Talmud, primarily consisting of rabbinic law; the Mishnah is divided into six orders.

MITZVAH   1. commandment from the Bible or the rabbinic tradition;   2. a good deed.

MUKTZEH   objects which are forbidden to be handled on Sabbaths and festivals.

NE'ILAH   the closing prayer of the Yom Kippur service.

NEROT   candles used to usher in or out the Sabbath and holidays; the mitzvah of lighting the ritual candles.

ONEG SHABBAT   a Shabbat gathering.

PARSHAH   the weekly portion of the Torah. The Torah is divided into fifty-four portions.

PARVE (also spelled pareve)   a Yiddish term for food which contains neither meat nor dairy products.

PASUK   a Biblical verse.

PESUKAI DEZIMRA   a collection of hymns from Psalms recited daily at the beginning of the morning service.

PIDYON HABEN   the act of redeeming the firstborn son of his mother.

ROSH CHODESH   the first of each month according to the lunar calendar.

SEFIRAT HA'OMER   the ritual of counting the days from Passover to Shavuot.

SELICHOT (Selicha—singular)   the penitential prayers.

SHABBAT/SHABBOS   the holy Sabbath.

SHABBOSDIK   in the spirit of the Sabbath day.

SHACHARIT   the morning prayer service.

SHALIACH TZIBBUR   one who leads the prayer service in a synagogue or minyan.

SHECHITTA   the act of ritual slaughter; also the laws pertaining to.

SHEHAKOL   the blessing said over certain foods and all beverages other than wine.

SHEHECHEYANU   the blessing recited in thanksgiving for certain acts or celebrations or experiences as they are enjoyed for the first time.

SHEMA, SHEMA YISRAEL   the central creed of Judaism; the affirmation of faith and belief in one God.

SHIVA   the first seven days of mourning.

SHMONEH ESREH   the eighteen (nineteen) benedictions; the central prayer of each of the three daily services, recited silently.

SHOCHET   one who is trained in the laws and performance of ritual slaughter.

SHOMER   one who keeps watch over the dead body until the funeral.

SHTAR PITURIN   a rabbinic document signifying that the woman has been divorced and is free to remarry.

SHUL (Yiddish)   synagogue.

SIMCHAT HABAT   a ceremony for celebrating the birth of a daughter.

SOFER   a scribe occupied in writing religious books and documents which are valid only if written by hand.

TAHARAH   the purification and preparation of a dead body by washing.

TAHARAT HAMISHPACHAH   the laws of ritual purity between husband and wife.

TALLIT   the prayer shawl.

TEFILLIN   phylacteries, worn by males for morning prayer.

TESHUVAH   the act of repentance.

TORAH   1. the five books of Moses;   2. the sacred texts of Judaism.

TREFEH   unfit for kosher use.

TZEDAKAH   charity; righteousness.

TZITZIT   a four-cornered garment with fringes.

YARMULKE   a skullcap worn as a headcovering.

YESHIVA   an academy for the study of the Torah.

ZEMIROT   songs sung during the Sabbath and festival meals.

SELECTED BIBLIOGRAPHY FOR A HOME LIBRARY

Below is a relatively short list of books that includes some of the classics. For a larger and more comprehensive bibliography, write to JWB Jewish Book Council, 15 East Twenty-sixth Street, New York, NY 10010.

I. The Basics

The Holy Scriptures: The Torah, the Prophets, The Writings. Philadelphia: Jewish Publication Society, 1982.

The Pentateuch and Haftorahs. Hertz, J. H., ed. London: Soncino Press, 1970.

The Soncino Books of the Bible. Cohen, A., ed. London: Soncino Press, 1947 and following.

Mishnayoth (The Mishnah). Blackman, Phillip, ed. London: Mishna Press, 1951.

The Babylonian Talmud. Hebrew-English ed. London: Soncino Press. Thus far, twelve volumes have been issued.

Ha-Siddur Ha-Shalem (Daily Prayerbook). Birnbaum, P., ed. New York: Hebrew Publishing Company, 1949.

The Mahzor: High Holiday Prayerbook. 1951 ed.; *Prayerbook for Three Festivals.* 1971 ed. Birnbaum, P., ed. Hebrew Publishing Company.

The Haggadah. There are scores of excellent Passover Haggadahs available. One should select an edition that is aesthetically tasteful and contains generous commentary on the text.

In addition to the traditional commentaries on the Bible, I would also recommend *The Torah: A Modern Commentary.* Plaut, Gunther, ed. New York: Union of American Hebrew Congregations, 1982.

II. Rabbinic Anthologies

Goldin, Judah. *The Living Talmud.* New York: New American Library, 1955.

Herford, R. Travers. *The Ethics of the Talmud: Sayings of the Fathers.* New York: Schocken Books, 1962.

Montefiore, C. G., and Loewe, H. *A Rabbinic Anthology.* New York: Schocken Books, 1960.

III. Jewish Philosophy

Belkin, Samuel. *In His Image: The Jewish Philosophy of Man as Expressed in Rabbinic Tradition.* New York: Abelard-Schuman, 1960.

Berkovits, Eliezer. *God, Man and History.* New York: Jonathan David, 1963.

Fackenheim, Emil. *God's Presence in History.* New York: The New York University Press, 1970.

Heschel, Abraham J. *God in Search of Man.* Philadelphia: Jewish Publication Society, 1955.

Rackman, Emanuel. *One Man's Judaism.* New York: Philosophical Library, 1970.

Schwartz, Leo. *Great Ages and Ideas of the Jewish People.* New York: Random House, 1956.

Soloveitchick, Joseph. *Reflections of the Rav.* Edited by Abraham Besdin. Jerusalem: Department for Torah Education and Culture, World Zionist Organization, 1979.

Twersky, Isadore, ed. *A Maimonides Reader.* New York: Behrman House, 1972.

Wouk, Herman. *This Is My God.* New York: Doubleday, 1959.

IV. Jewish Wisdom

Buber, Martin. *Tales of the Hasidim.* 2 vols. New York: Schocken Books, 1947.

Klagsbrun, Francine. *Voices of Wisdom.* New York: Schocken Books, 1980.

V. Contemporary Guides to Jewish Observance

Donin, Hayim Halevy. *To Be a Jew. A Guide to Jewish Observance in Contemporary Life.* New York: Basic Books. 1972.

Kitov, A. E. *The Jew and His Home.* New York: Shengold, 1963.

Klein, Isaac. *A Guide to Jewish Religious Practice.* New York: The Jewish Theological Seminary of America, 1979.

Seigel, Strassfeld and Strassfeld. *The First Jewish Catalogue.* Philadelphia: Jewish Publication Society, 1973.

Trepp, Leo. *The Complete Book of Jewish Observance.* New York: Behrman House/Summit Books, 1980.

VI. Prayer

Derovan, David. *Prayer.* New York: Yavneh Studies, 1970.

Donin, Hayim Halevy. *To Pray as a Jew.* New York: Basic Books, 1980.

Millgram, Abraham. 1971. *Jewish Worship*. Philadelphia: Jewish Publication Society, 1971.

Petuchowski, Jacob. *Understanding Jewish Prayer*. New York: Ktav, 1972.

VII. The Holidays

Agnon, S. Y. *Days of Awe*. New York: Schocken Books, 1965.

Blinder, Yaakov, ed. *Festivals and Fasts, A Practical Guide*. New York: Student Organization of Yeshiva University, 1978.

Eider, Shimon D. *A Summary of Halachos of Pesach* (I–IV). Lakewood, New Jersey, 1979.

Goodman, Philip, ed. Holiday anthologies: separate volumes for each holiday. Philadelphia: Jewish Publication Society.

Greenberg, Irving. Holiday guides: separate publications for each holiday. New York: National Jewish Resource Center.

Vainstein, Yaakov. *The Cycle of the Jewish Year*. Jerusalem: Department for Torah Education and Culture, World Zionist Organization, 1980.

VIII. The Sabbath

Greenberg, Irving. *Guide to Shabbat*. New York: National Jewish Resource Center, 1980.

Grunfeld, Isador. *The Sabbath*. New York: Feldheim, 1959.

Heschel, Abraham Joshua. *The Sabbath*. New York: Farrar, Straus & Giroux, 1973.

IX. Records and Books for Zemirot

Shiron. New York: National Jewish Resource Center.

Shiron. New York: United Jewish Appeal.

Oneg Shabbat with USY. New York: United Synagogue Youth.

X. Kashrut

Dresner, Samuel. *The Dietary Laws*. New York: Burning Bush Press, 1959.
Grunfeld, Isador. *The Jewish Dietary Laws*. London: Soncino Press, 1972.

XI. Marriage and Taharat Hamishpachah

Borowitz, Eugene. *Choosing a Sex Ethic*. New York: Schocken Books, 1972.
Feldman, David M. *Marital Relations: Birth Control and Abortion in Jewish Law*. New York: Schocken Books, 1974.
Goodman, Philip. *The Marriage Anthology*. Philadelphia: Jewish Publication Society, 1965.
Gordis, Robert. *Love and Sex: A Modern Jewish Perspective*. New York: Farrar, Straus, & Giroux, 1978.
Kaplan, Aryeh. *Waters of Eden: The Mystery of Mikveh*. New York: NCSY-Orthodox Union, 1976.
Lamm, Maurice. *The Jewish Way in Love and Marriage*. New York: Harper & Row, 1980.
Lamm, Norman. *A Hedge of Roses*. New York: Feldheim, 1966.

XII. Parenting

Blidstein, Gerald. *Honor Thy Father and Mother*. New York: Ktav Publishing House, 1975.

XIII. Speech

Kagan, Rabbi Israel Meir HaCohen (Chofetz Chayyim). *Guard Your Tongue.* Jerusalem: Pliskin Publishing, 1975.

XIV. Medical Ethics

Bleich, J. David. *Contemporary Problems.* New York: KTAV Publishing House, 1977.

Jacobovics, Immanuel. *Jewish Medical Ethics.* New York: Ktav Publishing House, 1959.

XV. Women

Greenberg, Blu. *On Women and Judaism. A View from Tradition.* Philadelphia: Jewish Publication Society, 1982.

Koltun, Elizabeth, ed. *Jewish Woman: New Perspectives.* New York: Schocken Books, 1976.

Meiselman, Moshe. *Jewish Women in Jewish Law.* New York: Ktav Publishing House, 1978.

XVI. Death and Burial

Lamm, Maurice. *Jewish Way in Death and Mourning.* Middle Village, N.Y.: Jonathan David, 1972.

Riemer, Jack, ed. *Jewish Reflections on Death.* New York: Schocken Books, 1974.

XVII. History

Roth, Cecil. A *History of the Jews*. New York: Schocken Books, 1970.

Grayzel, Solomon. A *History of the Jews*. Philadelphia: Jewish Publication Society, 1968.

Hertzberg, Arthur. *The Zionist Idea*. New York: Doubleday, 1959.

Sachar, Howard M. *The Course of Modern Jewish History*. New York: Dell, 1958.

Flohr, Paul Mendez, and Reinharz, Jehuda, eds. *The Jew in the Modern World*. New York: Oxford University Press, 1980.

Laqueur, Walter. A *History of Zionism*. New York: Holt, Rinehart & Winston, 1972.

Davidowicz, Lucy. *The War Against the Jews 1933–1945*. New York: Holt, Rinehart & Winston, 1975.

Wiesel, Elie. *Night*. New York: Hill & Wang, 1960.

In addition to these, every Jewish home should have a set of *Encyclopedia Judaica* (Jerusalem: Keter, 1972) which is an inexhaustible supply of information.

INDEX

abortion, 255–57
  general standard for, 255–56
  halachic rulings on, 256–57
  killing vs., 255
Adar, month of:
  happiness in, 387
  during leap year, 303
adoption, 250
afikoman, 430, 433, 434–35
agency, laws of, 285–86
aguna, 286
Ahasuerus, king of Persia, 387–
  388, 392, 395
Akdamot, 464
Al Chet (prayer), 339
Aleinu (prayer), 159
Al Hanissim (prayer), 384
aliyah, 79, 159, 221, 276
  blessings for, 266–68, 369
  of boy at Bar Mitzvah, 79
  on Simchat Torah, 369–72
Amidah, see Shmoneh Esreh
amniocentesis, 257
amud, 281
"Am Yisroel Chai," 369
Ani Ma'amin, 446
Antiochus IV, 375
aravah, 346–47, 350
arba kanfot, 189–93
Asarah B'Tevet, 305, 444, 469
Aseret Yemai Teshuvah, 313, 317,
  330–31, 341
  see also Rosh Hashanah;
    Shabbat Shuva; Yom Kippur
Atonement, Day of, see Yom
  Kippur

Av, ninth day of, see Tisha B'Av
avel, 297
avelut, 297
Avinu Malkenu (prayer), 325, 341
Avodah service of Yom Kippur,
  340
avodah zarah, 17
Ayshet Chayil, 66–68

ba'al tefila, 82
badeken, 221, 224
Barech, 432, 436
Bar Kochba, 439–40
Bar Mitzvah boys:
  aliyah given to, 79
  gifts for, 281
  Haftorah reading by, 81
  preparation of, 272–74
  Torah reading by, 80, 81
Bar Mitzvah ceremony, 265–76
  aliyah blessings in, 266–68
  father's blessing in, 268
  guests honored in, 268
  invitations to, 279–80
  keeping records of, 281
  selecting day for, 265–66, 271–
    272
  seudat mitzvah for, 265, 270–71
  synagogue decorations for, 280
Baruch She'p'tarani (blessing),
  268
Bat Mitzvah, 264–82
B.C.E., use of, 307
Ben-Gurion, David, 455–56
bentschers, 146, 351

besamim for Havdalah, 88–89
bet din:
  divorces obtained through,
    284–86
  vows annulled by, 319–20
bikkur cholim, 288
Birchot Erusin (blessings), 227
birchot ha'mitzvot (blessings),
  143, 154–56
Birchot Hashachar (blessings),
  156–57, 159
birchot nehenin (blessings), 143–
  154
Birchot Nissuin (blessings), 228–
  229
Birkat Ha'chamah (blessing), 306
Birkat Hagomel (blessing), 153–
  154, 236, 249, 345
Birkat Hamazon, 28, 35, 142
  for Brit Milah, 247
  for Chanukah, 384
  first paragraph of, 145–46
  Jerusalem recalled in, 450
  for Pesach seder, 432, 436
  quorum for introduction of, 75,
    270
  for Shabbat, 75, 85
  themes in, 146
  for wedding feast, 231
birth control, 257–63
  coitus interruptus for, 259, 261
  condoms for, 262
  diaphragms for, 262
  douching for, 262
  fallopian tubes tied for, 261
  IUDs for, 262–63
  oral contraceptives for, 263
  rhythm method for, 261
  spermicides for, 262
  sterilization for, 261
bitul chametz, 402, 407, 421, 422–
  424
  formula for, 422–23
biur chametz, 402, 406, 407, 421,
  424–25
blech, 43–44

blessings:
  for aliyah, 266–68
  by Bar Mitzvah's father, 268
  after birth, 236
  on bread, 70, 72, 85, 144, 145,
    324, 335, 357
  for Brit Milah, 246–47
  on cakes, cookies, crackers, 144
  for chametz search, 421–22
  on Chanukah candles, 382
  on children, 65–66, 323, 336,
    370
  on counting Omer, 440–41
  upon dressing, 188
  for eating in Sukkah, 156, 357,
    359, 365
  on elimination, 152
  for eruv tavshilin, 321–22
  on escaping danger, 153–54,
    236, 249, 345
  on fruit, 144
  on good news, 151–52
  before Hallel, 155, 453–54
  for hand washing, 71, 155
  on happy events, 152–53
  for Havdalah, 90–92
  on hearing of death, 152, 291
  on hearing thunder, 150
  on kriah, 291
  on lulav, 349, 359–60, 363
  on matzah, 432, 435
  after meal with bread, *see*
    Birkat Hamazon
  after meal without bread, 146–
    150
  on meat, fish, cheese, 145
  on meeting secular scholars,
    151
  on meeting Torah scholars, 151
  for mezuzah, 155
  in mikvah, 128, 155
  for morning, 156–57, 159
  on new clothes, 152–53, 188
  for Pidyon Haben, 252
  on recovery from illness, 153–
    154

on Rosh Hashanah candles, 323–24, 329–30
on seeing beautiful trees or animals, 151
on seeing lightning, 150
on seeing rainbows, 150–51
on seeing the sea, 151
on Shabbat candles, 57, 58–62
for shechitta, 98
on Sukkot candles, 352–53
on sun, 306
for taking of challah, 482
on tallit, 157–58
on tefillin, 275–76
for tevilah, 104–5
for Torah study, 155
on tzitzit, 190
in vain, 154, 199, 422
on vegetables, 144
for weddings, 227, 228–29, 231–232
on wine, 144; *see also* kiddush
on Yom Kippur candles, 336–337
blintzes, cheese, 489–90
blood:
  burial with, 289
  forbidden eating of, 97, 98, 100–101
Borchu (prayer), 159, 160
b'racha levatala, 154, 199, 422
Bris, *see* Brit Milah
Brisker, Chaim, 179
Brit Kedusha, 249
Brit Milah, 241–48, 253–54
  Birkat Hamazon for, 247
  blessings for, 246–47
  ceremony for, 245–47
  circumcision prior to, 248, 250
  Covenant with God and, 170–171, 241
  honorees at, 244
  "invitations" to, 243–44
  mother's role in, 247
  seudat mitzvah for, 245, 247
  on Shabbat, 241

Brit Nerot, 249
Brit Sarah, 249
burial, 288–93
  on Chol Hamoed, 294
  with Holy Land soil, 450
  on Shabbat or holiday, 289
burial societies, 289–90, 292

cabbage, stuffed, 494–95
cakes:
  carrot, 486–87
  sponge, 492–93
calendar, Jewish, 58, 301–7, 318–319
candlelighting:
  on Chanukah, 381–83
  for Havdalah, 88
  on Pesach, 431
  on Rosh Hashanah, 323–24, 329–30
  before Shabbat, 33, 36, 57–62, 324
  on Shavuot, 461
  on Shemini Atzeret, 365
  on Simchat Torah, 365
  on Sukkot, 352–53
  before Yom Kippur, 336–37
cantor, 82
caskets, 289, 290, 292
celibacy, 215
cemeteries, 292–93, 316
"Chad Gadya," 437
Chag Habikkurim, 459
  see also Shavuot
Chag Hamatzot, 401
  see also Pesach
Chag Ha-Urim, 378
  see also Chanukah
chai, 197
challah:
  matzah vs., 430
  recipe for, 481–82
  for Rosh Hashanah, 320, 322
  for Shabbat, 34, 43, 71–73, 85
  for Shavuot, 461

challah (*cont.*)
  for Sukkot, 357–58
  taking of, 111–12, 482
chametz:
  admixtures, 406
  burning of, 402, 406, 407, 421,
    424–25
  drugs and toiletries with, 404–5
  formation of, 402–3
  liquor as, 405–6
  pure, 406
  renouncing ownership of, 402,
    407, 421, 422–24
  search for, 406, 421–22, 425–26
  selling of, 402, 406, 421, 425–26
  time to abstain from, 424
chametz gamur, 406
Chanukah, 305, 306, 308, 374–86
  Birkat Hamazon for, 384
  blessings for candlelighting on,
    382
  eight days of, 377–78
  giving gifts on, 374, 383
  meal on, 381
  Shabbat coinciding with, 383
  Shmoneh Esreh for, 384
  special foods of, 383–84
  story of, 374–79
  as victory over assimilation,
    384–85
  see also menorah
Chanukah gelt, 374, 383
chanukiah, 379–80
charity, *see* tzedakah
charoset, 428–29, 430
chattan's tish, 222
chazan, 82
cheese blintzes, 489–90
Chevra Kadisha, 289–90, 292
chicken soup, 493
childrearing:
  corporal punishment in, 169–70
  parental respect in, 167–69
children, blessing of, 65–66, 323,
    336, 370
Chofetz Chayyim, 203–4

Chol Hamoed:
  burial on, 294
  of Pesach, 438
  of Sukkot, 357, 362–63
  tefillin worn on, 363
chuppah, 220, 226–27
Churban, 304, 305, 306, 430, 449,
    469–70, 472
circumcision:
  before Brit Milah, 248, 250
  ritual, *see* Brit Milah
clothes:
  blessing on, 152–53, 188
  for erev Yom Kippur, 333
  modesty in, 186–88
  for Rosh Hashanah, 322, 329–
    330
  for Shabbat, 47, 76
  for Sukkot, 350
  wool and linen mixtures in,
    189, 191
  for Yom Kippur, 335, 337
coitus interruptus, 259, 261
condolence greeting, 292–93, 294
condoms, 262
confession:
  on erev Yom Kippur, 333
  final, 288
  on wedding day, 222
  on Yom Kippur, 338–39
conversion, mikvah and, 250
corpses, 289–90
courts, Jewish, 284–86, 320
cremation, 290

Dama, story of, 182
Dayenu, 398
Day of Atonement, *see* Yom
    Kippur
Days of Awe, 317
  see also Rosh Hashanah;
    Shabbat Shuvah; Ten Days
    of Repentance; Yom Kippur
dead, honoring of, 287–93, 295
death, blessing on hearing of, 291
dew, prayer for, 438

diaphragms, 262
divorce, 283–86
douching, contraceptive, 262
dreydel, 384
dvar Torah, 223–24, 240, 270, 277

education, Jewish, 170–71, 174–
180, 465–66
"Ehad Mi Yo'deah," 437
Eichah, 474, 475
Eighth Day of Solemn Assembly,
see Shemini Atzeret
Elijah Gaon, 195
El Maleh Rachamim (prayer),
226, 292, 297, 446
Elul, month of, 309–16
cemetery visits during, 316
repentance during, 305, 311–14
Selichot said during, 311–12
shofar during, 308–11
embalming, 290
eruv, 31, 32, 42, 47–49, 315
eruv tavshilin, 321–22
eruv techumim, 32–33
Esther, queen of Persia, 388, 395–
396
Book of, 387, 389, 392–93, 395
fast of, 305, 306, 391–92
Ethics of the Fathers, 86–87
etrog, 346–50, 360–61
euthanasia, 288

fallopian tubes, tying of, 261
family purity, laws of, 120–36
family trees, 316
fasts, fasting:
on Asarah B'Tevet, 305, 444,
469
bathing prohibited on, 471
by firstborn sons, 426
on ninth of Tammuz, 470
on Rosh Chodesh, 222
after Rosh Hashanah, 330
on seventeenth of Tammuz,
304, 470

on Ta'anit Esther, 305, 306,
391–92
on Tisha B'Av, 277, 305, 306,
470, 472, 475–78
on Tzom Gedaliah, 305, 330,
470
on wedding day, 222
on Yom Kippur, 277, 337
feminism:
Haggadot and, 431
Orthodox Judaism and, 20–21,
35–36, 68, 73–74, 134, 369–
370
festivals, pilgrimage, 350–51, 458
kiddush for, 353–57
see also Pesach; Shavuot;
Sukkot
firstborn sons:
fast by, 426
redemption of, 251–53
fish:
gefilte, 483–84
kosher vs. non-kosher, 112
freedom vs. slavery, 401–2
funerals, 288–93

g'bruck, 407
Gedaliah, fast of, 305, 330, 470
gefilte fish, 483–84
gelila, 80
Gemarah, 86
get, 284–86
gittin, 284
gold, Yom Kippur and, 335
gossip, 198, 200, 203, 204
grudges, harboring of, 199, 201

hachnasat orchim, 50–51
hadas, 346–47, 350
hadran (prayer), 426
Haftorah, 80–81, 326, 340–41, 475
hagalah, 103–4
for Pesach, 409, 410–11, 414
hagbah, 80
haggadah, 428, 431–37
of Yom Ha'Atzmaut, 453

hakafot, 368–69, 370
Hallel (prayer), 358, 360, 384,
    436–37, 438, 453
    blessing before, 155, 453–54
Haman, 388, 393, 420
    Jews' enemies symbolized by,
        396–97
    noise at mention of, 392–93
hamantashen, 391
    recipes for, 484–86
hamotzi (blessing), 70, 72, 85,
    144, 145, 324, 335, 357
hand washing, ritual, 70–71, 324,
    357
    blessing for, 71, 155
    at seder table, 432
hash'cha'tat zerah, 259–60
Hatafat Dam Brit, 248, 250
hatarat nedarim, 319–20
Hatza'ad Harishon, 192
Havdalah service:
    candle for, 88
    during Nine Days, 472
    after Rosh Hashanah, 330
    after Shabbat, 59, 87–93
    after Simchat Torah, 372–73
    songs for, 92–93
    spices for, 88–89
    verses recited for, 89–92
"Hebrew" ethical wills, 183–84
Herzl, Theodor, 451
Heshvan, month of, 303
Hess, Moses, 451
hiddur mitzvah, 348
Hillel, 259
holidays:
    summary of, 304–5
    timeline of, 308
    see also specific holidays
Holocaust Remembrance Day,
    304, 307, 308, 443–48
holuptches, 351
Holy Letter, The (Nahmanides),
    120
Hoshanah Rabbah, 315, 363–65
    judgment sealed on, 315, 364

synagogue on, 364
    willow beating on, 364
Hoshanot, 360–61
hospitality, 50–51

idolatry, 17
Institute for Science and
    Halacha, 41
irui, 409, 411–12, 414–15
Israel, State of:
    birth of, 452, 455–56
    citizenship in, 452
    Oriental vs. Western Jews in,
        454
Israel Independence Day, 218,
    304, 307, 308, 440, 444, 449–
    456
Israel Memorial Day, 304, 307,
    308, 453
IUDs, 262–63

Jerusalem Reunification Day,
    218, 304, 307, 308, 440
Jewish education, 170–71, 174–
    180, 465–66
Jewish schools, selection of, 175–
    178
Jose bar Halafta, 216
Judah Maccabee, 377

kabbalat kinyan, 223
Kabbalat Shabbat, 62, 63
Kaddish (prayer), 160, 294, 297,
    446
    surrogate for saying of, 297
Kaddish zahger, 297
Kadesh, 432
Kalisher, Tzvi Hirsch, 451
kapparot, 333–35
karpas, 428, 430, 432, 433
kashering:
    of liver, 100
    of meat, 99–100
    for Pesach, 408–15
    of utensils, 102–4

kashrut, 95–119
  community fostered by, 97
  compassion for life in, 96, 98
  fish and, 112
  food shopping and, 107–12
  forbidden foods in, 97
  holiness and, 96
  as lifestyle, 95, 118
  milk and meat in, 98, 101–3,
    105–7
  rabbinic supervision in, 108–9
  registered symbols of, 108–9
  slaughtering method prescribed
    by, 98
  traveling and, 113–19
  utensil use and, 98, 101–5
  wine and, 109–10, 116
kavannah, 28, 140–41
Kedusha (prayer), 78, 160
kepah, 191, 193–97
ketubah, 219–20, 223, 227–28
ketubah de'irkesh, 223
kibbud av v'em, 167–69, 177, 181–
  183
kiddush
  for Friday night, 45, 66, 68–70,
    400
  for Pesach, 354–57, 427, 432
  for pilgrimage festivals, 353–57
  for Rosh Hashanah, 324
  for Saturday morning, 83–85
  for Shavuot, 353–57, 461
  for Shemini Atzeret, 353–57,
    365, 367
  for Simchat Torah, 353–57
  standing vs. sitting for, 357
  for Sukkot, 353–57, 359, 361
  in synagogue, 83
  women's recitation of, 70
Kiddush Hashem, 196–97
kiddushin, 215
Kiddush Rabbah, 83–85
kimpatur, 247
kiseh shel eliahu, 244
kittel, 225–26, 333, 364, 431–32
knaidlach, 494

Kol Chamira, 422–23
Kol Ha'ne'arim, 370–71
Kol Nidre (prayer), 338
Kolonymous ben Meshulam, 328
Korban Tamid, 377
Korech, 432, 435
kos shel ikkarim, 261
kriah, 291
kvatter, 244
kvatterin, 244, 245
k'vod hamet, 287–93, 295
k'vol'o kach polto, 409–10

Lag B'Omer, 218, 304, 306, 308
Lamentations, Book of, 474, 475
lashon hara, 198, 205
latkes, 374, 383
Law of Return, 452
leap years, 303
Lecha Dodi, 63, 294
lechem cherut, matzah as, 401
lechem oni, matzah as, 401
leyshev ba'sukkah (blessing), 156,
  357, 359, 365
libun, 103–4
  for Pesach, 409, 411, 414
licht-bentschen (blessing), 57, 58–
  62
liver, kashering of, 100
lulav, 346–50
  assembly of, 349–50
  blessing on, 349, 359–60, 363
  disposal of, 364
  in Hoshanot, 360–61
  women and, 348–49
lying, 198–99, 202–3

Maariv service, 62, 86, 87, 142,
  160, 162, 294, 338–39, 368
Maccabees, 377–78
machzor, 310, 315–16, 324
Maftir, 79, 266
Magen David, 197
Maggid, 432, 433–34
Magillah of Esther, 387, 389, 392–
  393, 395

Malbish Arumim (blessing), 188
Ma Nishtanah, 433–34
Maot Chittin, 420–21
marit ayin, 115, 117
maror, 428–29, 430, 432, 435
marriage, 215–32
  arranged, 173
  brokers for, 216
  contracts for, 219–20, 223, 227–228
  forbidden categories of, 220
  termination of, 283–86
  three methods of, 230
mashgiach, 108
matanot la'evyonim, 391
Mattathias, 376–77
matzah:
  baking of, 402–3
  as bread of affliction, 401, 430
  as bread of freedom, 401, 430
  erev Pesach abstinence from, 428
  Shabbat challot vs., 430
  shmurah vs. regular, 427–28
meat:
  kashering of, 99–100
  separation of milk and, 98, 101–103, 105–7
mechirat chametz, 402, 406, 421, 425–26
mechitza, 77
mechutanim, 217
Melaveh Malkah, 93
menorah, 379–81
  construction of, 380
  electric, 379
  lighting of, 381–82
  placement of, 379, 380–81
  use of light from, 379
mesader kiddushin, 227
me'sheh'bay'rach (blessing), 248, 249
meshulachim, 87
messianic era:
  prayer for, 59–60, 128, 324
  vegetarianism in, 96

mezuman, 75, 270
mezuzah, 17
  blessing for attaching of, 155
  Exodus and, 401
mikvah, 121–36
  blessing in, 128, 155
  bride's use of, 221
  conversion and, 250
  fee for, 129
  men's use of, 49, 56, 63, 333
  paramount importance of, 121–122
  tevilah in, 104–5
  waters used in, 125
  women's use of, 125–29, 221
  before Yom Kippur, 333
milk products:
  rabbinic supervision of, 110–111
  separation of meat and, 98, 101–3, 105–7
  Shavuot and, 461
milui v'irui, 409, 412
Mincha service, 62, 86, 87, 142, 160, 294, 340–41
minyan, 76, 77, 142, 163, 232
  for Kaddish, 294
  of women, 277–78
mirrors, covering of, 293
mishloach manot, 389–91
Mishnah, 86
mitzvah, beautifying of, 348
Modeh Ani (prayer), 138, 161
modesty in attire, 186–88
mohel, 234–35, 241, 245–47
  selection of, 242–43
months:
  ancient proclamation of, 318–319
  Babylonian names for, 303
  see also specific months
Mordecai, 388, 391, 393, 395
Moses, 400, 461, 468–69
Motzi Matzah, 432, 435
mourning period, 287, 293–97
muktzeh, 31, 36

Mussaf service, 82, 326–28, 340, 366

Nahmanides, 120
names, pasuk associated with, 279
naming of children, 236–40, 247, 248–50
Ne'ilah (prayer), 341, 437
Netaneh Tokef (prayer), 314, 327, 328
New Year:
    first day of, *see* Rosh Hashanah
    greetings for, 314–15
    of Trees, 305, 306, 450–51
niddah, 121–36
    childbirth and, 124
    defloration and, 218
    menstruation and, 121–24
    oral contraceptives as source of, 263
    proscribed conduct during, 122–24
nifsal me'achilat kelev, 405
Nine Days, 245, 472
Nirtzah, 432, 437
noodle puddings, 490–93

oaths, 199, 319–20
obstetrician, selection of, 234–35
Omer, counting of, 217–18, 304, 306, 438–42
onah, 259, 260
Onan, story of, 259
Oneg Shabbat, 75, 86
onen, 276
oral contraceptives, 261, 263
Orthodox Jews:
    cohesive family units of, 14
    communal structure of, 14
    diversity among, 14–15, 18, 32
    ethical behavior of, 19–20
    modern, 15–18
    secular life of, 16–17
    theological differences among, 14–15

parents:
    honoring of, 167–69, 177, 181–183
    responsibilities of, 167–84
    speech patterns of, 204–5
parshah, 76–77, 81, 278
parve, 107
Passover, *see* Pesach
pasuk, 279
Peel, Lord, 452
Pesach, 303, 304, 306, 308, 350, 398–442
    Birkat Hamazon for, 432, 436
    candlelighting on, 431
    Chol Hamoed of, 438
    cleaning for, 403–15
    food costs for, 416–17
    food preparation on, 350–51
    foods forbidden on, 402–3
    guests invited for, 421
    hagalah for, 409, 410–11, 414
    kashering appliances for, 408–415
    kiddush for, 354–57, 427, 432
    kitchen preparation for, 407–15
    libun for, 409, 411, 414
    pet feeding during, 405
    sermons on, 331
    Shabbat before, 420
    Shavuot and, 459
    shopping for, 415–17
    toothbrushes replaced on, 405
    Torah readings for, 438
    tzedakah before, 420–21
    utensils for, 407–8
    women and, 418–19
    see also chametz; matzah; seder
Pesukei Dezimra (prayers), 76, 159
pets, Pesach diet for, 405
Pidyon Haben, 251–53
pilgrimage festivals, 350–51, 458
    kiddush for, 353–57
    see also Pesach; Shavuot; Sukkot
pill, the, 261, 263

Pinsker, Leon, 451
Pirke Avot, 86–87
potato kugel, 487–88
prayer, 137–65
  at bedtime, 162
  content of, 142–43
  dress for, 141
  fixed times for, 139–40, 142,
    156
  functions of, 137–38
  Hebrew language for, 139
  kavannah in, 140–41
  longevity and, 164
  meditation before, 141
  in minyan, 76, 77, 142, 163, 232
  respect during, 141–42
  as service of heart, 138–39
  sitting vs. standing in, 160
  see also specific prayers
prayer book, 47, 161, 244, 253
  for holidays, 310, 315–16, 324
pregnancy, 234–36
procreation, 258–59, 260–63
profanity, 198, 202, 205–6
pru urevu, 258–59, 260–63
Purim, 305, 306, 308, 387–97
  drunkenness on, 393
  food exchanged on, 388, 389–
    391
  meal on, 391, 394
  parties on, 393–94
  Pesach cleaning starting on,
    404
  preparation for, 389
  relevance of, 395–97
  Shabbat before, 420
  story of, 387–88, 395
  tzedakah given on, 388, 390,
    391
pushke, 49–50, 384

rabbis:
  abortion and, 257
  binding decisions of, 102
  kashrut questions answered by,
    102, 104
  sermons by, 81–82, 331–32, 420

Rachtzah, 432, 434
rain:
  prayer for, 365–67
  Shmoneh Esreh and reference
    to, 366, 438
Rashi, 75
rhythm method, 261
ritual:
  evolution of, 254
  kavannah in, 28
  parental respect and, 14
  role of, 21
Rosh Chodesh, 222, 265, 306
Rosh Hashanah, 305, 306, 309,
    317–32
  blessing children on, 323
  candlelighting on first day of,
    323–24
  candlelighting on second day
    of, 329–30
  carrying on, 315
  cigarette smoking on, 320
  clothes for, 322, 329–30
  cooking for, 320–22
  fasting after, 330
  greetings after, 314–15
  greetings before and on, 314
  Haftorah reading on, 326
  Havdalah service after, 330
  household preparation for,
    320–24
  kiddush for, 324
  Mussaf of, 326–28
  on Shabbat, 329
  Shabbat after, 331
  Shacharit of, 325–27
  special foods for, 320, 322
  Tashlich on, 328–29
  Torah reading on, 325–26
  two days of, 317–18
  vows released on, 319–20

Sabbath, *see* Shabbat
s'chach, 345
seder, 20, 426–37
  Birkat Hamazon of, 432, 436
  four questions of, 433–34

Hallel during, 436–37
handwashing during, 432
meal of, 435
order of, 432
plate used for, 428–29
reclining during, 430–31
second night of, 437, 438
songs for, 437
table for, 427–31
wine for, 426–27, 429–30
seed, spilling of, 259–60
Sefirat Ha'Omer, 217–18, 304,
   438–42
Selichot (prayers):
   during Elul, 311–12
   during Yamim Noraim, 317
sermons:
   on Pesach, 331
   on Shabbat, 81–82
   on Shabbat Hagadol, 420
   on Shabbat Shuva, 331–32
seudah shelishit, 87
seudat havra'ah, 293
seudat mitzvah, 218–19, 222,
   230–31, 245–47, 265, 270–71
sexual pleasure:
   procreation vs., 259
   woman's right to, 259
sexual relations:
   extramarital, 215
   following childbirth, 124
   menstruation and, 122–24
   after mikvah, 124
   on Shabbat, 75
   during shiva period, 293
   on Tisha B'Av, 473
   yichud and, 229–30
   • on Yom Kippur, 338
Shabbat, 25–94, 241, 287, 306
   activities proscribed on, 30–38,
      40
   Biblical injunctions on, 26
   Birkat Hamazon for, 75, 85
   birth on, 235–36
   blessing children on, 65–66
   Brit Milah on, 241
   burials prohibited on, 289

candlelighting before, 33, 36,
   57–62, 324
carrying objects on, 31, 47–49
Chanukah on, 383
clothes for, 47, 76
conclusion of, 58, 59, 87–93
food preparation for, 43–46
foods, traditional, 44–45
gentile labor used on, 37–38
Havdalah service for, 59, 87–93
hospitality on, 50–51
kiddush for, 45, 66, 68–70, 83–
   85, 400
learning on, 86–87
medical emergencies on, 41,
   235–36
onset of, 57–59
paper tearing before, 40
before Pesach, 420
preparation for, 33–44
before Purim, 420
Rosh Hashanah on, 329
between Rosh Hashanah and
   Yom Kippur, 331
sample menu for, 53
sexual relations on, 75
shiva during, 294
shofar forbidden on, 309
slavery contrasted with, 400
sleep on, 85
songs for, 28, 35, 74, 87
Sukkot on, 363
table for, 34–35
tea preparation on, 45–46
tefillin on, 276
telephone use on, 40–42
timers, electrical, for, 37, 38
Torah reading on, 76–77, 79–
   81, 159, 265
tzedakah before, 49–50
warm food on, 43–44
wine for, 34, 43
yahrzeit commemorated on,
   297–98
Shabbat Chanukah, 383
Shabbat Hachodesh, 420
Shabbat Hagadol, 420

Shabbat Parah, 420
Shabbat Shabbaton, Yom Kippur
    as, 338
Shabbat Shekalim, 420
Shabbat Shuva, 331
Shabbat Zachor, 420
Shabbos clock, 37, 38
Shabbos goy, 37–38
Shabbos lamp, 39
Shabbos telephone, 41–42
Shacharit service, 76, 142, 156–
    160, 188, 294, 325–27, 400
shadchan, 216
shaleshudos, 87, 277
shaliach tzibbur, 82, 140, 160
shaloch manot, 389–91
Shalom Aleichem, 64–65
Shalom Nekevah, 240
Shalom Zachar, 240
shatnez, 189, 191
Shavuot, 304, 306, 308, 350, 457–
    467
    as agricultural holiday, 458–59
    Akdamot read on, 464
    all-night study session on, 462–
    464
    candlelighting on, 461
    challah for, 461
    decorations for, 461–62
    Jewish education and, 465–66
    kiddush for, 353–57, 461
    milk products eaten on, 461
    Pesach and, 459
    preparation for, 350–51, 460–62
    recipes for, 489–91
    Sephardic ritual on, 467
    Torah reading on, 464
shechitta, 98–99
Shehecheyanu (blessing), 152–53,
    188, 249, 252, 323, 337, 357,
    360, 368, 382, 431
sheh'hakol (blessing), 145
Shema Yisrael (prayer), 138, 158,
    159, 161–62, 288, 341
Shemini Atzeret, 305, 306, 352,
    365–67

candlelighting on, 365
charity given on, 367
kiddush for, 353–57, 365, 367
Mussaf of, 366
Tefilat Geshem on, 365–67
Torah reading on, 367
shemirah, 290
Shemirat Halashon (Chofetz
    Chayyim), 203–4
Sheva B'rachot (blessings), 228–
    229, 231–32
shevarim, 309
shinui, 235
shiva, 287, 293–96
    on Shabbat or holiday, 294
    telephoning during, 295
    visiting during, 295–96
Shivah Asar B'Tammuz, 304, 417
shloshim, 296–97
Shmoneh Esreh (Amidah), 82,
    140, 159
    on Chanukah, 384
    Kedusha in repetition of, 160
    rain phrase in, 366, 438
shmurah matzah, 427–28
shochet, 98–99, 101
shofar:
    blasts of, 309–10
    blowing of, 326–27
    during Elul, 308–11
    making of, 310–11
    purchase of, 310
    on Shabbat, 309
    symbolism of, 310
shomer, 290
"Shoshannat Yaakov," 394
shtar piturin, 285
Shulchan Aruch, 110, 193, 195
Shulchan Orech, 432, 435
shuls, *see* synagogues
sh'vut, 31
sick people, visits to, 288
siddur, 47, 161, 244, 253
Simchat Habat, 248–50, 253–54
Simchat Torah, 305, 367–73
    aliyot on, 369–72

blessing of children on, 370
candlelighting on, 365
Havdalah service for, 372–73
kiddush for, 353–57
Maariv of, 368
Torah reading on, 367–68, 369–372
siyyum, 221–22, 426, 472
slavery:
  freedom vs., 401–2
  Shabbat contrasted with, 400
sofer, get inscribed by, 285
Soloveitchik, Joseph, 16
sondek, 244, 245
speech, 198–207
  parents as role models for, 204–205
  profanity in, 198, 202, 205–6
  as reflection of faith, 206–7
spermicides, 262
sterilization, 261
stuffed cabbage, 494–95
suicides, 293
sukkah:
  blessing in, 156, 357, 359, 365
  construction of, 343–46, 348
  eating in, 353–59
  inclement weather and, 344, 359, 366
  women in, 361–62
Sukkot, 305, 306, 308, 342–67
  candlelighting on, 352–53
  Chol Hamoed of, 357, 362–63
  clothes for, 350
  decorations for, 345–46
  kiddush for, 353–57, 359, 361
  preparations for, 341, 343–52
  second day of, 361
  on Shabbat, 363
  songs for, 358
  see also Hoshanah Rabbah; Shemini Atzeret
sun, special blessing on, 306
synagogues:
  Bar/Bat Mitzvah decorations of, 280

decorum in, 280
on Hoshanah Rabbah, 364
informality in, 78, 82
junior congregation services in, 78
kiddush in, 83
mechitzas in, 77
on Yom Kippur, 338

Ta'anit Esther, 305, 306, 391–92
ta'avoret chametz, 406
tachrichim, 289
tahara, 289
taharat hamishpachah, 120–36
  Biblical injunctions on, 122
  human dimensions of, 129–36
  see also mikvah
tallit, 76, 78, 157–58, 189, 191, 267, 272, 276, 289
tallit katan, 189–93
Talmud, components of, 86
Tammuz, month of:
  ninth day of, 470
  seventeenth of, 304, 471
Tarfon, Rabbi, 182
Tashlich, 328–29
Tay-Sachs disease, 256–57
teachers, honoring of, 168
Tefilat Geshem (prayer), 365–66
Tefilat Tal, 438
tefillin, 141, 157–59, 190, 274
  blessings for, 275–76
  on Chol Hamoed, 363
  on Shabbat, 276
Tehillim, 290
tekiah, 309
Temple, destruction of, 304, 305, 306, 430, 449, 469–70, 472
Ten Commandments, 19, 458
  reading of, 464
Ten Days of Repentance, 313, 317, 330–31, 341
  see also Rosh Hashanah; Shabbat Shuva; Yom Kippur
teruah, 310
teshuvah, 202, 305, 311–14

Tevet, tenth of, 305, 444, 469
tevilah, 104-5
Three Weeks, 218, 238, 471
tichel, 187
tikkun leil Shavuot, 462-64
Tisha B'Av, 218, 276, 305, 306, 444, 470-78
    fasting on, 277, 305, 306, 470, 472, 475-78
t'naim, 217, 222
Torah:
    Bar Mitzvah boy's reading of, 80, 81
    cantillation of, 79-80, 273
    daily study of, 159-60, 174
    days for reading from, 265
    kissing of, 78-79, 267
    lifting of, 80
    moving of, 294
    Pesach reading of, 438
    reader of, 79-80, 81
    Revelation of, 26, 311, 458, 459-60, 464
    Rosh Hashanah reading of, 325-26
    Shabbat reading of, 76-77, 79-81, 159, 265
    Shavuot reading of, 464
    Shemini Atzeret reading of, 367
    Simchat Torah reading of, 367-368, 369-72
    Tisha B'Av reading of, 475
    weekly divisions of, 76-77
    wrapping of, 80
    Yom Kippur reading of, 340
trup, 273
tsholent, 44-45, 351
    recipes for, 488-89
Tu B'Shvat, 305, 306, 450-51
Tzafun, 432, 435
tzedakah, 280
    before Pesach, 420-21
    on Purim, 388, 390, 391
    before Shabbat, 49-50
    on Shemini Atzeret, 367
tzimmes, 486

tzitzit, 189-93
    Exodus and, 401
Tzom Gedaliah, 305, 330, 470

ufruf, 221, 268
U'rechatz, 432
utensils:
    kashering of, 102-4
    for Pesach, 407-8
    tevilah and, 104-5
uvdin d'chol, 31

vegetarianism in messianic era, 96
Viddui, 222, 288, 333
Vilna Gaon, 195
visits:
    during shiva, 295-96
    to sick people, 288
vows:
    Jewish view of, 199
    release of, 319-20

water, Hoshanah Rabbah prayer for, 364
weddings, 215-32
    Birkat Hamazon for, 231
    bride's dvar Torah at, 224
    canopy for, 220, 226-27
    confession on day of, 222
    dancing at, 230-31
    dates permissible for, 217-18, 439, 440
    fasting before, 222
    festive meal for, 218-19, 222, 230-31
    glass shattered at, 229
    groom's dvar Torah at, 223
    invitations to, 219
    nine-word formula for, 227
    processional, 225-26
    sharing costs of, 217
    shloshim and, 297
    witnesses for, 227
    Yom Kippur Viddui and, 222
wills, "Hebrew" ethical, 183-84

wine:
  kashrut and, 109–10, 116
  during Nine Days, 472
  for seder table, 426–27, 429–30
  for Shabbat, 34, 43
  see also kiddush
witnesses:
  for divorce, 284–85
  for marriage contract, 223
  for wedding ceremony, 227
  for yichud, 229
women:
  at Brit Milah, 243, 244
  hair covered by, 59, 186–88
  hakafot for, 370
  Kaddish recitation by, 297
  kiddush recited by, 70
  liturgy and, 162–63
  lulav and, 348–49
  minyan of, 277–78
  as onlooker vs. participant,
    369–70
  pants worn by, 186
  Pesach and, 418–19
  separate seating of, 77, 369
  sexual pleasure and, 259
  special mitzvot of, 111, 121
  in sukkah, 361–62
  tzitzit and, 192–93

Yachatz, 432, 433
yahrzeit, 297–98
Yamim Noraim, 317
Ya Ribon Olam, 74–75
Yehi Ratzon (prayer), 59–60, 128,
  324
yeshivas, selection of, 175–78
yichud, 229–30
Yizkor (prayer), 367, 438, 464–65
Yom Ha'Atzmaut, 218, 304, 307,
  308, 440, 444, 449–56
Yom Hadin, Rosh Hashanah as,
  325

Yom Hashoah, 304, 307, 308,
  443–48
Yom Hazikaron, 304, 307, 308,
  453
Yom Kippur, 303, 305, 306, 309,
  317, 332–41
  Avodah service of, 340
  candlelighting before, 336–37
  carrying on, 316
  closing service of, 341
  clothing worn on, 335, 337
  confession on, 338–39
  fasting on, 277, 337
  gold not worn on, 335
  Haftorah reading on, 340–41
  leather on, 188
  Maariv of, 338–39
  mikvah use before, 333
  Mincha of, 340–41
  mood of, 333, 339
  Mussaf of, 340
  Ne'ilah service of, 341
  prefast meal before, 335–36
  prohibitions on, 337
  sexual relations on, 338
  Shabbat before, 331
  as Shabbat Shabbaton, 338
  synagogue decor on, 338
  Torah reading of, 340
Yom Kippur Viddui:
  on wedding day, 222
  on Yom Kippur, 333
Yom Tefillin, 274
Yom Teruah, Yom Kippur as, 325
Yom Yerushalayim, 218, 304, 307,
  308, 440

Zecher Le'churban, 430
zemirot:
  for Shabbat, 28, 35, 74, 87
  for Sukkot, 358
zeroah, 428–29, 430
Zohar, 120, 462

ABOUT THE AUTHOR

Blu Greenberg is an author and lecturer whose previous book was *On Women and Judaism*. She lives in Riverdale, New York, with her husband and five children.